In Heaven as It Is on Earth

In Heaven as It Is on Earth

*Joseph Smith and the Early Mormon
Conquest of Death*

SAMUEL MORRIS BROWN

OXFORD
UNIVERSITY PRESS

OXFORD
UNIVERSITY PRESS

Oxford University Press, Inc., publishes works that further
Oxford University's objective of excellence
in research, scholarship, and education.

Oxford   New York
Auckland   Cape Town   Dar es Salaam   Hong Kong   Karachi
Kuala Lumpur   Madrid   Melbourne   Mexico City   Nairobi
New Delhi   Shanghai   Taipei   Toronto

With offices in
Argentina   Austria   Brazil   Chile   Czech Republic   France   Greece
Guatemala   Hungary   Italy   Japan   Poland   Portugal   Singapore
South Korea   Switzerland   Thailand   Turkey   Ukraine   Vietnam

Published by Oxford University Press, Inc.
198 Madison Avenue, New York, New York 10016

www.oup.com

Oxford is a registered trademark of Oxford University Press

Library of Congress Cataloging-in-Publication Data
Brown, Samuel Morris, author.
In heaven as it is on earth : Joseph Smith and the early Mormon
conquest of death / Samuel Morris Brown.
p.   cm.
Includes bibliographical references and index.
ISBN 978-0-19-979357-0 (pbk.)
1. Death—Religious aspects—Church of Jesus Christ of Latter-day Saints.
2. Church of Jesus Christ of Latter-day Saints—Doctrines.
3. Smith, Joseph, 1805–1844.   I. Title.
BX8643.D4B76 2011
236'.1097309034—dc22   2011002848

289.3
(Smith)
No B

1 3 5 7 9 8 6 4 2

Printed in the United States of America
on acid-free paper

For Kate, Amelia, Lucia, and Persephone

CONTENTS

PREFACE

This work began as an exploration of the role of angelic messengers in early Mormonism. As my pregnant wife, our toddling daughter, and I made our way through the town cemetery in Camden, Maine, imagining the life stories behind the laconic engravings on worn grave markers, I was struck by the fact that the angels of early Mormonism were visitors not only from heaven but also from beyond the grave. This recognition, coupled with my professional experience as a physician with life-threatening illness and death, fueled an expansion of the initial project into a broader view of Joseph Smith's vision of the complex and abiding interactions between the living and the dead. As I turned to familiar sources with an eye to the question of mortality, I discovered a rich network of interconnected narratives. This book is the final result of the investigations begun that day in Camden.

I am fortunate to have friends and colleagues (especially and alphabetically Lavina Fielding Anderson, Mark Ashurst-McGee, Philip Barlow, Kevin Barney, my siblings and their spouses, Diann Brown, Matthew Bowman, Kathleen Flake, Stephen Fleming, Lisa Gabbert, Terryl Givens, David Grua, Kristine Haglund, Blair Hodges, Kate Holbrook, Robin Jensen, Greg Kearney, Brad Kramer, Scott Neville, Jonathon Penny, Paul Reeve, Jana Riess, Brett Rushforth, Bill Smith, Jonathan Stapley, John G. Turner, and Kris Wright) who as readers and scholars have vastly improved my research and writing, though they are not to blame for any oversights and misinterpretations that persist. I specifically thank Glen Leonard for his support and encouragement when I began to study Mormonism. I am grateful to my editors, Cynthia Read and Charlotte Steinhardt, for their gracious wisdom, good humor, and support throughout this process. I also thank Bill Slaughter and his staff at the

Church History Library, The Church of Jesus Christ of Latter-day Saints, Salt Lake City, for their help with images, and Brett Dowdle, my able research assistant.

My work as an intensive care unit physician funded this research, and I am most grateful to the patients and families whose stunning courage in the face of death was a significant factor in my decision to undertake this work. These individuals and their wisdom have accompanied me throughout this intellectual journey.

I thank *Church History*, *Journal of Mormon History*, *Dialogue*, *BYU Studies*, and *International Journal of Mormon Studies* for permission to include material originally published in their journals. Portions of this work have been presented at meetings of the American Academy of Religion, Mormon History Association, BYU Studies Symposium, Mormon Scholars in the Humanities, Society for Mormon Philosophy and Theology, and Mormon Theology Seminar, among others.

I dedicate this book to my wife and children. I cannot imagine life or death without them. If indeed the Divine message is the eternity of a form of family intimacy, then I am of all men most blessed.

ABBREVIATIONS

APR   Joseph Smith, *An American Prophet's Record: The Diaries and Journals of Joseph Smith, Jr.*, ed. Scott Faulring (Salt Lake City: Signature Books, 1989).

CHL   Church History Library, The Church of Jesus Christ of Latter-day Saints, Salt Lake City, Utah.

D&C   *Doctrine and Covenants of the Church of Jesus Christ of Latter-day Saints* (Salt Lake City: Intellectual Reserve, 1981).

EJ   *Elders' Journal of the Church of Latter Day Saints*, Kirtland, Ohio, October–November 1837, Far West, Missouri, July–August 1838.

EMD   *Early Mormon Documents, ed. Dan Vogel*, 5 vols. (Salt Lake City: Signature Books, 1996–2004).

EMS   *The Evening and the Morning Star*, Independence, Missouri, June 1832–July 1833; Kirtland, Ohio, December 1833–September 1834.

EPB   *Early Patriarchal Blessings of the Church of Jesus Christ of Latter-day Saints*, H. Michael Marquardt, comp. and ed., (Salt Lake City: Smith-Pettit Foundation, 2007).

FWR   *Far West Record: Minutes of The Church of Jesus Christ of Latter-day Saints, 1830–1844*, Donald Q. Cannon and Lyndon W. Cook, eds., (Salt Lake City: Deseret Book, 1983).

GAEL   "Grammar and A[l]phabet of the English Language," MS 1294/5, CHL.

HBLL   L. Tom Perry Library Special Collections, Harold B. Lee Library, Brigham Young University, Provo, Utah.

HC   *History of the Church of Jesus Christ of Latter-day Saints, Period 1: History of Joseph Smith, the Prophet, by Himself, ed. B. H. Roberts*, 6 vols. (Salt Lake City: Deseret Book, 1953).

JD   *Journal of Discourses*, 26 vols. (Liverpool: LDS Bookseller's
            Depot, 1854–86).

JSPJ1   *Joseph Smith Papers, Journals,* vol. 1, *1832–1839,* ed. Dean
            C. Jessee, Mark Ashurst-McGee, and Richard L. Jensen (Salt
            Lake City: Church Historian's Press, 2008).

JSPR1   *Joseph Smith Papers, Revelations and Translations: Manuscript
            Revelation Books, Facsimile Edition,* ed. Robin Scott Jensen,
            Robert J. Woodford, and Steven C. Harper (Salt Lake City:
            Church Historian's Press, 2009).

JSR   H. Michael Marquardt, *The Joseph Smith Revelations: Text and
            Commentary* (Salt Lake City: Signature Books, 1999).

KEQR   *Kirtland Elders' Quorum Record: 1836–1841,* Lyndon Cook and
            Milton Backman, eds., (Provo, Utah: Grandin, 1985).

LB   Lucy Mack Smith, *Lucy's Book: A Critical Edition of Lucy Mack
            Smith's Family Memoir,* ed. Lavina Fielding Anderson (Salt
            Lake City: Signature Books, 2001).

M&A   *Latter Day Saints' Messenger and Advocate,* Kirtland, Ohio,
            October 1834–September 1837.

MS   *Latter-day Saints' Millennial Star,* Manchester, England, May
            1840–March 1842; Liverpool, April 1842–March 3, 1932;
            London, March 10, 1932–December 1970.

NewT   *Joseph Smith's New Translation of the Bible: Original
            Manuscripts,* Scott Faulring, Kent P. Jackson, and Robert
            J. Mathews, eds., (Provo, Utah: Religious Studies Center,
            Brigham Young University, 2004).

SelCol   LDS Church Archives, *Selected Collections from the Archives of
            the Church of Jesus Christ of Latter-day Saints,* 2 vols. (DVD)
            (Salt Lake City: Intellectual Reserve, 2002).

T&S   *Times and Seasons,* Commerce/Nauvoo, Illinois, November
            1839–February 1846.

WJS   *The Words of Joseph Smith: The Contemporary Accounts of the
            Nauvoo Discourses of the Prophet Joseph,* ed. Andrew Ehat and
            Lyndon Cook (Provo, Utah: Grandin, 1991).

WWJ   Wilford Woodruff, *Wilford Woodruff's Journal, Typescript,* ed.
            Scott Kenney, 9 vols. (Midvale, Utah: Signature Books,
            1983–85).

In Heaven as It Is on Earth

Introduction

Death has presided over life for all of human history. Whether and how the self can survive beyond the grave and what it means to live in the face of inevitable extinction are central religious and intellectual problems for almost all human beings and cultures. While various thinkers have claimed that no human can imagine her own death (a consciousness cannot conceive itself without consciousness), people have always wondered at and worried over the prospect of death, seeking explanations, condolences, and strategies when faced with the possibility that life will cease. In sociologist Peter Berger's eloquent phrase, "the power of religion depends, in the last resort, upon the credibility of the banners it puts in the hands of men as they stand before death, or more accurately, as they walk, inevitably, toward it."[1]

Contemporary Western societies have brought new technological tools to their struggle with death, but these tools have problems of their own. In modern America, at least 14 percent of gross domestic product is devoted to biomedical negotiations with illness, and, inexorably, death. Despite, or perhaps in part because of, vast financial and technical outpourings, a wide variety of voices have argued that the modern West has lost its ability to confront death.[2]

This was not always the case. Before a process dubbed the "Dying of Death" by which theologians, physicians, and others downplayed the significance of death in the late nineteenth and early twentieth centuries, Americans possessed a remarkably robust death culture with roots stretching from medieval Christianity through early modern England into the colonial churches and antebellum evangelicalism. These Americans knew death intimately, confronted it regularly, and brought significant cultural resources to these encounters. The early nineteenth century particularly distinguished itself with a potent emphasis on the deathbed, eternal community, and melodramatic bereavement, what

3

scholars have called the "good," "beautiful," or "happy" death, though I will suggest that "holy death" more adequately captures the meanings of these cultural phenomena.

Joseph Smith Jr. (1805–1844; see figure 0.1) is perhaps the most famous and successful of the alternative Christian voices to arise in the spiritual agitation of early nineteenth-century America. Smith has struck different observers as an imperialist, a satyr, a charlatan, a sectarian primordialist, a folk magician, an untreated frontal-lobe epileptic, and a hermetic magus.[3] There is some truth in many of these narratives about the Mormon founder, but most have failed to appreciate how concerned Smith was with death and its conquest. In his 1844 swan song sermon

Figure 0.1 Portrait of Joseph Smith Jr. Image courtesy of the Church History Library, The Church of Jesus Christ of Latter-day Saints.

commemorating the death of a Mormon elder, Smith proclaimed to his followers, "I will open your eyes in rel[ation] to your dead."[4] This statement is perhaps more accurate a summary of Smith's religious activity than almost any other.

While a handful of authors, most prominently Douglas Davies, have discussed death in Mormonism, most treatments have refracted Mormon death culture through the later Utah period; none has treated the cultural contexts and documentary record of earliest Mormonism in detail.[5] This study attempts to make sense of several questions. How did death affect the first generation of Mormons? What did these believers find in Smith's "dispensation" of divine light to prepare them for their encounter with the King of Terrors? What would their prophet's innovations and modifications of cultural themes have meant for them personally? Whereas Davies's elegant and persuasive treatment of the Mormon "culture of salvation" has drawn broad and compelling interpretive outlines for Latter-day Saint theology and practice, situating Mormonism anthropologically while describing the communal nature of Mormon salvation, this study paints a detailed portrait of the social and religious milieu in which Smith proclaimed his new religious tradition and his very specific responses to that world. When, following Davies, I refer to death "conquest," I mean a set of approaches to the meaning of life, a framing of aspirations for the afterlife, and controversies about the security or stability of salvation, as expressed in human struggles with mortality. When and under what circumstances life ends, how much of earthly experience will persist, and what constitutes preparation for death are problems that can be distinguished from the question of salvation per se. Framing Mormonism as an attempted conquest of death illuminates its theology and enriches the texture of the lived experience of believers.

The story of earliest Mormonism confirms historian Robert Orsi's argument that religion centrally creates, sustains, and interprets relationships, both "real" and "imagined," between heaven and earth.[6] The ideas that sustain these relationships come both from the lived experience of lay believers—what scholars call "lived religion"—and from theological claims made by Mormon leaders.[7] Though my sympathies are with the lived religion approach to history, Mormonism particularly demonstrates the limits to the asserted distinction between theology and lived religion. The leaders of earliest Mormonism are the types of generally marginalized voices that students of lived religion attempt to uncover. Joseph Smith Jr. particularly lived, breathed, and preached concepts familiar from lived religion: medical and paramedical practices, fluid application and development of ritual forms, folk beliefs that speak more to life's exigencies than formal theology. Because in early Mormonism the leader is often difficult to separate from the followers (a point that amused contemporary Protestant critics), I consider them together. These believers were coming to terms with and protesting pre-existing traditions as they attempted to discern their place in society and the world at large through the lens of divine revelation. Scriptures, sermons, poems, hymns, journals, and artifacts are all vital conduits both to understanding the aspirations of a group of people struggling on the fringes of American Protestantism to make sense of life and death and to appreciating the "cultural work" that Mormonism performed for them.[8]

In this study I have attempted to present a sympathetic and rigorous view of early Mormons, giving voice to the individuals and ideas I have encountered without molding them to the exigencies of devotion, polemics, or apologia. I have made no attempt in this book to assess the veracity of Joseph Smith's religious claims. I have, however, attempted to present Smith's concerns, ideas, and innovations as I believe he understood them. I explore the sacred texts he promulgated while leaving to the reader the question of whether he influenced the texts, they influenced him, or both. However they were created, these texts represented an important part of Joseph Smith's religious vision, and he cannot be understood without them.

I have largely ignored later developments in Latter-day Saint traditions in this study. I hope that readers of this book will experience what historian Peter Brown has called "salutary vertigo," an illuminating disorientation based in clarifying the foreignness of a seemingly familiar culture.[9] Some within the faith will find my analysis too secular, while some outside observers will complain that I have been too kind to the people whose stories I tell. A balanced treatment will necessarily brook such criticism, but I hope that the majority of readers will be served by this salutary vertigo.

In terms of nomenclature, I have intended to explore and present the idea-world that Joseph Smith and his followers inhabited. His followers I refer to variously as Latter-day Saints, Saints, or Mormons for stylistic reasons only. Given long-standing Mormon tradition, I occasionally refer to Smith as Joseph or the Prophet, to fit the flow of the prose. Because this story contains so many people surnamed Smith, I often use first names to refer to other members of the Smith family. Because this is a story about antebellum believers, I refer to the God (or LORD, in the King James idiom) of the Hebrew Bible, usually transliterated Yahweh, as Jehovah unless I am referring to a specific Hebrew text or phrase. With reference to America's Native peoples, I have employed a mixture of Mormon, antebellum, and modern terms. Where a specific culture group is identified, I have attempted to use the tribal name. Where several tribes or "native" as opposed to "white" peoples are intended, I have referred to them as Native peoples, occasionally by the Mormon name "Lamanites," and rarely by the term Indian, as dictated by the context. In attempting to re-create the conceptual world of early Mormonism, I have used the fraught term "patriarch" to describe a particular type of biblical figure or the Latter-day Saints when they identified themselves with such figures. By "patriarchal," the term early Latter-day Saints favored, I intend the collection of beliefs, rites, and mystical powers with which Smith announced he was creating a genealogical system to encompass the entire human family, based in a reinterpretation of the biblical patriarchs. Allowing these terms to bear the weight they bore in the early nineteenth century should contribute to the salutary vertigo induced by this study.

Joseph Smith claimed to be a translator-seer whose scriptures largely derived from grave artifacts. He first described entombed gold plates in the 1820s New York countryside, at a hill he called Cumorah. These plates, protected by their author—a resurrected proto-Indian named Moroni—gave voice to America's dead in the 1830 Book of Mormon, which the Saints affirmed as ancient scripture and critics rejected as an antebellum fraud. This scripture is bookended by two father-son pairs—Lehi and Nephi begin the narrative as they flee Jerusalem for America around 600 BCE, while Mormon (the prophetic figure who edited and compiled the writings of the American prophets up to his day) and Moroni conclude the narrative with the extinction of Nephite civilization by the savage Lamanites—whom antebellum Mormons considered to be ancestors of Indians—at a mass grave at Cumorah.[10] The scripture contains the story of still other gold plates, this time of the Jaredites, an earlier tribe that fled the Tower of Babel, retaining the ancient language of Eden in their flight to America. Though they called it Ramah instead of Cumorah, the Jaredites also died at the same hill that witnessed the Nephite extinction and contained the plates of the Book of Mormon for almost two millennia.

After the Book of Mormon emerged as a distinctive grave artifact in the late 1820s, Joseph Smith continued to explore relics and rituals central to the problem of death. In the 1830s, after moving to Ohio, Smith acquired and interpreted Egyptian mummies and their funerary papyri. Finally arriving in Illinois, where he founded a biblical-sounding utopia called Nauvoo, Smith elaborated his religious vision, encompassing an afterlife theology that could vanquish death, ensure permanent personal election, and maintain the human family intact forever in a sacerdotal structure. To this end, Smith drew on, adapted, and reformulated rites and doctrines from sources inside and outside normative Protestantism, yielding an intensely biblical system that combined elements of the Radical Reformation, Western esotericism, and Christian perfectionism. By the time of his death, Smith had revealed a polyvalent family system, a utopian communitarianism grounded in mystical traditions about Enoch, a temple liturgy that taught his followers how to negotiate the afterlife and promised them postmortal divinity, and a scandalously anthropomorphic God whom all humans could call Father. These surprisingly varied themes and innovations of early Mormonism find coherence in Smith's encounters with, and attempted conquest of, death.

I have subdivided the book into two parts that reflect the key themes of Joseph Smith's death conquest. The first concerns death and the dead, while the second describes Smith's construction of immortal communities. Joseph confronted death early and often in a culture much accustomed to premature mortality, a setting I describe in detail in chapter 1, situating the broader culture and the deathbed scenes that proved central to Smith family history. This death culture informed, even transformed, Smith's encounters with leitmotifs in antebellum America, including reverence for the corpse (chapter 2), the treasure quest and grave relics (chapter 3), and the hallowing of ground by interred human remains, particularly the ubiquitous grave mounds of Native peoples (chapter 4). In each of these cases, Smith derived a measure of connection to sacred ancestors that contributed to his final system of death conquest. These concerns provide an interpretive framework for understanding what has been misunderstood as an idiosyncratic variant of prophethood—seerhood—which Smith saw as the ability to vanquish the devastating silence of the grave (chapter 5).

In part II, I describe the types of specific communities—families—that Smith created in his conquest of death. In a four-chapter arc, I describe the temple cultus (an integrated body of rites, beliefs, and behaviors within a religious system), the capstone of Smith's conquest of death, moving from its origins in a modified covenantal theology and understanding of seals and the mission of the prophet Elijah (chapter 6) to the incorporation of translated Masonic motifs into a highly potent death conquest in Nauvoo (chapter 7) and the genealogical reformation of the Great Chain of Being toward which the temple rites directed believers (chapter 8). Because I believe the most notorious aspect of Smith's heaven family, polygamy, must be understood in the context of the genealogical Chain of Being, I cover polygamy— "celestial marriage"—in chapter 8.

Smith famously commented on multiple occasions that he would be happy in hell if only he could be there with his friends. In these coarse and scandalous statements Smith was defining heaven as the place where his loved ones would finally gather. In many respects the temple and related rites underscored this central insight. I conclude the narrative arc with an exploration of what I call Smith's divine anthropology, his incorporation of a heavily anthropomorphic God and deified humans into the upper echelons of a reformulated Chain of Being (chapter 9). In this divine anthropology stands an ontological rather than devotional *imitatio Christi*, a version of the Chain of Being in which Jesus pointed the way for humanity in its quest for perfection. In the divine anthropology, the traditional Christian view of merger into the body of Christ became a merger into the family of Christ, a merger that saw itself in Christ's life and teachings. This represented a radical, sacramental response to Protestantism. In place of Victorian piety, evangelical fervor, or Calvinist election, Smith assured his followers that he would take them to heaven himself through the rites and authorities of his priesthood power.

After investigating Smith's contexts and religious revelations, I explore the meaning of his death at the hands of a vigilante mob, deemed a martyrdom by the Latter-day Saints even before he had breathed his last on that afternoon in June 1844 (chapter 10). His community, suddenly bereft of its prophet, invoked the symbolically potent threads of martyrdom to come to terms with their "afflicting casualty." Simultaneously the community fractured along the lines of tension Smith had attempted to mediate, with the major group following his sacerdotal family and the other coalescing around his biological family. Smith's death was a test case for the theology he had been propagating throughout his religious career.

Figure 0.2 Portrait of William Wines Phelps. Phelps was Smith's amanuensis and recorded many of the most interesting of Smith's theological innovations early in the 1830s. Image courtesy of the Church History Library, The Church of Jesus Christ of Latter-day Saints.

Over and above the broad narrative of Smith's conquest of death stand a variety of interrelated themes and observations. These themes inform all of the chapters, unifying them as they come into dialogue with the concepts presented separately in each chapter. Because these themes are present in so many places, I highlight them here.

First is the sense in which Smith had a revelation to make, a set of religious messages that constantly overflowed the banks of his mind. In setting after setting, his message recurred. His mode of translation was a process of finding and assembling from many sources the clues and cues that supported this revelation. Whether he was observing burial mounds or scrying stones or the King James Bible (KJV) or Masonic liturgy or funerary papyri, Smith had a message whose details arose from careful and passionate reading informed by religious experience and spiritual insight. In this book it becomes clear why Smith included "translator" in his original title of "prophet, seer, and revelator," why he saw translation as central to his religious calling. This was more than just syncretism. Smith had a vision, a revelation—his followers believed a divine dispensation—and as his mind roamed over the conceptual landscape he inhabited, myriad phenomena came to speak of this great revelation. Smith was a translator rather than a parrot, an artist rather than a collator.

Second, Joseph Smith's struggle against death points out the impressive reach of an Antique-sounding view of cosmic integration within early Mormonism. At almost every turn the heavenly world informed, illuminated, and affected the earthly world and vice versa, what some term the metaphysical law of correspondence. By acting out the drama of the cosmos, Smith and his followers could change the course of the cosmos. The microcosm of earth life fed from and looked forward to the macrocosm of the heavens. The pedigrees of the sacerdotal heaven family mimicked and pursued the cosmic hierarchy of gods, angels, and astral bodies.

Third, understanding Mormonism requires appreciating the nature of Mormon biblical exegesis, from their strong appropriation of Isaiah and Ezekiel to provide internal evidences of the Book of Mormon to a cryptic prophecy in Malachi as the key to restoring the human family. In the Book of Revelation they discovered a variety of new ideas to structure their relationships and shape their views of the life to come. The nature of this approach, one I call "marvelously literal" exegesis in order to emphasize the supernatural ends to which a specific sort of literalism worked in Mormon hands, informs almost all of early Mormonism.[11]

The fourth motif is a person, William Wines Phelps (1792–1872; see figure 0.2). Largely forgotten among modern Mormons beyond his legacy as a hymn-writer, this lanky newspaper editor and self-made philosopher proved to be present at almost every crucial conceptual juncture in the early Mormon movement. A convert in 1831 drawn to the miraculous claims of the angel Moroni and the Book of Mormon, Phelps became editor of the first Mormon newspaper, then Smith's amanuensis, ghostwriter, collaborator, and linguistic coach. In these various roles Phelps documented and perhaps collaborated on a wide array of crucial doctrinal developments. Contrary to the historiographical tradition that maintains that most of Smith's theological innovations date to the 1840s,

Phelps was documenting many of these themes a decade earlier. Smith seems to have relied heavily on this confident older man with a dozen languages ostensibly at his command. Whether Phelps proved at times a muse rather than a cheerleader cannot be decided on the basis of current evidence, but the newspaperman's ability to be present at and be the voice for a wide variety of important theological developments is uncanny. Unlike the Pratt brothers, Orson (1811–1881) and Parley (1807–1857)—better-known systematizers of Smith's thought—Phelps found no place in the hierarchy of the Utah church. Kept at arm's length, Phelps pursued a career in jurisprudence, still promulgating the sort of energetic speculation he had pursued when Smith was alive, and he treasured the facility with ancient languages that Smith had aspired to. In these respects, Phelps represents an informative remnant of a particular strain of Mormonism that figured prominently during Smith's life but receded over the decades following his death.

Joseph Smith's is a complicated story with many twists and turns and possible interpretive approaches. His struggle with an almost universal concern over death provides a new vantage on the founder of a new religious movement. He did and said many things, grappled with diverse ideas, many of them framed in terms of a mythic lost perfection. However tempting it is to call him a Romantic expressing an excessive nostalgia for past epochs, though, Smith was not merely venerating the past. The Mormon prophet was actively seeking out the dead, both past and future, and placing them into direct family relationships with himself. The Joseph Smith who emerges from this treatment is a physical and resourceful, if often unusual, man roaring in the face of death, an epic "action hero" of death in the style of the ancients. He was a Heracles, a Beowulf, a Gilgamesh, an Odysseus—bound not to rout the underworld or bring down the heavens but to link the earth inextricably to them.[12]

PART ONE

DEATH, DYING, AND THE DEAD

These things spake God to Moses, from the mount
Whose name is veiled to ken of humankind;
And thus that prophet, but through unbelief
And cunning craftiness, at war with Light,
The fulness of his message sleeps till now,
When one like unto him and Him he typed,
Brings forth the buried meaning from its grave.
                              —Orson F. Whitney (1904)

1

"Melancholly Reflections"

Joseph Smith and Holy Dying

Nine months before his own death at the hands of a vigilante mob, Mormon founder Joseph Smith Jr. preached the funeral sermon for a prominent disciple, probate judge James Adams (1783–1843). Using the funeral sermon, as he often did, as a platform for broader purposes, Smith proclaimed to his followers:

> All men know that all men must die. What is the object of our coming into existence then dying and falling away to be here no more? This is a subject we ought to study more than any other, which we ought to study day and night. If we have any claim on our Heavenly Father for any thing it is for knowledge on this important subject.[1]

For an anticreedal folk prophet with little formal theology, this public requirement for ceaseless study seems extravagant, but his message was clear. Latter-day Saints were to become assiduous students of death.

In the Adams funeral sermon, as with much of his preaching, Smith demonstrated his strong desire to prepare his followers for death. A few months prior, he had preached in a Sunday sermon that "salvation is nothing more or less than to triumph over all our enemies...& the last enemy [i]s death."[2] In his swan song sermon of April 7, 1844, Smith proclaimed that "the greatest responsibility that God has laid upon us in this world [is] to seek after our dead."[3] These morbid-sounding refrains were the public face of Smith's near obsession with human mortality as the central problem of religious and social life. His solutions to the problem, what he called "the orders of Heaven," transformed the enemy death—"annihilation"—into a blessed state of heavenly community he termed "exaltation."[4]

Early Latter-day Saints embraced Smith's solutions to the problem of death. One Mormon, an aspiring if not particularly gifted poet, proclaimed that the Prophet's answer to death was wholly sufficient to recommend his religion, in an 1842 anti-Deist poem:

> Or what in death's dark hour can cheer
> The heart of man?
> I answer promptly without fear—
> *Religion can.*
> Call this delusion if you please—
> Enthusiastic fantasies,
> Or by still harsher names than these,
> And terms more rough;
> If it can bid our sorrows cease,
> *It is enough.*[5]

While Smith and his followers steadfastly maintained the truth of his religious system, he was surely sympathetic to the claims of this poem: let schooled theologians battle deists and evangelicals denounce the Prophet as a deceiver as they may, the Latter-day Saint religion provided comfort in the face of mortality. One of Smith's plural wives, the poetess Eliza Roxcy Snow (1804–1887), evoked the same theme in her "Apostrophe to Death," framing Smith's death conquest in military terms.

> The darkness that encompass'd thee, is gone;
> There is no frightfulness about thee now....
> since the glorious light
> Of revelation shone upon thy path
> Thou seem'st no more a hideous monster, arm'd
> With jav'lins, arrows, shafts, and iron barbs....
> Seen as thou art, by inspiration's light,
> *Thou hast no look the righteous need to fear.*[6]

Snow exulted in Smith's power in the face of death. Only "inspiration" and "revelation," code words for Smith's gospel, could dispel the darkness gathering around such a violent monster. Even as they pinned their hopes on their prophet, these early Latter-day Saints employed rhetoric and concepts familiar to other Christians, who saw Christianity as "an all-sufficient provision against the fear of death."[7]

The death culture Smith inhabited and inherited has been termed a culture of the "good," "beautiful," "triumphant," or "happy" death by various scholars.[8] Following the lead of the poet John Greenleaf Whittier (1807–1892), I prefer "holy" as a way to emphasize this culture's heavily sacramental, religious, and otherworldly emphases.[9] Though it defies simple description, the holy death featured a ritualized deathbed in which the decedent became resigned to death as an act of salvation, dramatic and conflicted bereavement, and a hope for heavenly reunions.

Although recent scholarship has seen holy death culture in primarily social or even military-patriotic terms, for those who lived and died within it, the religious meaning of holy dying predominated. Believers were saving and being saved by holy deathbeds. The features of this holy death were so stereotyped that they became something of a liturgy extending beyond any single denominational tradition, encompassing even those outside the main streams of American Protestantism.[10] Deciding what to call these performances—theater, drama, script, rites, or liturgy—seems less important than recognizing that they were remarkably uniform, widespread, and efficacious.

Holy dying prescribed roles and behaviors for three groups—the dying, the living, and the dead. The dying were to demonstrate their salvation through calm resignation and to preach saving sermons to the living. The living were to assist the dying in demonstrating their salvation and then to mourn and memorialize the dead in ways that supported the claim to salvation. The living were also to be regenerated by their encounters at the deathbed. The dead—whether angels or deceased friends and relatives—were to welcome the dying to the afterlife and confirm their salvation.

Through the rites of holy dying early Americans sought to negotiate the frightening transition into death while attempting to find the will of God in tragedy. Providentialism, the idea that God willed every important event in every life, whether as punishment or reward, dominated the experience of antebellum Christians. In early America the Providential worldview placed God behind every death, however premature or apparently cruel. Conflict between the Providential worldview and rising sensibilities about the importance of human relationships left participants deeply troubled and conflicted.[11] Death constantly broke up families, mocking human relationships. Simultaneously, Americans believed in the eternal worth of the relationships that death disrupted. This culture exclaimed most loudly and frequently what it feared most was not true— that Christianity could protect their identity and community against the specter of death. The holy death never overcame the central tension of dying in antebellum America, a tension Smith spent his life trying to resolve.

In this chapter I describe the cultural milieu in which Joseph Smith grew to adulthood. Holy death culture contextualizes and explains the problems Smith tried to solve. Understanding the limits of this culture— its failure to deliver reliable reassurances in the face of death—makes sense of the rich complex of beliefs, rituals, scriptures, and social relationships that Smith proposed over the course of his religious career.

Though by then remote from the Reformation itself, antebellum Protestants continued to see themselves as direct heirs of the Reformers. Those first Reformers argued that sacraments and ecclesiastical endowments rejected the efficacy of grace. If souls could be freed by the living from Purgatory, if sacraments had power to compete with the atonement of Jesus, then a theology of a salvation born of God's grace and beyond human control was stillborn. In the interests of establishing the primacy of faith over the "superstitions" of Catholicism, the Reformers rejected many treasured modes of confronting mortality—indulgences and Purgatory, masses for the dead, the sacrament of the deathbed (extreme unction), and the power of saintly relics.[12] Well into the nineteenth century, Protestants continued to define their death culture in opposition to the traditions of "Popery."[13] The needs that Christian ritual served, though, did not disappear with the Reformation. The problem of death had not gone away; the need for cultural and religious tools with which to confront mortality had not receded. Holy dying filled the vacuum left by Protestant reforms.[14]

The problem of death remained acute and severe throughout the antebellum period. Until what has been termed the "demographic transition" of the late nineteenth century, many Western societies experienced death rates of 3–4 percent per year, despite a remarkably young population. Antebellum America was no exception.[15] In a nation learning to treasure numeracy and the meaning of counting, death was a natural and common subject for analysis. One circulating paraphrase of a German public health physician's calculations put a daunting numeric face on the ubiquity of death. "It is computed by Dr. Caspar," the exchange papers announced, "that there are on the

Figure 1.1 Portrait of Lucy Mack Smith, Joseph Smith's mother and author of the family memoir in which many holy deathbed scenes are recorded. Image courtesy of the Church History Library, The Church of Jesus Christ of Latter-day Saints.

earth 960,000,000 human beings, and that the average deaths are 29,000,000 annually, 80,000 daily, nearly 3,700 hourly, and fifty-five every minute."[16] Morbid arithmetic put an objective, statistical face on an avalanche of personal experiences.

Joseph Smith's environs were no less dangerous than the rest of America. The Smith family knew premature death well. Joseph's mother, Lucy Mack Smith (1775–1856; see figure 1.1), lost seven of her eleven children, while in the next generation Joseph Jr. lost six of his eleven before dying himself in his late thirties, a death rate higher than the already significant nineteenth-century average.[17] Though mortality data for the Mormon settlements in Ohio and Missouri are sparse, there is little reason to believe they were any lower than for other frontier communities. Smith's most significant settlement, the

Mormon utopia at Nauvoo, Illinois, lost one in twenty of its population every year.[18] Of nearly four hundred deaths recorded by the city sexton for 1842–1843, only two were from "old age." Even in the absence of an epidemic—in which 10–30 percent of a settlement could die within a year—infections, the major cause of death, could strike down several members of a family at once as microorganisms spread from victim to victim.[19] Obituaries occasionally memorialized several members of a household at once. In the phrase of English immigrant John Greenhow (b. 1810), bereft of his wife and two children in a year, "death's shafts fly thick, and our friends drop off like leaves in autumn."[20]

The threat of death was even greater than its physical reality in early America. High mortality rates notwithstanding, there were many more dress rehearsals than actual deaths. A bout of dysentery, a chest cold, or a headache could rapidly turn fatal, even though they generally did not.[21] Unreliable, even dangerous, medical therapy meant that minor illness could end in death; every sickbed carried the specter of the deathbed.

Even when everyone involved was in perfect health, the lack of reliable communication networks and the significant risks of travel meant that death cast its shadow over every long-term farewell. Each parting threatened to be the last.[22] Migrants particularly might never see loved ones again, a point that struck Mormons, who were frequently dislocated from settlement to settlement on the frontier, especially hard.

The frequency of early death and familiarity with it are central features of the culture of holy dying. Peering from the other side of the demographic transition, it has been tempting for many scholars to believe that nineteenth-century Americans ritualized death simply because it surrounded them. Environmental determinism explains little, though: every historical person has died, often prematurely, and human cultures contain a multitude of approaches to this problem. Environmental determinism serves more as an apologia for the modern West than a credible account of the antebellum experience. Why did these people embrace the holy death over studied indifference, nihilism, secondary treatment of corpses, professionalized mourning, psychotropic ingestions, sacrifices of livestock, wrestling matches, or any of scores of other well-documented cultural solutions?[23] Death requires explanation for any culture; the form of that explanation is an expression of a particular culture at a particular time. Deathways both reflect and amplify impulses and ideas specific to their society.

Holy dying required considerable cultural maintenance. Early nineteenth-century Protestants, though lacking the detail of the late medieval *Ars moriendi* (devotional texts teaching the Art of Dying) or the formal liturgy of the Anglican *Book of Common Prayer*, had access to these traditions through reprinted works like Jeremy Taylor's *Rule and Exercise of Holy Dying*.[24] Spoken and printed sermons augmented such manuals, teaching believers what to expect and how to behave. The eighteenth-century Anglican James Hervey (1714–1758) contributed with his popular *Meditations and Contemplations*, a copy of which Joseph Smith owned.[25] Publishers printed funeral sermons of prominent individuals, disseminating words that echoed in every meetinghouse.[26] Biblical encyclopedias and school primers advised readers how best to approach their own demise.[27] Genres often merged: an account of Hervey's protracted deathbed, penned by a close friend, occupies a quarter of the preface to his *Meditations*.[28]

Over the course of the nineteenth century, literature played an increasing role in maintaining the culture of holy dying. Early in the century short stories—forgettable fictions detailing imagined deathbeds—circulated in newspapers, often framed by editorials about death. Almanac writers and newspaper editors contributed snippets or aphorisms to fill blank space between stories, sometimes as simple as "Every beat of the heart, is a rap at the door of the tomb."[29] Slightly longer works included famous stories and excerpts by Charles Dickens (1812–1870) or prolific and now-forgotten authors, scattered across the exchange papers.[30] By midcentury, novels had added their voices to the chorus, with characters like Harriet Beecher Stowe's (1811–1896) Little Eva or T. S. Arthur's (1809–1885) Little Mary Morgan. Even the humorist Mark Twain (1835–1910) had an offering in this genre, his caricatured Emmeline Grangerford.[31]

Midway between fiction and sermon stood written memorials, whether devotional paragraphs with a brief obituary, a poetic couplet, or a sustained memorial in the local newspaper. In these accounts, readers associated specific names with the generalized and ritualized experience of death.[32] While printed sources are most accessible to historians, oral sources and personal experience mattered a great deal. Responsibilities for maintaining this culture in practice fell on women. As Lucy Mack Smith did for her family, countless mothers across America taught rising generations how to live and how to die.[33] Through this work of maintaining culture, antebellum Americans learned how to prepare themselves to encounter the King of Terrors.

This culture of holy dying was the canvas on which Joseph Smith's life and religion were painted. Smith's early exposures to death, most centrally the death of his brother Alvin (1798–1823), serve as a useful frame for understanding both holy dying and early Mormonism.[34] In its repercussions in the lives of the Smiths, the uses, meanings, and problems of holy dying become clear.

Death and the Young Joseph Smith

Joseph Smith Jr. was born to Joseph Smith Sr. (1771–1840) and Lucy Mack Smith in December 1805, after a 1796 stillbirth, two sons, and a daughter. He entered a rural family well versed in the practice of holy dying. The best record of their family history, his mother's memoir, bears strong witness to this fact. Lucy Mack Smith filled her *Biographical Sketches of Joseph Smith the Prophet and His Progenitors for Many Generations* with stories of deathbeds, threatened deathbeds, miraculous resuscitations, and dramatic bereavement. She treasured passings, from that of her mother to that of a sister whom she carried in her arms on the verge of death, to that of another sister who recovered temporarily from her deathbed to pronounce Christ's love.[35] Joseph Sr. also displayed a near obsession with death that increased as he battled consumption and assumed prominence in his son's church in the 1830s. Neighbors in New York confirmed the Smiths' commitment to the principles of holy dying. One, in a critical reminiscence, paused to recall that the Smiths "were kind neighbors in sickness; & Hiram Smith in particular when my father died he was at our house all the time. & I had a brother died and he was as attentive then."[36] From the beginning, the Smiths knew and cared for death.

Holy dying provided an interpretive framework for Joseph Jr.'s childhood sickbeds. Afflicted during an epidemic of typhoid fever (Salmonella blood poisoning) that began in 1812, Joseph found himself near death twice. He later remembered that he "was attacked with the Typhus Fever, and at one time, during my sickness, my father dispaired of my life." With Joseph Sr. fretting over his ailing body, young Joseph developed an abscess "under the arm," which required surgical drainage. The procedure did not heal him, though, and the boy Smith acquired "a fever sore of the worst kind" in his leg. This common complication of typhoid fever (osteomyelitis, an abscess centered in bone) augured the possibility of amputation and perhaps death. Fortunate to live near an innovative surgeon, a founding professor of Dartmouth Medical School, Joseph Jr. underwent three ultimately successful operations, which Joseph remembered decades later as "the most acute suffering."[37] A limp reminded Joseph ever after of his childhood encounter with possible amputation and death, but the battle with typhoid was only the beginning of the Mormon prophet's brushes with death. According to his mother and disciples, Joseph narrowly escaped several assassination attempts in the 1820s: shots fired from the woods, death threats, and close pursuit on foot.[38]

Sometime around 1820, the embattled young Joseph underwent a theophanic regeneration experience later termed his First Vision. Smith reported seeing God in an otherworldly conversion he described as the attack of a diabolical, "physical" force followed by salvation from encompassing darkness. Many contemporary revivalists entered similar trances as they died to sin. Some of these Protestant worshippers lost control of their voices and bodies; some of them collapsed as if dead for a day or longer. Though less explicit than many of these trances, the First Vision shared their concern with stilled throats and descending darkness: the Prophet, his "tongue" bound, was "doomed to sudden destruction."[39] Only the appearance of divine beings averted certain death. With time, Smith saw his supernatural regeneration as signaling the beginning of a new biblical dispensation.[40]

After a hiatus in his supernatural life, Smith reported that in 1823 an angelic guardian named Moroni revealed to him a tiny stone crypt in the hill Cumorah, a glacial drumlin near Smith's home.[41] Cumorah contained various relics, including gold plates, the record of ancient America that became the Book of Mormon. Smith shared his angelic visions with his family, who embraced his religious calling. The angel would not share the sacred plates with the young Joseph on their first encounter, though. He required that Smith rendezvous again on the anniversary of the original visit, this time in the company of his older brother Alvin.[42]

Alvin, the Smiths' oldest boy and "auxiliary family head," looms over the family narrative like a mythic hero.[43] Dutiful, pious, and tender-hearted in his family's memory, Alvin may have mediated some tensions between the believing Lucy Mack and her unchurched husband, though such tensions were unlikely to be pathological.[44] Joseph Jr. for his part openly admired his brother, seven years his senior, and drew strength from Alvin's encouragement. The oldest Smith child was a logical choice to accompany the young prophet to Cumorah.

Tragically, the intended meeting of Joseph, Alvin, and Moroni never came to pass. In November 1823, the twenty-four-year-old Alvin abandoned his day's labors, "in great distress," "very sick...with the bilious cholick." An unfamiliar physician in a neighboring village arrived in place of the family doctor. For the colic, the replacement physician prescribed the standard "heroic" therapy, calomel, a toxic salt of mercury, which Alvin resisted until "by much persuasion he was prevailed on" to take the purgative. The family doctor arrived later, decrying the prescribed calomel, but it was too late, as "all the power [and] medicine which was afterwards prescribed by 4 skillful physicians could not remove it."[45] Alvin expired four days after he fell ill, probably of appendicitis, though his mother, spiting the first physician, may have correctly diagnosed fatal calomel ingestion.[46]

Alvin's passing illuminates several aspects of holy dying as it echoed across the Smiths' lives. The memories the family created of Alvin's deathbed emphasize how thoroughly holy dying shaped their worldview. Alvin and his family performed all the tasks required in the holy death— he approached death both conscious and resigned, exhibited the stipulated calm, and assembled an audience to whom he preached and exhorted. At his death a messenger from the other world collected his spirit, and his family began to grieve loudly and dramatically.

Glad not to have died in his sleep, Alvin approached death deliberately. According to Lucy he announced to the deathbed assembly his imminent demise and then turned to Joseph Jr. and summarized, "I am going to die now the distress which I suffer and the sensations that I have tell me my time is very short."[47] Divining his mortality in this particular sickbed, Alvin demonstrated his preparation for the moral contest of the deathbed and provided cues to his family. Alvin was not expressing fear, but proclaiming to his family that a holy death was under way.

Rather than inciting fear and melancholy, believers saw foreknowledge of death as a Providential gift. James Hervey representing generations before and after, called an unanticipated death "most pitiable" because failure to confront death robbed the event of its spiritual meaning.[48] Foreknowledge mattered because the contest for salvation was never far from the death chamber. Though the supernatural battles between angels and demons of the medieval deathbed had faded (Joseph Jr.'s recent conversion notwithstanding), new modes of achieving and proving salvation at life's end guided antebellum believers. Lucy's account of Alvin's final moments is canonical holy dying: remarkably self-assured, he announced, "Father Mother brothers sisters farewell I can now brathe out my life as calm as a clock." After this statement, he "immediately closed his eyes in death."[49] In these recollected phrases, his mother demonstrated Alvin's salvation. Despite the agony of death from an abdominal catastrophe, he displayed perfect equanimity.

Expiring as calmly as a clock—a timepiece measuring the spans of life and death in the determinism of Providence—Alvin embraced the otherworldly calm enjoined on Christians.[50] Hervey prefaced his popular "Meditations Among the Tombs" with the exhortation that the righteous should "look forward upon their approaching exit without any *anxious apprehension;* and when the great change commences, may bid adieu to terrestrial things, with all the *calmness* of a cheerful resignation, with all the *comforts* of a well-grounded faith."[51] Beneath these calm faces and tempered words raged the battle for salvation.

Resignation was the external evidence of victory in the moral contest at the deathbed, the fullness of conversion.[52] "Agony," that desperate synonym for life's final moments, originally meant "contest," and for many antebellum believers it remained so. Death represented the end of backsliding (for Arminians) or the last moment to demonstrate the grace of the elect (for more traditional Calvinists). Salvation was at stake.[53]

Different people chose different ways to express the sacred calm. Some sang psalms, others prayed or exhorted. Even as they occasionally cheered loudly in their "happy" version of the holy death, antebellum Methodists were careful to display Christian faith as they lay dying.[54] To fail in this project was to "die hard," a much feared outcome.[55] Though some Americans appropriated classical antecedents for this calm, by and large such resignation indicated victory in the struggle for salvation as it had for centuries.[56]

The earliest Latter-day Saints adopted the practice of calm resignation on the deathbed. In February 1831, Smith incorporated tenets of holy dying into the "Laws of the Church of Christ." In the biblicized language of the Laws, "it shall come to pass that they that die in me shall not taste of death for it shall be sweet unto them & they that die not in me their death shall be bitter."[57] Appropriating the language of a New Testament apocalyptic promise, Smith took control of the salvation drama of the deathbed.[58] His followers adopted this biblical amplification in their own memorials. The memorialist for eighteen-year-old Harriet Partridge (1822–1840) noted that "the words of the Savior were verified, in her case" before quoting the Laws. The memorial ended with the reminder that "blessed are the dead who die in the Lord."[59]

Amidst the "sweet" calm of holy dying, the dying had responsibilities not only to their own salvation but to their audience as well. They were to preach to the living.[60] In the fraught nights leading up to his passing, Alvin assembled his frightened family. During an initial round of exhortations, he told his sister Sophronia to "be a good Girl." As his final night settled upon him, Alvin "called for all the children and again exhorted them." He told Joseph Jr. to "set a good example for the children that are younger than you."[61] Though Alvin's exhortations were unadorned, the deathbed setting imparted to even simple platitudes a holy gravity. Even the humblest of Christians could command an audience in the death chamber; words from deathbeds echoed across the early American republic.[62]

The contest for salvation mattered enough that the living often assisted the dying in their performances. The living sought salvation for the dying in two interrelated ways: they urged conversion and resignation on the deathbed and reconstructed the deathbed in retrospect. Acts of interpretation made the promise of a sweet death a self-fulfilling prophecy.

In the death chamber visitors directed the sometimes reluctant decedent to play her part in the drama of salvation. Some Methodists cajoled the dying until the absolute final moment, needing ultimate confirmation that the believer had persevered.[63] Famous evangelists bragged of men they goaded into conversion in the very act of dying.[64] Though it was better for an individual to demonstrate salvation independently, even an assisted, grudging acceptance could suffice.

Survivors continued the work of salvation even after the loved one's death, by describing antemortal piety and deathbed calm. Mourners and memorialists at times invented details about the extent of calm or awareness in order to prove a decedent's salvation.[65] In difficult deaths, a single moment of calm awareness could be enough to reassure observers of the decedent's salvation.[66] Generally even the briefest of obituaries reassured readers that the dead had passed "without a struggle or a groan."[67] The spread of newspapers increased the power of written memorials to broadcast evidence of salvation from the deathbed.[68] When photography became available, postmortem portraits dominated the new technology, allowing families to create a permanent image of holy dying, the corpse posed in a state of quiet slumber.[69]

Memorials also emphasized the piety of the dead, testimonials designed to reassure writer and reader that the decedent had received salvation. Joseph Jr. in 1842 wrote heartfelt, clumsy lines of memorial poetry to his brother in a special journal: "In him there was no guile / He lived without spot from the time he was a child From the time of his birth, he never knew mirth He was candid and sober and never would play and minded his father, and mother, in toiling all day." Alvin, in Joseph's concluding phrase, "was one of the noblest of the sons of men."[70] By this memorial, Smith announced his unchurched brother's right to heaven, emphasizing Alvin's possession of pious virtues requisite to salvation.

Visitors to deathbeds also had obligations to themselves. Those who attended holy deathbeds came, often at the urging of their ministers, to save themselves; in these encounters participants rehearsed their own deaths.[71] Standing together with loved ones on the cusp of the afterlife they could see clearly their own path to heaven.[72] In the phrase of Hervey's eulogist, "the death-bed of the good man is a privileged spot."[73] The poem "Night Thoughts," by Edward Young (1683–1765), which often figured in antebellum death writings, announced: "The chamber where the good man meets his fate / Is privileged beyond the common walk of virtuous life / Quite on the verge of heaven."[74] Young saw the death chamber as privileged because it allowed a glimpse of afterlife and because the dying had a clearer vision than the living. The deathbed also reminded the living that mortal life was not permanent. Those who could not attend a deathbed clamored for news, seeking some mode of participation in the event.[75] Awareness of death turned the minds of the living to heaven. Joseph Smith, eulogizing an unexpectedly deceased missionary, reminded "all the Saints who are mourning, this has been a warning voice to us all to be sober and diligent and lay aside mirth, vanity, and folly and be prepared to die tomorrow."[76] Injunctions to live in constant awareness of one's own death paralleled the stern Calvinism of Puritan death culture and the ascendant Methodist understanding of the daily dying believer.[77] Just as a well-performed deathbed established the salvation of the decedent, so could it save the survivors.

A third group had obligations at the holy deathbed: visitors from beyond the pale of death. God, angels, and the already deceased were invited to the holy deathbed. As Alvin closed his eyes in death, he entered a space between life and afterlife, charged with supernatural power. According to Lucy, as he breathed his last, "one present said Alvin is gone an angel has taken his spirit to Heaven," an image that stayed with the Mormon prophet for the rest of his life.[78] This common trope of supernatural escorts from the death chamber cut across American history and society, from Puritans and evangelicals to folk believers and radical prophets.[79] Believers took the much-cherished phrase of British poet James Montgomery (1771–1854), "Angels wait my soul to carry," quite literally.[80] Such visitations strengthened hopes of salvation among worried Protestants, easing some of the loss of Purgatory to the Reformation.[81]

Increasingly enlightened Protestants, against the "enthusiastic" visions of folk prophecy and American Swedenborgianism, sought to constrain contacts with angels.[82] In a Protestantism fearful of the interference of pretended angelic visits caused by dark spirits or hallucinations, the deathbed represented a safe haven for such encounters, what some termed "the ministration of departed ones" in a vague merger of angels with the recently dead.[83] Protestant sermons often anticipated deceased friends as guides to heaven even as they disparaged visits from ghosts.[84] One Bible dictionary biblicized this cultural trope: angels at the deathbed were the modern version of Elijah's chariot of fire, drawing believers to heaven.[85]

The trope of angels gathering the believer at death was quite strong. When Lucy's sister Lovisa (1761–1780) recovered from an apparent deathbed and visited her father Solomon Mack (1732–1820), rather than gratitude at her recovery Solomon expressed wonderment at what he understood to be her ghost come to collect him. When Lovisa entered her father's house, Solomon cried out "in amazement Lovisa is dead and Loe her spirit has come to admonish me of my final exit."[86] Seeing his daughter—he believed she was dead—meant to Solomon that it was his time to die: Lovisa was the angel dispatched from heaven to gather up his spirit. Though both participants in this strange encounter were alive, the text was clear: the dead guided the dying to the next life. Angelic visits signaled both the mortal end and the hope of salvation—the angels would not come for a person headed to hell.[87] Early Latter-day Saint death chambers, as those of the generation before, were "full of Angels...to waft [the dying] home."[88]

Carried to heaven by angelic beings, the dying believer entered a place of supernatural reunions. The holy death strongly anticipated that people would recognize each other and rebuild communities in the afterlife. Contrary to the official theocentrism of Calvinism, post-Calvinist Protestants saw heaven as the place "where parting is no more," a tradition that only increased with the passage of time.[89] Revivalist hymns about "The joyful Meeting" of the blessed on "Canaan's happy shore" finally settled into the now famous hymn "Say, Brothers, Will You Meet Us," which reminded believers that "By the grace of God I'll meet you / Where parting is no more," by the 1850s.[90] Repeatedly Protestants consoled themselves with the thought that, if all the members of their families were converted, the families would be reconstituted in some way after death.[91]

The fragile prospect of heavenly reunions spurred much of the salvation emphasis of the deathbed. What threatened to make the separation of death permanent was the possibility that a loved one had not achieved salvation. Therein stood a crucial defect in the holy death culture's solution to the problem of death.

Grieving Providence

As the angels and their wards departed, the focus of the deathbed became the bereaved. Profound, public mourning defined holy dying as much as the behavior of the dying themselves. Lucy and her family knew their obligations and performed them well. When Alvin expired, his family "wept with one accord their irretrievable loss," a pattern they followed for all the deaths they endured.[92] Joseph Smith later reflected to an associate on the "many deaths" he had experienced, that they left "a melancholly reflection, but we cannot help it."[93] At times he indicated that he would rather have died than Alvin.[94] The Mormon prophet minced no words on the subject: "Alvin my oldest brother, I remember well the pangs of sorrow that swelled my youthful bosom and almost burst my tender heart, when he died." As Joseph Jr. began to record the story of his church, he and his brother Hyrum (1800–1844) inscribed a mark of dedication, "In Memory of Alvin Smith," and attached it to the manuscript of what became the official *History of the Church*.[95]

Early Mormons participated fully in the American folkway of mourning. Even as the 1831 Laws promised a sweet death to believers, they instructed faithful Latter-day Saints to "weep for the loss of them that die."[96] According to the Book of Mormon the requirement to "mourn with those that mourn" was part of an ancient baptismal covenant.[97] The Latter-day Saints complied with these instructions. In 1834 Oliver Cowdery (1806–1850), Smith's assistant in the late 1820s and early

1830s, editorialized an obituary: "We feel a willingness to weep with those that weep, and sympathize with those, who, in the providence of our Father are called to bid adieu to those who are united to them by the strongest earthly ties."[98] In 1842, Smith considered the death of a young man, noting that "I never felt more solumn it calles to mind the death of my oldest Brother who died in New York & my youngest Brother Carloss Smith who died in Nauvoo[.] It has been hard for me to live on earth & see those young men . . . taken from us in the midst of their youth."[99]

The passionate, vocal bereavement of holy dying, supporting and supported by a bountiful consolation literature, seems to have played three main roles: it provided a form of social immortality, it effected conversion among survivors, and, when performed competently, it demonstrated the superiority of belief over unbelief in the face of death.[100] Simultaneously, though, the bereavement of holy dying expressed a deep and abiding tension within the Providential worldview. The fact that death remained painful for survivors only heightened the tension, pointing out areas where holy death culture failed in its task. Antebellum Americans lived out the holy death so strenuously in part because they never fully resolved the tension out of which the culture arose. The complexity of the Mormon death conquest points out just how inadequate some found holy death culture to be.

If God oversaw and executed every vagary of human fate, and humans continued to die at the wrong time in great numbers, then how could God value the attachments that believers created with their loved ones? If, on the other hand, God did valorize human relationships, how could he possibly will that they end in high numbers and far earlier than they should? For a culture in which God still defined events, in which God's will could be expressed through a thunderstorm or the rustling of leaves, a business success or the loss of a loved one, determining God's will cost believers a great deal of rhetorical, intellectual, and emotional energy. Death, particularly premature death, was the event par excellence in need of Providential interpretation.[101]

Providence forced a search for the moral cause of every death. For the heirs of American Calvinism, premature death could be seen as an indication of moral laxness or of sinful attachment to the present world. Despite rhetoric about the blessedness of the holy death, believers often sought sin as the underlying cause of premature mortality.[102]

Many of the adjustments believers made are attempts to come out from beneath the burden of the Providential worldview, to explain why

God had killed a loved one. When believers called on Nature to mourn the passing of someone they loved, they tried to coax from God some reassurance that he did not glory in premature death, that he was no indifferent or sadistic ruler.[103] In the thunder and rain most often appropriated to this end in the antebellum period, God seemed to be apologizing for his Providence, weeping from the sky for the suffering of his children.

The power of death to express God's will is clear in the threatened 1842 deathbed of Eliza (1823–1845), the nineteen-year-old daughter of intermittent church co-president Sidney Rigdon (1793–1876). Reporting what would in the twentieth century be called a near-death experience, Eliza explained to her father that she had been spared to give him a message: he was to stop feuding with Joseph Smith. Eliza, enjoying her God-given return to life, made clear that other children had in fact lost their lives to their parents' apostasy. Of the dissident George Robinson (1814–1878), who had just lost a child, Eliza said, "as he had denied the faith, the Lord had taken away one of his eye-teeth, and unless he repented, he would take away another."[104] Describing Robinson's bereavement as God taking an "eye-tooth" blamed Robinson for his child's death and emphasized the risk of placing too much affection on a child. Eliza thereby implicitly blamed her temporary death on her father's fight with Smith.[105] Eliza's interpretation persuaded her father Sidney, a longtime believer in signs and wonders. To a large church conference Rigdon announced that he could never renounce the Mormon prophet, as he had "seen the dead raised." In the outcome of a daughter's sickbed rested a family's devotion to the Mormon movement.[106]

In one of the complex paradoxes surrounding death, the bereaved often worried that their mourning represented a punishable distraction from the glory of God. Attachments—to family, friends, possessions—had been encompassed by an uneasy disavowal of so-called *avaritia* since at least medieval Christianity.[107] For colonial Calvinists high child mortality was "a Testimony against our Immoderate Love to, and Doating upon our Children."[108] Such views persisted well into the nineteenth century, both in the South and the North.[109] One itinerant preacher called these "sublunary attachments" and prayed for liberation from them, worrying that one particular friendship would create "an idol in my affections" that would lead to a friend's early death.[110] The statesman Henry Clay (1777–1852) famously used this language to describe the 1847 death of his son in the Mexican War.[111]

Though Smith ultimately developed sacramental solutions to the problem of Providence, the pain of bereavement left him sometimes expressing wistful fear that God could punish excessive affection. In his eulogy for Ephraim Marks (1818–1842), Smith warned, "When we lose a near and dear friend, upon whom we have set our hearts, it should be a caution unto us not to set our affections too firmly upon others, knowing that they may in like manner be taken from us. Our affections should be placed upon God and His work, more intensely than upon our fellow beings."[112] Though less strict than his Puritan forebears, Smith emphasized the pain associated with loss even late in his career. To his wife Emma (1804–1878), he privately commented on the death of a niece: "I was grieved to hear that Hiram had lost his little Child I think we Can in Some degree Simpathise with him but we all must be reconciled to our lots and say the will of the Lord be done."[113]

The narrative of excessive love, while painful, was less difficult than believing that either the decedent or the survivors were guilty of gross iniquity. Providence could explain anything and for some individuals nothing, but for many believers there was no other option. In the melancholy phrase of Jonathan Edwards (1703–1758), "I find also by experience, that there is no guessing at the hands of providence, in particular dispensations towards me."[114]

The intense bereavement of the holy death clashed loudly with the peaceful demeanor expected of the dying, while survivors' mourning seemed to give the lie to the beauties of the afterlife. Doubt of the justice of God's plan might demonstrate worldliness, and the dying were thus not allowed public expression of sorrow. Reconciliation to God's will marked the saved; to protest it by grieving one's own demise could disrupt the salvation of the deathbed.

At times the tension spilled over into strange conflicts, the dying obligated to accept death, the bereaved to resist it. According to his 1838 obituary, James Marsh (1823–1838), fourteen-year-old son of a Mormon bishop, "said, 'if it is the will of God to take me, I do not wish to stay.' On seeing his parents' anxiety to save him, he said 'I do not wish to live only for the sake of my father and mother.'"[115] The Marshes grudgingly let James go, unable to resist his logic. Julia Ann Coltrin (1812–1841), almost thirty, called out to her husband Zebedee, *Let me go! Let me go!* as she died.[116] Even James Montgomery's gentle poem warned onlookers, "if ye love me, let me go," a sentiment present in a variety of deathbed accounts.[117] Mourning was not merely the expression of muted suffering, the antidote to the deliberate piety of the dying; it also served to further divide the living from the dead—the living had time to make peace with Providence and the will of God, while the dying did not. The departing prepared for a meeting with the just, while those who remained behind prepared for their sacred loneliness. Such conversations, where the dying downplayed sublunary attachments and the living clung desperately to them, demonstrated just how unnatural this claim was and how inevitable.

Antebellum America was not of one mind on the question of bereavement, however. Some antebellum Christians found the passionate mourning of the holy death distasteful, and some clergy forbade gloomy funerals or other paraphernalia of grieving.[118] Famed lexicographer and textbook author Noah Webster (1758–1843), in the primer used in Smith's district school in Palmyra, New York, answered the question "Is it not right to grieve for the loss of our friends?" with a stern response:

> It is certainly right; but we should endeavor to moderate our grief, and not suffer it to impair our health, or to grow into a settled melancholy.... We should therefore remember our departed friends only to imitate their virtues; and not to pine away with useless sorrow.[119]

Webster amplified a variety of voices urging that life go on, that Christian hope replace vocal grief. Some early Mormons mimicked Webster's admonitions, without much success.[120] However much propriety recommended that grief obey limits, most people were not inclined to be easily consoled. Decades later, with the "Dying of Death" in American culture, Webster's views would predominate. Before the Civil War, though, Webster pointed out but did not resolve a central tension of the holy death, the uncertain balance between grief and reassurance.

Even as many ignored calls to temper the bereavement of the holy death, antebellum Protestants and Mormons grieved with an eye to the public face of their convictions. Too much grief might cast doubt on the power of the Gospel to remove the sting of death. For Latter-day Saints, always under the microscope of their Protestant compatriots, injunctions to temper mourning came early. The 1831 Laws required that the Saints mourn "more especially for those that have not hope of a glorious resurrection," implying that mourning for the saved could and should be modulated.[121] Edward Webb (1815–1852), memorializing his brother

Lorenzo (1816–1839) in 1840, remarked that "while we mourn we do not mourn as though we had no hope, he died in the faith of the gospel and in hope of a glorious resurrection and immortality."[122] Joseph Smith repeated the refrain in an 1842 sermon occasioned by the death of a young child. After recounting the elements of the Mormon conquest of death, Smith commented: "notwithstanding all this glory, we for a moment lose sight of it, and mourn the loss; but we do not mourn as those without hope."[123] As they grieved, the Latter-day Saints consoled themselves that they were not as the hapless pagans whom Protestants mocked; or like the Protestants themselves, ever troubled by anxiety over salvation. The fact that Mormons mourned in public further intensified the tension inherent in grieving within the Providential worldview. Mourning too much risked offending God and proving to outsiders that Mormonism had not solved the problem of death.

Whatever the tensions underlying bereavement, the grief of the holy death performed important work for believers. It allowed them to commit loved ones to a form of social immortality, to affirm the importance of the dead to the living. What the pious resignation of the dying was not allowed to express, the loud tears of the bereaved could demonstrate. An 1830s Latter-day Saint summarized the problem poignantly: "perhaps we should be found wanting in feelings of respect and friendship were we not to notice the departure of our beloved brother, the loss of whom we view as an afflicting, though just providence."[124] In this simple phrase, this Latter-day Saint captured the tension of the Providential worldview. Providence "afflicted" believers; premature deaths wounded them. But the Providence of a given death, however painful, had to be "just."

Bereavement expanded the saving compass of holy deathbeds; mourners often turned their eyes heavenward. Smith underscored this point in an 1842 sermon, acknowledging the deaths from malaria and other infirmities and infections in early Nauvoo. "What chance is there for infidelity when we are parting with our friends almost daily?" he asked his sorrowful audience. He answered unequivocally, "None at all."[125]

At times mourners yearning for salvation seemed suicidal by modern standards. Readiness to die, though, was a hopeful expression of one's readiness for heaven. Believers were not suicidal, they were preparing themselves for heaven.[126] In Smith's phrase, "When men are prepared, they are better off to go home."[127] Non-Mormon John Lewis, mourning his daughter's death in 1830 New York, diarized about his hope that his entire family would soon "join the dear departed child in realms of endless bliss."[128] Participants in camp meetings, confessing the temptation to "backslide" would at times plead for Jesus to "take me home," to seize them before their conviction waned.[129] A grief so severe it seemed to flirt with suicide affirmed the rent in the fabric of human existence caused by the death of a loved one.[130] Simultaneously, grief that made peace with the griever's own death proved devotion. The hope more than anything was that they would be true until death.

Coming of age in the culture of holy dying, the Mormon prophet never fully recovered from Alvin's death. Though it would be overly simplistic to attribute all of Smith's religious activity to Alvin, this death cast a long shadow over Joseph Jr.'s career.[131] Joseph soon confronted the similar death of his father in 1840 from consumption; Alvin was the angel that carried Joseph Sr. home.[132] In constant negotiation with the inevitability of death, the intensity of human revulsion toward it, and the inscrutability of God's Providential will, Smith made his way through the founding of a new religion.

The culture in which Smith lived his life and revealed his religion situated and amplified his personal concerns with death. A reverent but troubled intimacy with death echoed across the length of his often surprising religious career. Smith proved dissatisfied with the adequacy of the culture of holy dying, though, recasting, reforming, and at times frankly rejecting the solutions of his peers to the problem of death. Smith's radical revision of holy death culture is the story of the rest of this book.

2

The Corpse and Its Rest

In Fayette, New York, immediately before the September 1830 second conference of his fledgling church, Joseph Smith issued a millenarian revelation on the fate of humanity at the return of Christ.[1] To the slumbering righteous Smith promised that "the earth shall quake, and they shall come forth...to be clothed upon" with new flesh.[2] Both Smith and the biblical writers he appropriated recalled the imagery of Ezekiel's famous dream to make their point. In this dream, Jehovah showed to Ezekiel a valley "full of bones" that were "very dry." At Jehovah's command, "the sinews and the flesh came up upon them, and the skin covered them above." In Smith's phrase, this promised resurrection would be perfect: "not one hair, neither mote, shall be lost."[3]

For the wicked, however, God promised a curse. For this divine malediction Smith invoked a grisly fate that precisely opposed the resurrection of the just, revising imagery from another Old Testament prophet. Where Zechariah (14:12) had prophesied consumption as a plague from Jehovah—"their flesh shall consume away while they stand upon their feet, and their eyes shall consume away in their holes, and their tongue shall consume away in their mouth"—Smith understood a very explicit curse of putrefaction: "I the Lord God will send forth flies upon the face of the earth, which shall take hold of the inhabitants thereof, and shall eat their flesh, and shall cause maggots to come in upon them; And their tongues shall be stayed that they shall not utter against me; and their flesh shall fall from off their bones, and their eyes from their sockets; And it shall come to pass that the beasts of the forest and the fowls of the air shall devour them up."[4] This revelation presents a striking picture— larvae eating tongues, eyeballs dropping from their orbits, flesh rotting from living bodies that fall prey to carrion feeders. According to the Mormon prophet, a putrefying plague effected by flies, maggots, and vultures awaited the wicked. These nauseating and frightful images seemed to be intended to discourage evildoing and strengthen the resolve of the righteous, not unlike some contemporary revivalist rhetoric.[5] This threat framed the promise of bodily integrity and corporeal resurrection as the ultimate gift of God and its loss to decomposition as God's greatest punishment. This revelation provides an important window into Joseph Smith's worldview and his relationship to the body, its demise, and the decay that inevitably followed.[6]

Smith's curse on the wicked contained two violations of the proper order of things. First, the unrighteous dead were to be consumed aboveground, deprived of the quiet and invisible skeletonization of the righteous dead, whose dry bones would be invested in flesh at the Last Day. Second, and more dramatically, the evildoers would begin to rot before they ever came to die. The wicked would live to experience the aftermath of their own physical death.

Smith returned to the theme of cursed putrefaction in an 1832 vision of the afterlife, in which he revealed that hell meant for the wicked that "their worm dieth not" in eternity.[7] Mormon apostle Orson Hyde (1805–1878), quoting this revelation in 1836, claimed that "they shall desire to die; but their desire shall not be granted."[8] In more concrete circumstances, the Saints cursed individuals suing them in court, praying that the money they acquired would "canker & eat their flesh as fire."[9] Eliza Roxcy Snow used the same imagery in an 1844 diatribe against the citizens of Missouri. "Rottenness has seized upon thy vitals," she told Missouri; "corruption is preying upon thy inward parts."[10]

In such images of live putrefaction, Latter-day Saints invoked ancient traditions about the fate of the persecutors of early Christians.[11] According to a preferred antebellum reference, the *Theological Dictionary* of Charles Buck (1771–1815), the judgments of God doomed certain persecutors to rot alive. Herod Agrippa, the king who beheaded John the Baptist, was "eaten of worms" before he "gave up the ghost," while the second-century Claudius Herminianus was "eaten of worms while he lived." As for "the most cruel" tyrant of his age, God "tormented [Emperor Galerius] with worms and ulcers to such a degree, that they who were ordered to attend him could not bear the stench. Worms proceeded from his body in a most fearful manner; and several of his physicians were put to death because they could not endure the smell."[12] John Foxe (1517–1587) in his *Actes and Monuments* (1565; widely republished in America as the *Book of Martyrs*) announced these tyrants' fates in similarly gruesome terms: emblematically, Chancellor Du Prat's stomach was "gnawn asunder by worms."[13] Mormons made explicit use of these age-old traditions. Smith's assistant Oliver Cowdery reprinted material from Foxe in the *Messenger and Advocate* in 1835, recounting the fate of Galerius: "the whole mass of his body was turned into universal rottenness."[14]

Smith had easy access to these traditions—he owned and consulted Buck's dictionary and had read and praised Foxe's work. But his thoughts on the specter of bodily decomposition also drew on personal experience and contemporary culture.[15] The corpse as a physical and cultural object contained, in the first hours of its existence, a hope against hope for miraculous restoration. With each passing hour, the corpse increasingly mocked that hope, as the body resisted all attempts to awaken it, an unresponsive image of a now absent loved one. Within a few days, depending on the weather, the putrefying corpse became repulsive, even malevolent. Finally, within weeks to years, depending on the temperature and depth of burial, the corpse became dry bones, semipermanent evidence of the coming resurrection. However incapacitated, the corpse performed a great deal of work for the living.

Tracking the corpse from life's final agony to troubled sleep to rotting matter to dry bones, this chapter elaborates Joseph Smith's interpretation and expansion of the antebellum cult of the dead body. Putrefaction occupied Smith's mind in continuity with long-standing Western traditions about decomposition as well as antebellum approaches to the corpse's fraught position between life and extinction. Sequentially, this chapter considers the power of the uncertain moment of death, exploring it in fears about premature burial and early Mormon attempts to raise the dead, and then investigates the Mormon obsession with the power of decomposition, exploring the Smith family's decision to disinter Alvin's body in late 1824 as a context for understanding the obligations owed to the corpse by antebellum believers. The chapter then considers Smith's contributions to an ancient and enduring debate about the necessity of material continuity for the integrity of the body at resurrection, ending with an exploration of the way early Mormons used surrogates of the corpse—usually locks of hair or canes made from coffins—to extend the power of the corpse. Early Mormons made theological and imaginative war with the threat of decay; their theologies of resurrection and embodiment represent answers to the grotesque liminality of the corpse and the persistent specter of decomposition.

The Uncertain Moment of Death

Questions about the meaning of the corpse were deeply personal for the Smith family. Alvin's body played a fateful role, both at his death in 1823 and again the next fall. In the domestic preparations for burial in antebellum America, bodies generally lay shrouded on a board spanning two chairs in a parlor or main room of the house for the day or two before burial (wealthy families could buy time with blocks of ice to cool the body). Alvin's corpse dominated the life of his family while it rested in the house. In a heartrending account stricken from her final memoir, Lucy recounted the effect Alvin's corpse had on her youngest daughter, whose fearful confusion mirrored that of her family. This namesake daughter, two-year-old Lucy, "would run out of the house and drag in a board and lay beside [Alvin's] corpse then take a white cloth and wrap herself in it and lay down on the board by his side."[16] This image of the living shrouded beside the dead had remained with Mother Smith for three decades. But young Lucy, mimicking her dead brother under a shroud, struck at the central irony of the newly dead body. The image of beloved Alvin remained in three dimensions, palpable, while the impulse of life had fled. Decomposition, lurking in the shadows, had not yet made the loss seem irrevocable, but her older brother would not rouse.

Central to the corpse's power and the fear of decomposition was the fact that decay marked irreversible separation from the loved one. Before the onset of decay, a corpse looked like nothing so much as a person sleeping, a metaphor the living often employed to describe death. Given the state of early nineteenth-century medical diagnostics, observers often remained uncertain about the timing or finality of death. This uncertainty fed into hopes that, early on, death might be negotiable.

Survivors invested considerable energy in the illusion of life that lasted for a day or more after death. An 1840s account of a Mormon burial highlights this phenomenon. At a funeral for a young woman, an observer peered into the "plain pine box lying upon the green sward." There he saw the "most delicately beautiful being that I ever beheld." Explaining the serenity of the child's face, the observer reported that "these friendless people gathered around the lovely remains of the young and beautiful martyr; and they 'gazed upon the face of the dead,' and looked upward, penetrating with the eye of faith the vail of the flesh, and assured that in the moment death was victorious, he had been destroyed."[17] When viewed with the eye of Christian faith, the beauty of the girl's corpse, unmarred by decay, served as witness to the reality of the resurrection.

Survivors often imagined corpses smiling, one final act of communication as they expired. Thus one Ohio Methodist reported that "a smile of joy lit up the brow of death...to give animation to her features after every trace of life had become extinct,"[18] and a sentimental fiction invoked the face of a heartbroken virgin: "The smile that animated her countenance while living, still seemed to play around her mouth."[19] One devotional piece instructed mothers of deceased infants to "See upon its placid brow a smile—oh! sweeter than the smiles of life!—is still resting. Ay, gaze upon it as thou wouldst gaze upon the face of an angel; for it is the signet which Heaven has impressed upon its own, sealing it for immortality. Gaze reverently, for it is the reflected glory of that unclouded smile, which beams from the brow of the Eternal."[20] In energetic sentimentalism, believers coaxed from the freshly dead reassurances of heavenly power, symbolic communications of a blessedness beyond death.

That corpses could still smile demonstrated the fraught ambiguity of the newly dead. In the minds of many, this ambiguity raised the possibility that they were not actually dead. Though cremationists later made more of the problem (in tangled logic but potent sentiment—ashes could not suffocate in their coffin), the matter of premature burial occupied many antebellum minds.[21] Claims to live burials or near misses made the rounds among all socioeconomic strata, both as fictional accounts and purportedly true occurrences. Some observers testified to finding corpses in unnatural positions or with signs of postmortem trauma as evidence of live burial. More common were amplifications of the narrative of a sufferer rousing from a coma after observers had decided she was dead, as with one famous corpse found lacing his shoes shortly after his wake.[22] There were practical reasons for this fear, though folk tradition exaggerated occasional medical missteps. Coma could be misinterpreted as death for long hours or even, rarely, days. Though such uncertainty about the time of death strikes the modern imagination as absurd, for antebellum Americans the first hours or even days of death were inherently uncertain.

Some individuals took more caution than others to be sure they had diagnosed death properly. Mormon observers recorded Judge James Adams to be "pulseless" for more than ten hours before proclaiming him dead.[23] One New York woman in 1807 waited with the corpse of her daughter "till an apparent change took place," before committing her to the grave.[24] Stories of live burial, probably rarely if ever true, served a mythic role, treating and broadcasting the central tension of the newly dead body, the most liminal of all entities. Objects or events that span established categories, existing in a process of sustained transition, exert considerable cultural and spiritual power. Such objects, termed "liminal" by anthropologists, threaten an entire classification system by uniting strongly opposing states such as life and death.[25]

Smith's Book of Mormon addressed the question of premature burial, invoking the stench of decay to solve the diagnostic problem of the deathbed. According to the narrative, a good-hearted but benighted Lamanite king named Lamoni heard the Gospel message and entered a deathlike conversion trance. After an almost three-day vigil, his people prepared to inter him in the royal sepulchre, but his wife objected. Seeking out the Nephite evangelist Ammon, the queen pleaded that her husband had "been laid upon his bed for the space of two days and two nights; and some say that he is not dead, but others say that he is dead and that he stinketh, and that he ought to be placed in the sepulchre; but as for myself, to me he doth not stink."[26] Ammon promised that "on the morrow" Lamoni would "rise again" from his trance.[27] His prediction came gloriously true on schedule. Not only did this account employ familiar tropes to describe the Christian conversion of an infidel king, it documented the power of God over death and the dramatic social power of the corpse. Ammon's ability to resolve the uncertainty of Lamoni's apparent deathbed, in the presence of malodorous evidence of decay, documented the prophet's power. In this particular deathbed narrative, anxiety about whether a loved one has truly died and the slow process of awaiting sure signs of decay ended well. The stricken king arose from apparent death. Lamoni's escape from premature burial became the exemplar for his people, who would thereby die and rise again: the entire kingdom converted, several others undergoing death-like trances.

Nineteenth-century readers would have found in the story of Lamoni scriptural confirmation of the power of the ambiguous status of the corpse. The possibility that some apparently dead bodies might in fact be alive also pushed toward the striking possibility, nourished by biblical narratives, that in the right setting the dead could actually rise long before the final resurrection.

Raising the Dead

The liminality of the recently dead body provided the backdrop for disputations about an improbable charism of New Testament Christianity. In 1857, the anti-Mormon pseudonymous writer Maria Ward reported a stunning scene she dated to her conversion in the 1830s. Ward had gathered with Mormons to observe a portentous but unspecified religious ritual. Into a room fraught with suspense Joseph Smith—"a tall, elegant-looking man, with dark piercing eyes"—entered, lectured on Bible miracles, and then led the assembly in silent prayer. As he arose, the Mormon prophet "uttered the solemn and impressive words...'in the might of the Spirit, I command you, bring forth your dead!'" Ward observed a "deep stillness" among the crowd followed by the entry of two men bearing "the body of a young and beautiful female, clad in the white habiliments of death, and looking, Oh! how ghastly and ghostly in the dim obscurity of the uncertain light. The limbs were stiff and rigid, the eyes and mouth partially open, and the whole aspect of the countenance that of death." The girl had died that afternoon, and her mourning father had requested the Prophet's intervention. The dead girl's mother threw herself at Smith's feet, pleading, "she was too young, too good, and too beautiful to die. Restore her, and I will worship you for ever." Smith then led his followers in a "Hallelujah Chant," an otherwise unattested Mormon hymn that ostensibly proclaimed that the Book of Mormon heroes Nephi and Lehi had restored the power to raise the dead.[28] As his followers swelled with holy enthusiasm, Smith "stood beside the apparently dead body. He pressed and stroked the head, breathed into the mouth, and rubbed the frigid limbs, saying in a deep, low tone, 'Live thou again, young woman.'" In an "electrical" display, the dead woman stirred and arose, in full possession of life. Her once pallid body now gave the lie to the deathly shroud that hung limply from her shoulders.[29]

Ward, despite her antipathy for Mormonism (she blamed Smith for the girl's death in the first place, as he had forbidden her marriage to a non-Mormon suitor) did not reject this apparent miracle, the quickening of the dead. She attributed Smith's powers to mesmeric energies, providing a common nineteenth-century explanation for the potency of healing or other miracles effected by physical touch. Whether the girl stirred from a coma or, as is more likely, the episode is a fiction meant to discredit Smith, the account addresses several vital issues surrounding the corpse in antebellum culture—the overwhelming liminality of the newly dead, the hazy uncertainty of the diagnosis of death, and the stakes of claims to religious power over recovery from a deathbed.

Notably, Ward's vignette also points to an actual practice of some early Mormons. From at least June 1831, sources suggest that early Latter-day Saints attempted to raise the dead. They also began to promise each other the charismatic powers necessary to effect the miracle.[30] Generally responses to the sudden death of young people, these efforts occurred sporadically but with much attention from outsiders. As early Mormons dealt with the culture of death and the weight of their anticipated restoration of the "fullness of the Gospel," they found biblical evidence that the faithful should be able to raise the dead. Smith's angelic patron, the immortal Elijah, had raised a widow's son, and Jesus both raised Lazarus and blessed his disciples with, among other things, the power to "raise the dead." The Book of Mormon confirmed the possibility of such miracles.[31] When Smith and his colleagues assembled and ordained the first group of twelve modern apostles in 1835, they explained that "all things should be subject to [them] through the name of Jesus Christ," including death.[32] Joseph Sr. bestowed the same powers on various recipients of ceremonial blessings from 1833 to 1840.[33] Father Smith emblematically informed Noah Packard (1796–1859) that he would "have power to rais[e] the dead[.] Mothers shall rejoice, having their children raised from the dead, and presented to them."[34]

The Latter-day Saints were not the only Anglo-American Christians to consider raising the dead. Seventeenth-century English Quakers gained notoriety for disinterring bodies in hopes of resuscitation, while the French prophet John Lacy (c. 1664–1730) made a public spectacle of attempting to raise Thomas Emmes from the dead.[35] Jemima Wilkinson (1752–1819), the prophetic founder of Vermont's early nineteenth-century New Jerusalem, reported that God himself had raised her from the dead, returning her to earth to provide blessings of health as the "Publick Universal Friend."[36] Critics of Wilkinson and similar visionaries made much of these attempts as fanatical delusions, attributing any publicized successes to fraud.[37] Even near the mainstream, though, glimmered the hope of such a miracle. John Wesley (1703–1791), following the church father Irenaeus in an argument with Conyers Middleton, claimed that early Christians could occasionally, "by great fastings and the joint supplication of the church," return the "spirit of the dead person" into the body. By implication, in rare instances, believing Christians could still raise their fellows from the dead.[38] Participants in the mighty revivals at Cane Ridge in 1801 pursued the same end.[39] These charismatic aspirations demonstrated the imminence of Christ's return and the validity of the supernatural power of the New Testament apostles. They also represented the extreme case of healing and a protest against the inevitability of putrefaction.

Other attempts to raise the dead derived more explicitly from a combination of overwhelming bereavement and folk supernaturalism. In 1830 New York City reformer Elijah Pierson (1786–1834), driven to religious excess by the mortal illness of his wife, Sarah, declared himself an avatar of his namesake, the prophet Elijah. When Sarah died, Pierson staged an attempt to raise her corpse before burial in place of a traditional viewing. He plied her body with rituals of healing, saying "we have anointed her with oil, and prayed the prayer of faith." Embarrassed by public failure when her corpse resisted his ministrations, Pierson abandoned his evangelical past, casting his lot instead with Robert Matthews (1778–1841), the controversial Prophet Matthias. At such a moment Pierson faced the limits of Protestantism and then moved beyond them, propelled onward by his grief.[40]

Despite precedents in the New Testament, the church fathers, and John Wesley, Protestant critics found Mormon resuscitations a choice trope for Smith's charlatanism. Whereas healings could be explained away—the sick did occasionally recover spontaneously—the dead did not naturally rise.[41] In tales of Mormon resurrection, Protestants espied frauds designed to win converts. Mormon seceder John C. Bennett (1804–1867) reprinted an emblematic story in his 1842 *History of the Saints*. A desperately ill stranger came to a farmhouse late one night, asking for a place to sleep before expiring in an upstairs bedroom. Coincidentally, Mormon elders arrived shortly thereafter, reporting that they "were empowered by God to perform miracles, even to the extent of raising the dead." The wily farmer, smelling a hoax, asked the Mormons to confirm that they could "bring any corpse to life" and then proposed to dismember the corpse in the interests of demonstrating the Mormons' power. Presented with the threat of decapitation, the dead stranger miraculously arose and confessed his complicity in a proselytization plot. Several aspects of the story, not least the threat of dismembering an innocent corpse, suggest it is fictitious, but the account clearly frames the issues surrounding the question of raising the dead. Death was so hard to diagnose that a simple Mormon elder could perfectly mimic it to strangers, resuscitation was the converting miracle par excellence, and the specter of disintegration—whether by dismemberment or putrefaction—threatened hopes of early restoration to life.[42]

At times the association of Latter-day Saints with early resurrection came to dominate Mormon death scenes, even when such a rite had not occurred. One of the better known instances reveals the complexity of these themes. Mormon elder Joseph Brackenbury (1788–1832) expired during a mission tour in New York, "from the effects of poison secretly administered to him by opposers." The assassins reportedly mocked Mormon failure to secure the protection of Jesus that "if [the disciples] drink any deadly thing, it shall not hurt [them]."[43] Mormons took the death hard, as "a trial to our faith."[44] Some newspapers announced that, after failing to prevent Brackenbury's death through healing rituals, fellow missionaries attempted to raise their martyr from the dead, an error perpetuated by misreadings by twentieth-century historians. Later nineteenth-century church historians, confessing Brackenbury's failure to survive poisoning, disputed this claim. Rather, following the lead of other contemporary reports, they argued that Brackenbury nearly fell posthumous victim to a nefarious "resurrection" by body snatchers. The official Mormon summary concludes, "Joel H. Johnson dreamed that some persons were digging up Brother Brackenbury's body, and was so exercised about it that he called up some of the brethren and went to the spot, about one mile distant, and he found a party of doctors at work, who had nearly cleared the grave of earth; the men fled with utmost precipitation."[45] While the Mormons struggled to preserve the sanctity of their comrade's corpse (either from professional resurrectionists or sacrilegious critics), outsiders framed their actions as charismatic excess bordering on necromancy.

Following the lead of their Protestant critics, many Latter-day Saints refused to endorse the practice of early resurrection. A doubting Mr. Rose challenged apostle David Patten (1799–1838) in May 1836, claiming that he would believe the Book of Mormon if Patten would "ra[i]se the dead." Rose met with harsh reproof "for his infidelity and unbelief."[46] Mormon itinerants Erastus Snow (1818–1888) and Benjamin Winchester (1817–1901) announced in their general defense of charismatic gifts that "neither do we make any pretensions to raise the dead; for it is not mentioned among the signs that were for the believer."[47] Oliver Cowdery, ever nervous about charismatic excesses, announced in 1836: "that we profess to be able to raise the dead, or ever expect to be . . . is utterly and unequivocally false."[48] Joseph Smith himself, despite likely temptation and his great religious power at Nauvoo, did not attempt to raise his father, his brother, or his children, even though he was present at their deaths. In a formal statement Smith published in the church organ at Kirtland, he kept open the possibility of raising the dead, though he left the matter explicitly in God's hands. In response to the question "Can they raise the dead," Smith answered, "No, nor any other people that now lives or ever did live. But God can raise the dead through man, as an instrument."[49] In a recurrent theme, early Mormons sought to distinguish themselves from the disrespectable folk and Christian traditions of magic and necromancy even as they continued to pursue their religious vision.

An intermediate view of Mormon raisings is evident in the first deathbed scene of Eliza Rigdon (see chapter 1). When Eliza returned from certain death to scold her father Sidney for his infidelity to Smith, Father Rigdon addressed the assembled church in Nauvoo to explain that despite all the miracles he had observed as an early Latter-day Saint, "never before had he seen the dead raised." As Eliza lay dying, "the doctor told him [Rigdon] she was gone, when, after a certain length of time she rose up in the bed and spoke in a very powerful tone...in a supernatural manner." Meeting every expectation of the holy deathbed, this young woman "called the family around her and bade them all farewell, with a composure and calmness that defies all description." She related the message God gave her personally, though the only sign of life in her "was the power of speech." This talking specter spent thirty-six hours hovering between life and death, then revealed to her father that if he were to remain loyal to Joseph Smith, God would return her fully to life, though she wished to remain in the land of the dead. Rigdon agreed with his daughter, declaring to the assembled church that "no person need therefore come to reason with him, to convince him of error, or make him believe another religion, unless those who profess it, can show that through obedience to its laws, the dead has been and can be raised."[50] Eliza's deathbed demonstrates the crucial uncertainty of diagnosing death in its first hours, the desperate extension of sickness into death, and the oracular power of those inhabiting the space between life and death.

In attempting to raise the dead, Mormons confronted a central tension of the deathbed. For death to be meaningful within the Providentialist worldview, it had to be according to God's will. If the dead could rise before the general Resurrection, the closure of a

Providential death became unstable. If a person continued dead merely because her loved ones had neglected to perform certain rituals or lacked adequate faith, then perhaps God had not willed the death in the first place. God had to have power to raise the dead, but exercising that power out of turn threatened human accommodations to death. Simultaneously such a miracle disputed the desirability of heaven. If heaven were truly beautiful, why would anyone want to come back? Eliza Rigdon and many others had been clear that there was no reason to doubt that heaven was better than earth. This was Oliver Cowdery's point when he adamantly denied that the Latter-day Saints "have a wish to call back, to this scene of suffering, those who are freed from it."[51]

The tensions attendant on divine resuscitation are apparent in a story from Zina Baker Huntington (1786–1839), Joseph Smith's plural mother-in-law. According to her son Oliver (1823–1909), Zina heeded the call to perform the vigil over a deceased neighbor, "a man of usefulness in the neighborhood." As she sat in the presence of death, she "was studying upon the power, faith and possibility of the dead being brought back to life now as well as in the days of the apostles." Filling herself with faith and strength, she "stepp[ed] to the corpse turned down the cloth that covered his face and called him to come to life." To her great amazement, "the dead man obeyed, and opened his eyes full wide and gazed into hers." In Oliver's phrase, "the scene was too much for her mortality" so she threw back the shroud, fled the room, and "that inanimate flesh remained as it was." Passing on this secret knowledge later in life, she explained to her children that she had been allowed the power to prove God's existence but the man's return to life was "not expedient," not consistent with the dictates of Providence, so God diverted her mind just before she finished the project.[52] The final flickers of life during the last agony and the some-times unpredictable behavior of the body in the precincts of death left room for such interpretations. This image of the haplessly and abortively raised dead would persist and expand in Mormon folklore into the twentieth century. When raised, the dead pleaded with the living to let them die again.[53]

While critics saw the practice as the absurdity of enthusiastic religion in the hands of charlatans and fanatics, Smith and his followers saw divine resuscitation as the greatest of biblical miracles. Even when they denied engaging in the practice, they maintained its possibility, the knowledge that if necessary God could reverse the irreversible. The practice of raising the dead recognized the horrifying liminality of the corpse, imbuing the difficulty of distinguishing coma from decease with a glimmer of hope for the return to life. Maintaining that God could reverse death under the right circumstances also served as a protest against putrefaction in the brief period before decay left its obvious mark on the body. What mattered most to the Saints was that in principle this miracle substantiated the hope of a literal, physical resurrection, and even if this occurred with some delay, they were content to know that it was well within God's power. The corpse, that infrastructure of the eternal body, would necessarily rise again.

The Threat of Decay

The onset of decay marked for many observers the time when hope for recovery ceased. This harbinger of unrecoverable death turned the breath of life into the stench of death. Decomposition occupied the mind of antebellum Protestants almost as much as it had concerned medieval Christians, with their rich depictions of rotting flesh and their intense reverence for the preserved remains of the holy dead.[54] Natural disasters or outbreaks of disease raised the specter of miasmata—tainted vapors released from corpses—infecting the living.[55] The risk of contagion from human remains served as an important argument in favor of the rural cemetery movement of the 1820s to 1860s, which moved the dead to idyllic rural parks, banishing them from urban settlements.[56] In the transition to the dry bones of Ezekiel's dream, corpses—generally revered and protected—induced fear and discomfort among the living. Decomposition also imperiled hope in individual persistence. In the words of a famed Huguenot preacher, "At length death comes and dissolves all the parts of the body, and how difficult it is to persuade one's self, that the soul, which was affected by every former motion of the body, will not be dissipated by its entire dissolution!"[57]

Strong images of corpses appeared in the Book of Mormon, published shortly before Smith's 1830 revelation on the fate of the wicked. A concern with rewards and punishments, particularly Jehovah's legendary willingness to destroy civilizations for wickedness, echoes across the pages of this biblical-sounding narrative of prehistoric American Hebrews. According to this scripture, a Lamanite army decimated a corrupt Nephite city named Ammonihah as an act of God's wrath for their fall from grace. "In one day it was left desolate; and the carcases were mangled by dogs and wild beasts of the wilderness." Their severe punishment, the inability to bury their dead properly, found expression in the stench of rotting flesh: "so great was the scent thereof that the people did not go in to possess the land of Ammonihah for many years. And it was called Desolation of Nehors; for they were of the profession of Nehor, who were slain; and their lands remained desolate."[58] Nehor, an anti-Christian demagogue whose followers settled Ammonihah, provided the eponym for this fate of the wicked. What appears at first to be a grisly description of the carnage of war is actually a pronouncement of God's curse. Repeatedly, wicked Nephites suffered the same frightening fate, a punishment that continued to visit backsliders to the bitter end of the Book of Mormon. In the final battles of the Book of Mormon civilizations, the Nephites were forced to leave the "flesh, and bones, and blood" of their slain warriors "moldering in corruption" on the battlefield. Their fate was a sign of the moral devastation of internecine battles of Nephite versus Lamanite.[59] These are only the most vividly described of several battles that ended in piles of corpses rotting in the open air like a textual gibbet warning the living of the rewards of wickedness.

For antebellum believers, decay marked the moment of no return, a mockery of hopes for bodily resurrection. Adelia Cole, a Mormon schoolteacher and poet, eulogized her mother and sister in a poem published in place of the weekly sexton's report in the Nauvoo newspaper:

> Once more I see their pulseless hands,
> Which oft my own have pressed—
> In silence blending with the dust,
> Upon their gentle breasts.

After briefly envisioning the body of the dead as the body of the living, Cole turned to the tragedy of dissolution.

> And oh, I see the earth worm glide,
> Upon those darkened eyes,
> Where dwelt in stainless purity,
> The splendor of the skies.
> And mark it, as it careless feeds,
> Upon those sacred lips.[60]

Lips that she should be kissing in filial devotion were instead consumed by relentless earthworms. This sacrilege weighed heavily on Cole, however natural and predictable the process. The aspiring Latter-day Saint poet expressed the preoccupation of her peers as she implicitly counterposed the Gothic horror of a face picked over by worms against the fragile promise of ultimate bodily resurrection. Could such a rotting face once again smile and touch cheeks with a loved one?

Though putrefaction was the enemy against which the Latter-day Saints and their peers railed, they found its inevitability difficult to resist. They understood putrefaction as a curse God visited upon the wicked even before they had died, but they also could not deny that decay overtook the bodies of their loved ones. For most, their anger and fear at the process by which loved ones merged into soil could only be sublimated by their hope for a future and final resurrection, a process of recomposition by which God wholly and precisely reversed decomposition.

A Brother's Corpse and the "Last Debt of Honor"

In the final accounting, putrefaction was a stage through which the body passed, a process that yielded the perdurable dry bones that would one day serve as the basis for the miraculous process of resurrection. For nineteenth-century believers, the Smiths and other early Mormons among them, this process and its end result had to be protected from the ravages of nature and ill-disposed humanity. The skeleton had to be protected.

After young Lucy's deep distress at Alvin's corpse during the first watchful day or so, the Smiths uneasily interred their beloved son in the Palmyra village cemetery (see figure 2.1), embarrassed and angered by the orthodox implication that Alvin, unchurched and unbaptized, was in hell and not in heaven.[61]

Their troubled peace with Alvin's death would not last long. Nearly a year after Alvin's funeral, his father published a six-week run of an advertisement in the local paper (see figure 2.2).

> Whereas reports have been industriously put in circulation that my son, Alvin, has been removed from the place of his interment and dissected; which reports every person possessed of human sensibility must know are peculiarly calculated to harrow up the mind of a parent and deeply wound the feelings of relations, I, with some

Figure 2.1 Alvin Smith's original grave marker from Palmyra, New York.
Image courtesy of Larry Porter; © Larry Porter.

of my neighbors this morning repaired to the grave, and removing
the earth, found the body which had not been disturbed.[62]

In his reference to "peculiar" calculations, Joseph Sr. recognized the
indisputable cultural importance of honoring the remains of the dead.
He criticized as inhuman those who were even involved in the propaga-
tion of rumors that Alvin's body had been stolen after burial and sent to
a medical school under cover of night.[63]

Despite the power of this momentous event, only two additional references to it remain, neither explicit. Lucy, remembering her eldest son
in her memoir, recalled that "Alvin was murdered by a quack physician;
but still he lay at peace," which emphasized the security of his resting
place as a probable nod to their confirmatory expedition.[64] In 1839,
Joseph Jr., at the time imprisoned in a Missouri jail for his role in the
Mormon War of 1838, complained in a letter: "after a man is dead he
must be dug up from his grave and mangled to peaces for no other
purpose than to gratify their splean against the religeon of god."[65] This
response to rumors that Missouri vigilantes had disinterred and defiled

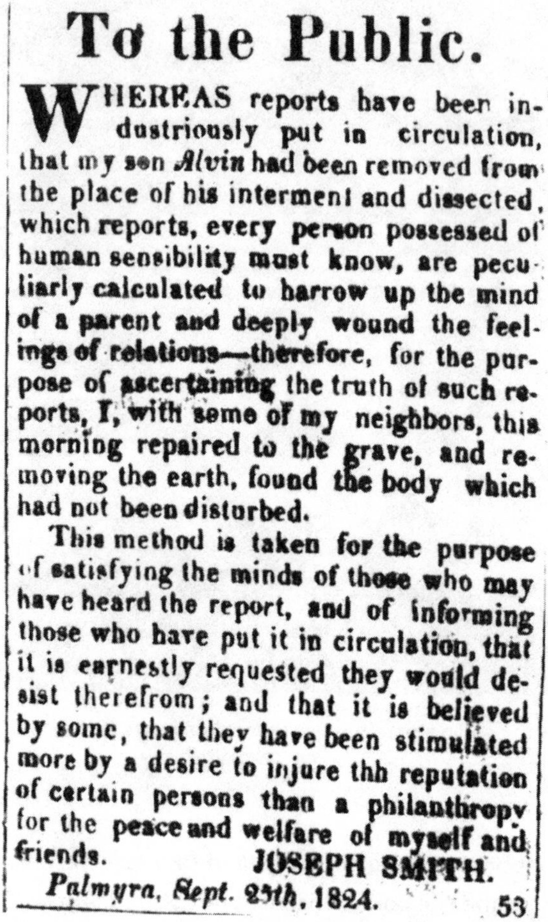

To the Public.

WHEREAS reports have been industriously put in circulation, that my son *Alvin* had been removed from the place of his interment and dissected, which reports, every person possessed of human sensibility must know, are peculiarly calculated to harrow up the mind of a parent and deeply wound the feelings of relations—therefore, for the purpose of ascertaining the truth of such reports, I, with some of my neighbors, this morning repaired to the grave, and removing the earth, found the body which had not been disturbed.

This method is taken for the purpose of satisfying the minds of those who may have heard the report, and of informing those who have put it in circulation, that it is earnestly requested they would desist therefrom; and that it is believed by some, that they have been stimulated more by a desire to injure thh reputation of certain persons than a philanthropy for the peace and welfare of myself and friends.   JOSEPH SMITH.

Palmyra, Sept. 25th, 1824.   53

Figure 2.2 In this notice in the *Wayne Sentinel* (October 27, 1824) Joseph Smith Sr. announced to his neighbors that the family had disinterred Alvin to prove that his body had not been stolen by resurrectionists. Image courtesy of the Church History Library, The Church of Jesus Christ of Latter-day Saints.

the corpse of Mormon militiaman Gideon Carter (1798–1838) merged with the known dismemberment of the elderly Thomas McBride (1776–1838) as he lay dead during an infamous massacre at Haun's Mill.[66] When Smith's younger brother, Don Carlos (1816–1841), published this letter the following year, he deleted the reference to exhumation, perhaps out of respect for painful family memory.[67] In the slaughter of his followers, Smith may have recalled the horror of the threats to the bodily integrity of his dearly beloved brother.

Though reports of actually purloined bodies circulated in New York and the Northeast in the 1820s, contemporary outsiders said almost nothing about the Smith disinterment.[68] Silence from Smith's neighbors, many of whom provided highly critical statements to a disaffected Mormon in 1833–1834, suggests their shared respect for the corpse and the grave.[69] The apparent rumors, to the extent they existed, clearly overstepped the bounds of propriety, and to exploit them, even in public defamation of an unpopular sect, would have violated social norms. While later writers have sought to connect the disinterment to folk-magical necromancy, witnesses closest to the events, both within and without Mormonism, maintained reverent silence. Though silence is the most fickle witness, the Smiths' neighbors appear to have respected the poor family's sacred duty to the corpse of their beloved son.

These rural New Yorkers had little choice. The sanctity of the corpse reigned supreme in early America, from colonization through the Civil War. Though Protestant reformers strenuously rejected Catholic death ritual, including rites for the dead and reverence for saintly relics, they worried anxiously over the physical status and location of the corpse.[70] Laws made explicit the belief that failure to obtain the security of an unmolested, marked grave represented a fate worse than death. Judges could and did punish particularly heinous capital crimes by consigning the executed criminal to dissection on the anatomist's table.[71] These early surgeons gave over the mutilated remains to unmarked graves or, according to popular rumors, to hungry dogs. In response to the limited supply of executed felons, body snatchers—dubbed resurrectionists—began to acquire unauthorized corpses for dissection. The poor equated the potter's field, the anonymous graves of the indigent, not only with the shame of the unmarked grave but with the predations of resurrectionists, who offered purloined corpses to the highest bidding anatomist, preying especially on marginalized populations. These body snatchers filled society with dread out of proportion to their actual economic activity, though they did in fact steal bodies, even on very rare occasions from the living (a practice called burking in honor of an entrepreneurial Scottish barman who murdered alcoholics and sold their corpses).[72] Bereaved families watched bodies until decay had set in, posted guards at cemeteries for the first several days after burial, or even threw quicklime on bodies—tolerating a minor desecration of the body to make it unusable for anatomists. When these measures failed, riots occasionally ensued. Thus in the 1820s and 1830s, empty graves motivated violent action against presumably guilty anatomists in towns across New England.[73] The much-lauded Anatomy Laws of the early nineteenth century did little to allay the concerns of the poor, whose "unclaimed" bodies could now be appropriated under the aegis of law.[74]

Even without the threat of body snatchers, many Americans feared the specter of improper burial. One early Mormon aptly and typically characterized secure burial as "the last debt of honor to the remains of the sacred."[75] The working poor invested money sorely needed to sustain their lives in order to obtain burial insurance as a hedge against the ignominious anonymity of the potter's field. Indeed, formal burial was the most important expense for many poor Americans in the early nineteenth century. Burial mattered to them even after they died: many ghost stories before the Victorian era centered on the improperly interred corpse— some ghosts were so fastidious that they objected to placement of their remains facing west instead of east, the pose preferred to greet the Archangel and/or the returning Christ at his Second Coming.[76] Even for those with proper, marked graves, the specter of failure to protect the body provided cause for expensive locking or reinforced coffins.[77]

The Smiths disinterred Alvin in late September 1824, within days of the anniversary of the visit with Moroni, the angelic guardian from whom Smith eventually retrieved the Book of Mormon gold plates at Cumorah Hill. According to Smith, Moroni refused him access to the plates in 1824, and Joseph left the hill with empty hands and a heavy heart—he was to return annually until he became worthy to receive the plates.

The close timing of the disinterment and Smith's disappointment at Cumorah does not seem coincidental. Friends and neighbors alike remembered that Moroni required Alvin's presence for Joseph Jr. to receive the plates. Only in 1827, when Joseph Jr.'s wife, Emma Hale, accompanied him to the great hill, did Moroni release the gold plates.[78] According to reasonable evidence, the Smith family sought to explain Joseph Jr.'s 1824 failure to obtain the plates by recourse to Alvin. Moroni would probably have accepted the explanation that Alvin had died and could not attend, unless his family had failed to protect his remains. Therein stood the problem—hidden from view beneath the ground Alvin's corpse might have fallen prey to resurrectionists. Both friends and critics seem to have suggested that Alvin was the key to the puzzle. Rather than see Joseph Jr.'s failure to produce the gold plates in 1824 as a disappointed quest, they appear to have seen it as a curse for their failure to protect Alvin. Not only had they failed to produce the required older brother at Cumorah, they had failed even to safeguard his corpse, a difficult admission to the angel, himself a dead man presumably also interred in western New York. The exhumation was necessary to set their minds at rest, both in general and with specific reference to their quest to obtain the gold plates. The problem of the plates in late 1824 provides context and perhaps partial explanation for Lucy's retrospective statement of bereavement: "With [Alvin's interest in the gold plates] before our minds we could not endure to hear or say one word upon that subject[,] for the moment that Joseph spoke of the record it would immediately bring Alvin to our minds with all his kindness his affection his zeal and piety[,] and when we looked to his place and realized that he was gone from it to return no more in this life we all wept with one accord our irretrievable loss."[79] The tie between Alvin, Moroni, and the Book of Mormon project pressed hard enough against Lucy's mind that as she wrote her memoir decades later she still could not disentangle them. She may have had the exhumation and the problem they hoped it would solve in mind when she remembered her family's response to the "irretrievable loss" of Alvin's death.

Joseph Jr. likely accompanied his father on this most personal of all digs—they had dug together for years, and exclusion of the younger brother from the excavation would have been hurtful. In the cool soil of western New York, Alvin's body had probably not fully skeletonized, particularly if he were buried more deeply than two feet. Though the stench of early putrefaction had dissipated, Alvin's corpse likely wore a ghastly mien, with missing eyes and nose but large patches of adipocere—an oily white coating—spread across his face and torso.[80] The experience combined the potent, even horrifying, image of decomposition with the intense reassurance that Alvin's remains were indeed safe. Mapping this experience with Alvin's remains onto twenty-first-century cultural norms is difficult. Antebellum Americans had a strong visceral revulsion for decomposition, but they were also prone to "gaze upon the mouldering bones" when the opportunity presented itself.[81] Most important, this discovery proved the safety of Alvin's remains, a great relief to his worried family. What does seem likely is that the image persisted for many years in Smith's mind. Memories of the experience almost certainly intruded on the attention of the Mormon prophet during the dictation of the Book of Mormon and the revelations that followed. The assiduous materialism of Smith's teaching on resurrection answered the obscene grotesquerie of Alvin's corpse.

These were not the only disfigured remains of an Alvin Smith that the Prophet would have to confront. Four years later, Joseph made plans to name his first son in honor of his dead brother, perhaps in hopes of fulfilling the older Alvin's original mission through the use of a necronym, a colonial custom on the wane among Protestants by the nineteenth century.[82] The child proved as tragic as his namesake uncle. The day after Smith had violated a promise to Moroni—by releasing the draft pages of the Book of Mormon manuscript to his insistent financier, Martin Harris (1783–1875)—this second Alvin was "still-born and very much deformed." The boy survived a few hours, and childbirth nearly killed Emma.[83] At the moment of the stillbirth, Smith did not yet know the fate of the pages he had loaned to Harris. After burying the disfigured body of the second Alvin, Smith left his wife on her sickbed to rush home to Palmyra to determine the fate of his manuscript. When Harris revealed that he had lost the documents, Smith suffered severe agitation. By Lucy's report, Joseph Jr. was "weeping and grieving like a tender infant untill about sunset we persuaded him to take a little nourishment."[84] The child Alvin haunted Joseph Jr., who, according to his mother, blamed himself for its malformation and demise, recalling the "monstrous births" of colonial American wonder lore.[85] The use of a necronym backfired catastrophically, the second failure to protect an Alvin associated with the gold plates. In the painful logic of Providence, God took the second Alvin to punish Joseph Jr. for his disobedience.[86] Though Smith would report later that God had forgiven him, these experiences of a grief that could not be healed by the standard Providentialist view left their mark on the Mormon prophet.

The Material Integrity of the Corpse

Scholars from various perspectives have attempted to situate Smith's assiduous materialism in established philosophical traditions.[87] He notoriously denied creation *ex nihilo*, taught that matter could never be created, taught that spirit was itself a kind of refined matter, and preached an embodied God. In his life and preaching Smith provided evidence and context for understanding his philosophical claims as based in his relationship to decomposition and the promise of physical resurrection. In important respects, Smith's preaching on the eternity of matter provided the theoretical structure necessary to allow for the complete reversal of decomposition. Having experienced the nauseous misery of decay first-hand, Smith readily embraced and amplified an account of physical existence that entirely negated its power: everything is matter, matter can never be destroyed, and the exact matter that constituted an individual during life will be returned at resurrection.[88]

Since Christ's return from the dead, Christians have struggled to understand what resurrection means. One camp, following Paul, anticipated that a new body would be as different from the physical body as a tree is from its seed. Others, following proof texts and folk beliefs, maintained that the resurrected body would be materially identical to the mortal body. Most Christians held the latter view of the body's "material continuity" through death from the second century through the late Middle Ages.[89]

Though philosophers and theologians had been discussing these problems for many centuries, it was the early modern English scientists and thinkers who framed the debate for nineteenth-century Americans. Most of these authorities denied any form of strict material continuity. Robert Boyle (1627–1691), for example, famously investigated "physico-theological" considerations regarding resurrection. In a fairly common *reductio ad absurdum*, Boyle returned to the ancient logical problem of cannibalism (deriving at least in part from the Roman custom of feeding Christian martyrs to animals and then butchering the animals for human consumption)—in whose body would the tissue be resurrected?[90] Boyle concluded, on the basis of this and similar arguments, that material continuity was logically absurd. John Locke (1632–1704), interacting with Boyle, his mentor, in his *Essay Concerning Human Understanding*, also argued for a physical resurrection without material continuity. For Locke, "the body of a man dead and rotten in his grave, or burnt, may at the last day have several new particles in it, and that without any inconvenience; since whatever matter is vitally united to his soul is his body."[91] Locke was working out a theory of the persistence of human identity on the basis of mind and the continuity of memory—material continuity was largely irrelevant. More speculative voices also enthusiastically rejected the necessity of strict material continuity. The Scottish gentleman philosopher Thomas Dick (1774–1857), in a popular work of amateur theology published as *Philosophy of a Future State*, maintained that the phrase "all flesh is grass" should be interpreted literally, supporting the free interchange of animal, vegetable, and human matter. In the convoluted style characteristic of many natural theologians, Dick invoked the fact that matter could never be annihilated to support his claim that human souls could also never be annihilated, turning the cycles of decomposition into evidence of the immortality of the human soul.[92] Mormons like Oliver Cowdery read and quoted from Dick, even if they did not entirely understand the argument.[93] Some observers found a metaphor for the egalitarian community of the afterworld in the idea that physical matter from various human bodies could combine together. James Hervey wrote that "crumbling bones *mix* as they moulder... [they] incorporate with each other in the grave."[94] The idea of death as a great leveler found new energy in scientific beliefs about nutrient cycles and the ecology of decomposition. American authors like Samuel Drew (1765–1833) and George Bush (1796–1859) also argued against material continuity, to much controversy.[95] Some nineteenth-century medical reformers, twisting a phrase of evangelical piety, termed the frequent turnover of particles the "daily dying body."[96] In a few short decades, images of Union and Confederate soldier skeletons picking through each other's remains on battlefields at the Resurrection would be further employed to mock the traditional belief.[97]

Though material continuity had dominated ideas about resurrection for many centuries, in the nineteenth century the system seemed logically unsupportable. Antebellum Christians dealt with the conflict between traditional and scientific views in various ways.[98] Buck's dictionary placed evangelical Protestantism in a compromise position, calling Locke's proposal "a mere quibble" while admitting that "it is true, indeed, that the body has not always the same particles, which are continually changing, but it has always the same constituent parts, which proves its identity; it is the same body that is born that dies, and the same that dies that shall rise again."[99] For a Protestantism tending toward the rational, conceding the untenability of strict material continuity was a price worth paying in order to maintain belief in the reasonable Providence of the Creator and the physical promise of the resurrection.[100]

Mormonism also contained a variety of ideas about the mechanics of resurrection. Mormon apostle Parley Pratt largely accepted Locke's view, though he required a small measure of material continuity. Committed to the physical resurrection, Pratt and other early Mormons nevertheless allowed modern biology to inform their views.[101] In 1841, Pratt explored the question of physical resurrection in the *Millennial Star*. Noting that many claimed the resurrection "comes in contact with the known laws of nature, and [is] therefore both unreasonable and impossible," Pratt espoused the view that the body is entirely transformed every ten years. Locke's continuity of consciousness, according to Pratt, could withstand at least four entire exchanges of physical matter. Ultimately, Pratt exclaimed, "it will be readily perceived that Paul and the Latter-day Saints, so far from being ignorant of the laws of nature, or coming in contact with the philosophy thereof, have rather reconciled or harmonized the revelations of God with the laws of nature."[102] Though he did little more than recite the work of Locke and Dick, Pratt exulted in the power of Mormon theology, even as he made claims contrary to Joseph Smith's own belief.

Orson Pratt, early Mormonism's favorite intellectual and one of its first apostles, followed his brother Parley's lead in reconciling with Locke. At the April 1843 church general conference, Pratt preached on the end times, including resurrection.

> Resurrection of the body is denied by many because it is contrary to the laws of nature, because flesh and bones are constantly changing, completely new in 7 or 10 years. If this is true a man in 70 years would have matter enough for 10 different bodies. Objector says this resurrection cannot be true, for if so, men would be quarreling which body belong to himself and others. Who shall have the best right to it.
>
> I do not believe that more than ¾ of our bodies is comprised of animal organization, but is purely vegetable. Hence through all the 70 years a man will have one or two parts, which will be the same original. If he receives the matter he was in possession of 50 years before he died, he has the same body. The people living in the house are the occupants of the house and the house though repaired all through its different parts from time to time even to new timbers throughout; yet it is said to be the same house still.[103]

Suggesting that the resurrected body could dispense with its unnecessary "vegetable" matter, Orson mainly echoed the scientific argument, with a nod toward the structural continuity espoused by Buck. Orson admitted the logical absurdity of resurrected bodies sharing substantial matter and used a homespun analogy to a home constantly under repair to make the point plain for early Latter-day Saints. Whether his audience understood the philosophical argument or not, they knew that they would be physically resurrected and would maintain their own identity in the afterlife.

Smith saw Locke and the philosophy he represented as a direct assault on the integrity of the biblical promise of physical resurrection. He followed Orson Pratt's sermon with an "addition" to limit his intellectual apostle's accommodationism. "Their is no fundamental principle belonging to a human System that 'ever goes into another in this world or the world to come.' . . . I care not what the theories of men are. We have the testimony that God will raise us up and he has power to do it. If anyone supposes that any part of our bodies that is the fundamental parts thereof, ever goes into another body he is mistaken."[104] Employing Pratt's argument even as he drew a line in the sand, Smith allowed the possibility that a body might contain surplus matter, that perhaps "vegetable" matter could be excluded from the resurrection body. However— and here Smith sharply dissented from Locke—no significant part of the material body could disappear. However circular the reasoning, Smith would not abandon the requirement for material continuity. Like many of his lay peers, Smith believed that to allow a reshuffling of physical material threatened a death powerful enough to destroy personal integrity and the promise of postmortal community. God promised a full and miraculous resurrection. Anything less was blasphemy, the "theories of men" directly opposed to Smith's revelations. The strength of Smith's conviction, in direct and poorly argued conflict with commonsense observations about the flow of organic matter, reflected the personal significance of his philosophy.[105]

Though Smith engaged the philosophy of resurrection directly in 1843, his views were reasonably clear as early as 1830. The Bible itself, reflecting variable resurrection theologies and with no clear statement of physical immortality (a point Boyle made strongly), did not reliably support any specific view of resurrection.[106] The Book of Mormon provided clarity where the Bible equivocated. A prophet named Amulek, in a public debate with a notorious anti-Christ named Zeezrom, focused on the resurrection as the sign of Christ's redemption of humanity, promising that in the resurrection "even there shall not so much as a hair of their heads be lost; but every thing shall be restored to its perfect frame, as it is now, or in the body."[107] Smith's Protestant critics understood well the significance of this claim in Mormon scripture. In the sarcastic phrase of Eber Howe (1798–1885), "the doctrine of personal identity and of the resurrection is explained by our chief judge and high priest, which if John Locke or the

Bishop of Worcester had read, that great matter of controversy between them would have been avoided."[108]

Smith reiterated the promise of the Book of Mormon in a revelation from 1832–1833. "They who are of a celestial spirit shall receive the same body which was a natural body; even ye shall receive your bodies, and your glory shall be that glory by which your bodies are quickened."[109] The eulogy for Elias Higbee (1795–1843) announced that "the same almighty power that first reared the piece, and took it down, can reassemble the loose scattered parts, and put them as they were, and then shall the victor's cry be heard: 'O grave where is they victory?'"[110] God's mystical power in effecting the reassembly of every atom of the dead was the proof of his power over death. The Higbee eulogy made explicit how threatening the loss of material continuity was to Smith's conquest of death.

The centrality of literal resurrection to Smith's assault on death provides necessary context for understanding his teaching on matter generally—the material integrity of the body through time appears to have been the cornerstone of Smith's much-discussed philosophical materialism. In 1833 Smith promulgated a revelation, which taught that "man is Spirit. The elements are eternal: And spirit & element inseperably connected receiveth a fulness of Joy; and when seperated man cannot receive a fulness of Joy. The elements are the tabernacle of God; yea man is the tabernacle of God."[111] Though the report is fragmentary and Smith seems to be drawing on diverse and sometimes conflicting philosophical traditions, this revelation demonstrates Smith's belief that the constituent elements of the physical body represent eternal elements, a house for the eternal spirit, which was itself a material mind. This emphasis on a unified whole speaks to Smith's commitment to material continuity in the definition of resurrection and immortality.

Smith's attachment to materialism as the philosophical reassurance that death would never truly threaten human beings only increased with time. The Mormon prophet preached in his 1844 King Follett Discourse that "God has materials to organize the world. Element[s] nothing can destroy. No beginning, no end."[112] The persistence of the human body corresponded to the general eternity of matter. John Taylor (1808–1887), Smith's close friend and third president of the main church, echoed Smith's teachings: "The component parts of man can no more become the flesh of beasts or fishes than gold can become silver, lead turn to iron, or copper to gold. Each is separate and distinct from the other."[113] Derisively pairing a Lockean view of resurrection with the presumed absurdities of alchemy, Taylor confirmed Smith's view that identity depended on physical existence.

The commitment to material continuity was so overwhelming that even spirit proved material in Smith's thought. As he clarified in an essay on enthusiasm in 1842 and a sermon in 1843, "the spirit is a substance …it is material," and "there is no such thing as immaterial matter. All spirit is matter but is more fine or pure."[114] Even when he invoked hermetic-sounding spiritual emanations, what he termed the "light of Christ," Smith seems to have intended a material entity.[115]

The materiality of spirit paralleled the materiality of the body in part because the body would in fact lose certain significant particles irretrievably. For all his insistence on the integrity of the corpse, Smith preached the utter annihilation of a crucial component of the mortal body. Blood, the ruddy tint whose absence signals the transition to death and the humor whose excess heroic physicians sought to control through phlebotomy, would never see resurrection. During a funeral sermon in 1843, Smith engaged Paul's letter on resurrection, interpreting the phrase "flesh and blood cannot inherit the kingdom of God" to mean that "Flesh and blood cannot go [to heaven] but flesh and bones quickened by the Spirit of God can."[116] This odd turn of phrase marked Smith's literal reading of Paul as specifically excluding blood from the resurrected body. Smith returned to the topic at greater length in 1844, extending his reinterpretation of Paul:

> Concerning Resurection Flesh and Blood cannot inherit the kingdom of god or the kingdom that god inherits or inhabits. But the flesh without the blood and the Spirit of god flowing in the vains in Sted of the blood for blood is the part of the body that causes corruption. therefore [sic] we must be changed in the twinkle of an Eye or have to lay down these tabernacles and leave the blood vanish away[.] Therefore Jesus Christ left his blood to atone for the Sins of the world that he might assend into the presents of the father for god dwels in flaming flames and he is a consuming fire he will consume all that is unclean and unholly and we could not abide his presents unless pure Spirits in us. for the Blood is the corruptible part of the tabernacles.[117]

This passage in Paul's letter to Corinthian Christians had occasioned substantial debate about the physicality of the resurrection for the duration of Christian history. The majority view in patristic and medieval thought largely ignored the implications of the claim that "flesh and blood cannot inherit the kingdom of God," given their emphasis on material continuity.[118] In the eighteenth and nineteenth centuries, more authors were willing to consider a spiritual reading of the new body described in Corinthians. Prominent writers endorsed a spiritual reading, recognizing but rejecting Smith's strongly literal interpretation.[119] For Smith, the scriptural phrase identified the corrupting element within the body. Smith's commonsensical interpretation of Christ's spilled blood—Christ left his blood in the earth as the mark of his now extinguished susceptibility to decay—presented Christ's body as a detailed, physical exemplar for the resurrection of believers.[120]

Despite a vibrant scholarly literature on the social, cultural, and religious meanings of blood in the medieval period,[121] relatively little is written about blood in the eighteenth and nineteenth centuries beyond a treatment of the culture surrounding the medical use of blood transfusions.[122] In his exegesis of blood, Smith drew most on Hebrew tradition refracted through prevalent physiological beliefs—blood was an animating force akin in complex ways to the animal spirits needed to keep a body alive.[123]

The similarity of coagulated blood (a sight familiar from traumas or therapeutic bloodletting) to the effluvia of putrefaction may have contributed to Smith's association of blood with corruption; the same could be said of the pungent smell of blood. Despite the physical association with putrefaction, Smith did not follow some radical Baptists and other fringe groups in forbidding the consumption of animal blood. It was enough for Smith to abolish blood from the resurrected body.

Smith's conception of blood solved a logical problem for believers in a strict physical resurrection. If the body were identical after resurrection, as material continuity required, what would prevent it from dying again? Older writers had described a process of supernatural hardening of matter, an inoculation against decay.[124] For Smith, the answer was that material spirit replaced blood within the body. Smith's insistence on the materiality of spirit seems to have relied at least in part on his understanding that this material spirit would replace blood within the vascular systems of the resurrected bodies of the Saints. The body would be purified of the possibility of physical corruption, the coagulating soup that filled the veins of mortals. Through the placement of spirit into vessels that once carried blood, Smith stamped out putrefaction forever.[125]

Smith never clarified whether the material spirit he preached was a portion of his "light of Christ," the integration of the individual's spirit into the resurrected blood vessels, or some other material. Orson Pratt attempted to solve this problem a decade later. Orson, sounding more medieval than modern, explained that a diet of the vegetable material of earth formed blood "having a constant tendency to decay," while "celestial vegetables" would create the heavenly blood substitute, Smith's material spirit.[126] Such details were not crucial to Smith; what mattered to him was that the replacement of blood by spirit ensured human invulnerability to decay.

Standard treatments of material continuity have emphasized its relevance to debates about dualism or the "mind-body" problem on the one hand and the meaning of the self or persistence of personal identity on the other. While these problems are aspects of the same underlying concern, they all fail to account for the communal nature of resurrection and identity in Joseph Smith's thought. Decomposition threatened community: it was the living, not the dead, who witnessed putrefaction. Smith was after "sociality," as he declared in 1843, not just physical persistence.[127] To him the abstruse debates about the cycling of matter among different bodies undertaken by his peers and predecessors distracted from the more important image of reunion on resurrection morning, of hands clasping and arms wrapping in embrace, of lips pressed against cheeks and loud salutations issuing from throats wet with emotion and heard with physical ears.

Surrogates of the Corpse

The skeletonized corpse became the dry bones of Ezekiel's dreams, the nucleus upon which God would work the miracle of resurrection. Continued access to components of the dry corpse or surrogates for it encouraged Latter-day Saints in their hope that God could recover their lost bodies and communities. They used these surrogates of the corpse not only to remember their dead but also to hope for freedom from sickness and evil.

The skeleton, in its impressive durability, supported the belief that God could keep track of the particles of matter that had constituted the physical body. Though antebellum culture lacked the supernatural physicality of martyrs' relics, believers still maintained contact with dry bones through fragments or surrogates, generally locks of hair, artifacts built from coffin wood, or images of the dead.

Though broader culture lacked specific rites of secondary treatment (manipulation of bodies after skeletonization), some individuals created their own. An enigmatic diary entry by Ralph Waldo Emerson (1803–1882) of March 29, 1832, is widely remembered. On that March day Emerson paid homage to his wife, who had died a little more than a year earlier from tuberculosis. Tersely, he noted, "I visited Ellen's tomb and opened the coffin."[128] The intimate encounter of a grieving man with the physical remnants of his wife replicated on a domestic scale a phenomenon observed with some celebrities. George Whitefield (1714–1770), international star of eighteenth-century revivalism, received eager pilgrims to his tomb for decades. His remains, despite Protestant antipathy for Catholic relics, bestowed wisdom and inspiration on Christian seekers, much as did the humbler gravesite of the widely revered David Brainerd (1718–1747), protégé of Jonathan Edwards.[129] Some twentieth-century historians saw this material culture of the deceased body as necrophilic, but such an appropriation of psychiatric terminology for sexual disturbance tells more about twentieth- than nineteenth-century society.[130] For these women and men, the dry corpse represented their most immediate access to loved ones and a potent reminder of their hope for a physical resurrection.

Though direct contact with skeletons was the exception rather than the rule, many Americans maintained physical contact with their dead in other ways. Grave markers in well-kept cemeteries helped, but such monuments were insufficient. Small portions of the body could be held back from burial without giving offense to the dead.

Different cultures reserve different fragments of the body. Some Europeans preserved the embalmed heart as a token of the body's permanence. This practice could be problematic, as in the sad plight of the Duke of Orleans, a quarter of whose heart was eaten by his Great Dane during the embalming process in 1723.[131] In Anglo-American culture, particularly by the nineteenth century, hair—more permanent and easier to secure—represented the preferred surrogate. Bones would await the resurrection in their graves, facing the rising sun, while hair, partaking of the adamant immortality of the skeleton, was a portable memorial that could remain on the person of a survivor. Hair made its way into lockets worn by survivors, the pages of family Bibles, or treasured spots in bureaus and on hearths.[132] Much as the fragmentary relics of the medieval period, these surrogates served as metaphors for and evidence of the persistence of the entire corpse. Objects both near at hand and manifestly immune to decomposition promised that the entire body could ultimately recover from decay.

Joseph Smith's followers participated in this culture of relics, retaining emblems from family and friends. The fortunate few, including Smith's first wife, Emma, even obtained hair from the Prophet or his brother Hyrum.[133] Apostle Wilford Woodruff (1807–1898) created a collection of "some Hair from the Heads of Joseph Smith the Prophet And all the Smith family of Male members also Mother Smith."[134] Woodruff combined the Smith hair with samples from living apostles, explaining that his "object was in putting a portion of each in the top of my staff as a relick of those noble men, master spirits of the nineteenth century, to hand down to my posterity, to deposit in the most Holy and Sacred place in the Holy temple of GOD."[135] Woodruff's sacred project recalls the practice of braiding a wreath from the hair of an entire family, though he explicitly tied his collection to Mormon temple theology.[136]

Fragments of the body were not always available, so images or other artifacts of the dead often served as surrogates. In many families death portraits were the most important artwork they owned.[137] The luxury of funeral portraits—a genre that supported many painters and the later development of photography—often stood out of reach. For some, death masks (see figure 2.3) filled the void. These plaster casts placed over the face of the deceased provided a semipermanent version of the skull, still encased in flesh.[138] For others, particularly as technology improved, daguerreotypes and other mechanical images played a similar role.[139] These images and impressions played the role of arresting decomposition, of capturing the dead forever in the liminal moments after death.[140]

Physical objects near the corpse could serve a similar role. The coffins used to transport the bodies of Joseph Jr. and Hyrum in 1844 became canes parceled among the Mormon elite. (One late tradition significantly if hyperbolically claimed thousands of such canes, as if recapitulating the New Testament miracle of multiplying loaves and fishes.)[141] Some mourners combined the varied media of physical memory. Dimick Huntington's cane preserved small portions of Smith's hair—possibly retrieved from his corpse during its 1844 reinterment—in a notch under glass (drawn from the coffin's viewing window) in the cane's knob handle, much as in Wilford Woodruff's cane.[142]

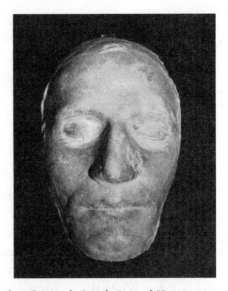

Figures 2.3a and 2.3b These death masks of Joseph Smith Jr. and Hyrum are maintained in the Church History Museum of the Church of Jesus Christ of Latter-day Saints to the present day. Image courtesy of the Church History Library, The Church of Jesus Christ of Latter-day Saints.

Physical emblems of the corpse wielded substantial power. Echoing the healings of cunning folk and medieval relics, early Mormons attributed to certain personal artifacts power over life and death. During the Mormon Reformation in Utah (1856–1857) apostle Heber Kimball (1801–1868) asked his listeners: "How much would you give for even a cane that Father Abraham had used? or a coat or ring that the Saviour had worn? The rough oak boxes in which the bodies of Joseph and Hyrum were brought from Carthage, were made into canes and other articles... and the devil cannot overcome those who have them."[143] The surrogates of the corpse could protect believers from their own death and return the sick to health. Not only did such relics protect against the devil, they protected bearers physically, much as they had for centuries of Catholics.[144] Kimball and many others used coffin canes and other physical emblems of Smith's body to perform miraculous healings over the years.[145]

Grave relics represent the last stage of the corpse before resurrection, and they are also the final destination of traditions about the power of the corpse in the Mormon tradition. The canes and locks or wreaths of hair are still available in museums and private collections in

Utah, even though the cultural and theological context in which they were removed from the early Mormon dead is gone. Through such physical emblems a modern audience may gain some sense of the incredible power the dead body wielded for early Mormons and their peers.

Like countless previous generations, the early Latter-day Saints searched the deceased body for clues to humanity's future. Grappling with the process of putrefaction whereby loved ones are drawn away from the living, Joseph Smith and his Latter-day Saints negotiated the tensions inherent in death and the hope for resurrection. The Saints proved rapt students of the corpse in all its phases, from the first uncertain moments when many might still dare to hope for resuscitation, to the pestilent onset of irreversible decay, to the dry bones that would be clothed with flesh at the last day. While the unarousable slumberer mocked their desire for community and the decaying corpse filled them with revulsion, the dry bones promised them that God could restore their bodies and their communities. To that end, the early Latter-day Saints solemnly and assiduously discharged their "last debt of honor" to the remains of their family and friends.

3

Relics, Graves, and the Treasure Quest

In 1833 William Stafford, a prominent Palmyra farmer, recalled that in the 1820s the Smiths

> had seen in my flock of sheep, a large, fat, black weather. Old Joseph and one of the boys came to me one day, and said that Joseph Jr. had discovered some very remarkable and valuable treasures, which could be procured only in one way. That way, was as follows:—That a black sheep should be taken on to the ground where the treasures were concealed—that after cutting its throat, it should be led around a circle while bleeding. This being done, the wrath of the evil spirit would be appeased: the treasures could then be obtained.

In this brief account, a highlight from a defamatory statement, Stafford derided Palmyra's most famous residents. While he intended to demonstrate the Smiths' ruthlessness in the pursuit of food and money (it was, he said, "the only time they ever made money-digging a profitable business"), Stafford elaborated important themes in early America's treasure quest.[1] He invoked the ritual death of an animal, circumscription of a special area, buried treasure, and the spilling of life blood, all to effect an interaction with the dead, in this case an "evil spirit," protecting treasure.[2] The accuracy of Stafford's story is not crucial. Whatever the fate of Stafford's black wether, his statement provides a vista of a culture important to Smith's early life. This culture cared a great deal about grave relics.

The Smiths participated in American folkways that maintained that the ground—the bowels of the earth—contained treasures interred by generations past. Before the rise of Mormonism, Joseph Smith Sr. and his sons made their names in treasure digs, and Joseph Jr. gained a reputation as Palmyra's treasure seer. Though much of the emphasis on Smith's magic derives from unfriendly sources, the documents (including a sardonic confession by the Prophet himself) confirm that the young Smith pursued buried treasure. Through native relics and their supernatural guardians, Smith began his career mediating between the living and the dead. As he turned to his religious calling, seer stones bridged the gap to his exploration of the Book of Mormon and a collection of Egyptian funeral papyri. In Smith's hands the treasure hunt was a negotiation with the dead over their legacy.

Discussions about the treasure quest have been casualties of the complex relationship between dominant Christianities and clusters of cultural beliefs disparagingly termed "magic" or "occult."[3] Clergy and Enlightenment agitators pushed to eliminate "magic" from polite society but were never more than partially successful among commoners.[4] In pursuit of fabled riches, treasure seekers prepared for encounters with malicious spirits, invoking ancient rites of control—magic circles and sacred oaths, the observation of holy silence, the shedding of animal blood—to defend themselves against forces from the other world.[5] The association of this folkway with America's social margins made involvement a perilous threat to respectability.[6] In response to social opprobrium, participants in contested practices and beliefs often protested and obfuscated.

After their heavy involvement in the practices in the early and middle 1820s, the Smiths ultimately disavowed most of their explicit connections to the world of folk magic and the treasure quest. Representing family, community, and the legal system, his uncle Jesse accused Joseph Jr. of "the necromancy of infidelity," an accusation outsiders repeated for decades.[7] The intense stigma associated with the treasure hunt pushed Smith and his family into later denials of involvement.[8]

While insiders have tended to see the treasure quest as unrelated to Smith's later career except as an index of his spiritual flexibility, his capacity to receive and disseminate startling religious innovations, outsiders have generally seen Smith's angelic visits and gold plates as the grand and fraudulent culmination of an adolescent treasure-hunting career.[9] These extreme views are misleading. The Mormon prophet's quest for buried treasure emphasized the dead and their secreted artifacts, as did the religion-building that soon followed. Smith searched and dug to discover what only burial in the earth could keep hidden from prying eyes and grasping hands. Smith's later attempts to secure prophetic respectability should not obscure the critical continuities between his early quest and his later ministry. Right up to the end of his life, Smith explained that "it has always been my province to dig up hidden mysteries."[10]

Meanings of the Treasure Quest

Few American historians have looked far beyond the world of folk magic or financial privation for interpretive motifs in the treasure quest.[11] Dreams of wealth and financial security certainly beckoned to many if not most treasure seekers, a point made by the critical reference to "money-digging" or "money-getting."[12] One Maine contemporary captured the easy melding of the artifact and its monetary value as "the treasures that have been left by those that have been before us," which could yield "a sudden and boundless fortune."[13] Still, dismissive accusations of greed provide only a limited view of a rich culture.

Treasure digging is essentially a form of grave-robbery, a sacrilege against the dead. The archetypal treasure hunt is the looting of a royal tomb or the retrieval of necklaces, gorgets, or arrowheads from an Indian burial site.[14] Scholarly interpretations like colonial historian Alan Taylor's otherwise compelling view of a "materialistic faith" underlying the treasure quest fail to appreciate the meaning of these interactions with the remains of the dead.[15] Though economic aspirations played a role, a complex of supernatural communications mediated by the dead and their resting places underlies the treasure quest, particularly in Joseph Smith's practice. This connection emerges as a major theme in Smith's treasure questing when simple questions are asked of familiar documents. What was the treasure? Where was it secreted? Whose treasure was it? When approached from this perspective, the treasure quest was not just an act of economic opportunism; it was also a quest for the dead and their relics.

Proto-Mormon seekers were clear about their goals: they sought "hidden treasures in the bowels of the earth."[16] Lucy Smith more expressively reported that her son's "buisness" was "to tear open the bowels of the Earth and drag to light the precious things of the Earth."[17] Images of the "bowels of the earth" evoke retrieval by excavation, even exhumation. The bowels of the earth had from time immemorial housed the remains of the dead, a point echoed in the etymology of the word "human," from an Indo-European root meaning earth or soil.[18] The valuables Smith pursued were not to be found in rivers or forests, lakes or mountaintops. They did not lurk in the nests of bewitched birds or the trunks of enchanted trees. They were inhumed.

Native Relics

Native peoples and their grave mounds strongly connected the treasure quest to the dead. Americans of the early republic frequently encountered the remnants of earlier civilizations, which filled the antebellum frontier.[19] In the words of Unitarian minister Thaddeus Mason Harris (1768–1842), touring Ohio for his health in 1803, "vast mounds and walls of earth...are scattered over the whole face of the country. You cannot ride twenty miles without finding some of the mounds, or vestages of the ramparts." On the same trip Harris penned a poetic memorial to the Grave Creek Mound on the Ohio River near Wheeling, Virginia:

> Behind me rise huge a reverend pile
> Sole in this desert heath, a place of tombs.
> Waste, Desolate; where Ruin dreary dwell,
> Brooding o'er sightless skulls and crumbling bones.[20]

The earth that Harris witnessed contained the bodies of the dead. Harris in poetry expressed what Smith would emphasize throughout his career, that the American landscape contained untold millions of bodies. Popular New York author Josiah Priest (1788–1851)—a favorite of Mormons and their peers—proclaimed that the "mounds in the west are very numerous, amounting to several thousands."[21] Such mounds were close to the Smith family: by one estimate there were eight significant mounds within twelve miles of their Palmyra home.[22] A contemporary writer called neighboring Ohio, where the Mormons relocated in the 1830s, "nothing but one vast cemetery of the beings of past ages."[23]

Not only were graves common, so was the act of turning the earth. The inhabitants of the agrarian communities of the early republic regularly cleared forests, plowed fields, dug wells, and planted crops, inserting implements into hard soil. Because Indian groups had long inhabited America, the spades white farmers propelled into the soil often discovered strange artifacts. Each clunk of metal against stone held the possibility of new contact with lost civilizations. Not just stones, but arrowheads, gorgets, or even skeletons could clang against the blade of a shovel in the early American republic.

Burial mounds represented more than treasure troves. Smith wanted to understand the artifacts, to know the people who had left them. He sought the wisdom and legacy of the ancients. One editorial in *Times and Seasons* asked readers to "look at the mounds of America, and reflect what noble spirits must have actuated the hearts of the living for the dead."[24] The Latter-day Saints knew that the trinkets in graves were the personal effects of the dead. A popular hymn to Natives reprinted in the Nauvoo newspaper invoked the sentimentalized image of the dying Indian and promised that "All in thy grave shall buried be / Which pleased—they please thee yet!"[25] Smith made explicit his belief in an intimate connection between hidden treasure and human burial when he stated that Indian burial mounds were "undoubtedly...made to seclude some valuable treasures deposited by the aboriginees of this land."[26] Echoes of this quest's religious and funerary aspects are present in Smith's 1833 blessing of his father, in which he promised the elder Smith the "blessings of heaven above...and the blessings of the deep that lieth under."[27] God, Joseph promised his father, would bestow blessings from within grave mounds as easily as he could from his heavenly habitation.

Smith further connected burial sites to treasure by presenting many Indian mounds as treasure caves, using terms appropriate to royal tombs.[28] The Smiths' neighbor William Stafford reported that Joseph had claimed that "nearly all the hills in this part of New York, were thrown up by human hands, and in them were large caves...he could see within the above mentioned caves, large gold bars and silver plates—that he could also discover the spirits in whose charge these treasures were, clothed in ancient dress."[29] Lorenzo Saunders recalled an even more explicitly mortuary cave, explaining that "a king of one of the tribes...was shut in there in the time of one of their big battles."[30] In both accounts, the key motifs of tombs, treasures, and the spirits or remains of the dead take center stage. While these reminiscences are from affidavits critical of the Smiths, friendly sources corroborate the claim of treasure caves within New York burial mounds.[31] Easy identification of past civilizations with sacred treasures continued to play across Smith's religious activity, a fact reflected by the Mormon claim that "sepulchral ruins" or "monuments of antiquity" were in fact "sacred archives" of lost peoples.[32]

Guardians and the Dead

The treasures Smith and his colleagues sought did not arrive in their location by the vagaries of geology. This treasure was not the gold that created the Gold Rush two decades later. Human hands had interred these treasures. According to various traditions, Captain Kidd and other pirates, the Spanish, pygmy miners, Celts, the Mound Builders, and proto-Aztecs (Kiantonians) all had buried treasures in rural New York and Ohio.[33] While treasures of Native groups were the most plentiful, they served as an entry point into a varied collection of lost peoples secreting their relics in the ground.

The ancients did not abandon their treasure, which explained another significant component of Smith's treasure experience. In many cases the treasure guardian of folklore was an individual interred with the treasure, representing "the ghosts of men sacrificed by the treasure buriers."[34] One treasure chest Smith sought was explicitly guarded by the Indian murdered and buried to protect it.[35] Not all such guardians were human: they could take the shape of toads, bears, or even giants. Notably, though, animal guardians generally represented shape-shifting by the spirits of the human dead.[36] Many of the dark ritual overtones of the hunt—animal sacrifice, magic circles drawn or bled into the ground, spells and invocations—are familiar as methods to subdue apparitions of the dead generally.[37] The spilt blood of the animal, even if only metaphorical, paralleled the blood of the treasure's guardian.

The gold that Smith sought bore the imprint of humans—breastplates, spectacles, inscribed plates, coins. Even an 1825 mine quest in which the Smiths participated included artifacts of human fabrication: they expected to discover "a valuable mine of either Gold or Silver and . . . coined money and bars or ingots of Gold or Silver."[38] For technology-poor frontier people, ore may have been less useful than coins or ingots. Minted coins might resolve financial troubles faster than gold or silver ore. As Smith understood treasure, though, this convenience was not the point.

Fascination with the legacy of the dead is apparent in Smith's 1836 quest to Salem, Massachusetts, some years after his best known treasure seeking. Smith and several of his followers sought a cache in the basement of an old home in Salem, though they were quickly disappointed. A revelation Smith received in response to their failure promised that God was "not displeased" and had "much treasure in this city" for them. The revelation further instructed the party to "inquire diligently concerning the more ancient inhabitants and founders of this city, for there are more treasures than one for you, in this city."[39] The revelation turned the party's minds from the buried treasure to the people who would have buried it, the men and women who had founded Salem two centuries earlier. In this warning, the Mormon prophet revealed the easy equivalence of physical relics and metaphorical treasure as wisdom from the long-dead settlers of the famously magic-plagued town.

Smith does appear to have sought at least one treasure superficially unrelated to the dead. As part of his employment with Josiah Stowell (b. 1770)—the man whose nephew initiated criminal proceedings against Smith in 1826 for "disorderly" behavior—he searched for salt springs. While this may simply reflect an artifact of his employer's preference, even this salt was tied to the ancient inhabitants of the Americas. By a contemporary newspaper account, the salt was the "hidden treasure" of local Indians. While not a human-made artifact per se, the mineral was an "important secret" passed from generation to generation among the Natives, linking the dead to the living through oral tradition.[40] Though Smith reportedly also told fortunes, dowsed for water, and occasionally found missing objects for neighbors in his role as a seer, his greatest efforts were devoted to the quest for objects buried within the earth. These were the applications that persisted into his religious career.

The Book of Mormon as Grave Artifact

After Smith's religious calling around 1820 he continued with the life of an adolescent, which was interrupted in the fall of 1823. He reported that an angel named Moroni described a record engraved on gold plates buried in the nearby hill he called Cumorah (see figure 3.1).

A glacial drumlin on the Robinson property between Manchester and Palmyra, New York, Cumorah was, according to early Mormons, a massive grave mound.

The plates, Smith announced, told the story of three waves of migration from the Old World to the New, all of them peoples of the Hebrew Bible. (None of them—contrary to popular misconception—represented the famous lost ten tribes of Israel.) One group, the Jaredites, fled the disruption of the Tower of Babel (see chapter 5) before dying in bloody conflict. The next group, the Mulekites (the "people of Zarahemla"), lost themselves in the expanses of ancient America, serving primarily as an example of the

Figure 3.1 The Hill Cumorah in western New York, the site at which Smith reported obtaining his gold plates. Early Mormons believed Cumorah was a mass grave memorializing the extinction of two early American civilizations. Image courtesy of the Church History Library, The Church of Jesus Christ of Latter-day Saints.

fate of a people who abandoned their traditions. Finally came the people of Lehi, who dominate the Book of Mormon narrative. Lehi's favored son, Nephi, a prophet in his own right, led a righteous people called Nephites, whereas his impious brother Laman founded the wicked Lamanites. Over the course of almost a thousand years, these Nephites and Lamanites waged wars that ultimately led to the destruction of the Nephite peoples. The Lamanites survived as the precursors to at least some of the Native groups inhabiting America when European "Gentiles" arrived. The record interred at Cumorah awaited the rise of an American prophet.

The marks of the treasure hunt and the uneasy dance with desecration are visible in Smith's initial encounter with the plates. In his later narratives, Smith focused considerable attention on the conflict between the two currents in treasure seeking, one the venal and sacrilegious quest for easy money, the other the reverent pursuit of the artifacts of the dead. When he first "saught the Plates to obtain riches," he experienced the wrath of the dead.[41] Their anger came in the form of "a shock...produced upon his system, by an invisible power."[42] At this critical moment, the dead, represented by the angel Moroni, were angry with young Joseph for treating their offering as an object of material wealth.[43] In more general terms, Smith agreed with what Oliver Cowdery had written, that "if ever these sacred things are obtained they must be by prayer and faithfulness in obeying the Lord."[44] The book itself emphasized this mandate: this treasure was not to be spent. Moroni, Mormon's son, warned modern readers, "I am the same who hideth up this record unto the Lord; the plates thereof are of no worth, because of the commandment of the Lord. For he truly saith that no one shall have them to get gain; but the record thereof is of great worth; and whoso shall bring it to light, him will the Lord bless."[45]

The Grave Mound at Cumorah

Book of Mormon societies ended catastrophically, with great shedding of blood. The record these people left in an "angel guarded home"[46] represented "hidden treasures of wisdom & knowledge, even divine revelation, which has lain in the bowels of the earth for thousands of years" or "the hidden things of the ancient mountains."[47] Treasure required the dead, and Cumorah had them in spades: Smith taught that the hill was a massive burial mound.[48]

The Book of Mormon gave names to the peoples whose dead filled the mass grave at Cumorah. They were Jaredites and Nephites, the two extinguished peoples of ancient America. Both groups had named the hill, the Jaredites calling it Ramah and the Nephites calling it Cumorah. Both groups fell at the hands of wicked cousins—Lamanites destroyed the Nephites, while rival Jaredite factions annihilated each other. William Phelps, proclaiming in 1835 that "Cumorah...must become as famous among the latter day saints as Sinai was among the former day saints," taught that

> Cumorah, the artificial hill of north America, is well calculated to stand in this generation, as a monument of marvelous works and wonders. Around that mount died millions of the Jaredites; yea, there ended one of the greatest nations of this earth. In that day, her inhabitants spread from sea to sea, and enjoyed national greatness and glory, nearly fifteen hundred years.—That people forsook the Lord and died in wickedness. There, too, fell the Nephites, after they had forgotten the Lord that bought them. There slept the records of age after age, for hundreds of years, even until the time of the Lord.[49]

According to Phelps, these records slept as the ancients whose story they chronicle, in the "artificial" hill, a giant grave mound. Mormons knew whose treasure Smith had found.[50]

Phelps was only following the Book of Mormon narrative. As the prophet-general Mormon anticipated the final battle of the ancient Nephite civilization, he requested of his Lamanite opponent that his entire civilization be allowed to assemble at and around Cumorah.[51] Once this gathering had occurred, the Lamanites extinguished the Nephites in a gory round of battles that killed, by Mormon's estimate, 230,000 people (twenty-three units of "ten thousand" each, possibly a figurative term). Mormon did not spare his readers many details of the carnage. His compatriots' "flesh, and bones, and blood lay upon the face of the earth, being left by the hands of those who slew them to molder upon the land."[52] Among the heaps of rotting flesh, he and his son soon interred the record of their people. According to Cowdery, "in this vale lie commingled, in one mass of ruin, the ashes of thousands, and in this vale was destined to consume the fair forms and vigorous systems of tens of thousands of the human race blood mixed with blood, flesh with flesh, bones with bones, and dust with dust! When the vital spark which animated their clay had fled, each lifeless limb lay on one common level—cold and inanimate."[53] Mormon's account had its desired effect: Latter-day Saints could easily imagine the many dead who collapsed at Cumorah.

The Nested Jaredite Narrative

The final Nephite-Lamanite battle is the best known source of bodies for the burial mound that contained the gold plates. According to the Book of Mormon, the hill witnessed the demise of a Hebrew civilization more ancient than the Nephites. The story of the hill then called Ramah requires a detour into a nested narrative that illuminates the meaning of the Book of Mormon as artifact. Separate from and prior to the people of Lehi, a group of Hebrew pilgrims abandoned the Near East during the chaos of the Tower of Babel, led by Jared and his brother Moriancumer. God guided the Jaredite people across the ocean in wooden submersibles illuminated by sacred stones, two of which appear to have been the interpreters Smith used to translate the Book of Mormon. The history of this civilization was recorded on plates kept by Ether, the last Jaredite prophet and an obvious type for Moroni.

Prefiguring the internecine wars of Lamanites and Nephites, the Jaredites came to their collective end in battle. In this civilization's bloody twilight, Coriantumr, the last warrior king, attempted to repent and experience conversion, but his opponent Shiz would not relent. Finally he "gather[ed] together all the people upon all the face of the land, who had not been slain" at Ramah (that "same hill where my father did hide up the records unto the Lord" according to Moroni).[54] In a showdown filled with warriors "drunk with anger" and "howlings" of despair punctuating battles that decimated all but Ether, Coriantumr emerged the nearly vanquished victor and "fell to the earth...as if he had no life." An expedition from the Mulekite people found his barely animate corpse. Coriantumr's death stretched for "nine moons" among his rescuers, after which he fulfilled Ether's curse that he "should receive a burial by...another people receiving the land for their inheritance."[55] Coriantumr's exile from an ancestral grave reflected and amplified the destruction of an entire people.

In addition to the walking corpse of a king, the Mulekites discovered Ether's plates of gold in the company of breastplates and swords, relics of battle Smith would find with his Book of Mormon plates. These Jaredite records reposed in "a land which was covered with bones of men" and promised to give "a knowledge of this very people who have been destroyed," just as the plates Smith found at the same hill centuries later.[56] These plates were the "record of the people whose bones they had found," a clear echo of the plates of Mormon.[57] This Mulekite band was later discovered by a group of Nephites, and the plates of Ether were brought to a priest-king named Mosiah, who wielded seer stones to overcome the silence of the grave (see chapter 5). Coriantumr simultaneously possessed within himself the cultural valences of the prophesied interactions between Indians and Joseph Smith. Barely alive and slated to be buried far from the sepulchres of his fathers, the last Jaredite king saw his land taken by another people. Situated on the cusp of death, he passed the records of his people to a seer who could interpret them. This encounter with the Jaredite dead and their artifacts is important enough to be reiterated at several different points in Mormon's scripture.[58]

That Jaredite and Nephite civilization ended in the same mass grave suggests the Jaredite account in Ether as an explanation of the meaning of the gold plates. Two sets of records, one within the other, were "hid[den] up...in the earth" among the bones of the dead at Cumorah Hill. Long-dead men carved these books to immortalize their voices. Moroni likely buried his father, Mormon, at Cumorah along with the records.[59] The Book of Mormon burials probably underlie various images of cave tombs and interred kings in the New York countryside that circulated among Latter-day Saints, tying them to the new scripture.

After their deathly slumber, the buried plates would rise again. Moroni employed such resurrection imagery in his prophecy that the Mormon scripture would "be brought out of darkness unto light, according to the word of God; yea, it shall be brought out of the earth, and it shall shine forth out of darkness."[60]

The gold plates were not the only relics passed to Smith. Moroni had interred a breastplate, a supernatural compass, and the Sword of Laban (see figure 3.2).

Figure 3.2 This depiction, an 1893 engraving by Edward Stevenson, of Joseph Smith's encounter with Moroni highlights the other artifacts included with the Book of Mormon plates. Image courtesy of the Church History Library, The Church of Jesus Christ of Latter-day Saints.

This sword, stolen by Lehi's son Nephi, played an important role in Book of Mormon narratives. With the sword, Nephi beheaded his enemy Laban in order to obtain the "brass plates," a scripture containing Lehi's genealogy in an early version of the Hebrew Bible.[61] The sword thus represented blood shed to assure the continuity of scripture across generations. For the first generation of Latter-day Saints this sword assumed apocalyptic and even political meaning. Brigham Young (1801–1877) stood in for others when he preached that "this sword will never be sheathed again until the kingdoms of this world become the kingdom of our God and his Christ."[62] Cumorah's relics were to echo across the entire globe.

Seer Stones

Special "scrying" stones were the best known emblems of the seer's work. These stones, which accompanied Smith through much of his formally religious career, illuminate the connections between treasure and the dead, between Smith's early quest and his later religious activity.[63] The stones included both visually distinctive rocks and Native artifacts inaccurately denominated gorgets.[64] Seer stones could discover the location of other stones or treasures, especially when enclosed in the hollow of a hat pressed over the seer's face. These seer stones, critical to Smith's project, are often passed over as minor folk magic emblems, mineralized versions of the divining rods occasionally pressed to similar tasks. Stones may have been a consolation prize for some—the clank of a spade leading to something other than treasure. Importantly, though, seer stones and their treasure were integrated into and then removed from the earth. Though seers occasionally discovered stones in dry riverbeds, Smith generally disinterred his, maintaining that "men can pick stones out of this Earth ... & see knowledge of futurity."[65]

Joseph Smith possessed several seer stones, probably a brown stone, a white stone, a green geode, and—probably later—at least one gorget. The brown and white stones were most important[66] and had been buried deep within the earth. The first, apparently the brown stone, guided him to the more potent white stone, which he disinterred while digging a well, possibly combined with, or a front for, a treasure dig.[67] According to Brigham Young's reminiscence, Smith found the stone "in an Iron kettle 15 feet under ground," a depth amplified in a later retelling to thirty feet.[68] Just as treasures were interred, so were the obdurate fragments of earth that provided access to them.

From early on Smith situated these special stones within Bible narratives. The Urim and Thummim—oracular jewels in the Israelite priestly breastplate—were the sacred archetype for seer stones.[69] In William Phelps's phrase, the "Urim and Thummim" were "the spy-glass of a seer." Phelps exulted that "The Urim and Thummim, Seer stones, Teraphim, and Images, whatever name is given to them; are found in the United States of America."[70] Such stones sat beside Moroni's gold plates in their stone sepulchre in Cumorah. (Early Mormon descriptions favor two stones set in a large figure-of-eight frame like a pair of "spectacles.")[71] Armed with these stone relics of America's sacred past, Smith undertook the translation of the gold plates.[72]

Throughout his career Smith made clear that seer stones were central to the process of revelation itself. Rereading Revelation 2:17 in 1843, Smith saw the apostle John receiving his great Apocalypse through such stones, just as Smith's scriptures had come.[73] He preached that such stones were the birthright of the righteous, as "every man who lived on earth [is] entitled to a seer stone, and should have one."[74]

Just as others had seen crystal balls as microcosms of the earthly globe, so did Smith see in seer stones—special fragments of earth—clues to the mystical power of the entire earth. In 1843 he instructed his followers that the "Urim & Thummim is a small representation" of the earth, and the "earth when it is purified will be made like unto crystal and will be a Urim & Thummim."[75] These stones, able to communicate eternal truths, held within themselves the future meaning and power of the earth, which would itself be transformed into a large seer stone after it had been purged of the dead at the Great Judgment. Such geologic relics even extended back to God's physical presence, as Smith maintained in an exegesis of Revelation 15:1–4: "God and the planet where he dwells is like crystal, and like a sea of glass before the throne. This is the great Urim & Thummim whereon all things are manifest both things past, present & future and are continually before the Lord."[76] Smith's ultimate understanding of the Urim and Thummim extended well beyond that of his Protestant peers.[77]

When Smith approached the gold plates he often draped Moroni's sacred relics in a makeshift linen shroud and then stared toward the stones within his hat.[78] Though outsiders see this as sure evidence of fraud, Joseph stated that he had been commanded to respect the sanctity of the gold plates by the dead man who interred them. Although the image is largely suggestive, it is nevertheless striking: the Prophet, his face buried atop his Urim and Thummim stones, sitting beside the beshrouded plates, recovering from them the voices of the dead. From the inky blackness that mimicked death he resurrected the stories of the dead.

In the Book of Mormon Smith purified the treasure quest of the taint of filthy lucre, providing the kind of treasure that exemplified the deep meanings of the quest, themes that persisted throughout his religious career.

The Egyptian Book of the Dead

The close intersections between grave relics and Smith's religious career did not end with the publication of the Book of Mormon. America's dead were not the only ones to occupy Joseph Smith's attention. With his compatriots, Smith cherished the civilization of the pyramids. Egypt loomed large in the worldview of nineteenth-century America, spurred by the Napoleonic seizure of Egyptian national artifacts and an ongoing quest to decipher hieroglyphics. Starting around 1820, mummies began to arrive on American shores, touring the new republic as embalmed celebrities. Antebellum America at times seemed to hum with Egyptomania—mummy teas and medicinal nostrums, fictional treatments of resurrected mummies, touring mummy exhibits, the metaphysical weight of the Rosetta stone, omnipresent images of the Nile, even ideas about the meaning of race all partook of this fascination with things Egyptian.[79] For many nineteenth-century Americans, Egypt represented the source of human culture: writing, the arts, astronomy, and magic.[80] Some even saw in Egypt the direct source of ancient American civilization.[81]

Applying humanity's beginnings to their individual ends, antebellum Americans modeled their death culture on Egypt, claiming that its death emphasis, indeed its dead themselves (the astonishingly preserved mummies), represented humanity's ancient response to the eternal problem. America's cemeteries, particularly in the rural cemetery movement of the 1830s and 1840s, made this connection explicit—in the phrase of one advocate, "Egyptian architecture is essentially the architecture of the grave... [and is] particularly adapted to the abode of the dead."[82]

Smith, whose Book of Mormon claimed to be written in Egyptianized Hebrew, believed strongly in the continuity between ancient America's Israelites and Egypt through the two patriarchs he most closely associated with Egypt, Joseph and Abraham.[83] The discovery of America's indigenous mummies only made such associations stronger. One garbled report of mummified Indians in the Mammoth Cave system in Kentucky elicited an editorial by Smith: "This art was no doubt transmitted from Jerusalem to this continent, by the before mentioned emigrants, which accounts for the finding of the mummies, and at the same time is another strong evidence of the authenticity of the Book of Mormon."[84]

Near the middle of his career, Joseph obtained direct access to Egypt's dead. In June 1835, Michael Chandler (1797–1866), an Irish-American entrepreneur, arrived in the Mormon capital of Kirtland, Ohio, to meet Mormonism's prophet. Visiting nearby Cleveland with an exhibit of road-weary Theban mummies and their funeral papyri, Chandler had caught word of Smith's notoriety as a translator of hieroglyphs. Although the showman probably recognized that the mummies were unlikely to survive further travel and hoped to dispose of them profitably, he may have been genuinely curious to hear what the New York prophet had to say about his charges. In any event, Chandler did not leave Kirtland disappointed. Chandler issued a certificate attesting Smith's skill with hieroglyphs, then sold the Mormon founder four of his "posthumous travelers" and their attached papyri for the formidable sum of $2,400 (five times the annual income of a typical family farm).[85]

These mummies commanded immediate and sustained interest among the Latter-day Saints and their neighbors. So did the papyri the deceased visitors clutched to their chests. Smith and his followers identified the papyri immediately as the records of Abraham and Joseph in Egypt (see chapter 5). The disinterred grave goods that Chandler brought to Kirtland recalled for Smith the core meaning of the treasure quest. Piggybacking a letter to Sally Phelps (1797–1874) on her husband William's announcement of the purchase of the papyri, Joseph Smith wrote that William would "return and teach... hiden things of old times... the tre[as]ures hid in the sand."[86] This Old Testament allusion, an apparent reference to miraculous bounty in a desert, was one the Smiths understood as explicitly representing the treasure quest.[87] Chandler had brought to the Mormon seer a treasure of incomparable value, the type of grave relic the Bible sanctioned and anticipated.

The papyri, "obtained from the catacombs of Egypt sixty feet below the surface of the Earth," finally provided Smith with a durable physical relic of the ancient dead, an opportunity he cherished.[88] Outsiders and some insiders had long complained about the absence of the original Book of Mormon artifact, the gold plates. Of the gold plates at most a scrap of paper remained containing transcribed hieroglyphs, and outsiders mocked Smith's claim that Moroni had recovered the plates for safekeeping. Smith's eagerness to display "the ancient reccords in my possession" to all comers suggests his awareness of their potency as artifacts. He personally exhibited the papyri almost daily from October to December 1835.[89] According to Phelps, Smith's most active collaborator on the Egyptian project, the papyri "will make a good witness for the Book of Mormon. There is nothing secret or hidden that shall not be revealed."[90]

Oliver Cowdery took the comparison between gold plates and papyri further, explicitly reporting that extracts from the reformed Egyptian of Smith's original gold plates matched hieroglyphs on the Chandler papyri. The "history of the Nephites" was inscribed in the same script as the papyri.[91] In a fraught cultural exchange a half decade later, Mormons made a gift of papyrus fragments to Pottawatamies.[92] They seem to have believed that this gift brought the papyri full circle, returning hieroglyphic relics to their rightful heirs, the Book of Mormon peoples.

Smith was not satisfied to identify the papyri only. As in most of his encounters with the dead, he sought specific identities. In a statement later erroneously attributed to the Prophet, the measured assistant president Oliver Cowdery attempted to distance the church from claims that Smith named the Chandler mummies, but reasonable evidence supports Smith's designation of the mummies as a pharaonic family.[93] The family included a king named Onitas (or Onitah) and his powerful daughter Kahtoumun.[94] When Smith and Phelps set about decoding the papyri (see chapter 5), they clarified that Kahtoumun was a queen who possessed the "record of the fathers" and the secrets of the "art of embalming," and Onitas was her father.[95] There is in this apparent creativity the same hunger to know the dead by name that Smith evidenced his entire life.

The mummies and papyri became a fixture of Mormonism throughout Smith's life. His mother curated an exhibit of the mummies, while Smith proudly displayed the papyri to learned visitors. In 1842 Smith published the Book of Abraham, which joined the Book of Mormon as an account of once-lost sacred history. This book, widely criticized for the disconnect between the extant Egyptian hieroglyphs and the text Smith translated from them, illuminates the close associations between the dead and early Mormonism. This book is a scripture that Joseph Smith translated from funerary texts wrested from the hands of embalmed corpses disinterred from the sands of Egypt. Smith saw corpses buried with a message from the culture most intimately associated with death, and from it he recovered an intensely cosmogonic story of Abraham. Coming face-to-face with the unresuscitated dead, the Prophet discovered the origin and meaning of life.

Critics understood well the importance of the relics of the dead to Smith. In 1843 a group of Illinois hoaxers produced the so-called Kinderhook plates, a collection of inscribed metal sheets with "bell shape[d]" outlines similar to the Native gorgets believed by some to be military armbands. Claiming that in April 1843 Robert Wiley explored a burial mound, apparently following a dream meant to mimic Smith's encounters with Moroni, Dr. Harris of Kinderhook announced in an affidavit that a team excavated to ten feet, removed two feet of charred rock, then "found plenty of charcoal and ashes; also human bones that appeared as though they had been burned; and near the eciphalon a bundle was found that consisted of six plates of brass," news that spread in the press to Nauvoo.[96] The Latter-day Saints took the bait. John Taylor introduced the find in the *Nauvoo Neighbor* as "additional testimony to the Book of Mormon." In their account, the Mormons emphasized that the plates were discovered "on the breast of" a corpse buried "about six feet from the surface of the earth."[97] Though Smith's lieutenants reported his intention to translate the plates and his assessment of their authenticity, no such translation has been found. The story certainly persuaded Taylor, who printed a facsimile of the plates and sold them for 12.5 cents, with "an account of their discovery."[98] In their response to this hoax (definitively demonstrated to be a fraud only in the 1970s), Smith and his inner circle remained true to the themes of their prior revelation: America's dead had a story to tell, and that was the treasure that lurked in their burial mounds. That is how John Taylor introduced the Kinderhook affidavits to his Mormon audience, claiming "there are more dreamers and money diggers, than Joseph Smith, in the world" in reference to men who claimed to find plates among the bones of the dead.[99] In claiming this shared identity, Taylor emphasized his prophet's proud record as an interpreter of the relics of the dead. Although the hoax was not ultimately successful in tripping up Joseph Smith, the effort nevertheless illuminated the persistence of Mormon ideas about the power of the grave and its relics.

In the transition from gold coins and ingots of bullion to ancient swords and breastplates, thence to gold plates and the cosmogony of funerary scrolls, Joseph Smith Jr. made his way from marginalized treasure seer to prophet, revealing two books of scripture and a new religious system in the process. Whatever his ultimate credibility, Joseph was ever in pursuit of the dead and their legacy. Through this quest he managed to revise and amplify themes within folk magical culture that demonstrate the great religious power of the dead.

Through entombed artifacts, Smith revealed to his followers, and perhaps to himself, the full spiritual and metaphorical power of the treasure quest. Though Smith's chief biographer is correct that he had largely disentangled himself from the less esteemed aspects of folk magic by the late 1820s, substantial continuities persist. These continuities are religiously much richer than the simple equation of his first scripture with a charlatan's quest for buried gold or a training period for a prophet.[100] Smith found great religious power in the contents of the graves beneath his feet.

4

Hallowed Ground

Tombs, Indians, and Eden

Before the cholera outbreak that concluded their 1834 efforts to recover Mormon lands in Missouri, the members of the Mormon expeditionary force called Zion's Camp traversed western Ohio, "wandering over the plains of the Nephites, recounting occasionally the history of the Book of Mormon, roving over the mounds of that once beloved people of the Lord, picking up their skulls & their bones, as proof of its divine authenticity."[1] This expansive reference to Indian graves in a private letter masks the details of a dramatic encounter—the Camp discovered a burial mound, on the top of which "there was the appearance of three altars, which had been built of stone, one above another, according to the ancient order; and the ground was strewn over with human bones." According to participant Heber Kimball, this scene "caused in us very peculiar feelings, to see the bones of our fellow creatures scattered in this manner, who had been slain in ages past. We felt prompted to dig down into the mound, and sending for a shovel and hoe, we proceeded to move away the earth" (see figure 4.1). Much to their delight, the Mormon militia discovered there "the skeleton of a man, almost entire."[2]

The dry corpse, its femur broken, sheltered an arrowhead within its torso. Smith pronounced the skeleton the remains of Zelph, an eminent Lamanite warrior who served under a theretofore unknown prophet-general, Onandagus. Zelph, not mentioned in the Book of Mormon narrative, was "known from the hill Camorah or east sea to the Rocky mountains."[3] Zelph had perished in the terrible battles that heralded the end of Nephite civilization.[4] This brave's bones had lain silent for a millennium and a half, awaiting the seer who could reveal their history.

Figure 4.1 A retrospective depiction of the 1834 disinterment of Zelph, from "The Mormons," *Harper's New Monthly Magazine* 6:35 (April 1853): 610. This disinterment illuminates meanings of Smith's interactions with grave relics and his ability to see Mormon futures in America's pasts. Image courtesy of the Church History Library, The Church of Jesus Christ of Latter-day Saints. I thank Lachlan Mackay for this reference.

The Zelph incident is often passed over as a minor curiosity or a particularly egregious example of Smith's imaginative flights of fancy.[5] However, Zelph's story is pregnant with meaning: in this almost necromantic act, Smith demonstrated to his followers the nature of their relationship to the mortal remains of America's ancient civilization. A warrior's disturbed bones provided access to lost multitudes. One participant aptly summarized the revelation: "Joseph had a vision and the Lord shewed him that this man was once a mighty Prophet and many other things concerning his people."[6] Seeing in an unknown Book of

Mormon hero a kindred spirit—Smith, too, was a prophet in the Book of Mormon tradition—the Mormon prophet placed himself, his followers, and modern Indians on sacred ground and within a sacred narrative. In this act Smith confirmed that the Nephites had possessed the land, pockmarked with graves, over which the Saints marched to reclaim their Missouri Zion.[7] In a very real sense, Smith was a modern Onandagus, and his followers on Zion's Camp modern Zelphs. While they might die, as Zelph manifestly had (and several of them did, from cholera, at the end of the expedition), their mission would not be in vain.[8]

There may be a personal valence to this experience. Joseph may have recalled his brother's corpse as he valorized Zelph's skeleton. Less than a decade after Alvin's disinterment, memories of his fallen brother may have crowded Joseph's mind as he handled the remains of a warrior from America's sacred past. The prophet's hands running over the now dry bones of another human corpse connected the personal with the epic, a type of spiritual image with which Smith often inspired his followers.[9]

Repeatedly in Smith's relationships with America's soil, the personal, the social, and the historic intermingled. In this revelatory encounter with Zelph's bones, Smith made clear his desire to connect the living and the dead, an effort inextricably tied to human relics and the land that contained them. This chapter explores the meanings Smith and his followers found in ancestral graves and their residents, broadly conceived. Smith seized on Indian grave mounds not only in his quest for the secrets hidden in the bowels of the earth but also for their connection to the sacred past. From the putative mound of Cumorah Hill through the Ohio mounds of Zion's Camp and Kirtland, to the sacred hills of Missouri's primal landscape, Smith situated every early Mormon settlement among America's ancient graves.[10]

Smith's relationship to graves encompassed a sepulchre built beside his Nauvoo Temple, a robust identification with Natives both living and dead, and his identification of the American frontier with the Garden of Eden. These intertwined themes illuminate the meanings of Mormon Indianism and primitivism and the Mormons' revision of the Vanishing Indian belief of their peers to understand their own prospects for resurrection. They also illuminate the ways human cultures personalize their lands and histories by creating relationships with the dead, both real and imagined.[11]

The House of the Dead

Reverence for the location of human remains came naturally to Smith: proper burial near one's people was central to holy death culture for Americans in the early nineteenth century. Emblematically, Boston jurist Joseph Story (1779–1845) declared at the 1831 founding of the Mount Auburn cemetery (first of America's rural cemeteries) that "there is nothing that wrings the heart of the dying…and the surviving, with sharper agony, than the thought, that they are to sleep their last sleep in the land of strangers." Story anticipated that Mount Auburn would allow the dead to have "communion" with each other and with the living.[12]

The seeming permanence of the Mormon settlement at Nauvoo, perhaps coupled with the development of Smith's temple, resulted in an amplification of prevalent beliefs about the necessity of community burial. In homiletic musings about the overseas death of missionary Lorenzo Barnes (1812–1842)—whose English village grave became a site of Mormon pilgrimage—Smith made explicit his reverence for mortal remains and the site of their interment.[13]

> When I heard of the death of our beloved hero Barnes it would not have affected me so much if I had the opportunity of burying him in the land of Zion. I believe those who have buried their friends here their condition is enviable. Look at Joseph in Egypt how he required his friends to bury him in the tomb of his fathers….It has always been considered a great curse not to obtain an honorable buryal and one of the greatest curses the ancient prophets could put on any one was that a man should go without a burial.[14]

A complementary account of the sermon captured the personal, physical impulse that underlay postmortal proximity for Smith, who taught "the importance of being buried with the saints & their relatives in as much as we shall want to see our relatives first & shall rejoice to strike hands with our parents, children &c when rising from the tomb."[15] For Smith the physical reality of resurrection was undoubted, but believers had obligations to ensure that their bodies were adjacent to each other when the great day came. While Smith was well within prevalent cultural expectations to demand such considerations, his answer to this problem was more assiduously literal than many of his peers.

As Smith's theology of resurrection developed further, its physical and personal aspects were amplified to a remarkable extent. Smith appears to have taught his followers that their physical proximity in graves not only sweetened the resurrection, it made resurrection possible. Many early Latter-day Saints believed that at Christ's Second Coming they would lay hands on each other and raise each other from the dead. Through Smith's priesthood the joyous handclasps of the resurrection, "striking hands," were the medium by which resurrection physically occurred. Rather than occurring spontaneously in the presence of the returning Christ, resurrection required the laying on of hands by priesthood-wielding Mormon elders. Having loved ones interred nearby was critical to the timely efficacy of the ordinance of resurrection—mismanaged burials could impair the central miracle of Christ's Second Coming.[16]

The fact that Alvin slept far away in the Palmyra graveyard and a mythically large number of his followers moldered without a "decent grave" after their ejection from Missouri bothered Joseph Smith greatly.[17] In a grandiose if culturally coherent act, Smith began work on a family sepulchre in the 1840s. He called this structure (see figure 4.2), located on the Nauvoo Temple grounds, the "Tomb of Joseph" in a reflexive and biblical reference to the Egyptian patriarch.[18]

Smith had not had the resources to accomplish such an undertaking in Ohio or Missouri. Nauvoo would be the settlement permanent enough for, and made permanent by, a Smith family sepulchre. Referring to this burial chamber in a eulogy of his father, Smith proclaimed, "Sacred to me is his dust, and the spot where he is laid. Sacred to me is the tomb i have made to encircle o'er his head."[19] In the eulogy for Lorenzo Barnes, Joseph reported a vision of the power of this family tomb.

> So plain was the vision I actually saw men before they had ascended from the tomb as though they were getting up slowly, they take each other by the hand. It was my father and my son, my Mother and my daughter, my brother and my sister. When the voice calls suppose I am laid by the side of my father. What would be the first joy of my heart? Where is my father, my mother, my sister? They are by my side. I embrace them and they me.[20]

This resurrection scene, occurring at the parousia, seems to display no substantial awareness of the returned Christ. In defiance of the theocentric tradition that emphasized God's majesty over human relationships,

Figure 4.2 Architectural drawings for the Tomb of Joseph, situated on the Nauvoo Temple grounds. The reason for the water channel beneath the tomb is not certain but appears to be drainage from the baptismal font in the temple. Image courtesy of the Church History Library, The Church of Jesus Christ of Latter-day Saints.

Smith highlighted in resurrection the loving embrace of family and friends. Christ would return and superintend the process, but ultimately resurrection was a story about families reunited. In his dream and the sermons he preached, Smith made clear that this Tomb of Joseph was a familialization and reification of the broader culture he invoked in eulogizing Lorenzo Barnes. The need to have one's dead interred nearby was not merely a mode of respect or a statement of community standards, it was a necessary component of the sacramental, communal act of resurrection.[21]

Smith fully intended to assemble his family in the tomb. In 1842 he instructed: "let my father, Don Carlos, and Alvin, and children that have [been] buried be brought and laid in the tombs I have built."[22] Much as did the families who would pick through Civil War battlegrounds for remains to return to their hometowns two decades later, Smith hoped to disinter Alvin one last time, moving all his family's corpses to the Tomb of Joseph.[23] This, sadly, was not to be. His plans thwarted, Smith died before the tomb was completed, before he could relocate the Alvins or his stillborn twins from their remote graves. Adding insult to injury, Smith could not himself be buried there for fear of desecration of his remains (see chapter 10).[24] Ultimately, only one sister-in-law was buried in the sepulchre. After Smith's death and the forcible eviction of Mormons from Nauvoo, the location of the tomb was lost for many decades.[25]

The act of adjacent burial made strong statements about the nature of created community. In valorizing a new place of burial, antebellum Americans torn from their natal lands emphasized the centrality of graves, both actual and imagined, to the development of community. The society Smith created, encompassing life and afterlife, provided his followers with the reassurance that despite their risky migrations into the frontier and the desertion of their extended families, they would not be buried alone. On the morning of the resurrection, they would discover their friends, even their prophet, rising from the soil beside them. Such reassurance helped to limit the brutal allegations of those, like the Anglican academic Henry Caswall (1810–1870), who bemoaned the high mortality of English immigrants to the Mormon Zion "far from the graves of their fathers, remote from the ministers of the true faith," who "ended their days in want and wretchedness, and were buried without that respectful solemnity which in England is not denied even to the pauper from the workhouse."[26] In comparing all Mormons to inhabitants of the potter's field, Caswall denigrated the Latter-day Saints harshly, speaking to a profound and widely experienced fear. Latter-day Saints in response emphasized the cemetery logistics of their new faith and community. When faced with the crucial question of where to be interred, many said they would be buried with the Latter-day Saints. In place of the churchyards of England that Caswall believed they should inhabit, the Saints chose to be buried, where possible, near Smith and his family. In a late echo of the medieval practice of burial *ad sanctos*, Mormon convert Josiah Richardson (1783–1842), dying of cancer in his thigh, chose to be "intered at Montrose [Iowa] burying ground (according to his wish to be buried with the Saints)" rather than in his ancestral burial ground.[27] Other Protestants on the periphery espoused similar desires. The independent if mostly Baptist itinerant Nancy Towle (1796–1876), often plagued by thoughts of interment far from home, was prone to muse, "I could have staid:—and there with them been buried" as a way of acknowledging how well she liked a given audience for her preaching.[28]

The potent bond of a community gravesite was one of several claims that sites of inhumation made on antebellum Americans. A cult of the cemetery, centuries if not millennia old, connected survivors to the dead.[29] In their encounters with the graves of loved ones, survivors evoked, honored, and mourned the dead, and the gravestones and interred bones served a purpose similar to the relics of medieval Christianity. Adelia Cole, the aspiring Mormon poet who conjured the horrors of decay in "My Mother's Grave," wrote:

> 'neath that cold but hallowed turf,
> My mother's ashes lie.
> There, there she's lain for two long years,
> Beneath that sacred spot.[30]

This "sacred spot" of "hallowed turf" had been made so by the presence of human remnants, sleeping until the Resurrection. This phrasing is not merely metaphorical—the combination of humanity and soil wielded religious power alongside its sentimental gravity. For Cole, the presence of her mother's corpse, now dissolved into bone and ashes, created a new space. To this spot Mrs. Cole came to mourn and confront her own mortality; she also came to locate herself in the cosmos.

Soil mixed with human remains was no longer merely soil. This sacralizing view of the graveyard could serve as a circumlocution for decomposition, framing it as an act of integration rather than dissolution. Mormons and others reprinted the anticipation of Methodist lay poet Otway Curry (1804–1855) that after death "I shall blend with the ancient / And beautiful forms of the Earth."[31] The Book of Mormon periodically referred to dissolution into "mother earth" as a euphemism for death.[32] Many antebellum believers drew comfort from imagining incorporation into the soil in place of the horrors of decomposition. Simultaneously, this image physicalized the metaphorical power of remains to sacralize earth. Earth was not just earth when it contained the dead.

Holy Land and the Sepulchres of the Fathers

The power the interred dead wielded was not simply personal or familial. Just as individuals located themselves on the basis of family graves, entire civilizations staked claims and set bounds on the basis of ancestral tombs.[33] The early Latter-day Saints often drew on such traditions. Dealing with mass expulsion from Missouri, the Mormons waged a publicity campaign in hopes of securing compensation for lost property and physical suffering. The most literate of the Saints wrote formal petitions to the legislatures or militias of their states of heritage. (Frontierspeople often maintained an identity with the state from which they or their parents emigrated.) In establishing their credentials for the state bodies, the petitioners emphasized family graves. Sidney Rigdon in his letter to the Pennsylvania legislature addressed "the state of his nativity, and the place of the sepulchers of his fathers."[34] Noah Packard, addressing the Massachusetts government in 1844, similarly called upon "the land of the sepulchers of his ancestors."[35] These flourishes wielded rhetorical power to establish bonds of kinship with the states Mormons hoped would succor them.

Simultaneously the graves of those dying in Zion became the "sepulchers of the fathers" for new generations. A version of the language of ancestral sepulchres came to play in the crisis following the murder of Joseph and Hyrum Smith in June 1844 (see chapter 10).[36] Initially Brigham Young refused to consider departing from Nauvoo, arguing that the church could not abandon the remains of the Smith family. He preached in August 1844: "let us stay here where the bones of Joseph, Hyrum, Samuel, Don Carlos, and Father Smith are. . . . I would rather have the dead body of the Prophet than some men who are alive."[37] John Taylor announced in his eulogy of the dead brothers: "in life they were not divided, and in death they were not separated!"[38] In the deathly proximity of the brothers stood a lesson to their ecclesiastical heirs: the Mormons would no more abandon Joseph Smith than his brother Hyrum had. Young and his apostle-colleagues used precisely this line of argumentation to reject Sidney Rigdon's proposal to move the church to Pittsburgh. Nothing could substitute, the apostles argued, for a church built physically on the graves of prophets, "the very ground where sleeps the ashes of our deceased friends."[39] Soon, though, political realities forced Young to admit that the Mormons who were loyal to him would be forced to leave Illinois or face the threat of civil war. As he prepared to abandon Smith's physical Zion, Young sought what he could of the Prophet's remains. Smith's widow, Emma, disgusted by Young's continuation of polygamy, refused him access to the remains, which she had buried in a secret grave. Her refusal enraged Young, who announced in a pivotal church conference in October 1845 that the fallen prophet had made Young promise to bury him in the Tomb of Joseph. According to Young, "Joseph once said with outstretched arms 'if I fall in battle in Missouri, I want you to bring my bones back + deposit them in that sepulchre. I command you to do it in the name of the Lord.'" Young portrayed

Emma's refusal to disclose the location of Joseph's corpse as violation of a covenant. In harsh words to a grieving widow, Young announced: "if she will not consent to it, our garments are clear[—]then when he wakes up in the morning of the resurrection he shall talk with them & not with me—the sin shall be upon her head not ours."[40] Smith's commitment to burial in the family sepulchre was public knowledge in Nauvoo, which gave Young an advantage against Emma, but the chief apostle's demands fell on deaf ears. Mrs. Smith prevailed, and Young was forced to abandon the relics of his former leader when the Mormons were driven out of Nauvoo in 1846.[41]

Young's failure to obtain the bodies mattered. When he attempted to persuade the Smith matriarch, Lucy, to migrate to the Great Basin with him, she protested:

> Here lays my dead my husband & children I want to lay my bones here so that in the resurrection I can raise with my husband & children—if so be that my children go [West with Young]—And I would to God that all my children would go—they will not go without me & if I go I want to have my bones fetched back to be laid with my husband & children.[42]

Lucy borrowed Old Testament images her prophet-son invoked for the family tomb in Nauvoo to argue with Young. She recalled during the same speech the illness of her son William (1811–1893) during the Missouri Mormon War of 1838. From a sickbed he reported a dream to his mother in which thousands of men attacked a Mormon settlement. Frightened by his illness and the associated nightmare, Lucy recalled her son pleading: "[If] I die . . . I want you to carry my corps[e] wherever you go."[43] Lucy's voice was not alone—her last surviving son had reiterated the desire that the entire family be buried together.

The remains of the Smith family needed to stay together so they could resurrect one another. The Smiths and their Latter-day Saints feared the abandonment of their corpses in death just as they feared being alone in life. They sought assurances that their religious faith and community would not disrupt family ties. In response to Lucy's request, Young announced to the assembled, "Mother Smith proposes that she will go with us if we will promise to bring back her bones in case of her death & deposit them with her husbands I propose that we as a people shall pledge ourselves that if she do go with us and die we will bring her bones back &

lay them by the side of her husband according to her wishes." The assembly accepted the proposal unanimously.[44]

The contention over the Smith family remains at Nauvoo points to a broader phenomenon of geographical self-identity grounded in the interred remains of loved ones and ancestors. In this encounter and in many others, Mormons' relationship to the house of the dead proved broader than their desire to be buried with loved ones nearby. The relationship between the living and the soil that contained their predecessors extended into attempts to come to terms with the topography and history of "the land now known as America."[45] Identifying the interred ancestral dead with a land's past and future proved crucial to Mormon views of America's Native peoples and the world's history. The imaginative linking of graves with lands took Mormons to America's lost ancestors and thence to the ancestors of all humanity.

America's Ancestral Graves

Early America offered a special opportunity to explore the meaning of ancestral remains for nationhood. The western frontier of the early republic contained a multiplicity of grave sites, burial mounds of the culture groups generally designated the Adena and Hopewell (more generically Mound Builder) societies. Like Europe's castles, the mounds testified of a lost and splendid age.[46] For others, these structures vied with Egypt's pyramids and sarcophagi for antiquity, imparting to the American republic a historical gravitas it otherwise lacked.[47] Mounds also amplified prevailing images of the ubiquity of death. These were the "place of tombs" and "sightless skulls and crumbling bones" that the traveling writer Thaddeus Mason Harris conjured in 1803.[48] Josiah Priest taught that many centuries if not millennia of dead rested within the Grave Creek mound, giving the gravesite a historical scope that it imparted to America.[49] The frontiers of the nineteenth century bore the mark of an ancient civilization; early Americans lived among a dead other than their own.

These lands, the "inheritance of the saints," were "consecrated ground" for early Mormons.[50] Even in Nauvoo these ancient graves were never far away. When they first arrived in Illinois in 1839, the Twelve Apostles toured local burial mounds and "visited about 20 mounds," including "the grave of a Lamanite Chief."[51] According to one description, "a number of tumuli, or ancient mounds, are found within the limits of the city, proving it to have been a place of some importance with the extinct inhabitants of this continent."[52] Henry Caswall noted that across the Mississippi, "upon an eminence," recent Sauk and Fox gravesites served as shrines.[53] Even after they had been exiled from the United States entirely, the Latter-day Saints continued to situate themselves in "the country of the Lamanites."[54] Each major Mormon settlement claimed a holy proximity to Native graves.

The quest to discover Indian origins is difficult to separate from the need to understand ancient grave sites and, particularly for Joseph Smith, to possess the relics of the American dead. To borrow historian Catherine Albanese's perceptive phrase, Native "ghosts trod in his mind and in the countryside around him."[55] What connected those "ghosts"— Smith would call them angels (see chapter 9)—to the living were the omnipresent grave ruins. Similar in many respects to those of his peers who were interested in the historical or philosophical meaning of the vast social and political changes imposed on Natives in the aftermath of the War of 1812, Smith discovered powerful testimony of the meaning of America and its ancient dead in the Mound Builder ruins.[56] In his prophecy upon the bones of the once-mighty Zelph lies a neglected and misunderstood story of American beginnings and civilizations that illuminates the complex history of Mormon Indianism. Natives and their graves allowed the Latter-day Saints to confront death, to sacralize and primordialize their physical environment, and to prepare for the Resurrection of the Just at the coming of Christ. For Smith in particular, who discovered the long-lost name of the American Indian—Lamanite— America was sanctified by the presence of the Native dead.[57] William Phelps's early history of Mormonism demonstrates both the temporal scope of the narrative, comprising all of American history, and the mystique of the ancient dead. In answer to his rhetorical question of where the mighty generations who inhabited America before the Mormons had gone, Phelps answered: "Numbered with the dead! Numbered with the dead! Numbered with the dead!" Naming the shroud that covered those dead Lamanites, he called out in print, "O grave! Grave! How many mysteries thou hidest!"[58] For the early Latter-day Saints, Native graves contained America's history.

The early Mormons drew strength from the graves of the ancestors who had trod and perhaps died on the sacred paths the Mormons followed in their own peregrinations.[59] In one particularly strong metaphor, the Mormons literally sprang, like their scripture, from the remains of the dead. In Oliver Cowdery's early church history, he recalled the fertility of the soil near Palmyra, "which gives a prospect at once imposing, when one reflects on the fact, that here, between these hills, the entire power and national strength of both the Jaredites and Nephites were destroyed." In his fecund image of a civilization rising from the ruins of its predecessor lurks the possibility that the flora of western New York had been fertilized by the remains of the ancient dead.[60] Regardless of the reach of Cowdery's metaphor, something crucial to the Latter-day Saints did spring from the graveyard of Cumorah: a new American scripture interred with the Nephite and Jaredite dead. For the Latter-day Saints the Book of Mormon contained the secrets of the peoples among whose bones it was buried.

The architectural and funereal relics of ancient America manifestly had a story to tell; the stony silence of the mounds could not long be tolerated. Josiah Priest explained to his readers: "we can see their vast funeral vaults, enter into their graves and look at their dry bones; but no passage of history tells their tale of life; no spirit comes forth from their ancient sepulchers, to answer the inquiries of the living."[61] According to Priest, white Americans had no real record "beside that which is written in dust, in the form of mighty mounds, tumuli, strange skeletons, and aboriginal fortifications."[62] Had he been a Latter-day Saint, Priest would have realized that Joseph Smith had discovered such a record in his Book of Mormon.[63] The scripture's guardian angel agreed: Moroni introduced his father's gold plates as "an account of the former inhabitants of this continent and the source from whence they sprang" in Smith's 1839 account of their encounter.[64]

Grave mounds also served to support the Book of Mormon, which explained them.[65] Even as Latter-day Saints knew of prior traditions about Indian origins, the association between the grave sites and ancient America's scripture cast a long shadow over early Mormonism.[66] William Phelps, equating Jaredites with the biblical giants of Genesis, exclaimed: "whenever we hear that uncommon large bones have been dug up from the earth, we may conclude, That was the skeleton of a Jaredite."[67] The sacred story of America's dead would not be restricted to the sites of Mormon habitation, though. As the humbler mounds of North America were upstaged by the complex ruins of Central and South America, the Latter-day Saints embraced them as new external evidences of their scripture. Mormons eagerly embraced reports from

Mesoamerica by explorers like John Stephens (1805–1852) and Frederick Catherwood (1799–1854), with ringing endorsements in church periodicals. Repeatedly, the ruins of the Americas proved the truth of Mormon scripture and religion. Some believers even credited their personal conversion to the presence of these ruins, a Mormon parallel to widespread Protestant fascination with the archaeology of the Holy Land as proof of the Bible's validity.[68]

Even as the grave monuments supported the Book of Mormon, so did the Book of Mormon, at least for Latter-day Saints, support the graves. In the aforementioned memorial to Lorenzo Barnes, Smith tied the sanctity of the burial ground directly to his translated scriptures. "The place where a man is buried has been sacred to me. This subject is made mention of in [t]he Book of Mormon and Scriptures to the aborigines. The burying places of their fathers is more sacred than any thing else." By this association, Smith intended to demonstrate the perfect continuity of the death cultures of the ancient Indians and antebellum Christians, the relevance of his scripture and its peoples to the present problem of death.[69]

Identifying with Native Pasts and Futures

A variety of American observers, most poignantly William Cullen Bryant (1794–1878) in his poem "Thanatopsis," imagined the final moments of the last survivors of America's ancient civilizations. For this wistful Romanticism these observers found support in a variety of archaeological and scholarly voices.[70] In many respects America's lost dead represented a mythic past for the citizens of the new American republic. For Smith, Native identity was both mythic and quite personal. The Book of Mormon was no generic revelation, no statement of white geopolitics. Smith knew its major voices—Nephi, Mormon, Moroni—by name.[71] He reported that these prophets had visited him personally. In the phrase of Parley Pratt (later attributed to Smith), the reconceptualized Natives were "one of the most important points in the faith of the church of the Latter Day Saints."[72] The sense of personal intimacy Smith felt with America's Native peoples shows in his mother's proud reminiscence that Joseph Jr. often described their "dress, mode of traveling & the animals upon which they rode ... with every particular."[73]

Central to the meaning of these sustained encounters with Native groups was the simultaneous existence of the exotic living and their dead.[74] This juxtaposition proved productive for Latter-day Saints facing a world on the verge of extinction as well as their own very uncertain life spans: Mormons revised America's Vanishing Indian narrative to situate their own suffering and death.[75] The graves divulged to Smith the secrets of the origins of Native populations, and the records of the dead established bonds between white Latter-day Saints and modern Natives. Smith was not just parroting his peers: the genealogy of Lamanites is more complex than merely an account of Israel's lost tribes. America's ancient inhabitants, the Vanishing Indians of the nineteenth-century frontier, and Joseph Smith himself were all descendants of Joseph of Egypt.[76] Through the ancient heroes of the Book of Mormon, Smith announced a direct genealogical connection with the imperiled Natives inhabiting the early American republic.

Ancient American remains spoke to the Latter-day Saints in a variety of ways. Because Natives lived in threat of extinction among the ancient graves and ruins of their past glory, they seem to have represented the death that stalked everyone in antebellum America. At times the Latter-day Saints envisioned the death of ancient Americans in very concrete terms. Oliver Cowdery, representing his coreligionists in a recitation of the battles at Cumorah, relived the death of Nephites vividly and specifically. "Mormon, with a few others, after the battle, gazed with horror upon the mangled remains of those who, the day before, were filled with anxiety, hope, or doubt. A few had fled to the South, who were hunted down by the victorious party."[77] In the imagined mental states of Nephites the day before their death stood the grim contrast of lifeless corpse and human aspiration that antebellum Americans confronted several times a year. In 1833 Phelps sang a glossolalic hymn that an elder interpreted, with Phelps's approval, as containing "Ideas &c. concerning the travelling of the Nephites their toils troubles & tribulations &c."[78] Natives provided an imaginative kinship framework for dealing with death on scales simultaneously large and small. Modern Mormons and ancient Lamanites were both part of Joseph Smith's family. Cowdery, writing about Cumorah, captured its power to induce reflection on the death of the Nephites and the miserable sorrow of violent deaths.

here may be contemplated, in solitude... scenes of misery and distress—the aged, whose silver locks in other places and at other

times would command reverence; the mother, who in other circumstances would be spared from violence; the infant, whose
tender cries would be regarded and listened to with a feeling of
compassion and tenderness; and the virgin, whose grace, beauty
and modesty, would be esteemed and held inviolate by all good
men and enlightened and civilized nations, alike disregarded and
treated with scorn!—In vain did the hoary head...ask for mercy;
in vain did the mother plead for compassion; in vain did the help-
less and harmless infant weep for very anguish, and in vain did
the virgin seek to escape the ruthless hand of revengeful foes and
demons in human form—all alike were trampled down by the feet
of the strong, and crushed beneath the rage of battle and war![79]

This melodramatic language was almost identical to the language the
Latter-day Saints used to describe the fate of their coreligionists in
Missouri.

An early hymn called "Moroni's Lamentation" illuminates the relationship between the Native dead and the Saints' personal and corporate
experience with death. This anthem chronicled Moroni's great loneliness
as he "gazed upon his Nephite men; / And women, too, which had been
slain, / And left to moulder on the plain." The hymn held a mirror to the
desolation felt by antebellum Americans surrounded by death in general,
and Mormons experiencing the sometimes deadly violence of vigilante
mobs in particular.

> My heart is pained, my friends are gone,
> And here I'm left on earth to mourn.
> I see my people lying round,
> All lifeless here upon the ground.
> Young men and maidens in their gore,
> Which does increase my sorrows more.

Facing the piles of corpses that overlapped the hill where he would inter
the Book of Mormon, Moroni elected to embrace death himself,
pleading:

> Lord, take me home to dwell with thee;
> Where all my sorrow will be o'er,
> And I shall sigh and weep no more.[80]

The witness of corpses and graves to the lonely bereavement of the living turned Moroni toward the next life, just as similar feelings on a smaller scale turned antebellum whites toward the afterlife. The heaven Moroni anticipated was the heaven antebellum believers knew, a place free from sorrow and parting. "Moroni's Lamentation" and similar acts of publicly remembering the Native dead only strengthened the Mormons' sense of identity with their Lamanite cousins. Emphasizing the extent of this identity with the Native dead, as they struggled in 1838 to inter the bodies of their coreligionists slain during the Haun's Mill Massacre, Latter-day Saints sang this hymn as a funeral dirge, seeing in the bodies of their dead the same vision that haunted Moroni as he prepared to bury his gold plates.[81] For the Latter-day Saints, identifications with dead Lamanites and Nephites aided the process of conceptualizing death, both personal and corporate.

Smith's identity with America's Native peoples persisted beyond modern applications of scenes from the Book of Mormon. Just as they saw themselves in the ruins of American civilization, the Latter-day Saints also saw their hope for future glory in a quest for Indian supremacy. Both the Native civilizations already dead and those threatened by present extinction would live again, just as would the faithful believer. As the tension of the Missouri conflict mounted in the fall of 1838, Mormon Daniel Crandall (1808–1883) made explicit the association between the funerary monuments of the American frontier, the Book of Mormon refraction of Native history, and the redemption of Indians.

> The land appears like swelling waves
> That flow upon the main—
> There view the natives' lonely graves,
> And thousand warriors slain....
> While mournful voices, thrilling round
> All nature seem'd to weep—
> And lifeless bodies strew'd the ground,
> In Death's cold arms they sleep.
> O Lord! Are these forever doom'd,
> In watchful silence rest—
> Their bleaching bones without the tomb,
> And waiting souls not blest.
> But lo! Methinks I truly hear,
> An Angel's swelling them;...

> While waving through unsullied air,
> And sounding loud his voice;
> Bids Jacob's sons to now prepare
> And ever more rejoice.[82]

The key elements of Mormon Indianism are present in this poem: the Nephite viewing his dead compatriots; whites witnessing the disinterred bones that testified, much as Zelph did, to past glory and ancient misery; the promise that Moroni's ascent from the grave prefigured an Indian return to glory.

The distinctive Mormon view of Native pasts and futures did not develop in a vacuum. Traditions about an Israelite origin for America's Native peoples were as old as European colonization.[83] Nearest in time and location to Smith and his peers were Ethan Smith (1762–1849; no relation) and Josiah Priest.[84] Other Anglo-Americans used Natives for various ends, whether as "noble savages," as support for American exceptionalism, or as fictionalized braves who proved the existence of an indigenous American literature.[85] Joseph Smith integrated the Indians into his apocalypse, merging their fate with his at the end times. God would gather the Lamanites with the rest of Israel in preparation for the return of Christ.[86]

As Mormonism came into being, the politics of Jacksonian white supremacy disrupted scores of Native civilizations, killing and displacing a variety of cultures.[87] Mormons had a way of turning familiar social narratives against their compatriots, a facility made clear in their divergent vision of Native futures. From the Mormon perspective, Indian Removal was not punishment; it was the beginning of the gathering of Israel. In an 1832 letter to the church at large, William Phelps and colleagues announced that "the government of the United States is settling the Indians, (or remnants of Joseph) immediately to the west," adjacent to the Mormon Zion.[88] Phelps, one of the first Mormon missionaries to the displaced tribes near Fort Leavenworth, elsewhere reported: "our government has already gathered many of the scattered remnants of tribes and located them west of the Missouri, to be *nationalized* and *civilized*. . . . I rejoice to see the great work prosper."[89] Another editorial on Removal commented that "it is really pleasing to see how the Lord moves on his great work of gathering the remnants of his scattered children."[90] The Latter-day Saints used the pregnant term "gather" quite specifically, as a divine act of recovering communities through migration. Gathering described the identical process by which the Saints were moving to Zion. This vision of Removal meant that "phoenix-like...the Indians begin to raise out of their fourteen hundred years of darkness and error."[91] Parley Pratt had argued strongly to the same effect in the early 1830s.[92] Though they employed the racist language of their peers, they invested it with new meaning. In the complex logic of Mormon Indianism, the Book of Mormon foretold this event: the "Gentiles" (American Protestants) would save the Lamanites after they had scattered them.[93] From the Mormon perspective, Indian Removal was an unwitting tool in the hands of God, gathering Natives for their impending merger with the Latter-day Saints. As the Saints gathered on the frontier, so did their Native kin, both under God's direction.

In Mormon theology, Natives were a "remnant" of Joseph or Jacob. This remnant served as the nucleus for the gathering of Israel in preparation for Christ's return. To an extent unparalleled by other religious bodies, Mormons evangelized Indians through the attempted creation of community. Whereas most other Protestant missions were understood by the mainstream as acculturating Natives to expedite seizure of their land, the Latter-day Saint mission announced that proselytizing the Indians would recover to them their ancestral lands through God's miraculous restoration of their former state.[94] The Saints' view was opposite that of their white peers. Native proselytization came early to Mormons, whose scripture was, according to an 1828 revelation, to be disseminated to the full spectrum of Lehi's people—to "the Nephites, and the Jacobites, and the Josephites, and the Zoramites...the Lamanites, and the Lemuelites, and the Ishmaelites." Indeed, "for this very purpose are these plates preserved...that the Lamanites might come to the knowledge of their fathers."[95] The need to restore the remnant was a central message of the Book of Mormon—the record of the sepulchres had to return to its rightful heirs. When it returned, it promised the restoration of their societies and their lands. Moroni, the final prophet of ancient America, wrote: "I would speak somewhat unto the remnant of this people who are spared, if it so be that God may give unto them my words, that they may know of the things of their fathers." Moroni declared to them their genealogy and required that they attend to the records of their ancestors in order to participate in the immortality promised by Jesus, who "hath gained the victory over the grave."[96] The title page of the Book of Mormon proclaimed that the book was written "to the Lamanites, who are a remnant of the house of Israel." The Book of Mormon told both Indians and Mormons that they belonged to America, and America belonged to them. Lehi, Nephi, Mosiah, Alma, and a score of other sacred kin had claimed it for them.

Once the record of the remnant of Jacob had been published in 1830, attempts at conversion began in earnest. The first major mission of Smith's church was to Native groups, patterned after a similar mission of Nephites to Lamanites.[97] After setting the stage with a September 1830 revelation, Smith dispatched Parley Pratt and Oliver Cowdery in 1831 "unto the Lamanites [to] preach my Gospel unto them."[98] They would also, in fraught language Cowdery borrowed from Josephus and biblical history, plant the "pillar" to mark the temple of the New Jerusalem.[99] These itinerants headed west to preach to the Lamanites, an activity in which they were soon joined by other early Mormon evangelists.[100] They came to tell Natives that the Book of Mormon was the "record of their forefathers."[101]

Early on Smith anticipated the restoration of direct personal ties with Natives. When he dispatched his first missionaries to the Indians, he instructed them to "take unto you wives of the Lamanites and Nephites, that their posterity may become white, delightsome and Just." Intermarriage was not an uncommon strategy for Christian missionaries attempting to "civilize" Natives, although in Mormon hands it bore a different meaning. Little if anything came of these instructions to intermarry, but the prospect expressed ideas about the possibility of a genetic bond that could hasten the apocalyptic recovery of Indian destiny.[102] Conflicts with federal Indian agents and the cultural void between Native groups and Mormon primitivism meant that Pratt, Cowdery, and colleagues made few willing converts among the relocated tribes, though they did found their New Jerusalem "on the borders of the Lamanites" (Jackson County, Missouri), as specified by a revelation from Smith.[103] Along the way the missionaries laid claim to Kirtland, Ohio (by converting Sidney Rigdon's congregation of Restorationist ex-Baptists), which became church headquarters as the body of the church slowly moved to its Zion among the Lamanites.[104]

Though numerically unsuccessful with Natives, the mission bore significant fruit. In Kirtland, several white proselytes engaged in charismatic exercises that strongly emphasized identity with Indians.[105] One observer remembered that "some would slide or scoot on the floor, with the rapidity of a serpent, which the[y] termed sailing in the boat to the Lamanites, preaching the gospel."[106] These exercises imaginatively fulfilled the prophecy of the Book of Mormon that Europeans would bring the Gospel across the great ocean.[107] Other enthusiasts went "through all the Indian maneuvers of knocking down, scalping, ripping open, and taking out the bowels." Adopting images of tribal warfare in enacting the sacred theater of dying to sin, those Mormons secured Native identities. In revivalistic fervor they preached to people they understood as Native kin, seeing the ecstasies of glossolalia as the key to proselytizing Lamanites.[108] They "fanc[ied] themselves addressing a congregation of their red brethren; mounted on a stump, or the fence, or from some elevated situation."[109] A contemporary outsider noted that "while in these visions they [Mormons] say that they can see the Indians on the banks of the streams at the West waiting to be baptized; and they can hear them sing and see them perform many of the Indian manoeuvres, which they try to imitate in various ways...if any one of their brethren or sisters talk to them in Indian it will so please them that they will laugh and set out many Indian capers and motions."[110] Like some Shakers, these early Latter-day Saints merged their fascination with Indians with the outpourings of God's spirit.[111] Unlike the Shakers, they claimed genetic relationships and a shared ancestral ground. Though they also sometimes understood glossolalia as the language of Adam (see chapter 5) in the early 1830s Latter-day Saints often saw themselves speaking ecstatically in recognizable Indian dialects.[112]

As interested as he was in the Indianist content, Smith worked to suppress the extremes of enthusiasm in Kirtland.[113] The commitment to supernatural proselytism, however, continued in Ohio and Missouri. Joseph Sr. often promised believers that they would receive gifts of xenoglossia or supernatural transportation to allow them to convert the Lamanites.[114] Hopes for success continued: in 1835 Phelps believed that Native peoples would rush "like doves to their windows" to hear the Mormon message.[115] More conservative voices within the Kirtland movement also emphasized the evangelistic duties to "the remnants of Joseph" or "Josephites,"[116] and Native proselytism continued through the Nauvoo period.[117] As Joseph Smith gained prominence, his power to collaborate increased, and he officially received Native delegations, encounters that later Mormons memorialized graphically (see figure 4.3).

Employing the paternalistic language of his peers (most notoriously Andrew Jackson), Smith referred to Natives as his "children," himself as their "father." In contrast to other whites, Smith corroborated claims to family ties through his Book of Mormon.[118] Mormons did not forget their

Figure 4.3 A depiction of Smith preaching to Native groups. Mormon proselytism of Indians represented several distinctive ideologies of race and apocalypse. Image courtesy of the Church History Library, The Church of Jesus Christ of Latter-day Saints.

obligations to Native America. Immediately after Smith's death, Parley Pratt issued a statement in which the Saints pledged themselves to "refine, purify, exalt, and glorify [American Natives] as the sons and daughters of the royal house of Israel and of Joseph."[119]

Mormon Indianism led to conflict with white neighbors, particularly their apocalyptic emphasis on Indian restoration.[120] Vigilantes quickly banished Mormons with violence similar to that visited upon Natives. As the Saints themselves experienced a form (albeit much less severe) of removal in 1838, the year of the Cherokee Trail of Tears, the Mormons' sense of shared identity grew, as did their yearning for both groups to be restored to their promised lands.[121] Smarting from the loss of their Missouri Zion beside the gathered Indians, the Saints anticipated the day when "the outcasts of Jacob [will] be brought back to dwell upon the lands of their inheritance."[122] These code words for their God-given right to Missouri included both Mormons and the Indians they claimed as joint heirs of the American frontier. The outcast remnant would be restored. Even as they employed the racist and paternalistic language of their peers, Mormons foresaw a bright and conjoint future with Lamanites.[123]

The Latter-day Saints recognized the yearning Indians, separated from their ancestral graves, as kindred spirits. Wilford Woodruff's memory of an Ojibwa chief's statement in New York emphasized the experiences they shared—exile from community grave sites. The chief pleaded: "Give them a Tarritory that thay Can Call their own where the Children can point to the graves of thair fathers & say we can now live in Peace and be drivan no more. We can visit the graves of our fathers with none to drive us from them."[124] Twice-removed from the Saints' Missouri paradise, Woodruff found the chief's statement persuasive. Mormons were not the only observers to worry over this point: the English critic Frances Trollope (1779–1863), harshly criticizing Americans for their duplicity toward Indians, bemoaned their loss of "the sacred bones of their fathers."[125] The upsetting of sacred attachments to ancestral graves concerned a variety of observers; none pursued the solution quite the way the Mormons did. The identity of ancestry that the Book of Mormon offered through America's burial mounds pushed back still further, toward the first people, the first graves, and the first human settlements.

The Garden at Eden

Mormon evangelization of Native groups and settlement in geographical proximity to the centers of Indian Removal arose from and fueled a strong sense of identity with America's Natives, heavily dependent on the grave markers of a lost civilization. For Joseph Smith and his Saints, the connection to lands sanctified by ancestors continued well past Lehi and his sons, beyond the Jaredite survivors of Babel, reaching a time before known scripture. Smith was not just defining Indian origins. His concern for Natives and their ancient dead derived from a broader project to track the bodies that sanctified America's soil. Through the ruins of ancient America, Smith was discovering human origins. Whereas other Americans sought to separate Indians from the Adamic creation, Smith not only included Native Americans with the family of Adam, he reenvisioned Indians on a path back to Adam and his home in Eden. From early in his career Smith taught that the Garden of Eden was located at or near the Mormon New Jerusalem in Missouri.[126] The site of Lamanite gathering stood near Adam, his deathbed, and probably his grave.

Stitching together ancestors and land, Smith revealed a place called Adam-ondi-Ahman (see figure 4.4) in the first human language.[127] By 1837–1838 Smith had revealed that Native ruins on adjacent elevations that Mormons named Spring and Tower hills in Missouri's Grand River Valley marked the spot.[128] Adam-ondi-Ahman, Smith revealed, was Adam's home after the Fall. As his life drew to a close, Adam "called his progeny together" in the Valley of Adam-ondi-Ahman to give them his "final blessing." An antebellum audience would have immediately recognized this as a deathbed farewell. They would have understood Adam's urgency—waiting too long, he might miss his opportunity to address his progeny. Playing the role of departing father, Adam looked over his assembled family and "predicted whatsoever should befall his posterity unto the latest generation."[129] All of the earth, including Joseph Smith

Figure 4.4 Named Adam-ondi-Ahman in the original human language, Smith described this valley on Missouri's Grand River as the crucial location of Father Adam's life and death and of the Second Coming of Christ. Image courtesy of the Church History Library, The Church of Jesus Christ of Latter-day Saints.

and his followers, were present in Adam's mind at that deathbed farewell at Adam-ondi-Ahman.

Revising and interpreting the Book of Daniel, Smith identified Adam as the "Ancient of Days," the patriarch of all humanity who would report to God at the parousia. According to Smith, God would return to Adam-ondi-Ahman for this event. The location of Adam's deathbed farewell was the sacred place where humanity would reunite to part no more forever.[130] In a reminder of the intense personalization of these events for Smith, he foresaw his own father, Joseph Sr., participating in the events of the Apocalypse alongside Adam in the sacred valley.[131]

Adam's choice of a hill for his farewell paralleled the association between mounds and graves in the Book of Mormon. A hill could, as in Jesus's Sermon on the Mount, allow Adam's voice to carry to a large crowd. Old Testament stories of Mount Zion emphasized elevations as holy places. But hills were not just hills for the early Latter-day Saints; they were monuments of lost civilizations.

Like other Native mounds, the hills at Adam-ondi-Ahman contained evidence of ancient human habitation and burial. According to one reminiscence, Smith identified a long stone wall ("30 feet long 3 feet thick, and about 4 feet high above the ground") discovered during surveying as "the remains of an Altar Built By Father Adam whare he offered Sacrafice after he was driven from the Garden of Eden." Adam never strayed far from the spot, as "it was upon this Altar whare Adam blessed his sons and Posterity Before his death."[132] Another observer marveled that "I saw it [the altar] as Adam left it as did many others, & through all the revolutions of the world that Altar had not been disturbed."[133] The stones in the wall, indistinguishable from Native grave relics, emphasize the extent to which the story of Hebrew Nephites and Lamanites was the story of all humanity.[134] While other Protestants saw Adamic altars as a way to bypass Catholic "superstitions" in establishing precedents for communion tables, the Latter-day Saints gained possession of actual, physical remnants of the altar Adam constructed.[135]

The hills and altars of Adam-ondi-Ahman contained Adam's life and death. In perfect parallel to the beleaguered Latter-day Saints cast out of their Jackson County Eden, this First Day Saint came to the Grand River Valley as an exile from paradise. According to one contemporary, Smith "inform[ed his] followers that it was the place to which Adam fled when driven from the garden of Eden in Jackson County and that Far West was the spot where Cain Killed Abel."[136] The Mormons followed, in other words, the path of their first parents in their exile from Zion. Just as Adam trudged wearily from Jackson County to Adam-ondi-Ahman, so did the Latter-day Saints. Once again the sacralized landscape allowed the Saints to identify strongly with their dead ancestors, to explain their own discomfiture as an antitype of sacred history.

In fact, Smith's followers maintained for decades that Adam was buried at Spring Hill, interpreting the altar as a grave marker. By 1844 outsiders knew well this narrative of Adam-ondi-Ahman as the location of "the bones of Adam and Eve."[137] The tradition was sufficiently public that outsiders considered it a mark of local distinction.[138] One late source even maintains that the name Adam-ondi-Ahman means "Adam's grave."[139] Though Smith was not explicit about the grave in extant documents, the first father clearly had died, and many Mormons reasonably assumed that he died near the site of his deathbed farewell. This Adam-ondi-Ahman, filled with grave mounds, ancient altars, and the memory of Eden, equated dead ancestors with the lost civilizations of America and the world. Though some other Christians had attempted to locate Adam's grave in various places (e.g., at Mount Calvary), Smith's identification of its location in America was highly distinctive.[140]

In an Eden among the ruins of Indian civilization, Mormon Indianism comes full circle. The Native peoples who figured as metaphor for omnipresent death and would rise up again in an archetypal resurrection pointed to a sacred mound where humanity's first parent bid his family farewell. At this place the entire human family would be restored at the end of time. Smith's Indian Eden placed his followers in primordial time and space, as it emphasized their power over death.[141]

Identifying America as Eden was in itself no great innovation. Many Americans of the early republic, indeed many of the original Anglo-European colonists, considered North America a modern-day Eden.[142] Fleeing relatively overpopulated areas of the Old World, colonists discovered what they erroneously regarded as limitless pristine forests, untouched by civilization.[143] Eden narratives served well the creation myths of a new nation, which often saw itself as a modern Israel.[144] Simultaneously, Christian speculation about the location of the paradise at Eden abounded. Buck's conservative *Theological Dictionary* summarized myriad proposals, including "the third heaven, in the orb of the moon, in the moon itself, in the middle region of the earth, above the earth, under the earth, in the place possessed by the Caspian sea, and under the arctic pole," as well as Mesopotamia. Buck worried, as did many others, that such speculation was fruitless, a position even the highly creative Josiah Priest endorsed.[145] The New World Eden was almost always metaphorical for antebellum Americans. A few scattered thinkers defied standard ideas with remarkably literal interpretations in the spirit of Joseph Smith, perhaps most notably James Leander Scott's spiritualist community at Mountain Cove, Virginia, in the 1850s.[146]

While other American Eden visions implicitly eliminated Native peoples, seeing their land as available for white colonization, Smith recovered Eden on the American frontier in part because the Indians, his remnant of Joseph, had lived and died there. Joseph Smith's Eden was more literal, more personal, and more firmly grounded in the conquest of death than the Edens of his compatriots. In his Eden the Mormon prophet interwove narratives about hallowed ground, Indian Israelitism, and the meaning of ancestral sepulchres.

Figuratively alongside the grave marker of Adam on Spring Hill and the mass grave of Cumorah/Ramah with its associated record, Smith placed his own monumental tomb, named for the Egyptian Joseph who united the Lamanite and Mormon remnants of Israel. These memorializing grave markers situated the living, protected the dead, and united them all. In the Indians, a mythic community spanning the living and the dead, potential converts and entombed skeletons, Smith descried the origins of all humanity. Simultaneously he saw the place to which they would return in the grand cycle of life. In the rising of the Indians from their graves stood the promise of an end to all endings and a view of the first beginning.

5

Seerhood, Pure Language,
and the Silence of the Grave

Around 92 BCE, according to the Book of Mormon, an aging monarch named Mosiah faced the unusual problem of four worthy heirs but not a single interested contender for his throne. All four sons were missionizing and little interested in secular affairs. In the strange interplay of church and state characteristic of that society, Mosiah thus bestowed his kingdom on the son of the high priest, passing the crown in a ritual pregnant with the meaning of Book of Mormon history. Assembling his subjects, he transferred the records of his people to his successor. There was no scepter, ring, or crown; the authority of this state was its written legacy, engraved on metal plates. In addition, Mosiah transferred another set of plates, this one acquired from America's refugees from the Tower of Babel, the Jaredites.

Mosiah's people cared a great deal about these undecipherable plates. They were "desirous beyond measure to know concerning those people who had been destroyed" at Mount Ramah. To the daunting task of translation—the plates were recorded in the pure language of Eden—Mosiah brought to bear sacred relics, two stones "fastened into the two rims of a bow." The prophet-editor Mormon, reflecting on the account centuries later, editorialized that these stones "were prepared from the beginning, and were handed down from generation to generation, for the purpose of interpreting languages." These stones, Mormon explained, made Mosiah a seer, as "whosoever has these things is called seer, after the manner of old times." With these mystical interpreters in hand, Mosiah "translated and caused to be written the records which were on the plates of gold." These stones, in Mosiah's hands, recovered the story of the people of Jared, from the preservation of their language at Babel to their ultimate destruction.[1]

Mormon's son Moroni incorporated the Jaredite plates into the Book of Mormon as the Book of Ether. The Nephite king Mosiah had received the Jaredite plates by means of the third set of Hebrew pilgrims to the New World, the Mulekites. Named for the biblical king Zedekiah's son, the Mulekites had fled the Babylonian exile like Lehi's family but then languished in the Americas because "their language had become corrupted; and they had brought no records with them." Geographically isolated in the vastness of early America, they spoke no idiom that Mosiah and his followers could identify, despite having a shared ancestry only a few hundred years earlier. This language barrier notwithstanding, the Mulekite people "rejoice[d] exceedingly, because the Lord had sent the people of Mosiah with the Plates of Brass which contained the records of the Jews." The Mulekites also brought a "large stone" with "engravings on it" from which Mosiah decoded the history of the last king of the Jaredite people.[2] These engravings were tied, as was the Book of Mormon, to the remains of the dead (see chapter 4); they told the story of the people whose "bones lay scattered in the land northward."[3] Mosiah's task as a seer was to interpret ancient records culled from a battlefield graveyard. Without a seer, the Jaredite voices were lost forever; only the seer's power could recover their lost history—"the Lord and not man, had to interpret, after the people were all dead."[4]

This odd transfer of royal power—a charismatic monarch uses seer stones to recover the records of a lost civilization, translates a remnant of Adam's language for a civilization that has lost its ancestral language, then hands the records and thereby his kingdom to the high priest's son—frames central motifs in earliest Mormonism. Seers gave voice to the dead through their access to a pure form of language. Through Joseph Smith, a latter-day seer, Mormons heard voices issuing from the dust. Smith chose "translation," a richly multivalent concept, to describe the way a seer recovered lost voices. In this vein Smith translated Egyptian funerary papyri, gold plates, and the King James Version of the Bible. Such translation was no mere work with lexicon and grammar, no scholarly decryption of a Rosetta stone: it was a religious experience of connection. For Smith, scripture represented recovery of the voices of the dead through access to a language beyond language.

The Silent Grave

Joseph Smith and his followers inhabited a culture with two powerful images of silence: the silence of the grave and the stilling of supernatural voices. The silence of the grave, imitated in certain forms of revivalistic worship, stood as one of the starkest markers of the impact of death. This was a personal, familiar silence. On a broader scale, advocates of the American Enlightenment worked to still the voices of God that had been treasured for centuries, if not millennia, by believers. God, according to these rationalist partisans, would never reach humans, even with his still, small voice. Seeing, not hearing, was believing. Silence represented a threat to antebellum believers on many levels, but silence was the problem a seer could resolve.

The perfect stillness of the newly dead, bereft of breath and speech, extended to the decomposing corpse within the earth. For antebellum America, as for most human cultures, silence served as a trope for the alienation of the dead from the living. Joseph Sr.'s father, Asael, penned a statement to be read after his death to preserve his voice "when my Tongue shall be mouldered to Dust in the Silant toom."[5] The Book of Mormon patriarch Lehi similarly urged his children to "hear the words of a trembling parent, whose limbs ye must soon lay down in the cold and silent grave."[6] The Methodist Otway Curry reminded antebellum believers in his "Kingdom Come" that the "voices [of the dead] are lost in the soundless / Retreats of their endless home."[7] Death meant silence, and silence evoked death.

Some early Americans toyed with the silence of death in energetic worship. In revivalistic conversion some believers died to sin, their bodies resting in trances that could fool observers into proposing medical consultation, pulmonary resuscitation, or even burial.[8] As they rose from this mimesis of death, sacred mourners recovered their voices and often shouted praises to God.[9]

Divine encounters also mimicked death's silence. Smith remembered that during the converting experience termed his "First Vision," the dark power that "overcame" him "had such astonishing influence over me as to bind my tongue." Prepared to "abandon" himself to mute "destruction," at the last moment Smith was saved from death and its attendant silence by divine visitors.[10] The Book of Mormon narrative incorporated several such trances. An angel induced a regenerating trance in one Alma, the wayward son of a high priest. Alma later remembered that "it was for the space of three days and three nights that I could not open my mouth, neither had I the use of my limbs."[11] Upon his recovery, he began to evangelize with his friends, the sons of King Mosiah. In another tale, the dramatic conversion of King Lamoni by Ammon (see chapter 2) relied heavily on deathlike trances; Ammon seemed particularly susceptible, falling into a trance at the sight of his brothers after a long absence.[12]

Another silence threatened antebellum America, a stilling of heavenly voices related to the dissemination of Enlightenment views. Sounds in the environment—wind, thunder, rustling leaves, the crackling of tree branches, or the distant whining of beasts—had communicated messages from God for many generations of Christians. Believers had precedent in the New Testament for their beliefs—Saul became Paul when a voice came to him on the way to Damascus; the Apostles were filled with power by a rushing wind of fiery tongues on the day of Pentecost. In the Hebrew Bible, Elijah recognized God in a still, small voice. By the late eighteenth century, Enlightenment agitators had declared war on supernatural sounds. Skeptics broadcast doubt about the veracity of heard experience, the reliability of the voices of God and angels.[13] Once intelligent, even personable, ghosts became mumbling apparitions, malarious emanations.[14] The enervating silence of the rational world, coupled with the cessationism preached by most Protestants, threatened God and his angels with the very stillness that afflicted the dead.

The dark silence of sin, the immobile tongue of the corpse, and the closed heavens represented different facets of the same problem. Communication between heaven and earth, between the dead and the living, was desperately imperiled. Seerhood promised to overcome each of these perils.

Hearing Voices from the Dust

The man who could recover the lost voices of the ancients was a seer, a prophet trained in the arts King Mosiah wielded on behalf of his people. The Book of Mormon explained that "a seer is greater than a prophet" because "a seer is a revelator, and a prophet also; and a gift which is greater, can no man have."[15] A statement the day he organized the church declared Smith "a seer, a translator, a prophet, an apostle of Jesus Christ, an elder of the church."[16] In 1835 Smith reiterated that he was "the Lords Seer whom he hath appointed in Israel."[17] Besides "Prophet Joseph" or "Brother Joseph," "Joseph the Seer" was probably the most common epithet for their leader, a title Mormons proudly advertised to outsiders.[18]

Early in the Book of Mormon, the hero Lehi proclaimed that "Joseph truly testified, saying: A seer shall the Lord my God raise up, who shall be a choice seer unto the fruit of my loins." In the same passage Lehi clarified that the mission of the seer was to connect the living with the dead: "he shall do a work for the fruit of thy loins, his brethren, which shall be of great worth unto them, even to the bringing of them to the knowledge of the covenants which I have made with thy fathers...unto him will I give power to bring forth my word unto the seed of thy loins."[19] During his deathbed farewell, Lehi told a son named Joseph about a special prophet who would bear that same name centuries later. According to Lehi, Joseph of Egypt had prophesied that Joseph Smith was to be a seer who would "write the writing of the fruit of thy loins."[20]

Smith's use of the title "seer" situated him in a complex of meaning in the early nineteenth century. In antebellum folkways, seers were people blessed with supernatural sight. Such visionaries were not rare, despite their disrepute in educated or orthodox society, overlapping with scryers, cunning folk who could see things invisible to the natural eye, often but not exclusively the location of buried treasure.[21] As discussed in chapter 3, prior to his religious career Joseph Jr. was known as a village seer or scryer in this folk tradition; for most of his adult life critics used this interpretation of seerhood to denounce him as a magician or necromancer, at the time synonymous terms.[22]

Boundaries between folk and established religion were hazy then, as always, despite the strenuous protestations of most clergy. In a culture steeped in the language and images of the King James Bible, seerhood echoed from the Old Testament, most familiarly in Saul's quest for Samuel, where seer was defined as an "old" term for prophet. Famed Bible commentator Matthew Henry (1662–1714) saw "seer" as indicating the insight required of a prophet (a "wise man") or merely a synonym for prophet.[23] Particularly sagacious Protestant clergy might merit the title as an honorific, though for them it lacked the visionary aspect of the biblical reference.

Smith's campaign to separate himself from what he saw as immature involvement in magical culture was already well under way before the Book of Mormon was published. Why, then, did the Mormon prophet retain the title that would identify him to some contemporaries as a treasure seeker, even as he distanced himself from the stigma of the treasure hunt? The biblical precedent mattered a great deal. Smith took few positions he could not justify from biblical exegesis, however idiosyncratic. Smith appears also to have seen seerhood as the sacred essence of his scripture-making vocation. For Smith a seer found what was lost, gained access to "the minds of the Ancients."[24] Smith recovered the voices of America's dead—Jared-ites, Mulekites, Nephites, and Lamanites—before turning to the dead of Israel and Egypt. In the process Joseph the Seer made his way to the ances-tors of humanity, including Adam, Enoch, Abraham, Moses, and Noah. Not entirely hermetic magus or Romantic hero, as a seer Smith was reconnect-ing to the long dead in a literal and highly personal way. His quest was social, in the many ramifications of that word.

Smith was careful to distinguish his religious behaviors from what he saw as base imitations. The Book of Mormon explained the relationship between sacred seerhood and wicked necromancy, even as it affirmed that seerhood was first and foremost a mode of communication from beyond the grave. Nephi reprinted and interpreted Isaiah's pronounce-ment: "when they shall say unto you: Seek unto them that have familiar spirits, and unto wizards that peep and mutter—should not a people seek unto their God for the living to hear from the dead?"[25] The seer, as opposed to the necromancer, would operate "with an eye single to his glory, or the welfare of the ancient and long dispersed covenant people of the Lord."[26] Even as their vocations blur in the eyes of some observers, the necromancer was a showman and a charlatan, the seer a man of God supporting communication between the dead and their heirs.

Wilford Woodruff, representing his colleagues in Smith's inner circle, rhapsodized:

> Truly the Lord has raised up Joseph the Seer of the seed of Abraham out of the loins of ancient Joseph, & is now clothing him with mighty power & wisdom & knowledge.... The Lord is Blessing Joseph with Power to reveal the mysteries of the kingdom of God; to translate through the urim & Thummim Ancient records & Hyeroglyphics as old as Abraham or Adam."[27]

Woodruff honored Smith as an heir to the Egyptian patriarch gifted to see in dreams the fate of his people. These "records & Hyeroglyphics" proved essential to larger projects "as old as" the fathers of humanity. In the hands of the seer such memorials promised connections to a long-bygone past and the people who lived it.

In an essay published in the *Times and Seasons*, Phelps adulated his leader, explaining to the Saints that "a prophet is commonly called a foreteller, but a seer reveals matters past, present and future."[28] John Taylor remembered Joseph in those terms in a devotional hymn: the Mormon seer "gazed on the past, on the present too;— / And open'd the heav'nly world to view."[29] In his exposition of the superiority of seerhood over prophethood, the Book of Mormon evangelist Ammon explained to a proselyte that "a seer can know of things which are past, and also of things which are to come, and by them shall all things be revealed, or, rather, shall secret things be made manifest, and hidden things shall come to light."[30] Though the miraculous predictions and social criticism of prophethood were never far from Smith's self-definition, in seerhood he and his followers emphasized their connections to the sacred past.[31] Even their eschaton would prove to be more than anything a reunion with past generations. In this sense Smith was more Romantic than millenarian, although his Romanticism was overwhelmingly familial. Romanticism sought imaginative connections with a mythically pure past, a protest against the world that Romantics saw around them. Theirs represented a generally poetic yearning for lost purity and clarity. Smith radicalized and concretized the general concepts of Romanticism. Smith's seerhood spans the gap between the otherworldly apocalypticism of the revolutionary prophets and the sentimental necromancy of the séance spiritualism that preceded and succeeded him, respectively.

The Mormons' favorite Bible proof text strongly framed seerhood. In language appropriated and interpreted by the Book of Mormon, Smith's New Translation of the Bible, and Smith's own self-image as a seer, Isaiah's obscure prophecy of a sealed book of voices whispering from the dust like ghosts (Isaiah 29) defined scripture and seerhood. After predicting the destruction of Jerusalem, Isaiah addressed the fallen city: "Thou shalt speak out of the ground, and thy speech shall be low out of the dust, and thy voice shall be, as of one that hath a familiar spirit, out of the ground, and thy speech shall whisper out of the dust" (29:4).[32] The KJV euphemism occasionally distracts modern readers, but the image of ghosts speaking from the grave was clear.

Though the majority of the Book of Mormon's notoriously voluminous Isaiah extracts are taken verbatim from the KJV, the use of Isaiah 29 is distinctive.[33] The Book of Mormon forced a particular reading of this passage that both situated early Mormonism within biblical prophecy and provided context and justification for Smith's definition of seerhood. Multiple voices within the Book of Mormon confirm this view of Isaiah

29 as an explanation for the entire Book of Mormon.[34] Whereas Isaiah's reference to the "clos[ing] of the seers" comes late in the chapter, the Mormon redaction draws the missing seers out of turn to the foreground.[35] The Book of Mormon would be the "words of those who have slumbered in the dust"; through the stories and sermons of the prophesied record, ancient America's peoples would "speak as if it were from the dead."[36] God's seal kept the texts safe from prying eyes and, like an inviolable sepulchre, ensured that none molested or destroyed those texts during their slumber in Cumorah.

In the buildup to his redaction of Isaiah 29, Nephi appropriated Isaiah's images, comparing his society to ancient Jerusalem:

> After [the Nephites] shall have been brought down low in the dust, even that they are not, yet the words of the righteous shall be written, and the prayers of the faithful shall be heard, and all those who have dwindled in unbelief shall not be forgotten. For those who shall be destroyed shall speak unto them out of the ground, and their speech shall be low out of the dust, and their voice shall be as one that hath a familiar spirit; for the Lord God will give unto him power, that he may whisper concerning them, even as it were out of the ground; and their speech shall whisper out of the dust.[37]

These "words of the righteous" were the plates that Moroni presented to Joseph Smith after more than a millennium of interment. The dust represented the burial mounds of America, and Isaiah prophesied through Nephi that the dead would overcome the silence of their graves in whispers that would echo across the American continent.

Moroni employed the same image when he described his own forbears. "Those saints who have gone before me, who have possessed this land, shall cry, yea, even from the dust will they cry unto the Lord." Moroni made his interpretation explicit: "it shall come even as if one should speak from the dead."[38] The book seems to worry that faithless interpreters might lose the plain reading and repeats it several times.

The characters seem to force a particular reading of the Book of Mormon, modeling how to understand "the saints who have gone before." The Book of Mormon incorporated this imagery into personal deathbeds. When Nephi came to die, he envisioned his future offspring. "My beloved brethren, all those who are of the house of Israel, and all ye ends of the earth, I speak unto you as the voice of one crying from the dust."[39] Moroni similarly warned that "the time speedily cometh that ye shall know that I lie not, for ye shall see me at the bar of God; and the Lord God will say unto you: Did I not declare my words unto you, which were written by this man, like as one crying from the dead, yea, even as one speaking out of the dust?" Moroni recognized his posthumous voice speaking "unto the fulfilling of the prophecies." For these ancient visionaries facing their own extinction, the scriptures they were recording became the medium to preserve their voices to "hiss forth from generation to generation."[40]

Early Latter-day Saints saw themselves as the audience, in company with contemporary Natives, for the Book of Mormon. They celebrated in song their "heavenly treasure: a book full of merit: / It speaks from the dust by the pow'r of the Spirit."[41] In the phrase of another hymn, Parley Pratt's "An Angel from on High,"

> Sealed by Moroni's hand
> It has for ages lain
> To wait the Lord's command
> From dust to speak again.[42]

Editorials in church periodicals confirmed the Isaianic reading for decades.[43] In Phelps's phrase, the Book of Mormon survived "for the living to hear from the dead."[44] In an audacious letter to the British monarch, Parley Pratt explained that through the Book of Mormon "a nati[o]n whose 'bones are dried' and whose ruined temples and monuments have reposed for ages in silent, solemn, and awful grandeur, has now spoken from the dust."[45] Death would never still their voices.

Mormons vividly enacted their reading in 1828. Martin Harris, the visionary farmer who funded publication of the Book of Mormon, carried samples of hieroglyphs extracted from Mormon's plates to professors Samuel Mitchell (1792–1868) and Charles Anthon (1797–1867) in New York City. The parties have sharply conflicting memories of the encounter, but by the end Harris was persuaded to bet his farm on the printing of the Book of Mormon, perhaps in response to Anthon's admission that he could not read a "sealed" book. For Mormons Harris's encounter meant that "the 29th Chapter of Is[a]iah" was "fulfill[e]d."[46] While Isaiah is now thought to have been decrying arrogant piety and casuistry or commenting on the complexity of evolving oral traditions with his reference to a sealed book, Mormons saw only the distinction between the wisdom of men and the inspiration of a seer. No one but a seer could read "the words of a book that is sealed" to recover, like Mosiah, voices from the dust. No mere scholar could uncover these long-extinguished voices.[47]

Some have seen the Mormon use of Isaiah's prophecy—particularly the notion of sealed books and the reference to a "familiar spirit"—as an admission of occultism.[48] This oversimplified view misapprehends ante-bellum biblicism, folk religiosity, and the death vision of Smith and his peers. While there are parallels to esoteric traditions in the quest for the voices the dead, Smith's interpretation drew on a marvelously literal reading of Isaiah. For the Latter-day Saints, spirits crying from the dust were prophets, lost ancestors, rather than ghoulish specters. Necromancy was a corruption of the miracle of seeric scripture in the Mormon view.[49]

The Book of Mormon warned of the consequences of failure to create and preserve scripture. Early on, Nephi obeyed a divine command to murder his kinsman Laban in order to recover the "brass plates," the ancient records of his people, "that we may preserve unto our children the language of our fathers."[50] The fate that might have befallen the Nephites fell instead on the Mulekites. Bereft of their ancestral records, the Mulekites dwindled and perished, a pattern for the Lamanites some five hundred years later. Disoriented and incoherent as a people, the Mulekites' only hope was Mosiah the Seer. Through seerhood Mosiah would recover those lost stories.

Joseph Smith carried the Book of Mormon narratives through his entire religious career. Lamanites and Mulekites were a lesson to all peoples: if there is no memorial, no ethnic scripture, there can be no civilization. Whereas his compatriots constructed narratives about the backwardness of preliterate societies and Romantics yearned for an earlier time, Smith uncovered the mystical power of primal language and the devastation that attended its loss.

Books of Remembrance

Speech is not the same as text, a point scholars have been making for some time.[51] In many cultures, text extinguished or constrained the power of the spoken word. On Smith's reading of seerhood, though, the text preserved the voice. The Book of Mormon proved to be only one of many seeric scriptures. Even Abel, the Bible's archetypal witness, required scripture to allow him, "being dead," to "yet speak."[52] Smith's scriptures were a kind of divinely supported remembering. This capacity to reach across boundaries was inherent in the written word. In an editorial later attributed to Smith, William Phelps wrote: "the art of writing is one of the greatest blessings we enjoy.... By these means the thoughts of the heart can act without the body: and the mind can speak without the head, while thousands of miles apart, and for ages after the flesh has mouldered back to its mother dust."[53] John Good (1764–1827), whose *Book of Nature* circulated in western New York and whom Mormons quoted, asked, "without this [writing], what to us would be the wisdom of past ages, or the history of former states? The chain of nature would be broken through all its links, and every generation become an isolated and individual world."[54]

For the Latter-day Saints, the practice of preserving the records of past generations dated from Eve and Adam in the Garden. According to Smith's preamble to the Pentateuch (the Book of Moses), Father Adam and Mother Eve kept a "book of remembrance" that was "recorded in the language of Adam, for it was given unto as many as called upon God." Though Smith never gained access to the text itself, his New Translation of Genesis made clear that the Book of Remembrance was the first human scripture. Adam used the book to teach his offspring "to read and write, having a language which was pure and undefiled." Centuries later, address-ing the readers of the New Translation, the mysterious Enoch reported that "the first [human being] of all we know, even Adam. For a book of remembrance we have written among us, according to the pattern given by the finger of God."[55] The sacred book provided both a memorial and a way to preserve language so that later generations could read it. Adam's Book of Remembrance was not an esoteric manual of hermetic secrets but a memorial scripture, a vessel to preserve the ancient dead, their voices, and the language they spoke.[56]

Though he never disclosed any details of Adam's and Eve's Book of Remembrance, Joseph Smith revealed and created many records mod-eled on the image of this archetypal book, holy texts meant to preserve the authors for future generations. Smith had been intending to produce something like this book from at least 1832, when he honored "the saints whose names are found and the names of their fathers and of their chil-dren enrolled in the Book of the Law of God."[57] While he initially saw the Book of the Law of God as a version of the much-discussed biblical Book of Life—a supernatural list of the names of the saved—Smith rapidly expanded this concept into physical records he had his people keep as sacred and probably salvific books of remembrance.[58] For Latter-day Saints, these books included the Patriarchal Blessing Book, the Book of the Law of the Lord, and several others.

Starting in 1833 with his ordination as patriarch to the church, Joseph Sr. issued to faithful Mormons personalized scriptures, revelations of past and future called patriarchal blessings, explicitly modeled on Father Israel's deathbed blessings of his sons (see chapter 8).[59] These blessings, often received at meetings reminiscent of Methodist love feasts (communal meals centered around an expanded Lord's Supper, spiritual discussion, and singing), contained impressive promises to believers. By 1835, Joseph Jr. directed that these blessings be compiled into a special ledger called the Patriarchal Blessing Book, and set his scribes to the task of transcription. In the Patriarchal Blessing Book, Latter-day Saints found their lives predicted, blessed, and memorialized. Blessings in the ledger often betray an awareness of the Patriarchal Blessing Book as an instance of the Book of Life. Joseph Sr. told Amoranda Murdock that she would have her "name registered in the Lamb's book of life," while Amos Fuller discovered that the patriarchal blessing was his entry into a book of remembrance.[60] When the patriarch himself prepared to pass to the next life, Joseph Sr. blessed Hyrum as a way of memorializing the dead Alvin: "his seat is vacant this day, but his spirit is at rest. Wo be to the man who sought his fall, by which means he was deprived of leaving seed to rise up in his inheritance to call him blessed. I therefore, that his name may not be forgotten, make this mention of him, in thy blessing, that it may be recorded with the same, for my posterity to look upon." This blessing of the living Hyrum was explicitly designed "to perpetuate the memory of thy brother, who was an upright man."[61] Repeatedly the Saints recorded such benefactions for the ages to follow. Collected into their special ledger book, Mormons saw these blessings as having something of the power of other scripture. Through these patriarchal blessings, early Latter-day Saints secured prospectively the status Joseph Smith had bestowed on Adam, Abraham, Moses, and Nephi—they were recorded in Scripture.

At the end of 1841, Smith designated one of his official diaries the Book of the Law of the Lord. Though the book did not circulate widely, it was meant to secure the status of its contents for future generations. Over the course of 1842, this volume combined memorial poetry, free-form tributes to close friends, both living and dead, and a financial register meant to secure the good name and future salvation of donors.[62] For Alvin, Joseph Jr. wrote a stanza of memorial poetry, then recalled that "he was one of the noblest of the sons of men: Shall his name not be recorded in this book? Yes, Alvin: let it be had here, and be handed down upon these sacred pages, forever and ever."[63] In this act Smith fulfilled the deathbed blessing Joseph Sr. gave Hyrum; Alvin's memory was "perpetuated" for his "posterity to look upon."[64] Joseph made a similar claim in this personal Book of Remembrance for his older brother Hyrum: "thy name shall be written in the Book of the Law of the Lord, for those who come after thee to look upon, that they may pattern after thy works."[65] He remembered others as well—his father and several of his closest followers—memorializing some of the living in prospect, as if they were dead. With these stylized obituaries, the Book of the Law of the Lord became a scriptural memorial. This practice was similar in purpose but more ambitious in extent than the family Bibles of contemporary Protestants, used to track vital statistics for all their kin and sometimes to store other family information.[66] Though Mormons kept genealogical records in their own family Bibles, they also possessed a history dating to the Garden of Eden that no Protestant could lay claim to.

The Mormon books of remembrance served at least two purposes. Most simply these books guaranteed the persistence of the deceased in shared memory. They also provided a protection against Judgment, a reassurance vital to the Mormon revolt against Protestantism. In place of the uncertain state of election or the impermanent status of Arminian regeneration stood ink on paper in sacralized volumes. These early Mormon books point toward the broader, complex meanings of word and text in the religious life of early national America. In an address a year after Smith's death, apostle Heber Kimball combined both social immortality and salvation, informing Latter-day Saints that "you will be judged out of the books kept by the church; and they will be of great consequence to look upon in the morning of the resurrection. What a pleasure it will be for our children to look upon these books, while we are in our graves, sleeping."[67] The mixed goals of survival and persistence of relationships appeared in seeric scripture. Though the formal Book of the Law of the Lord was not published in toto, the *History of the Church*, of which extracts from the Book and its associated records formed the nucleus, continued this tradition, a sacralizing memorial to the earliest Mormons (an early version of the *History* contained explicit genealogies of the church presidency).[68] Hyrum Smith, having taken the reins from his father, Joseph Sr., merged patriarchal blessings with these general records. Hyrum told Addison Pratt (1802–1872), Mormon evangelist to the Pacific Islands, that "your acts [will] be written in the Chronicles of your brethren."[69] This impulse at least in part underlies the Mormon obsession with maintaining lists of names of those who have participated in salvific rites, a practice that began in earnest in the 1840s.[70] Whereas a wide variety of revivalists and prophetic radicals sought the Book of Life in vision, Smith's Latter-day Saints actually wrote several volumes of it. Joseph the Seer had given them that power. In place of angels taking endless notes of evangelicals' behavior sat the Mormon elders, books of new scripture open on their writing desks, recording the lives and deeds of those to be saved.

Smith did not restrict memorial scripture to Americans, ancient or modern. Every righteous people would prove, at the time of Apocalyptic gathering, to have kept a Book of Remembrance.[71] Smith's scriptures were only the first of a flood of seeric records yet to be discovered.[72]

The Mormon use of written memorials to protect and preserve the dead recalls practices throughout Christianity, ancient and contemporary. In medieval Catholicism, obituaries played this role, ecclesiastical documents providing security for the dead in the afterlife.[73] Though many people still honored older traditions, and Catholicism continued to gain strength in America, the dominant use of written memorials in the antebellum period was by Protestants—from the Calvinists of colonial New England to the Edwardsian New Lights of the First Great Awakening to the dominant evangelicals of the Second Great Awakening. Protestants sought to expunge from Christianity "superstitious" excesses, replacing them with sentimental awareness of the power of social immortality, particularly in pious biographies.[74] Devotional biographies, emblematically Jonathan Edwards's revision of David Brainerd's diary, continued to support Protestant devotions through the Second Great Awakening.[75] Antebellum believers also created their own memorials, such as Nancy Towle's self-conscious memoir. Towle made the point explicit in her reminiscence of a sickbed on a return visit to her family. She prayed that God would spare her to finish her memoir so that "when my voice is lost in death, may my labors still exist." She anticipated that her memoir was "for the benefit of many—when I might be sleeping in the dust."[76] Many Christian believers hoped that the written word could preserve memories; few were as assiduously literal about the process as the Latter-day Saints.

Hieroglyphs, Pure Language, and Humanity's Parents

In parallel with the memorial books of the dead recovered by Joseph Smith, the earliest Mormons revered the language in which humanity's first books were penned, the pure language of Adam. It was not enough only to discover the lost records of the dead; they would need to be translated, just as Mosiah interpreted the Jaredite records. Throughout his career, Smith invested considerable energy in hieroglyphs. Primarily through encounters with his funerary papyri, Smith revealed that holy pictographs could break through the strictures of language to liberate the voices of the dead.

For Smith each act of translation, a reminder of the linguistic barriers separating every people from every other, pointed back to a sacred past when translation was not necessary, when the original language in which God named Adam united all creation. This was the language of the Jaredite epic history and the language in which Adam wrote the Book of Remembrance. According to Christian and Mormon tradition, this original language became corrupted and fell from its primeval purity as a result of the curse of Babel. It was against this curse of Babel that Joseph Smith battled.

Inscrutable hieroglyphs kept mysteries and life stories of the ancients hidden from view, the dead in shadow. For Smith, translation could not be separated from seerhood, nor seerhood from translation. Though he would ultimately merge the "translator" of his official 1830 title into "seer," translation remained central to Smith's identity through the end of his life.[77] At some level Smith was enjoying the Romanticization of ancient languages and the evidential power of his apparently miraculous aptitude with them. Whatever other influences were present, and despite his attempts to study Hebrew and Greek formally, Smith grappled with hieroglyphs metaphysically, religiously. Instead of writing treatises of systematic theology like Jonathan Edwards, Smith proffered translations of lost texts. Scholarly fads could come and go, the theologies of learned divines could rise and fall, but the identities, mysteries, and truths of the ancient world would transform the Latter-day Saints. The seer would be the one to reveal those truths, hidden in the lost language.

The Bible in Babel

Understanding Smith's victory over the corruption of language requires appreciating how he understood the enemy. Mutual unintelligibility paralleled and enhanced the devastating silence of the grave. Like many other thinkers in Jewish and Christian traditions, Smith seized on the biblical Babel to explain the linguistic drift separating generations. According to Genesis, God cursed an arrogant scheme to build a tower on the plain of Shinar with the "confusion of the ancient language."[78] Early Latter-day Saints saw Babel's curse as the original source of a painful diversity of language and religion. The Saints were not alone in their concern about fallen language.[79] Where many thoughtful peers saw a philosophical point about the limits of formal theology, Smith understood a central threat to the integrity of the human family, a fundamental truth about the way societies flourished and collapsed.

The Book of Mormon displays an abiding concern with Babel. The Jaredite narrative of the seer Mosiah that began this chapter, important enough to be highlighted in both the copyright notice and the "Testimony of Three Witnesses" in the first edition of the Book of Mormon, strongly frames the Babel narrative. In the book of Ether, the patriarch Jared pleaded with his brother Moriancumer to "cry unto the Lord, that he will not confound us that we may not understand our words," a wish God granted to this Moses for the New World, who according to Ether was the first person faithful enough to see the physical hand of God. In the odd and multivalent phrase of Smith's scripture, "Jared and his brother were not confounded," and they migrated to America, with their language—the language of prelapsarian scripture—intact.[80]

Smith continued his pursuit of pure language after the publication of the Book of Mormon. When he turned to the Christian Bible he saw in it the stamp of Babel, the corruption by interlopers in the original text.[81] After the Book of Mormon, Smith's first translation task was to restore from the Authorized Protestant Bible (the KJV) the plain meanings of the "sacred penmen," to recover the lost "fulness of the Scriptures."[82] This project, the New Translation,[83] answered competing restorationists like Alexander Campbell (1788–1866), who believed the Christian system could be derived entirely from Bible texts, if only they were correctly translated from extant Hebrew and Greek manuscripts. In contrast, Smith's New Translation was not just a criticism or revision of the KJV, it was the application of seeric power to it. Joseph the Seer both recovered its plain meaning in brief textual emendations and discovered texts lost in their entirety. The New Translation at once defined scripture and beckoned toward a world of recoverable memorials to the lost dead. Smith was uncovering Enoch, the prototypical immortal, and providing Moses with an opportunity to explain and introduce his accounts of Creation.

Though final analysis of the texts is limited by their unfinished state (Smith completed most of his work by 1833 but continued to revise the translations until his death), the New Translation illuminates the seeric project. Modern scholars see the New Translation as an exegetical commentary or pseudepigraphic scripture, but Smith would not have accepted this distinction.[84] The Mormon seer spelled out the significance of his New Translation: he was unearthing "many important points, touching the salvation of man," that "had been taken from the Bible, or lost before it was compiled."[85] As opposed to Campbell's 1826 *Sacred Writings* or Noah Webster's 1833 *Common Version*, the New Translation used the KJV as a conduit to a lost age, missing truths, and dead heroes.[86] Though he was certainly "translating time," Smith was also giving a voice to the dead in his New Translation of the Bible.[87]

By the mid-1830s, Smith had translated the Book of Mormon, the Bible, and a supernatural parchment (a description of the fate of John the Evangelist).[88] In 1835 he became a translator of physical hieroglyphs. As his seeric project turned to Egyptian funerary papyri, Smith appropriated a centuries-old quest to expand the metaphysical reach of his seeric quest.

Re-forming Egyptian

Smith's exposures to hieroglyphs, ancient languages, and supernatural translation blossomed with the 1835 arrival of Michael Chandler's mummies and papyri. The timing of Chandler's visit could not have been more opportune. Smith had been concerned with ancient Egyptiana since the 1820s, with his gold plates "filled with engravings, in Egyptian characters" that Latter-day Saints denominated "Reformed" or "short-hand" Egyptian.[89] Whereas we saw in chapter 3 that the mummies and papyri held great meaning as grave relics, the language they contained proved more important still. Hungry for hieroglyphs, Smith and his colleagues "literally chopped open" the mummies to liberate the papyri, an act of aggression that cultured visitors found appalling.[90] He and his spirited amanuensis and sometime ghostwriter, William Phelps, almost immediately began attempts to decode the hieroglyphic message of the papyri, the stories of Joseph and Abraham.[91]

Two important texts derived from Smith's sustained encounter with the papyri. The best known is the Book of Abraham, an account of terrestrial creation and cosmology narrated by Abraham himself in the spirit of the Christian Apocrypha.[92] A set of related documents provides more insight into Smith's quest for pure language. These documents, a collection of ostensibly grammatical documents written by Phelps and Smith, have been called the Kirtland Egyptian Papers (KEP).[93] Within these documents, the best known manuscript is a bound notebook whose spine reads "Egyptian Alphabet" and whose title page declares it a "Grammar and A[l]phabet of the Egyptian Language" (GAEL; see figure 5.1).

Designed as a lexicon—with terms, transliterations, glosses, and the like—GAEL entries attempt to clarify the sacred meaning of glyphs. These documents, as much as if not more than the Book of Abraham, provide a crucial window on Smith's beliefs about hieroglyphs as the language of the dead and the power the translator-seer derived from them.

Early Latter-day Saints made much of the funerary derivation of the Abraham papyri. Parley Pratt wrote that the papyri had "slumbered in the bosom of the dead,"[94] while Oliver Cowdery called them "hiden records that have been obtained from the ancient bur[y]ing place of the

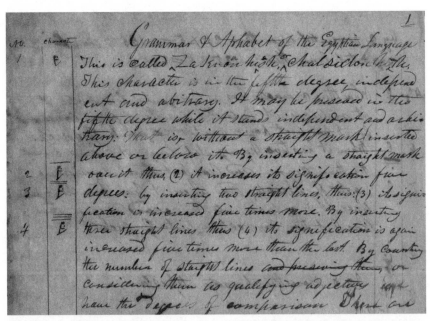

Figure 5.1 The Grammar and A[l]phabet of the Egyptian Language associated hieroglyphs with transliterations and definitions. Part of the broader Egyptian project, the Grammar illuminates the meanings of the early Mormon quest for pure language. Courtesy of the Church History Library, The Church of Jesus Christ of Latter-day Saints.

Egyptiens."[95] The papyri had not come from a library or a secret society; they had been disinterred from an ancient tomb. For Smith the hieroglyphs he owned served as a sort of metaphysical grave relic; the association between the papyri and the grave was direct and persistent. Smith and Phelps summarized their encounter with the corpses in 1843, claiming that "although dead, the papyrus which has lived in their bosoms, unharmed, speaks for them in language like the sound of an earthquake. *Ecce veritas! Ecce cadaveros!* Behold the truth! Behold the mummies!"[96]

The language by which Smith's mummies spoke like "an earthquake" served, as it had for many other Westerners, as the archetype of mystically potent language. Though Jean-François Champollion (1790–1832) had deciphered the Rosetta stone by 1822, culture changed slowly, and the mystique of those inscrutable pictograms persisted—if increasingly metaphorically—inspiring the literati of the American Renaissance, Emerson and his Transcendentalist peers, and a host of others. Champollion's phonetic Egyptian was slow to find traction among Americans because hieroglyphs had so long been understood to function as secret pictographic codes rather than a phonetic system.[97] Though attributed to the German Jesuit Johannes Kircher (1602–1680), by the nineteenth century this belief had moved well beyond the esoteric literature from which it sprang.[98] Noah Webster defined hieroglyphs as follows:

> In antiquity, a sacred character; a mystical character or symbol, used in writings and inscriptions, particularly by the Egyptians, as signs of sacred, divine, or supernatural things. The hieroglyphics were figures of animals, parts of the human body, mechanical instruments, &c., which contained a meaning known only to kings and priests.[99]

Mormons imbibed this tradition of hieroglyphs as secret code publicly as early as 1833.[100] Few voices disputed the general wisdom that hieroglyphs concealed ancient mysteries. In this tradition the esoteric quests of hermeticism entered the mainstream as cultural commonplace. Without ever opening books like the kabbalistic *Zohar* or the hermetic *Divine Pymander*, the devoted student could approximate the awesome power of holy words through Egyptian hieroglyphs.[101] Though only the very rare Mormon was an actual kabbalist, most of them saw hieroglyphs as confirmation of the ancient mysteries Smith could discover, wedded to the records of the dead.[102] Wilford Woodruff, touring the British Museum, admired the papyrus collection "more...than any thing" else, realizing that the papyri contained "many glorious things Sacred & historical concerning the early ages of the world Abram & the Prophets &c.," if only they could be "translated."[103]

Central to the mystique of hieroglyphs was their pictographic nature. As no phonetic language could, hieroglyphs represented actual objects in nature.[104] Understanding hieroglyphs as pictographic ciphers for the mysteries of human origin and religion provides the most immediate context for understanding the KEP. The GAEL overflows with creative pictographic interpretations of Egyptian characters. As the simplest example, a dot represents the human eye (*Iota*, "the eye or to see or sight"), and similar references to vision in association with dots or circles are scattered throughout the manuscripts; a "compound" of *Iota* looks like an eye with a horizontal lash.[105] Geographic interpretations are also represented in a convex arc translated as the earth's horizon (*Sue*, "the whole earth," and by extension "the whole of anything") or a concave arc as its antipodes (*Toan tau ee tahee tahee toues*, "under the sun; under heaven; downward...going down into the grave; going down into misery = even Hell").[106] Many of the KEP glyphs are semantic and syntactic composites of simpler glyphs: forms and meanings were combinative. A stick figure (*Ho hah oop*) represents Jesus, an "intercessor"; his left leg is the glyph for delegation (*Jah-ni-hah*), anticipating the Book of Abraham account in which Jesus is chosen as God's legate to earth in the cosmological drama.[107] In many cases, Phelps's and Smith's interpretations combine physical and metaphorical meanings, as in the case of the glyph *Zi*, which means both "upright" (it looks like an upside-down *T*) and "modest and chaste being taught most perfectly."[108] The identical glyph is later transcribed as *Zub* (see figure 5.2), extending another pictographic interpretation, this time vertical ascent: "leading up or to: the time for going up to the altar to worship; going up before the Lord[;] being caught up."[109]

Funerary illustrations within the Chandler papyri confirmed the connection between pictures and objects in the minds of Phelps and Smith. Smith offered interpretations of these illustrations, published in the *Times and Seasons* as "Fac-similes" (the name by which modern Latter-day Saints know them), similar to the approach employed within the GAEL. Circulating as published predecessors to the anticipated

Figure 5.2 This hieroglyph suggests the image of ascent and is interpreted within the GAEL as indicating "worship" or "having been caught up." Courtesy of the Church History Library, The Church of Jesus Christ of Latter-day Saints.

Egyptian Grammar (despite plans in 1843, it was never published), these facsimiles spanned the hieroglyphic project and the ultimate Book of Abraham.[110] These illustrations—"the figures at the beginning" of the official Book of Abraham—were the very definition of hieroglyphs, pictures telling sacred stories.[111] In support of this project, the Book of Abraham revealed an ancient name—*Rahleenos*—for hieroglyphs themselves.[112]

In their visual, material interpretations of glyphs on papyri, Smith and Phelps emphasized the strict correspondence of primal languages and objects in Nature, mediated through ancient pictograms. In this respect early Latter-day Saints differed little from other thinkers, including Emerson. According to Emerson, words in their originals, the "roots" extending into "outer creation," held the secrets to inner states, supernatural wisdom, and perhaps the origins of humanity. They are "the original elements of all languages."[113] By conflating idealized words with the bare essence of physical existence, Emerson proposed a transformative language based in deep reality. Something like this is the implicit argument of Smith as the translator of hieroglyphs. The Mormon prophet honed an impulse akin to Emerson's Romantic quest for primordial language. Whereas Emerson was seeking individual enlightenment, though, Smith emphasized recovering the secrets of the dead from ancient records and their constituent scripts.

Belief in the power of primal language extended well beyond Emerson and Smith to include a variety of learned sources.[114] The gentleman geologist Emanuel Swedenborg (1688–1772) embraced this model of hieroglyphs in the eighteenth century. For the Swedish mystic "everything harbored hidden correspondences; all the world was a hieroglyph."[115] Although theories of magic often emphasize the centrality of metaphysically potent language, in hieroglyphs such potent language came much closer to the mainstream than the term "magic" would suggest.[116]

For many students of language and its history, the primal language of Eden lurked behind Egyptian hieroglyphs. For these thinkers, Adam's naming of animals at Eden (Genesis 2:19–20) represented both the creation of language and the archetype of the sacred correspondence between divine language and physical reality.[117] Merging the spoken word with the pictogram, many claimed that the names bestowed by Adam on animals arose necessarily from their physical appearance.[118]

Whereas others invoked snippets of Bible text, increasingly obsolescent scholarship, and commonplaces about pictograms in their pursuit of language's mystical origin, Joseph Smith actually believed he could recover the language of Eden. He found that language in his scriptures, in the charismatic act of glossolalia, and in direct revelations to his mind. His Book of Mormon contained words and names from that language in its Book of Ether.[119] When his earliest disciples spoke in tongues, they were speaking the "pure Adamic language, that which was spoken in the garden of Eden."[120] While others (like Shakers, early Methodists, some Quakers, and scattered Scottish Presbyterian revivalists) saw the recapitulation of a New Testament miracle of Pentecost, in Mormon glossolalia Smith also espied connections to the language spoken by the parents of all humanity.[121] Orson Pratt followed Smith's lead in proclaiming that Adamic was "a language that is spoken by higher orders of beings than ourselves" and was "that same language that was spoken for nearly two thousand years after the creation."[122] Controlling such a language, the Saints could create associations with the ancient dead.

Beyond glossolalia, the Book of Mormon, and the Egyptian papyri, Smith created other explicit connections to the lost language of Adam. Smith actually employed this Adamic language on several occasions. Using the name for God (Ahman) in an 1832 revelation, Smith revealed to his disciples the Adamic name for angels, Jesus, and humans.[123] Later in the 1830s, Smith bestowed Adamic names on sacred locations within Missouri, including Adam-ondi-Ahman and Zomar.[124]

Tying Adam's language into his own religion-making, Smith emphasized that the "first word Adam spoke" was brought to the first father via the Urim and Thummim seer stones, the central relic in Smith's early prophetic activity (see chapter 3). God created these stones, the Jaredite narrative suggested, to preserve the Adamic language for future generations. As Moriancumer prepared his people for their escape from Babel, he saw God's finger transform a collection of white stones into sacred lanterns and "interpreters" because "the [Adamic] language which ye shall write I have confounded." These supernatural stones preserved the Jaredites by illuminating their ships during the transoceanic flight from Babel, then made their way slowly to the sepulchre on Cumorah where Smith recovered them in 1827.[125] The stones that spared the Jaredites (Smith suggested they were called *gazelem* in the pure language) assisted Smith in his translation of the Book of Mormon and portions of the Book of Abraham.[126]

As in so much of early Mormonism, the sacred past of pure language was heavily personalized. The glyphs of GAEL and the pure language underlying them led inexorably to a particular place and a particular people, the first family in Eden. Through the Egyptian project, Smith revealed the true history of the Garden's occupants—the mysteries of Egypt framed his revisions of the Genesis creation accounts. Eve, according to the Book of Moses, was the individual wise enough to see that death was the best solution to the palpable paradox of life in the Garden of Eden.[127] Adam, the "first man" and "Kingly power" known in the GAEL as *Phah eh*, stands at the beginning of human history, and the origin of human language.[128] When Phelps and Smith found a glyph reminiscent of *beth*, the Hebrew pictographic letter meaning "house," they said that it meant "the place appointed of God for the residence of Adam; Adam ondi = Ahman)."[129] Just as Adam's deathbed and grave consecrated the Missouri frontier, so did Adam's language establish and memorialize human origins. He was the archetypal ancestor speaking through archetypal scripture.

The KEP are not just concerned with first things and first places. The hieroglyphic interpretations are most concerned with the creation of genealogical relationships. Even the grammatical theory of the documents supports a genealogical reading.[130] The preface to the GAEL refers to "degrees of comparison" or "connecting parts of speech" that increase in their "signification," continuing "until there are as many of these connecting parts of speech used as there are connections or connecting points found in the character."[131] In this reading of "degree," glyphs ramified their meanings like pedigrees charting descendants. The glyph translated as "degree" (*Zip Zi*; see figure 5.3) refers to "all women: it took its origin from the earth yielding its fruit. And from the first woman who bore children; and men were multiplied upon the earth."[132]

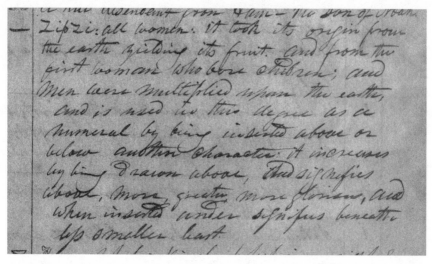

Figure 5.3 This interpretation of the mark used to indicate "degrees" within the KEP ties together the grammatical and procreative imagery of the Egyptian project. Courtesy of the Church History Library, The Church of Jesus Christ of Latter-day Saints.

Signification and connection, the grammatical claims of the KEP, arose as metaphors for human reproduction, closely tied to Eve and Adam.[133] One glyph, a reference to one of the female mummies, tracked Kahtoumun's progress through these grammatical degrees as she progressed from "princes[s]" to "married" and then "widowed queen," to the queen who bore the "record of the fathers" and the "art of embalming."[134] This female mummy represented Eve and her power through the generations, the figure who secured for Smith the mummies and papyri of the Egyptian project.

The glyph *Zool* confirmed the genealogical extent of the KEP, directing readers of the grammar "from Abraham back to his father and from Abraham's father back to his father and so on back through the line of his progenitors."[135] Smith and Phelps emphatically focused their attention on modes of connecting to long-dead ancestors, as exemplified by Adam and Abraham.

Smith's hieroglyphic journey comprehended the primordium within the ancient family, but his pure language was not solely retrospective. Seerhood served as the basis for a marvelous future even as it decoded a sacred past. By returning to Eden—humanity's home, first parents, and language—the early Mormons prepared themselves for the eternities.

God would "turn to the people a pure language, that they may call upon the name of the Lord," according to Zephaniah.

More conservative nineteenth-century authors like Methodist Adam Clarke (c. 1760–1832) saw the return of pure language as a statement about orthodox religion, while Alexander Campbell saw in it the power of his superior exegesis.[136] The noted Edwardsian theologian Samuel Hopkins (1743–1803) also believed in a common language for humanity in preparation for Christ's return as the fulfillment of Zephaniah's prophecy.[137] Mormons saw Zephaniah's prophecy as a claim about the return of humanity's first language at the Millennium.[138] In this respect they were not unlike Swedenborg, who anticipated a period of "a more intimate fellowship with saints and angels," a coming time when "angels shall converse with men as familiarly as they did with Adam before the fall."[139] The ancient past pointed to the glorious future.

The association of Eden's pure language with the coming age was more than simply a millenarian interpretation of a passage from Zephaniah. The Mormons believed that something sacred had happened in Eden that needed to be revisited. In an 1833 editorial, Phelps had announced: "the Spirit of God upon all flesh, will cause all to fill the place of its creation, as in the day when all was named by Adam in the garden of Eden."[140] Eden connected believers directly to the afterlife, a point emphasized in the GAEL. In an extension of *beth* as *E beth ku ain tri eth*, Phelps and Smith proclaimed Eden "a future place of existence, a place of residence beyond this earth" or "the earth in its most sanctified state as it shall be—eternity."[141] The primordial was to be the postmortal paradise. Eden showed the path to heaven.[142] As would often be the case with Smith, the secrets of the future were inextricably tied to the dead, their language, their family associations, their graves and memorials. The seer arrived at the future by way of the past.

Eden, broadly represented in Adam-ondi-Ahman, also signaled the familial valences of the Mormon eschaton at the site of Adam's deathbed. In the Grand River Valley, Smith revealed in a creative exegesis of Daniel's apocalyptic prophecy (Daniel 7:9–27), Adam, "the Ancient of Days," would assemble all of humanity at the site of his former deathbed to present them as a united family to the returning Messiah. Many early Latter-day Saints made explicit plans to participate in this gathering at Adam-ondi-Ahman; Smith used this image to describe his own father's deathbed.[143] The connection of the Millennium with Adam's return as the father of the human family is clear in the 1836 phrase of Cowdery's brother Warren: "the period is fast approaching when time itself shall be swallowed up or as the revelator expresses it, should be no longer, when Adam and his youngest son will be contemporaries."[144] This image of Adam standing with the most modern of his offspring is central to Smith's vision of human connectedness. Father Adam would hold in his arms a nineteenth-century child, and they would be united by both common blood and language. Beside Adam's grave near the primordial garden, believers would reunite to speak together Zephaniah's pure language and embrace the coming Christ. In the Egyptian project, an Adam-obsessed grammar of pure language that reflected the holy seership of the Mormon prophet, Smith provided potent symbols and concepts to prepare his people for this dramatic event. Then the sectarian babel of religious pluralism would give way to domestic unity in humanity's first home. Drawing on traditions about Egypt, mummies, Eden, and hieroglyphs, Smith demonstrated to his followers the shape of things to come.

Amid the trauma of the Missouri Mormon War of 1838, his imprisonment for his role in the war, and the settling of malarious Commerce, Illinois, Smith's translations faded from his daily routine. Despite distractions, he struggled to return to translation. The Egyptian project resulted in partial publication of the Book of Abraham in 1842.[145] Even with publication of these early chapters, the project remained on his mind through his final years. In 1843 Smith's lieutenants pleaded for funds to "prosecut[e] . . . the translations which he is anxious should be in the hands of the brethren as speedily as possible."[146] At the same time that the temple rites began to absorb the themes of seerhood, the "key words" of the temple cultus fleshed out the sacred names of the pure Adamic language (see chapter 7). To the day he died, Smith was the translator and seer predicted in his scripture.

Joseph, son of Joseph, the American seer, led his people on a journey across millennia, one whose milestones were people, the ancient dead. The textual maps he created were written monuments to the dead, their homes, their language, even, in some mystical sense, their very names. These maps created and enabled networks of belonging in which his followers could see themselves as the immediate kin of biblical heroes. As he reinterpreted seerhood, scriptures, and translation, Smith personalized and familialized the ancient past and the mystical future. *Gazelem* stones in hand, he saw and heard from Adam and Eve. A critical public called him a necromancer, but Joseph Smith knew better. As Isaiah had promised, God gave him eyes to see and ears to hear the voices of America's and the world's ancestors. The seer could unseal the grave and hear voices, sacred words whispering from the ground that led back to Father Adam and beyond.

PART TWO

EVERLASTING COMMUNITIES

Jesus Christ...was a Saviour to the Brethren and now we are to
be Saviours of men of our brethren to redeem our dead friends
and the friends of those who will not save their own friends to
Exalt ourselves untill we are all linked together again.
                            —George Laub, Journal (1845)

'Tis true he'd lose a parent's love, his home,
His heritage, his all; but would he not
Become a Son of God, and have a claim
To glory and inheritance, that still
Should be when every earthly good had past.
                        —Thomas Ward, "A Fragment" (1843)

6

The New and Everlasting Covenant

On March 10, 1844, Joseph Smith preached a sermon following the burial of his friend King Follett (1788–1844), killed by accidental rockfall while building a well. To an assembled crowd, Smith proclaimed: "If you have power to seal on earth & in heaven then we should be crafty...go & seal on earth your sons & daughters unto yourself & yourself unto your fathers in eternal glory...use a little Craftiness & seal all you can & when you get to heaven tell your father that what you seal on earth should be sealed in heaven. I will walk through the gate of heaven and Claim what I seal & those that follow me & my Council."[1] These instructions, an idiosyncratic combination of folk wit, biblical allusion, perfectionism, and a complex challenge to the waning theocentric heaven of Calvinism, thrilled early Latter-day Saints. Smith's use of "crafty" (revised to "wise" for the official history) probably meant resourceful rather than conniving, though the latter reading is not unreasonable.[2] More to the point, the God Smith's followers would control is a caricature of the Calvinist Creator, whom Smith specifically derided in the same sermon, rather than a representation of the God the Latter-day Saints actually worshipped. The confrontation between the Saints and the capricious being they saw as the God of Calvinism is central to the Mormon death conquest.

Apostle Wilford Woodruff proclaimed the sermon "one of the most important & interesting subjects ever presented to the saints."[3] He was right: the sermon dramatically illustrated central aspects of Smith's theology and eschatology. Standing figuratively over the corpse of a loyal follower, Smith instructed his followers to require of God through their "Craftiness" that he honor the eternal persistence of their relationships. This funeral sermon pointed toward something grander than the immortalized hearth that soon prevailed in broad swaths of mid-nineteenth-century Protestantism as the "domestic" heaven. Smith's vision of a human family united as sacerdotal kindred unfolded in the temple that Smith came to associate with the prophet Elijah and his special powers.[4]

All the exegetical theology, metaphysical energy, and earnest perfectionism of Smith's temple system served the end of creating a sacerdotal heaven family that would be stronger than the caprice of death and the Protestant God. The development of the temple is a complex story unfolding over a tumultuous decade, one sensitive to the contexts of antebellum Christianity. The temple cultus became the ritual and theological locus of the Mormon death conquest. The story of the cultus combines disparate elements of earliest Mormonism—charismatic gifts, the residue of Puritan covenant theology, sacramentalism, and the assurance of salvation. Through this cultus Smith armed his followers to fight a caricature of the Calvinist God, a malevolent being who arbitrarily denied sure salvation and the eternity of human society. From precedents in 1830s Ohio to the full-fledged cultus of 1840s Nauvoo, these strands combined into a ritual system that provided both "words against death" and a society against death.[5] Using terms like *endowment, washing, anointing,* and *solemn assembly*—more often types of rites than any single occurrence—the Latter-day Saints prepared themselves for the afterlife.

The complex story of the temple unfolds across two chapters. This chapter traces temple worship up to Smith's 1838 imprisonment at the end of the Missouri Mormon War; the next chapter picks up the story in Nauvoo as Smith brought the temple system to its fruition.

Binding Up: Seals and Covenants

The first strands of what became the temple cultus appeared early in Mormonism as interpretations of "seals" and "covenants," fraught terms current among Anglo-American Protestants. Sealing among Protestants ranged from the abstract seal of Christ all the way to wax seals given to believers to document their salvation. Fundamentally, sealing referred to a way of recognizing a believer as belonging to God. The complementary term *covenant* encompassed binding agreements between God and humanity or among humans, as well as sacred societies, groups of people united by God's good will and given special powers as a religious community. Sealing and covenant intertwined at the foundation of Smith's temple.

Early Seals

Images of seals arose early among the Latter-day Saints.[6] Initially Mormons engaged the sealed book of Isaiah 29 that only a seer could decode, drawing on ancient traditions about wax seals on sacred documents that identified them as issuing from a particular individual and protected the contents from undetected modification.[7] Scriptural seals contained clues to the broader meaning of seals as markers of identity and protection. Sealed records tantalized Latter-day Saints, from the Book of Mormon—where sealing implied something like burial—to Smith's 1832 exegesis of Revelation.[8]

For many American Protestants, sealing referred to the way God had identified believers as belonging to him, a sense present in the Book of Mormon as well.[9] Puritans understood the Lord's Supper or baptism as "the Lord's seal," an outward sign of regenerating grace, much like a wax seal on a letter.[10] For Puritans, these seals bore the strong sense of membership in a community. Accenting individuals over communities, John Wesley and many early Methodists saw seals as the internal stamp of a believer's rebirth. Such Christians were "sealed" by the "holy spirit of promise," a concept difficult to disentangle from their theology of adoption (see chapter 8). Many Protestants also understood sealing in evangelistic terms, as securing converts so that Christ would recognize his own at his Second Coming.[11] While antebellum Protestantism contained a wide diversity of views, at their core seals represented the promise of Christian identity and salvation, a security against life's inherent uncertainty.

Many millenarians, the Saints among them, saw seals in terms described in John's Revelation as an actual mark upon the foreheads of believers.[12] Interpreting the 1830s from the perspective of 1840s Nauvoo, Smith announced "the necessity of the Temple that the Servants of God may be sealed in their foreheads."[13] Some imaginative groups took the physicalization of seals further still. Joanna Southcott (1750–1814), a British prophetess to whom Smith was often compared, distributed to loyal followers "a *sealed written* paper with her signature . . . by which they are led to think they are *sealed against the day* of redemption."[14] In each of these interpretations, from the wholly conceptual to the assiduously physical, seals represented marks of God's ownership of human beings that protected them against the end times.

As did many Protestants, Mormons also saw baptism as an evangelist's seal.[15] One patriarchal blessing promised: "Thou shalt command

the waves when about to sink and be a . . . means of saving ships crews, &
they shall know that it is by the power of God and believe and thou shalt
baptize them in the briny deep, seal them up to eternal life and send
them to Zion."[16] The power of such an evangelist merged the physical
rite of baptism with the metaphysical promise of the seal of salvation.
The mild sacramentalism of this view of seals increased steadily with
time.

The different meanings of seal often merged in early Mormonism. As
the Saints considered the burden of proselytizing the world, they staged
several conferences over the course of 1831—most notably in April,
June, and October—in which they prepared to seal up the work of global
evangelism.[17] At the October conference, the various meanings of seal
were present, from the outward sign of a church covenant to assured salvation, from an evangelist's binding testimony to a supernatural entry in
the Book of Life. At this meeting, church leaders pledged to "cleanse ourselves and covenant before God," and Smith reassured them: "our names
are sealed in the Lamb's Book of life." According to Smith, "the order of
the Highpriesthood is that they have power given them to seal up the
Saints unto eternal life." Participants nervously anticipated the day
"when we have a testimony that we are sealed," while Sidney Rigdon
partially explained that the "Holy Spirit binds their hearts from Earth to
Heaven." Several elders relished the prospect. One wished "to be sealed
with the Holy Spirit of Promise," while another believed "it was the will
of the Lord to seal his saints."[18] The language of seals could also be used
for condemnation. The next month, Smith wrote a preface for the *Book of
Commandments* bestowing "power" on his elders "to seal both on earth
and in heaven, the unbelieving and rebellious."[19] The rebellious, rather
than being marked as Christ's, would be marked as belonging to the
devil.[20] Seals determined afterlife status before death.

Smith's father exemplified the radical power of sealing in early
Mormonism. As church patriarch, he often sealed recipients. He told
Mary Elliot (b. 1810), "I seal thee up unto eternal life in the name of
Jesus," while he told Henry Garrett, "I seal thee unto lif[e]." Their names
were "written in heaven"; their "salvation" was "sealed on high."[21] As they
recorded these blessings in the Patriarchal Blessing Book, Mormons
recalled the seals of the Book of Life. Other patriarchs followed suit,
"register[ing]" the "name" of recipients "in heaven."[22]

Seals were always personal, reassuring individuals of their election,
but seals were also communal. In 1832, Smith reflected of a session of

Sunday worship that the spirit was "binding there souls to gethe[r] that nothing but death can break asunder."[23] The disclaimer served as a reminder that Smith did not yet feel that he had solved the problem of the vulnerability of relationships to death. This admission did not suggest a lack of effort, even in the early 1830s. In an early, partial response to this problem, Mormon elders sealed congregations to eternal life. Reynolds Cahoon (1790–1861) recorded in November 1831 that he "Blest the Children in the name of the lord & sealed the Church unto eternal life."[24] Orson Pratt did the same in 1833, while Smith himself did so in 1832 and 1834.[25] For the Latter-day Saints, durable community was never far from the miraculous seal on the individual believer. The sealing of entire churches mirrored the incorporation of individual blessings into the Patriarchal Blessing Book. This image of created community steadily increased over the coming years.

Covenants

Mormon congregational sealings of the 1830s drew on the precedent of the church covenants of Reformed Protestants. Such covenants established a community of the elect as well as rules for participation and membership for a given congregation.[26] For the Congregationalists of the Second Great Awakening, covenants continued the legacy of the federal salvation of Puritanism, itself the legacy of Israel's national covenant in the Bible.[27] Salvation came to all participants in such covenants federally—as a church community—rather than individually.

The Baptists who surrounded Smith in western New York generally understood covenants as the specific commitments that, when entered into, constituted the creation of "a church in gospel order."[28] Methodists were widely known for "yearly covenants" to renew their shared commitment to God.[29] The itinerant Nancy Towle, when she found a particularly responsive community, urged them to join "in covenant, to seek eternal life, at the loss of all things; and to meet me, in a better world."[30] Though simpler than the federal theology of the Puritans, the covenant theology of frontier Protestants situated religious communities in sacred history.

The early Latter-day Saints employed covenants in interconnected ways. Mormon covenants ranged from vast to small, from the holy to the mundane. The 1831 Laws of the church predicted establishment of "church covenants, such as shall be sufficient to establish you, both here, and in the New Jerusalem."[31] The church was to be led by "articles and covenants," which provided the authorization for priesthood offices and outlined the functions of the church.[32] In 1835 the biblical-sounding *Book of Commandments* became the *Doctrine* (a catechism called the *Lectures on Faith*) *and Covenants* (the revelations regulating the church and providing the supernatural basis for its operation). On a smaller scale, and like many Protestants, the Mormon "Bretheren renued thair Covenant" when spiritual exigencies required it.[33]

Some Mormon itinerants entered into modified versions of church covenants in which they pledged to be loyal to each other for the duration of a mission tour. These pledges during the difficult course of itinerancy occasionally became contentious, as when John Page (1799–1867) abandoned a covenant to accompany Orson Hyde all the way to Palestine.[34] The covenants of small churches and itinerant elders evolved within the communitarian experiments of 1830s Kirtland. At the early Mormon headquarters, covenants represented spiritual and financial contracts regulating the behavior of participants.[35]

While concrete examples of covenants abounded in early Mormonism, the Latter-day Saints also had a strong sense of covenant as an abstract term. They were in good company. Many orthodox Calvinists saw covenant primarily as a reference to the "covenant of grace," in opposition to the "covenant of works."[36] For some Christians, like founding Quaker George Fox (1624–1691), the "new and everlasting covenant" referred to the power of Jesus's New Testament, the end of the Mosaic law.[37] For most others, it was either Christ's end to the Mosaic law or a reference to the millennial restoration of Israel and the church, when Jerusalem would receive its true Messiah.[38] Mormons, on the other hand, interpreted their church as a "new and everlasting covenant." As Smith struggled in 1830 to explain his requirement that baptized Christians be rebaptized by Mormon elders, he explained in God's voice that "all old covenants have I caused to be done away; this is a new and an everlasting covenant, even that which was from the beginning."[39] The "new and everlasting covenant" ultimately served as a coded phrase for polygamy (see chapter 8), but the phrase initially encompassed the divine dispensation under which the Mormon Church operated and the enduring community it made possible.[40] The language of new and everlasting covenant as membership in Smith's new church dominated the early uses of the term and appeared in many letters home from itinerant elders.[41]

Dying Mormons employed the new and everlasting covenant to protect themselves spiritually. Robert Thompson (1811–1841), for example, departed "life in the triumphs of faith, bearing testimony, in his dying moments of the truth of the fullness of the gospel of Jesus Christ, and of the faith of the new and everlasting covenant; rejoicing greatly, that his time had come, when he too could go, and be at rest in the paradise of God."[42] Thompson and his friends drew from the covenant the strength to confront death with the hope that their community would persist beyond the grave.

Beginnings of a Kirtland Cultus

Ideas about seals and covenants began to coalesce into a cultus in 1833. Mormons used a generally Protestant term, "School of the Prophets," to describe several educational and fraternal endeavors beginning in the winter of 1832–1833.[43] These fraternal orders became stepping-stones from general church covenants to Mormonism's ultimate temple cultus.

The School of the Prophets began with a December 1832 revelation, called the "Olive Leaf," that announced the Kirtland Temple into which the School merged. By stipulation of the Olive Leaf, the president of the School would open each meeting with a "prayer upon his knees before God ... in token or remembrance of the everlasting covenant." After this formalized greeting, the president was to raise his hands over his head and "salute" his colleagues formulaically: "Art thou a brother or brethren? I salute you in the name of the Lord Jesus Christ, in token or remembrance of the everlasting covenant, in which covenant I receive you to fellowship, in a determination that is fixed, immovable, and unchangeable, to be your friend and brother through the grace of God in the bonds of love, to walk in all the commandments of God blameless, in thanksgiving, forever and ever. Amen."[44] Early Mormon leaders thereby bound themselves in a covenant or "determination" intended to last "forever and ever." In this period, Smith blessed his father that he would "receive councel in the house of the most high that he may be streng[t]hened in hope that the goings of his feet may be established for ever."[45] The biblicized reference to the "goings" of Joseph Sr.'s "feet" circled back to the hope of seals—believers wanted the surety of salvation that would allow them to face death with equanimity or even hope. In this eternal fraternal order stood the image of the sacerdotal heaven family that came to dominate the Nauvoo Temple cultus of the 1840s.

In the first three years of the movement's existence, Mormons had recast covenant, appropriated the mythic power of sacred seals, and begun the creation of communities that could span the chasm of death. Still, something was missing. To the themes of covenant, sacred community, and seals of salvation would soon be added a restoration of the charismatic "endowment of power" received by the apostles in the Book of Acts, comprehending both miraculous power and ecclesiastical authority.

Pentecost and the Enduement of Power

Much like early Methodists and some Baptists, early Mormons sought the immediate, miraculous presence of God. They hoped to work the miracles that the New Testament apostles had worked. Over Mormonism's first half decade, the quest for the immediate presence of God and his power began to shape ritual, liturgical, and devotional forms with a sacerdotalism foreign to most Protestants. Over several years, Mormons made interrelated attempts to secure an "endowment of power" from God, initially a reference to a type of experience rather than a specific event or rite. In a holy season that stretched across several months in early 1836, they enjoyed memorable success at achieving their endowment.

In most religious movements, including Mormonism, spiritual power proves difficult to control.[46] Near the Saints, the Shakers experienced a brief Era of Manifestations (c. 1837–1842) but rejected charismata when they threatened the movement's disintegration.[47] Though the push toward the extremes of enthusiastic worship by the ex-Baptist core of Mormon Kirtland caused Smith to disavow the most energetic displays of God's immediate presence, he instructed his disciples that miracles must follow authorized ministers.[48] Frank enthusiasm was not the solution, but neither was the formalism of the orthodox Protestant churches. The tension over early Kirtland worship only made the question more acute. When would the Saints acquire incontrovertible proof of their calling, the power that authorized and empowered the first apostles to preach the Gospel? With time and several false starts, Smith and his Saints came to believe that their endowment would arrive when they gathered like the New Testament apostles in Jerusalem, this time in America.

Smith set the stage for endowment as early as 1831, when he instructed followers to "go to the Ohio" to be "endowed with power from on high."[49] This call for an endowment (or "enduement," following the KJV) derived from biblical precedents, primarily the New Testament Pentecost.[50] Christ, returning after the crucifixion, required of his disciples that they "tarry" in Jerusalem, "until ye be endued with power from on high." Following this injunction, Christian leaders gathered in Jerusalem, by tradition at the temple, and awaited the promised power. That power arrived in a miraculous wind, with tongues of fire flickering above their heads. The apostles spoke in foreign languages, a portent of their international evangelism. Peter then explained to an astonished crowd that the miracle had fulfilled a prophecy in the Book of Joel. The Pentecostal endowment attracted several thousand proselytes to the fledgling church, according to the New Testament.[51]

Within mainstream Protestantism, the endowment of power referred primarily to the New Testament account. Some thought it referred to personal inspiration or the conversion experience, while others ignored it entirely.[52] Among certain populist sects, endowment meant a call from above, the filling of the believer's emptied soul by the Holy Spirit.[53] With time and some controversy, the endowment of power became intertwined with sanctification and the Holiness movement of the latter nineteenth century.[54] Few stood with Smith's interpretation in the 1830s.[55]

The New Testament precedent of the apostles in Jerusalem rapidly led Mormons to the conception of a New World temple to match the Old World original where the apostles had gathered. After the disappointment of a false start on a temple in the center of their Edenic Zion in western Missouri, Joseph Smith announced in the Olive Leaf revelation a new Solomonic structure in Ohio.[56] Outwardly a Georgian Gothic meetinghouse with an adjacent cemetery, the Mormon temple contained distinctive internal architecture. Work began on the Kirtland Temple (see figure 6.1) in the summer of 1833 and continued through 1836, at great expense to the financially stressed church.[57]

The power to evangelize the earth and establish God's kingdom would not come easily. Smith prepared his itinerant elders for their mission work with traditional education as well as spiritual power. The Olive Leaf clarified that the temple would be a "house of learning" as much as a "house of glory."[58] To this end, Smith had Sidney Rigdon write the *Lectures on Faith* as a catechism for the mystically fraternal School of the Prophets.

Figure 6.1 The Kirtland Temple, dedicated in 1836, was the centerpiece of religious life in Mormon Ohio. The dedication season was crucial to the development of the Mormon temple liturgy. Both temples built under Smith's supervision had burial grounds or tombs adjacent to them. Image courtesy of the Church History Library, The Church of Jesus Christ of Latter-day Saints.

The *Lectures* and their school anticipated the temple's emphasis on empowerment through knowledge. As the School progressed, it came to encompass English grammar and composition, world history, Hebrew, and for some the study of Greek and German.

Washing Feet and Bodies

Simultaneously with his educational efforts, Joseph Smith interpreted religious power in increasingly sacerdotal and sacramental terms. He introduced rites and fleshed out the contours of a church hierarchy. In January 1833, church leaders gathered in the School to become "clean from the blood of this generation," a state they achieved through "the ordinance of the washing of feet," a sacrament known among other radical sects as "feet-washing" and among Catholics or high church Protestants as *pedilavium*.[59] Acting out the narrative of John 13, in which Christ washed his disciples' feet after the Last Supper, the Saints were to share the Lord's Supper, "gird" themselves, and wash each other's feet, starting with the Prophet.[60] In his New Translation, Smith saw *pedilavium* as "the costom of the Jews under their law; wherefore Jesus done this that the law might be fulfilled."[61]

The washing of feet was a familiar primitivist ordinance among descendants of the Anabaptists, some radical Methodists, and a few strains within the Baptist tradition; various Catholics practiced *pedilavium* within the liturgical calendar. All of these groups followed New Testament precedent; some cited the practice among the early church fathers.[62] Most mainstream Protestants, including mainline Methodists, rejected the practice as an outward ordinance that distracted believers from faith, a sacramental blight imported from Catholicism. Those who practiced the ritual saw foot-washing as a rite of initiation or regeneration, grouping it with rites like baptism and the Lord's Supper.[63]

As in most rites of early Mormonism, both personal and communal salvation were at stake in the washing of feet. Mormons were declared worthy of heaven as individuals, cleansed of sin. Simultaneously they affirmed the discharge of their evangelizing duties to the world, connecting this fraternal rite to the parallel practice of "dusting their feet" to seal a testimony against hostile or unbelieving communities.[64] Standing apart from the world as they washed each other's feet, they confirmed—the future standing with the present—that they had called out from modern Babylon those who would be saved with them in the celestial kingdom of God. They also communicated their "fixed determination" to each other "in life or in death" as an ecclesial community.[65]

Priesthood played an increasingly prominent role in the Kirtland rites of the early 1830s. Foot-washing followed ecclesiastical seniority, and as the temple grew, Smith revealed that the temple would contain two sets of nine pulpits arranged in three rows to reflect the governing structures of the church, the officers of the Aaronic and Melchizedek priesthoods. These pulpits (see figure 6.2) adorned the east and west walls of the temple, a miniature version of the temple compound planned for their Zion in Missouri.[66]

As the temple neared completion, the elders began further preparations for a holy season that would constitute their endowment of power. In October 1835 the hierarchs made plans for the "first elders" to participate in a "solemn assembly" for the "organization of the school of the prophets, and attend[ing] to the ordinence of the washing of feet."[67] As they prepared for the ceremony a month later, the leading elders forecast that "we shall finally roll into the celestial kingdom of God and enjoy it forever." Initially excluding "private" (nonordained) members from foot-

Figure 6.2 This complex of pulpits within the Kirtland Temple reflected the Mormon priesthood hierarchy. Smith reported an encounter he had at the top of these pulpits with God and the patriarch Elijah in 1836. Image courtesy of Library of Congress.

washing, Smith explained that the rite "was never intended for any but official members."[68] These "official" itinerants were to purify themselves through this rite, to make themselves "clean every whit."[69] Spirits ran high as they pursued individual and corporate salvation.

Smith intended the fraternity that enclosed the rising priesthood hierarchy to be the vessel for the promised endowment. In December, Smith prayed to God to "prepare him and all the Elders to receive an endument, in thy house, even according to thine own order from time to time as thou seest them worthy to be called into thy Solemn Assembly."[70] During the same period, Smith reiterated that the School in its various instances was to merge into the temple and "that glorious endowment that God has in store for the faithful."[71]

The organization Smith hoped for would allow the Latter-day apostles to evangelize the world, to "go forth in my name unto all nations." He repeatedly and strenuously urged them to "prepare their hearts for the solem assembly and for the great day which is to come."[72] Employing the language of the New Testament, he advised his disciples that "you need an endowment brethren in order that you may be prepared and able to overcome all things, and those that reject your testimony will be damned the sick will be healed the lame made to walk the deaf to hear and the blind to see through your instrumentality."[73] The evangelistic aspect of the Kirtland Temple experience so dominated discussion that some recent converts worried that they would be unworthy to participate because they had not yet completed a mission tour.[74] The rites of the Kirtland endowment were designed to expand the size of the church community.

Ritual cleansing returned in force for the Kirtland holy season. In November 1835, Smith reinstituted foot-washing, desiring that it be in "a place prepared, that we may attend to this ordinance, aside from the world."[75] As the winter advanced, the ritual washings expanded from feet to the entire body. With time Smith clarified that ritual washings prepared participants for the associated rites of anointing. In preparation for a January 1836 anointing meeting, participants "after pure water was prepared called upon the lord and proceeded to wash each other's bodies and bathe the same with whiskey perfumed with cinnamon. This we did that we might be clearn before the Lord for the Sabbath, confessing our sins and covenanting to be faithful to God." Oliver Cowdery referred to the rite of washing as a "purification."[76] Participants in this meeting were very self-conscious of their biblical mimesis, reflecting "how the priests anciently used to wash always before ministering before the Lord," and performing a physical exegesis of the New Testament announcement that "ye are washed [and] ye are sanctified."[77]

Frontierspeople bathed rarely if ever.[78] Many disputed the safety of bathing, worrying that cold water risked infection, while warm water was dangerous and difficult to secure in needed quantities. The contemporary physiology reformers, emblematically Sylvester Graham, proposed bathing (often in cold water) as a mode to spiritual salvation through the manipulation and purification of the body.[79] Various versions of hydropathy circulated in Anglo-American culture, involving even John Wesley in its discipline.[80] The way the Saints washed themselves in Kirtland contained both medical and religious valences, pointing to associations between religious ritual and health.

Church leaders repeated similar washings during the meeting on January 21, 1836, with a "sweet smelling oderous wash."[81] The Saints seem to have been merging the "sweet spices" compounded to make "a perfume" for the priestly altar with the "holy anointing oil" for the priest's head, sacred liquids described together in Exodus.[82] The Old

Testament was not the only apparent context for whiskey baths, though. A metaphysical health code received during the second month of the School of the Prophets, the revelation called the Word of Wisdom, taught that "strong drinks" were reserved for "the washing of your bodies," a matter confirmed by unanimous vote in December 1836, which decreed that "liquors" could only be used for "wine at the Sacraments & for external Washing."[83] According to the Word of Wisdom, alcohol washing, coupled with other health practices, protected the Saints from the "destroying angel," a figure associated with both personal deaths and the Apocalypse. The connection of health and ritual purification highlighted the association between healing and immortality and the rites of the temple cultus.[84]

The rapid evaporation of alcohol from the skin, which causes a distinctive and stimulating sensation of cooling, may have played a role in the mystical physicality of the process of purification. Some described the visitation of the spirit as like "warm-water": topical alcohol was an able physical mimic of this spiritual experience.[85] Mormons were not alone in employing "stimulating baths." Popular remedies recommended whiskey baths to restore health, while physicians from herbalists to "heroic" allopaths sanctioned the stimulating application of alcohol to skin. James Ewell's Medical Companion recommended a whiskey bath for "nervous fever," an imprecise term applied to a variety of possibly life-threatening infections, while others treated swollen legs or "restlessness" similarly.[86] The Mormons, for their part, merged mystical purity with health in their practice of alcohol washing.

Anointing and Endowment

With their bodies rightly bathed and perfumed, these Latter-day priests of Solomon's Temple prepared to receive their anointings in recapitulation of an Old Testament priestly rite. Smith began this process in January 1836, with a significant meeting of official members.[87] Smith's diary notes that "we attended to the ordinance of washing our bodies in pure water, we also perfumed our bodies and our heads, in the name of the Lord." Then at "early candlelight" he gathered with "the presidency" in "the Chapel" in order "to attend to the ordinance of annointing our heads with holy oil." The assembled elders first approached Father Smith, "all blessing him to be our patraark, to annoint our heads." Having started with the patriarch, they then turned to each other, anointing according to position in the hierarchy.

As part of this grand meeting, Smith reported a vision that situated their temple within the themes of covenants and seals. In the vision, Smith witnessed members of his natal family, including Alvin, in the bosom of Abraham, inhabiting the celestial kingdom of God. Beyond his family, Smith "saw the 12, in the celestial kingdom of God" and "all of the presidency in the Celistial Kingdom of God, and, many others who were present." Smith's vision of heaven, like a glimpse of the pages of the Book of Life, displayed the composite nature of the heaven family in Mormonism. Hierarchs and siblings came together in this celestial reunion. The church leaders Smith was anointing had as valid a claim on the heavenly community as Smith's own family. Ritually transformed by scented whiskey and olive oil against their skin, the Latter-day Saints saw their way clear to salvation and community in the afterlife.

Few other Americans embraced anointing the way the Latter-day Saints did, in such assiduously physical terms. Protestants generally emphasized divine chosenness and immanence of the spirit in an evangelist, a metaphorical reading. Baptist historians in western New York described a particularly moving annual meeting in which itinerants "appeared to have received a new anointing," which meant that they "came together in the fullness of the blessing of the gospel of Christ."[88] The Reformed Methodist William Pitts (b. 1774) described anointing similarly.[89] Few actually applied olive oil to skin the way Mormons did, however familiar the Old Testament practice was.[90]

Oliver Cowdery claimed the elders were being "annointed with the same kind of oil and in the man[ner] that were Moses and Aaron."[91] There was plenty of material for the Mormons to draw on, all firmly situated within the Old Testament temple cultus. The Book of Exodus taught Latter-day Saints, who saw themselves as standing in for Aaron and his sons, that "their anointing shall surely be an everlasting priesthood throughout their generations."[92] Following the pattern of Aaron, they would "be hallowed" by the anointings they received.[93] Even the Book of Mormon provided precedent, as the Jaredites—the ancient people who survived Babel's curse—used anointing as a chrism to consecrate their kings.[94]

The choice to begin the anointing process with Joseph Sr. in the January meeting was consistent both with Smith's great admiration for his father and perhaps with a literalizing exegesis of Exodus 40:15, in which Moses anointed Aaron before turning to Aaron's sons. Participants found themselves transformed by these sacred washings and anointings. In Oliver Cowdery's phrase, "the heavens were opened to many, and great and marvelous things were shown." Over the next two weeks, the priesthood hierarchy engaged in several more episodes of anointing, often accompanied by fasting, glossolalia, "feasts" of Eucharistic bread and wine, and prayer meetings extending well past midnight.[95] In a primitivistic, sacramental way, the revival of the Kirtland church was in full swing.

For Mormons, anointing included a strong connection to healing the body. Olive oil was not just a ritual prop or mark of ecclesiastical authority; it was also a balm of healing. On the explicit example of James 5:14, Mormons saw oil as a medium for faith healing.[96] In scattered events in the early 1830s, Saints healed each other with such a balm. In the January 1836 prayer meeting, this oil acquired sacerdotal authority and an invigorated healing potency. The use of oil for healing increased dramatically after the Kirtland holy season.[97] The importance of charismata to early Mormon evangelism almost certainly played a role in this connection—endowed elders needed to prove God's approval of their mission through miraculous healings[98]—but the new temple rites affirmed a ritual power for oil that almost certainly contributed to the expanding role of anointing and sealing in faith healings.[99] Joseph Sr., empowered by his anointing of January 1836, blessed myriad Latter-day Saints with the preservation of physical health and control over death. As one example among many, he blessed Noah Packard in late 1837: "The destroyer shall not have power over the[e] to take thy life because of the sealing power."[100] This blessing merged protection from the destroying angel emphasized in the Word of Wisdom health code with the power of seals that stood at the base of the entire temple cultus.

The day after the initial anointing meeting, participants experienced another Pentecostal outpouring: "the congregation shouted a loud hosannah the gift of toungs, fell upon us in mighty power, angels mingled their voices with ours, while their presence was in our midst, and unseasing prasis swelled our bosoms for the space of half an hour." As they shouted their unceasing praises to God, these Latter-day elders recalled the Methodist shout tradition, even as they moved beyond it in a temple intended to replace and restore the one destroyed in Jerusalem.[101] On January 28, when church leaders assembled to "seal the blessings which had been promised to them by the holy anoint[in]g," Sylvester Smith (1806–1880) "saw a piller of fire rest down & abide upon the heads of the quorem."[102] Despite repeated outpourings of Pentecostal power, though, Smith continued to insist that more was yet to come.[103] Smith and his closest followers continued preparations for the March 27 dedication of the Kirtland Temple at a "solemn assembly" around the time of the church's sixth anniversary.[104]

Over the course of the next two months, anointings with oil became a staple of the weekly priesthood meetings, a method for confirming ordinations and initiating new Mormons into their respective priesthood bodies, called quorums.[105] In February "anointing blessings were sealed by uplifted hands and praises to God," which referred to specialized prayers and formulaic shouts of Hosannah.[106]

These special shouts, an applied exegesis of Revelation 7 and Matthew 21, continued the theme of seals as declarations of divine ownership even as they transformed the practices of Protestant revivalists.[107] Sealing shouts remained prominent through the dedication of the Kirtland Temple. William Phelps penned a hymn, "Hosanna to God and the Lamb," that represented and intermingled with the sealing shouts of the early anointings. In this hymn ever after connected to temple worship, Phelps announced that the Saints would "wash and be wash'd, and with oil be anointed / Withal not omitting the washing of feet: / For he that receiveth his PENNY appointed, / Must surely be clean at the harvest of wheat." A similar hymn looked forward to the time, presumably hastened by temple rites, when "The Saints immortal from the tomb / With angels meet again."[108] The Kirtland rites again pointed toward assured immortality and the hope of security at the apocalypse.

The awakening in the Kirtland church over the first months of 1836 encompassed physiologic privations, acts of ritual and physical cleansing, and frequent celebrations of the Lord's Supper with plentiful bread and wine in the spirit of Methodist love feasts.[109] Through participation believers sought validation of their belief in Mormonism and knowledge of their salvation status, drawing comfort from the promise of seals and covenants. Despite the distinctive trappings of Mormon primitivism and sacramentalism, the sought-for endowment subsumed what Protestants might have called the regenerating witness or the new birth. Following the encouragement of their prophet, many Latter-day Saints even sought a glimpse of Jesus's face.[110] The Latter-day Saint endowment experiences fit within visionary and revival culture even as they augured the increasingly angel-emphatic tone of Mormon temple worship.

The Kirtland holy season also allowed Smith to constrain enthusiasm with sacerdotal power.[111] Through the Kirtland holy season the Mormon Church organized its ecclesial hierarchy. From hierarchical pulpits to sealing and anointing through priesthood quorums to the sequence by which anointing and endowment occurred, Smith used the Kirtland holy season to establish the church's hierarchy.[112] The tiered pulpits of the east and west walls of the temple, visible to all, served as a constant reminder of both the existence and breadth of the hierarchy.[113] The great spectacle of the day of dedication in late March followed the hierarchy, beginning with a special dedication and consecration of the pulpits.[114] The official account of the day carefully described the occupant of each pulpit, arranged according to priesthood authority (the only deviation from protocol was Joseph Sr. taking his son's presidential seat).[115]

The hierarchs arrayed in their respective pulpits, the dedication—the "solemn assembly" of the Saints—could begin.[116] The centerpiece of the ceremony was a dedicatory prayer Smith wrote with Cowdery and others. In this prayer, Smith announced the goal of the Kirtland holy season.

> Let the anointing of thy ministers be sealed upon them with power from on high: let it be fulfilled upon them as upon those on the day of Pentacost: let the gift of tongues be poured out upon thy people, even cloven tongues as of fire, and the interpretation thereof. And let thy house be filled, as with a mighty rushing wind, with thy glory. Put upon thy servants the testimony of the covenant that where they go out and proclaim thy word, they may seal up the law.[117]

In the prayer, Smith made clear the intended purpose of the preparatory anointings practiced in the months leading up to the dedication. In addition to the heavily apostolic vision of the endowment, Smith recalled the power of the physical rites, pleading with God to "turn away thy wrath, when thou lookest upon the face of thy anointed." Anointings marked the Saints as those whom God would save. Recalling the assured salvation associated with seals, Smith pleaded, "Let these thine anointed ones be clothed with salvation."[118]

The Saints promptly staged another dedication to accommodate those who could not fit in the temple the first time, a ceremony that exceeded the first one "in sublimity and solemnity as well as in order."[119] Almost the entire Mormon population of Kirtland participated in the various events that culminated their holy season.[120]

The endowment of power the Saints acquired in the holy season surrounding the dedication of their temple was simultaneously private and corporate, personal and communal, charismatic and hierarchical. Though women participated in the general fervor, the endowment narrative generally favored ordained men—it was largely focused on preparing elders for proselytizing missions.[121] The spiritual experiences of some women, though, underscore a strongly personal view of the "grandure and sublimity" of the "spirit of their endowment," a parallel to the regenerating grace or new birth of evangelical Protestants.[122] This side of endowment was a renewal of commitment, a visitation of the spirit that suffused the worshipper with holy power. Because of this intensely personal aspect, endowment came to different people at different times and places.

Two weeks in late March and early April 1836 represented for many the fruition of the promised endowment. Many faithful participants characterized the events as the return of the day of Pentecost, down to the tongues of fire above their heads.[123] This was a Mormon revival both more powerful and more orderly, in the views of its leaders, than the ones at Red River and Cane Ridge that had amplified the Second Great Awakening three decades earlier. Participants saw angels, spoke and sang in tongues, and received personal and communal supernatural visions. Some saw God or Jesus.[124] The Saints celebrated the Lord's Supper with the liberal outpouring of bread and wine, as if they wished to receive the same criticism the New Testament apostles had of being "drunk with wine."[125] Anticipating the full range of biblical miracles from simple faith to raising the dead, they received at a minimum the gifts of healing the sick, speaking in tongues, receiving the ministering of angels, and prophesying during the frenetic weeks surrounding the temple dedication. "We had a most glorious and not to be forgotten time," remembered one participant, while Smith's diary called it "a penticost and enduement indeed, long to be remembered."[126]

About a month later, Smith clarified that the endowment represented a collection of rites and experiences that could be repeated as needed to prepare elders to proselytize. On April 30, ten "Elders with a Priest were anointed in the Lord's house with fasting and washing of feet according to the order given for the endowment of God, in the last days by the Prs. [Joseph Smith] and assistant."[127] Personal regeneration, rites of cleansing

and anointing, and worshipful prayer and shouting in the temple constituted the endowment of power required to dispatch Mormon itinerants
to the four corners of the earth.

The elders who missed the 1836 holy season received an opportunity
the next spring. Then, with considerable anticipation and anxiety, they
followed the instructions in Phelps's "Hosanna" hymn. Wilford Woodruff
recalled that he and his colleagues "wash[ed] our bodies from head to
foot in soap & watter we then washed ourselves in clear watter next in
perfumed spirits," "that our bodies might be prepared for the anointing."
Setting their souls right, Woodruff and colleagues "expressed our feelings to each other" as they washed and perfumed. After charismatic outpourings within the context of priesthood hierarchy, participants stayed
in the temple, "according to our Covenant," prayerfully refusing to eat or
sleep until the miraculous endowment had been received.[128] Mormons
anticipated that such an endowment would occur at every anniversary of
the church's founding, another echo of the holy seasons of Reformed
revival. Unfortunately, mass defections and the Mormon War of 1838
scuttled those plans; when the endowment returned, it did so in the context of the Nauvoo cultus.[129]

Elijah and Election in Common

During the Kirtland holy season Smith reported an encounter with a
specific angel who became critical to understanding the temple cultus.
On April 3, the Sabbath following the second dedication ceremony, Smith
and Cowdery drew a set of veils around their pulpit to pray. In fulfillment
of their earnest pleas, they saw the face of God, followed by a visit from a
mystical figure called Elias. What happened next shaped the temple
cultus for nearly two centuries. "A great and glorious vision burts [burst]
upon them." Standing above the pulpit was "Elijah, the Prophet, who was
taken to Heaven without tasting death." This biblical patriarch announced
that "the time has fully come which was spoken of by the mouth of
Malachi, testifying, that he should be sent before the great and dreadful
day of the Lord come, to turn the hearts of the fathers to the children,
and the children to the fathers." Elijah then told Smith and Cowdery that
"the Keys of this dispensation are committed into your hands."[130] In this
interaction Elijah, whose presence had been felt in Mormonism intermittently since the 1820s, assumed center stage in the temple cultus.

Standing atop the tiered pulpits of the temple's west wall, this physical-ized exegesis of Malachi 4 provided the Saints with a scriptural foundation for an effort to create durable connections among all generations of humanity.[131]

Elijah was a natural patron for the death-defying cultus. He was "the immortal prophet" who had been "wafted to the fair climes of immor-tality" without tasting death.[132] Elijah's immortality bestowed special status, which—coupled with his reanimation of a child—tied him closely to the conquest of death in a variety of traditions, including Judaism, Western esotericism, and Christianity.[133] For antebellum Protestants Elijah primarily represented a figure to introduce Christ's Second Coming, a harbinger of the end times. For Smith this relatively innoc-uous figure was called Elias, a doppelganger of the Mormon Elijah (Elias is the Greek transliteration of the Hebrew name Elijah). This Elias filled the roles that Protestants associated with Elijah. The Elijah that Smith preserved for Mormons by splitting off Elias had a grander role to play in the cosmic drama. This Mormon Elijah provided the cement to unite the society of heaven, an extension of sealing power that secured election for the Saints both individually and corporately.[134]

Images of Elijah as patron of immortality extended into Mormon life. The fact of Elijah's miraculous control over death emboldened Joseph Sr. to bless one aspiring believer with these words: "thou Shalt have power over death & the grave & not sleep in the dust, but if thou wilt seek with all thy heart thou shalt be able to translate & be with Elijah in the Kingdom of heaven."[135] Other believers learned that they would, follow-ing the precedent of Elijah's magic chariot, "waft" themselves to the presence of God.[136] Joseph Jr. employed this imagery in his retelling of a dream he had of prominent Mormon William Marks (1792–1872). A guardian angel dispatched an Elijah chariot to save Marks, who was threatened by physical destruction.[137]

Elijah's power extended into a dramatic priesthood, a word that Latter-day Saints understood then as both a sacerdotal order and a mystically efficacious power. Though Mormon priesthood orders were still devel-oping, Smith called Elijah's the "patriarchal" or "Abrahamic" priest-hood.[138] In 1840 Smith posed and answered a rhetorical question. "Why send Elijah[?] because he holds the Keys of the Authority to administer in all the ordinances of the priesthood and without the authority is given[,] the ordinances could not be administered in righteousness."[139] This priesthood, drawing on images of Abraham's countless seed, allowed

Elijah and his Latter-day Saints to create new, eternally durable relationships.

The priesthood power that Elijah brought to the Latter-day Saints was inextricably linked to covenant theology in several distinctive exegeses of Malachi's prophecy that the immortal prophet Elijah would "turn the hearts of the children to the fathers and the hearts of the fathers to the children." In an 1844 sermon, Smith returned to the translation of the book of Malachi—a book he had termed "correct" in the KJV at the conclusion of his New Translation in 1833.[140] "Turn," he announced, was better rendered "bind or seal," absorbing the KJV's rendition of Malachi into Mormon covenant theology.[141] An obscure word in the Authorized Bible found new life in the Mormon temple. In this sealing stood the maturation of the covenants and seals of the first years of the church's existence. In 1843, Smith taught that Elijah "shall reveal the covenants of the fathers in relation to the children.—and the children and the covenants of the children in relation to the fathers."[142] Elijah established such covenants that believers "may have the priviledge of entering into the same in order to effect their mutual salvation."[143]

Through Elijah, the Saints expanded the themes of sealing and covenant in an assault on the two prevalent modes of addressing the prospect of salvation. At an important level the strands of sealing, covenant, and Elijah converged on a solution to a particular, vexing problem: the uncertainty of salvation in the largely post-Calvinist landscape of antebellum Protestantism.

The promise of one's own salvation had long been an elusive and paradoxical goal in American Protestantism. A Calvinist legacy could theoretically leave the dying believer uncertain of salvation even on her deathbed—to know heaven before the Judgment was to commit the sin of pride.[144] Some particularly stern antebellum Calvinists even disabused the dying of belief in their own salvation on actual deathbeds.[145] The heaven of Calvinism, hard enough for a believer to achieve individually, could never reliably accommodate a family whole.[146] The doctrine of election formally required that parents admit uncertainty as to whether their children would be saved at all.[147] Even if they were saved, their bonds would be attenuated at best in the presence of an all-encompassing God.[148] From the perspective of populist critics, Calvinism suffered, among other things, from its view of an "Angry God," who bestowed salvation independent of human merit in the divine act called election. The way populist Protestants and sectarians viewed Calvinism was as important to American religion as how Calvinists actually understood their orthodoxy. In practice many Calvinists lived happily with the promise of irresistible and undeserved grace, and Calvinist theologians like Samuel Hopkins predicted a heaven a thousand times more populous than hell.[149] For critics, though, this theology promised only an inscrutable, alien God and a salvation as forcefully denied as water to the thirsty Tantalus of Greek lore. In the view of these anti-Calvinists, the orthodox God arbitrarily, perhaps even maliciously, denied election. This was the God Smith promised his followers they could control.

The standard antebellum response to Calvinism was the Arminian philosophy, which was most closely associated in America with Methodism.[150] For Arminians, so named for the patron of this theology, a Dutch theologian named Jakob Harmenszoon [Jacobus Arminius] (1560–1609), any believer could turn her soul over to Jesus and receive a regenerating grace that claimed her a place in heaven. However, with the power to accept grace came also the power to reject it. Called "backsliding," the prospect of losing grace—impossible under Calvinism, which maintained the Perseverance of the Saints, the belief that once saved, a Christian is always saved—became a frightful specter. Methodists particularly were known for their frenetic flight from backsliding, one that could continue right up to the final gasping breaths of believers on their deathbeds. When Arminianism combined with the evangelical mandate, the stress could become particularly intense, as worshippers fretted over their ability to persuade friends, family, and strangers to accept God's grace. Having secured one's own salvation only made the issue of loved ones' salvation all the more acute. Many Arminians worried constantly over the fate of their kith and kin, reckoning that any backsliding of loved ones threatened the integrity of their heavenly community.[151]

Though many Latter-day Saints had favored Methodism before the rise of Mormonism, Smith ultimately rejected Arminianism almost as severely as he did Calvinism. The perpetual flight from lost salvation mocked the power of covenantal seals and priesthood power. In strong terms, Smith preached in 1844: "I do not believe the methodist doctrine of sending honest men, and noble minded men to hell, along with the murderer and adulterer."[152] For Smith election was never just about individual salvation. Sealing the righteous individual to an isolated salvation was insufficient for a prophet who proclaimed "let me be resurrected with the Saints, whether to heaven or hell or any other good place.... What do we care if the society is good[?]"[153] He made his hunger for

persistent intimacy explicit in his eulogy of Lorenzo Barnes: "More painful to me [are] the thoughts of anhilitation than death. If I had no
expectation of seeing my mother, brother[s], and Sisters and friends
again my heart would burst in a moment and I should go down to my
grave."[154] Later that year he made similar comments at the funeral of
Elias Higbee. "There is a thought more dreadful than that of total annihilation That is the thought that we shall never again meet with those we
loved here on earth...this thought I say of being disappointed in meeting my friend in the resurection is to be more dreadful than of ceasing to
suffer by a cessation of being."[155] Smith seems never to have doubted the
physical reality of the resurrection. His fear of death was almost exclusively of the possibility that it would disrupt human relationships. He
strongly preferred extinction to eternal loneliness. The faithful could not
be saved without their loved ones.

The solution lay in the temple cultus and Elijah's sealing priesthood.
Something as fragile as regeneration could not justly be the measure of
eternal community. When Smith referred to the durable solution to
Calvinist election he used a New Testament reference to "calling and
election."[156] He identified this "calling and election" as available through
the "Holy Spirit of promise" by which believers are "sealed up unto the
day of redemption."[157] Smith had been promising something like this to
his followers at least since 1835, though the language changed over
time.[158] In his 1844 Elijah sermon, Smith announced that "the spirit &
power of Elijah is to come after [Elias] holding the keys of power building
the Temple to the cap stone placing the seals of the Melchezedeck priesthood up on the house of Israel."[159] For some populist sects, "calling and
election sure" was a synonym for the stage in a Christian's life called sanctification, the level beyond regeneration.[160]

Smith explicitly equated his Elijah with the promise of vanquished
election. To his followers he preached that "we are sealed with the Holy
Spirit of promise ie *Elijah*."[161] He made the point in his characteristi-
cally emphatic way: "could I tell the fact as it is all that heard me would
go home and never say one word more about God or Christ or religion
until they had received that assurance from Heaven which would set
their souls at rest by placing all beyond a doubt."[162] Another sermon on
Elijah was more explicit. "Here is the doctrin of Election that the world
have quarreled so much about but they do not know any thing about
it," he preached; "Elijah is sufficient to make our Calling & Election
sure."[163]

Over the next eight years, Elijah and his prophesied "binding" of the generations came to dominate the temple cultus. With its strong emphasis on seals to salvation, preservation of the body, and the evangelistic mandate of the New Testament, the endowment season in Kirtland constituted and confirmed a holy community invulnerable to the predations of time, distance, and death. In Nauvoo these themes found consummation in a ritually and theologically rich temple system that added a liturgy to guide believers from death to heaven and definitively assure their salvation.

Negotiating Death and Afterlife in Nauvoo

For all their charismatic and sacramental power, in retrospect the Kirtland rites provided only a sketch of the path to heaven. In later years Mormons called the Kirtland liturgy "initiatory" to the dramatic amplifications in Nauvoo. After the second major Kirtland endowment during the church conference of April 1837, further development of temple liturgy was delayed by hostilities with neighbors and disaffected Saints, the Mormon War in Missouri, an extended imprisonment of church leadership, and multiple forced migrations. Cast out to Illinois, the Saints regrouped over the course of 1839. There, for the first time, Smith founded a Mormon utopia from the ground up. He rapidly appropriated an obscure term for "beautiful" from the Psalms, "Nauvoo," for the unwanted, marshy settlement of Commerce on an elbow in the Mississippi River.[1]

Reflecting the ongoing centrality of the temple to Mormonism, Smith announced ambitious plans to replace the Kirtland Temple with a larger structure intended to draw heads of state to the Mormon kingdom on the Mississippi. The incongruity of such grand plans with the high mortality rates that Mormons attributed to geographic dislocations and endemic malaria are stunning and important. The Latter-day Saints settled Nauvoo in the midst of death and built the city in defiance of death. Though he did not live to see the structure completed, Smith used Nauvoo and its temple (see figure 7.1) to unveil rites that brought the promises of the Elijah theology to concrete fruition.

These new ritual forms and the theology behind them drew on themes, ideas, and aspirations that had been present in Mormonism for years. The liturgical development in Nauvoo, however dramatic it might seem at first blush, was remarkably incremental, filling in gaps, expanding the reach of prior teachings and practices. The end goal, the conquest of death

Figure 7.1 The Nauvoo Temple, built in the 1840s, towered over the Mormon city, both architecturally and religiously. Image courtesy of the Church History Library, The Church of Jesus Christ of Latter-day Saints.

through the creation of a society immune to its ravages, remained the same.

The Nauvoo cultus created a society comprising the living and the dead, the mortal and the immortal. Such a society was no mere fraternity or congregation. Because the temple society included supernatural members, the mortals among them required the ability to tell angelic friend from demonic foe. Drawing on New Testament precedents, Smith employed a charism called discernment and a version of the new names of the Book of Revelation to prepare his followers for their entry into the immortal community of the afterlife.

In Nauvoo Smith also studied, amplified, and revised—translated—the symbolic systems of Masonry to augment the ritual foundation for his afterlife theology.[2] Just as he had appropriated hieroglyphs as a means to the end of cosmic enlightenment, Smith plumbed the hidden reaches of Masonic traditions. Importantly, Masonry served as a natural vehicle to frame and express ideas Smith had been working with for years. The tradition Smith translated is a reasonable starting point in the consideration of the death conquest of the Nauvoo Temple cultus.

A Fraternity of Earth and Heaven

Masonry, a significant political and social force in the colonial, revolutionary, and republican periods, left a substantial mark on American history. Probably arising in Britain as fraternal societies in the early seventeenth century whose antecedents—based in medieval artisans' guilds—had existed for perhaps a century or more, Masonic societies were extant throughout Europe and Britain and made their way in significant numbers to America by the middle to late eighteenth century.[3] Many of America's early leaders participated in Masonic lodges: Benjamin Franklin's rise in society was due in no small part to his participation in the fraternity, and George Washington was probably early America's most famous Mason.[4] The Masonry of the revolutionary generation was a paracivic fraternal organization, a social club for largely white male property owners.[5] The fraternity allowed upwardly mobile men to combine together, create political networks, and experiment with solidarity outside established churches. Simultaneously, Masonic lodges provided respite from the sectarian strife of the American religious landscape, an aspiration shared by many religious reformers of the day.[6] For those so inclined, Masonry also provided powerful and ancient symbols that connected their fraternal congresses with the builders of Solomon's Temple, the mythic lost temple of Enoch, the ancient patriarchs and Greek philosophers, and, in the views of many, Father Adam.[7] The esoteric and the common always coexisted in Masonry.

American Masonry had drifted and diffused some by the 1820s, even as it simultaneously grew more explicitly populist and religious (complex transitions mirrored in the ongoing tension between "Modern" and

"Ancient" Masonry). Simultaneously, Masons embraced the rising belief in the great power of knowledge for nonelites.[8] Despite their increasingly religious and progressive views, Masonry elicited mounting resistance among nativists, evangelicals, and even many populists suspicious of "secret combinations" and threatened by the specter of extrademocratic power.[9]

In 1826 an event dramatically amplified national tension over Masonry, creating in the process the Anti-Masonic Party, a major political force—the first third party—that merged into the Whig Party six years later. The event was the murder of William Morgan (1774–1826), a seceding Mason whose former brothers attempted to block publication of his exposé of induction rituals.[10] The censorship campaign culminated in September with his abduction and presumed murder. Kidnapped from the Canandaigua jail—about fifteen miles from the Smiths' home—Morgan became a martyr of national prominence. Public response to the crime decimated the fraternity. In some states lodge participation declined by as much as 90 percent.[11]

Masonry proved difficult to put down, though. After a quiet half decade of torch-carrying by a small cadre of stalwarts, Masons began to regroup slowly in the 1830s, with an increasing emphasis on the higher degrees, those following after the three basic ones that culminated in the degree of Master Mason.[12] By the 1840s, Masonry had returned to a reasonable degree of popularity, a renascence soon to be followed by a massive wave of fraternal associations that dominated American public life in the last decades of the nineteenth century.[13]

Joseph Smith enjoyed a rich and sustained encounter with Masonry, a story that has been obfuscated by both apologists and critics. The few scholars who have engaged the topic have noted similarities in hermetic spirit between the Latter-day Saint and Masonic movements but have failed to acknowledge the wide dissemination of hermetic-sounding ideas in American culture or to investigate the broader contexts of Smith's system.[14] Defenders of the Latter-day Saint churches have most often denied any substantive association, distancing themselves from the opprobrium generally directed at Masonry while simultaneously rejecting allegations of plagiarism. Alternatively, they have maintained that Masonry is an ancient counterfeit of the rites actually practiced in Solomon's Temple, a poor (if prospective) copy of Smith's temple rituals.[15] Critics have maintained that Smith brazenly plagiarized the rites of the fraternal organization of which he became an important if highly unorthodox member, casting doubt on the authenticity of the entire Mormon ritual system.[16] Beyond such polemicization, there are a variety of barriers to a reasoned and persuasive treatment of the intersections of Masonry and Mormonism. Not least among these barriers is the fluidity of Masonic rites, orders, and structures, a remarkable diversity shrouded in a blanket of partial secrecy.[17]

Seceding Masons, betraying their former brethren, published a variety of exposés meant to disclose the secret rites.[18] Devoted Masons countered with their own coded primers, "monitors," designed to maintain the rites in their pure form.[19] Though monitors were preferred, in some places Masons actually used exposés to aid in learning their rites of initiation. Even when sanctioned texts functioned as intended, Masonry contained a variety of orders, systems that varied by national origin and the drift of time, without the standardization that later observers might expect of an esoteric society. No two sources were entirely consistent; interpretations of texts were still less standardized. There was not one Masonry but many, even in the United States. To maintain that any specific belief is Masonic is to say relatively little, as Masons self-consciously attempted to encompass all learning. Still, certain broad generalizations do apply to most of American Masonry, and occasionally Latter-day Saints made clear how and where Mormon belief and practice intersected with Masonry.

Notwithstanding the dynamism of Masonic ritual structures and the uncertainty of the documentary witness (mirrored by even more extreme constraints on publication of the Nauvoo Temple liturgy), a fruitful sketch of the intersections of early Mormonism and Masonry remains possible. The Mormon prophet grew up around Masonry. His older brother Hyrum (Hiram may have been the intended spelling) was a Mason in the 1820s, as were many of the Smiths' neighbors. In the aftermath of the Morgan affair, Joseph Sr. spent a night in jail with one of Morgan's imprisoned abductors.[20] To not be at least dimly aware of Masonry in western New York in the middle to late 1820s was impossible. This need not and likely does not imply any rigorous esoteric training derived from these encounters, but the young Joseph Smith was almost certainly aware of the basic social structures and at least one version of the founding myths of Masonry.

Despite this contextual familiarity, direct borrowings from Masonry are uncertain in the first decade and a half of Smith's religious career. The Book of Mormon, translated in the years after Morgan's abduction, reflects the complexity of any relationships that might have existed at that time. Published in 1830, the first Mormon scripture included a sustained narrative about a band of robbers and murderers named for the bandit leader Gadianton who recovered and employed "secret combinations," a common term then in use to describe purported conspiracies like those of Jesuits or Masons, practices ostensibly dating from Cain's slaughter of his brother Abel.[21] Though a minor part—one marked by no specific awareness of Masonic rites and traditions—in the broader narrative arc of wealth, greed, and pride as the cause of societal degeneration, the Gadianton robbers recur over centuries, united by their secret covenants to perform murder and mayhem. Early American readers noticed these narratives, immediately interpreting the Mormon scripture as an "anti-Masonick Bible." Alexander Campbell in his essay "Delusions" saw the Gadiantons as further evidence that the Book of Mormon was Smith's sophomoric attempt to broach "every error and almost every truth discussed in New York for the last ten years."[22]

Joseph Smith never answered accusations that he had written an anti-Masonic manifesto except to emphasize what he understood as the real messages of the Book of Mormon—the centrality of Christ to human history, the recovery of the heritage of Native peoples, the restoration of miracles, the dangers of rising capitalism, and scripture as memorial binding generations. The Mormon description of these Gadianton bandit groups did not conform to the typical 1820s imagery of Masonry as a powerful conspiracy of white landowners, while questions of public versus private loyalty, orthodox worship, and the transparency of government are perennial issues refracted through rather than defined by the Masonic controversies. Though several early converts were active anti-Masons, Mormons did not use the Book of Mormon as their critics maintained they intended to. Not even William Phelps, an anti-Masonic newspaper editor and politician before his 1831 conversion to Mormonism, found the Mormon scripture useful as an anti-Masonic tract.[23]

Later observers have maintained in parallel that the Book of Mormon and its origin story contain secret echoes of Masonic narratives: the plates interred in the hillside represented Enoch's hidden temple and his triangular golden record, and the Liahona compass paralleled Enoch's cosmic globe, inadvertent pro-Masonic echoes in the anti-Masonic Bible.[24] The comparisons are not entirely persuasive: they ignore the rich idea worlds beyond Mormonism and Masonry, including other traditions of buried wisdom and maps of the cosmos circulating in folk culture from which both Masons and Mormons drew.[25] That contemporaries reasonably versed in Masonry and harshly antipathetic to Mormonism and Masonry did not make these comparisons suggests a lack of traction for this interpretation. Smith's engagement of formal Masonry during this period seems to have been relatively minor.

Missouri Mormonism in 1838 did witness a near miss with Masonic fraternal forms—an impromptu trial of a secret society failed the Saints terribly. Called the Danites or "Sons of Dan" (borrowing a title as Masons and many other Americans were wont to do from an obscure biblical reference) this group, founded to purge Mormon settlements of dissenters, became a sort of guerrilla militia during the Mormon War. When Sampson Avard, the group's notorious leader, came to trial, he both turned against Smith and sketched the outlines of a secret organization designed to protect Mormons in conflict with their neighbors.[26] In this case Mormons seem to have adopted an organizational pattern from the Masons, employing distinctive loyalty oaths and a secret distress signal, though without other apparent Masonic trappings.[27] Under serious criticism, Smith disavowed any connection to the band, although he had supported its beginnings earlier in the year.[28] (His somewhat erratic assistant president Sidney Rigdon appears to have been more directly involved.) After Smith's imprisonment in Liberty, Missouri, the main vestiges of Danitism that remained were the hunger for secrecy and loyalty, themes the Latter-day Saints would treasure when they formally engaged Masonry in the early 1840s. The rites and origin stories of Masonry figured little at this point in time.

Though some authors have suggested Masonic influence in Kirtland (perhaps in the hierarchical pulpits of the temple or the offices of the developing priesthood), there is no persuasive evidence to support this claim.[29] The one apparent use of Masonic phraseology generally adduced, a reference to "the master of assemblies," is actually a common scriptural allusion employed by a variety of Protestants.[30]

The Kirtland-era encounters with Egyptian papyri suggest the time course of Smith's close awareness and use of the fraternity. The Egyptian project serves as a natural point for comparison with Masonry. Masonry resonated with the hieroglyphic culture that Smith had pursued for years. Webb's *Freemason's Monitor* announced that "the usages and customs of masons have ever corresponded with those of the Egyptian philosophers, to which they bear a near affinity. Unwilling to expose their mysteries to vulgar eyes, they concealed their particular tenets, and principles of polity, under hieroglyphical figures; and expressed their notions of government by signs and symbols which they communicated to their Magi alone."[31] Though Masonry would have imparted additional authority to cultural commonplaces, it had no monopoly on hieroglyph culture. This description of hieroglyphs differed little from Noah Webster's *American Dictionary*. In an editorial in the church organ explaining the meaning of the Mormon papyri, Oliver Cowdery, the son and brother of Royal Arch Masons (the Royal Arch was a supplemental degree of the Ancient York Rite, one of two supplemental systems of Anglo-American Masonry), exulted that "Enoch's Pillar, as mentioned by Josephus, is upon the same roll" as the portion of the Book of Abraham, which recorded life in the Garden of Eden.[32] Masons revered Josephus, and their founding myths centered on Enoch's pillar; it is reasonable to see Cowdery as affirming Masonic narratives in this reference. The Saints shared this affection for Josephus—Hyrum Smith owned a copy of his collected works, while Cowdery's reference tied Masonic traditions back to the broader culture that Masonry arose in and referred back to.[33] Some limited Masonic awareness appears to have been present at this stage.

The KEP and the Book of Abraham contain few if any explicit Masonic references, however. Only in 1841–1842, around the time of Smith's formal induction into the fraternity, did explicitly Masonic phrases appear, specifically in the illustrations Smith called facsimiles. The mystically powerful names of the latter 1830s became in these depictions "grand key-words," an identifiably Masonic term.[34] In the 1830s, Smith's study of hieroglyphs reflected his seeric quest for the pure and holy language of the ancient dead (see chapter 5). In the 1840s, when he finally engaged Masonry, his Egyptian project demonstrated that the fraternity could provide another interpretive context for the hieroglyphic quest. The ideas had not changed much, but the language used to describe them had.

Few fragments of Masonry are clearly discernible in Mormonism before the move to Nauvoo, though Smith did develop in that period an unexpected and dramatic personal association. In perhaps one of the stranger turns in American religious history, Joseph Smith took William Morgan's widow, Lucinda née Pendleton (1801–1856), as a plural wife.

The martyr's widow had married George Harris (1780–1857), a former Mason and friend of her dead husband, a half decade after Morgan's death. The Harrises had then joined the Mormon movement together in 1834. By the late 1830s, perhaps 1838, Joseph Smith had apparently married Lucinda in parallel with her continued civil marriage to George Harris.[35] An intermittent anti-Masonic campaigner known to have owned a copy of an exposé in Nauvoo, Lucinda and her civil husband probably discussed Masonry with Smith.[36]

Despite these various prior encounters, events of the 1840s demonstrated how little attention Smith had previously paid to Masonry, formally conceived, before the move to Nauvoo. Smith had access to Masons, exposés, and monitors for years. What pushed him from vague familiarity to active participation is not certain; some of the drive was its theological utility, providing a backdrop for the promulgation of several innovative revisions of and protests against Protestant theology. The role of political concerns in the adoption of Masonry is not entirely clear. Smith's explicit goal for Nauvoo was for international prominence, an ambition that Masonic connections could potentially support. Early on, Mormons could reasonably expect that the fraternity would open doors for them and provide protection from politicians and vigilantes.[37]

Beyond political aspirations, though, Masonry provided a vehicle for expressing themes Smith had been developing for years. The Mormon prophet seems to have toyed with Masonry until he found a use for it, to have held it at bay until he had something to reveal with it.[38] Personal relationships with public figures may have catalyzed this process. Beyond a critical mass of rank-and-file Mormon Masons, Smith welcomed to the fold James Adams, a prominent politician in Springfield, Illinois, and deputy grand master for the state, and John C. Bennett, a wandering opportunist and lover of pomp who hitched his wagon to Mormonism's star for a fateful two years before an explosive, acrimonious defection.[39] Whatever the proximate cause, within a year of their arrival in Illinois Mormons had founded a private lodge, with a dispensation granted in October and the first formal meeting December 29, 1841.[40] Other lodges were soon planted in the fertile soil of Mormon Nauvoo.

In an unusual but not unprecedented act, the Illinois Grand Master Abraham Jonas (1801–1864) raised Smith to the status of Master Mason over the course of March 15–16, 1842.[41] Despite this apparent reprieve from memorizing the induction catechism—one that yielded cries of political opportunism against Jonas and upset many Illinois

Masons—Smith proved an able student of the material.[42] In his first sustained encounter with the Masonic fraternity's esoteric quest, Joseph Smith appropriated new symbols to describe concepts he had been preaching for years, and he seized the opportunity with considerable enthusiasm. James Cummings (1780–1847), the Mormon Master Mason who officiated at Smith's induction, reportedly commented that his prophet seemed "to understand some of the features of the ceremonies better than any mason, and made explanations that rendered them much more beautiful and full of meaning."[43] By the spring of 1842, Smith's formal translation of Masonry had begun.

Death-defying Rites

The basic degrees of the Ancient York rite—Entered Apprentice, Fellow Craft, and Master Mason—offered Smith a panoply of symbols and images. Though not formally available in Illinois, Royal Arch rites also seem to have been available to him, possibly through conversations with Masons or circulating exposés. Masonic degrees, highly symbolic and physical catechisms and induction rituals that emphasized self-mastery, group loyalty, and progressive enlightenment, proliferated among the brotherhood. The degrees were generally limited to the three basic degrees that "entered," "passed," and "raised" initiates, and the four higher degrees—Mark Master, Past Master, Most Excellent Master, and Royal Arch Mason—of the Royal Arch (named for the temple's sacred ninth arch), which "exalted" them.[44] In receiving such degrees, candidates rehearsed obligations to their brethren and committed themselves to secrecy and loyalty. Stripped to the waist, blindfolded, and led by a rope around his neck, a "candidate" endured a series of symbolic threats to his safety in order to prove his loyalty, questing toward greater light in a vaguely deistic perfectionism. In this quest the candidate answered a set of stylized questions to confirm his worthiness and acquire secret knowledge. As important as the words uttered was the "furniture," physical objects that moderns would call props—aprons, scepters, miters, ropes, chairs, and swords. The rites of the higher degrees of Royal Arch Masonry were even more theatrical than the basic degrees of Ancient York Masonry, with rich costumery including robes and crowns, breastplates, multicolored veils, trapdoors, and a voice issuing from a burning bush.[45]

How much of this was the pageantry of a fraternity and how much formal esoteric discipline is controversial. Most modern scholars

separate American Masonry of Joseph Smith's day from formal hermeticism—lodges did not read the *Zohar*, Rosicrucian texts, or Jakob
Böhme (1575–1624). Many Masons were participating in a social club,
despite rising interest in a mythic past.[46] Joseph Smith, though, clearly
saw the mystical power underlying the rites and catechisms. Although
Masonry for the large majority of participants was not as hermetic as
some twentieth-century writers have imagined, Masons acted out and
engaged several interrelated themes, comprising at least four major
motifs: immortality, the sacred power of names, cosmology, and fraternal bonds. Each of these resonated with many Latter-day Saints,
Joseph Smith foremost among them.

Death played a dramatic role in Masonic ritual; the fraternity employed
symbols with strong ties to interment and excavation even from its origins in the seventeenth century.[47] The founding myth, explored in detail
in the third degree of Master Mason, contained "the traditional account
of the death and several burials, and resurrection of Hiram Abiff, the
widow's son."[48] According to the story, which circulated in many permutations, conspiring men murdered Hiram Abiff, the architect of Solomon's
Temple, in pursuit of the secret name of God. As he fell dead, Abiff called
out "O Lord, my God. Is there no help for the widow's son?" a phrase his
followers repeated when they themselves encountered mortal threats.
Unfortunately there was no timely aid for the archetypal widow's son,
and the name of God perished with the sacred builder (some Masonic
panegyrics position Abiff as a figure almost as mighty as Jesus). In part
to recover the holy name, faithful builders sought their lost leader, finally
discovering his corpse in a secret tomb deep within the temple. As they
sought to lift him from his grave, they embraced the corpse, only to discover that his flesh slid off the bones. Central poses and grasps required
of Master Masons were meant to simulate the physical contact that
allowed the extraction of the body from its secret grave within Solomon's
Temple, which had become a sepulchre of sorts by token of Abiff's interment.[49] Such an encounter involved whole bodies in the prescribed close
embrace of a candidate by his examiner.[50] The imagination of death
during the third degree could be stunningly physical, even olfactory: the
due-guard (a sort of phrase of protection) of the third degree was "to
guard their nostrils against the offensive effluvia which arose from the
grave."[51]

In their interpretations of the founding myth, Masons incorporated
prevalent cultural elements surrounding death. Impersonating Abiff

provided a way for Masons to experiment with their own deaths and anticipated resuscitations. Appropriating Hamlet's soliloquy to remind themselves of the lifelong journey toward death, Masons mused: "we are traveling on the level of time to that undiscovered country from whose bourne no traveler has returned."[52] In more general terms they commented "how swiftly the sands run, and how rapidly our lives are drawing to a close…thus wastes man." In their culminating third degree, Masons were reminded that they had "this night represented one of the greatest men that ever lived in the tragical catastrophe of his death, burial, and resurrection." The ritual furniture could bring death to their imagination as well: "the scythe is an emblem of time, which cuts the brittle thread of life, and launches us into eternity." In the midst of this death-beleaguered walk, Masons pledged commitment to an aspiration that was in many ways indistinguishable from that of Protestants. They prayed that they would "die in the hope of a glorious immortality," a fairly typical evangelical phrase that hearkened back to the yearning for election.[53] Different branches of Masonry toyed with death in more and less dramatic ways. In one account of the Knights Templar degree, participants drank from a human "scull," an act "emblematical of the bitter cup of death, of which we must all, sooner or later, taste."[54]

There was another important way that Masons experimented with death. This experiment spoke to the question of whether men controlled their destinies, as they proved themselves willing to sacrifice their lives, to make them forfeit, in the interest of their fraternal community. Just as they simulated raising Abiff, so did they simulate their own deaths if they strayed. The penalty for disclosing the secrets of Masonry was dismemberment followed by denial of proper burial. Their bodies would be burned, their ashes scattered, at a time when burial represented a sacred duty and cremation an anti-Christian desecration.[55] Candidates acted out this gruesome fate, hands drawn across throats like decapitating knives, with hands against the abdomen in a mimesis of evisceration, a practice that offended many outside observers.[56] For participants, these ritual executions underscored the power that Masonry could have over life and death. By pledging their mortal fates to the fraternity, candidates bestowed on the order a symbolic power over life and death. Some of the bloodiness of these images may have derived from the quest to avenge Abiff's murder in other ritual enactments. In fact, in higher degree Masonry, one could advance by exacting bloody revenge on Hiram Abiff's killers.[57]

Alongside and interleaved with the fascination with death and its transcendence stood the Masonic quest for potent words. The Masonic faithful raised the widow's son in order to discover the lost word he carried to his grave. In the first three degrees, candidates learned "new names" for the various handgrips and passkeys required for advancement.[58] Connecting images of death to secret names, the Master's Word of the third degree derived from exclamations made as Masons disinterred Abiff. As with so much of Masonry, there are several versions of the story. The word was proposed variously to be Mal-ha-bone, Mahalbyn, or Machbenah. One source called it "*Macbenah, which signifies, The Builder is smitten.*" Others made more explicit the physical image of Hiram Abiff's decomposing corpse—they interpreted the word to mean "the flesh is off the bones." A more complex interpretation may have been "Muscus Domus Dei Gratia," a phrase Masons translated as "thanks be to God, our master has got a Mossy House."[59] Most of the interpretations emphasized death, the grave, and putrefaction: the sacred word was literally a secret of the grave.

In the advanced degrees, candidates navigated the arches of Enoch's lost temple. The central quest of Royal Arch Masonry was the recovery of God's sacred name, the "grand omnific word." This word was triune—sacred and biblical-sounding names for God, most commonly "Jah-buh-lun, Je-ho-vah, G-o-d."[60] Masonry thereby protected and secretly disclosed God's once unpronounceable name. A giant *G* representing both the science of geometry and the first letter of the grand omnific word hung over the throne of the lodge master, a constant reminder of the power of names. Though reverence for the power of names and metaphysically potent language is by no means limited to the hermeticists, some Masons explicitly recognized their kinship with kabbalists.

As they learned the secret names of the world's past and prepared for their own mortality, Masons also embraced the cosmos. Astronomy, a discipline and diversion that spanned physics and metaphysics, represented a merger of the authority of science and the secrets of the heavens.[61] Astronomy was a sign of education, spanning almanacs and learned treatises. Frontier newspapers published brief astronomical lessons and advertised tutoring in astronomy.[62] The belief in sacred geometry as the order of the universe allowed Masons to see themselves and their fates in the stars. In the first degrees, candidates learned that "by [Masonry] we may discover how the planets move in their orbits, and demonstrate their various revolutions. By it we may account for the return of seasons, and the variety of scenes which each season displays to the discerning eye. Numberless worlds surround us, all formed by the same Divine Architect, which roll through the vast expanse, and all conducted by the same unerring law of nature."[63] Masons conjured the All-seeing Eye, God's supervision of the universe, as the one "whom the Sun, Moon and Stars obey, and under whose watchful care even Comets perform their stupendous revolutions, [and who] pervades the inmost recesses of the human heart, and will reward us according to our merits."[64] Such Masonic ideas differed little from the religious astronomy of natural theologians and the rising scientism of the nineteenth century.[65]

Owning the lost name of God, situating themselves in the cosmos, joining a fraternity more powerful than death, the Masons who were so inclined were awash in metaphysical power. Such Masons could try out titles that honored their quest for knowledge and boundless advancement, becoming not just Masons but princes, kings, and priests.[66] Intentionally mimicking Solomon's selection of twelve knights to rule the tribes of Israel, Masons could bear titles like "Prince of Jerusalem" or "Prince of Masons." The titled pageantry united the other metaphysical themes in a celebration of human potential. This expansive view of participants' future fit well with the perfectionism entertained by many early Methodists and other extreme sectarians, as well as the Latter-day Saints.[67]

A Latter-day Liturgy

Such were the major thematic structures of the Masonry with which Joseph Smith became closely acquainted in the 1840s. The acquaintance proved fruitful. On May 4, 1842, Smith gathered nine loyal followers, most of them Masons, in the upper room of his store, the place where he had entered the fraternity six weeks earlier. He welcomed them to a makeshift stage, one he had reconfigured from its basic Masonic decoration.[68] To his baptisms for the dead, his ritual washings and anointings, his celestial sealings of men to women (see chapter 8) he added new rites that incorporated sacred translations of Masonic rituals alongside dramatic narratives from Latter-day Saint scriptures. (Smith's translation mirrored in its own way the early Christian reappropriation of the Jewish seder into the sacrament of the Eucharist.)[69] Smith's new rites took initiates from the earth's creation on the cosmic stage and the first family in the Garden of Eden to their postmortal exaltations in the celestial kingdom.[70] Instead of the widow's son, the mythic builder Hiram Abiff, Mormons identified in these rites with their first parents, Eve and Adam. Along the way they made commitments to God and their church community as they negotiated passage through life's stages with men representing angels rather than mythic builders. They also received sacred vestments ultimately termed temple garments—the garb of angels—and new names partially patterned on the Book of Revelation.[71] These rites created a secret and venerated group called by many names but best known as the Anointed Quorum. This quorum, the descendant of the Kirtland School of the Prophets, became a major force in 1840s Nauvoo.[72]

Both Masonry and Nauvoo Mormonism shared features with ancient mystery religions, whether participants intended them to or not. Textual memories of these religions were certainly available to the spirited seeker. The Eleusinian mysteries are perhaps the archetype of the immortalist mystery religions.[73] If the fragmentary traditions are reliable, participants in the Eleusinian mysteries gathered in temples to pledge their devotion to the harvest goddess Demeter and her daughter, the resurrection goddess Persephone. Participants imbibed mind-altering substances and enacted rites to secure personal immortality.[74] The story of the temple and religion at Eleusis circulated in Atlantic print culture, both in histories of ancient Greece and speculative treatments of ancient mysteries. Though the conservative Warren Cowdery defamed the pagan rites of Eleusis in the *Messenger and Advocate* in 1837, Nauvoo Temple rites came to enact a Mormon version of an ancient and recurring quest.[75]

If Elijah was the patron of the temple's sealing power, then Adam, Mormonism's Ancient of Days, was the personal face of its catechism. In the Nauvoo Temple cultus, the Saints participated again in Eden's sacred drama. When Smith revealed the endowment in the upper rooms of his red brick store, his assistants forested the sacred chambers with local trees.[76] No longer able to live in their Missouri Eden, they re-created the primal garden in the sacred precincts of the temple. Smith's disciples continued to employ physical objects to evoke the primal forest for the formalized endowments of 1845–1846 performed in the newly dedicated temple. According to William Clayton, they "decorated and set up with shrubs and trees in pots & boxes to represent the Garden of Eden."[77] In this temple, church members often sang Phelps's exultant hymn

"Adam-ondi-Ahman," a celebration of the Missouri Eden and its fate.[78] Temporarily assuming the identities of Adam and Eve, Smith's followers connected themselves via the temple to their lost Zion and the sacred ground of their ancestors.[79] In that state, the Saints rehearsed the key events of Smith's revision of the Genesis cosmogony. In place of Solomon's Temple and Hiram Abiff, Joseph Smith employed the story of cosmic origins he had been elaborating for years without Masonry. The secret codes of Masonry mimicked the pure Adamic language; the Mormon pantheon supplied the truly omnific word. The connections to Adam that the Nauvoo liturgy amplified both personalized the Fall and situated human life on a cosmic scale. By returning to the beginning, the Saints could see the glorious ending.[80] The cosmic catechism also placed believers in the same vast expanse as the Egyptian project, with its revelation of Abrahamic astronomy.[81] In their mind's eyes, Latter-day Saint participants may have recalled the great visions of Enoch, Moses, and Abraham that Smith revealed in his scriptures. Each of these patriarchs experienced a grand ascension vision in which the entire compass of the human family presented itself to his senses.[82] In the Nauvoo rites, to a limited extent, believers gained similar visions of the temporal and spatial history of the universe.

The Nauvoo Temple endowment represents an expression of Smith's sacred worldview phrased as an amplification and reform of Masonry. Just as the KJV had come to hide the "plain and precious" truths of antiquity, so, too, had nineteenth-century Masonry. Whether early Latter-day Saints saw the same designing Hebrew scribes behind both obfuscations is not certain, but Masonry had certainly apostatized from its original in Smith's view. Mysteries of the cosmos and afterlife were buried in Masonry's myths, furniture, intimate greetings, and ritualized utterances. The hermetic catechism and its ritual context were a hieroglyph for Smith to restore and interpret, an artifact that required the attention of a seer, a text in need of translation.

This was certainly how the actual participants understood it.[83] The early Saints believed the temple to represent, at least in part, rites preceding Masonry as those rites had been practiced by their ancestors. Benjamin Johnson (1818–1905) reported that Smith revealed that "Freemasonry, as at present, is the apostate endowment, as sectarian religion is the apostate religion."[84] Willard Richards (1804–1854) reported that "Masonry had its origin in the Priesthood."[85] Joseph Fielding (1797–1863), a devoted English convert whose sister married Hyrum

Smith, called the temple rites "the true Origin of Masonry," while Masonry was a "stepping stone" to the temple.[86] Heber Kimball, noting to Parley Pratt in 1842 that "thare is a similarity of preast Hood in masonary," quoted Smith as teaching that "masonary was taken from preasthood but has become degenrated, but menny things are perfect."[87] Latter-day priesthood, the ancient order of the world, was reflected in fragments of wisdom hidden within Masonry.

Both friends and foes often compared the Anointed Quorum to Masonry. William Clayton (1814–1879), eager to be included, called it "J[oseph]'s lodge," while the critical John C. Bennett called it "Order Lodge" and depicted it without factual basis as a typical Masonic lodge marred by sexual depravity.[88] Despite similarities, the Latter-day Saints managed to distinguish Masonry from their temple worship. As the Masonic fraternity expanded to include perhaps five hundred Mormon Nauvooans, the Anointed Quorum remained elite and compact.[89] The nine slowly became sixty-five by the time of Smith's death.[90] Being anointed was never seen by participants as equivalent to or derivative from being raised to Master Mason or even exalted to Most Excellent Mason. The cultus of the Anointed Quorum was not, to its participants, mere Masonry: it was the mechanics of the celestial fraternity—impervious to death—to which Masonry only alluded and aspired.

Existing as the antechamber to the Anointed Quorum, Masonry per se served a variety of social goals in Mormon Nauvoo. As in other communities, Masonry occupied an important place in the culture of the city. One lodge met in Smith's office quite publicly; its meetings were announced in the newspaper.[91] Smith saw the Masonic Temple built before his own was completed. On April 5, 1844, two days before Smith's most famous sermon, the Latter-day Saints dedicated their Nauvoo Masonic Hall in a great spectacle.[92] As part of this structure, Mormons recapitulated in small part the story of Enoch, placing treasured emblems of Smith's mystical translations—the facsimiles from the papyri and the Kinderhook plates—in a copper box buried inside the cornerstone.[93] At times God himself, the figure behind the mystical capital G hanging over the master's throne, seemed to agree that he was the grand architect of Masonry, as when he spelled out G-O-D with a serpent in the sky above Cincinnati in the spring of 1843, an account of which Mormons reprinted in their papers.[94] Ultimately the Mormon lodges in and around Nauvoo counted almost a thousand Master Masons.[95] While these social ends were public and highly valued, Masonry was most important to the extent that it prepared Latter-day Saints for membership in the Anointed Quorum.

Soon a variety of factors, including fear of Mormon dominance, led the Illinois Grand Lodge to reject Smith, the Latter-day Saints, and the predominantly Mormon lodges in and around Nauvoo. Despite this mounting resistance among the Masonic hierarchy, Smith remained committed to the fraternity. As he faced a deadly vigilante mob, he issued the first words of their distress signal (potent enough to have saved at least one revolutionary soldier from loyalist forces during the War for Independence), though without receiving the covenanted assistance.[96] His Masonic brethren considered him an impostor and a corrupting influence on the "ancient landmarks" of their tradition, and some likely participated in the mob that shot him dead.[97] Their betrayal rapidly led to deep anti-Masonry among Mormons and a collective forgetting of the once vibrant intersections between a fraternal organization with hermetic roots and a radical Restorationist church led by a prophet-seer.

Emphasizing the question of plagiarism, as critics often do when discussing Masonic Mormonism, distracts from the more interesting consideration of the ways Smith translated Masonic rites to serve the ends of his death conquest. A model of Mormon temple liturgy that posits that Smith merely copied Masonry misapprehends both Smith and his religion. Nor, though, is the separation between Masonic and Mormon rites proposed by some Latter-day Saint writers entirely persuasive.[98] The cosmic catechism of Mormonism is similar to the Masonic initiation. The two liturgical systems shared underlying goals. Masons sought to transcend death and achieve a glorious immortality through their rites, creating a society more powerful than death. They cared deeply to know the names of God and the universe around them. So did the Latter-day Saints. Smith employed Masonic symbols, catechisms, and language to explain elements of his vision of life and afterlife. However, the cosmic catechism that translated Masonic induction rituals was only one part of the larger cultus. The Masonic-sounding rites integrated with covenantal seals, baptisms for the dead, ritual cleansings and anointings, and the novel heaven family, a reminder that Smith's system was always much larger than Masonry. In place of the esoteric Romanticism of Masonry, Smith proposed an astoundingly literal and genealogical system. The dead were not dead for Smith. The Nauvoo rites were not pageants but potent religious rituals—enactments in the human microcosm that echoed across the universal macrocosm, determining the postmortal fate of participants. For Smith heaven was achieved, even created, in his Anointed Quorum. Instead of a fraternity of men, however powerful in their future imaginings, members of the Anointed Quorum joined a sacerdotal kingdom and family.[99] The inclusion of women, a rank heresy for American Masons, proved the centrality of family structures to this project. While Kirtland had seen women restricted from certain rites, all Latter-day Saints were eligible to receive the Nauvoo endowment. Through this liturgy Smith familialized the afterlife. Ancestral connectedness proved central to the temple cultus in a way that Masonic hermeticism never quite achieved.

Discernment

The literal involvement of supernatural beings in a ritual fraternity that obliterated death propelled Smith and his followers into a sometimes treacherous realm. Creating relationships with the dead was risky business. Angels could be dark as well as light. Entry into the temple community required the ability to identify other members of the community and exclude outsiders. The fraught act of distinguishing good from evil angels paralleled and exemplified the more mundane problem of telling friend from foe on the early American frontier.[100]

Mormonism and Masonry were sharply, even centrally, concerned with discerning the authorized from the interloper. For both groups, handclasps were not just social pleasantries; they pointed to a complex set of themes that Mormons and radical Protestants understood within the rubric of "discernment of spirits," borrowing language from Paul.[101] Cousin George Smith (1817–1875) remembered twenty-five years after the Mormon prophet's death that "there was no point upon which the Prophet Joseph dwelt more than the discerning of Spirits."[102] George was right to highlight the theme, as Joseph Smith pursued it for most of his religious career. According to Oliver Cowdery, Smith received the gold plates only after Moroni gave him a special vision of the devil's minions who, in retrospect, had been the cause of his desire to sell the plates for money. The angel blessed the Mormon seer with the pronouncement that he would "know hereafter the two powers and never be influenced or overcome by that wicked one."[103] By the spring of 1831, in response to enthusiastic worship in Kirtland, Smith made his view of discernment public in two separate revelations. The first, a restatement of Paul's treatment of spiritual gifts, emphasized the orderly integration of charismata into worship. In the second, Smith turned specifically to the problem of the "false spirits, which have gone forth in the earth." He urged his followers to turn from their enthusiastic exercises to evangelism "by the Spirit, even the Comforter which was sent forth to teach the truth."[104] If an 1842 reminiscence was intended literally, the devil disguised as an angel of light had threatened Smith in the late 1820s; only the intervention of the Archangel Michael saved him.[105]

Handclasps figured prominently in Smith's response to the possibility of dark angels. An 1839 sermon trained apostles how to "detect the devel when he transforms himself nigh unto an angel of light." "When an angel of God appears unto man face to face in personage & reaches out his hand unto the man & he takes hold of the angels hand & feels a substance the Same as one man would in shaking hands with another he may then know that it is an angel of God, & he should place all Confidence in him."[106] A sermon in the winter of 1840–1841 reiterated that "If an Angel or spirit appears offer him your hand; if he is a spirit from God he will stand still and not offer you his hand. If from the Devil he will either shrink back from you or offer his hand, which if he does you will feel nothing."[107] Explaining how it was that traditionally insubstantial beings could seize them by the hand, Smith reassured his followers that "such personages or angels are Saints with there resurrected Bodies." When they performed the Nauvoo liturgy, Mormons were not "operative" Masons establishing guild monopolies, they were angels-to-be socializing with angels, clasping hands with their supernatural brethren.[108]

There is an audacious literalism in Smith's instructions for identifying angels, the expectation that Latter-day Saints would be encountering supernatural visitors, and that they could and should shake hands with them. The American habit of shaking hands, belittled by the eminently English Frances Trollope, represented equality and mutual respect, reassurance of the fraternity of the common man.[109] At times handclasps cemented interpersonal covenants.[110] That angels were prepared to clasp hands with Mormons communicated great respect within a supernatural fraternity. Not only were angels, like all human beings, physical, they were members of the same society. For this exchange to work, though, angels had to be corporeal, a truth Smith had advocated for years; only Satan's demons were denied embodiment (see chapters 2 and 9). In Nauvoo, Mormons were practicing encounters with angels and establishing their eternal relationships to each other.[111] Simultaneously, they were putting the devil down, flaunting their power over incorporeal demons.[112]

Many radical or visionary Protestants worried over the dangers of false spirits. Mainstream believers used the same trope, but their work was much easier—enthusiastic outbursts and apparently miraculous events were caused by false spirits (most believers had not yet transitioned to psychological models for explaining enthusiasm).[113] For the Latter-day Saints this was not just the perennial question of deciding the source of inspiration, though; it was also a question of supernatural community.

As he introduced the Nauvoo liturgy, Smith emphasized to the leading women, recently organized into the Female Relief Society (a cross between an evangelical reform league and a para-Masonic body that prepared women for participation in temple rites), that *keys*—a complex term suggesting special codes, or insights, or modes of power required to decide and govern that drew on biblical, sacerdotal, and Masonic contexts—bestowed the power of discernment. "The keys of the kingdom are about to be given to them [church authorities], that they may be able to detect every things false," he explained in April 1842.[114] Three days later, Smith again preached that "the keys are certain signs and words by which false spirits and personages may be detected from true, which cannot be revealed to the Elders till the Temple is completed.... The devil knows many signs but does not know the sign of the Son of Man, or Jesus. No one can truly say he knows God until he has handled something, and this can only be in the Holiest of Holies."[115] The latter phrase, a reference to an assembly of Master Masons in Masonry, was in Smith's hands a more direct allusion to the Old Testament. Three days later Smith taught his followers how to greet, try, and satisfy the angelic beings they could expect to encounter through their lives and afterlives. Smith's pronouncements highlighted the three major themes of discernment: the physicality of angels—whose hands believers could clasp and with whom they could create societies; the management of mystical experience; and the nature of secret human societies.

Angels were not the only visitors who could hide nefarious intentions beneath a misleading facade. Just as demonic angels could deceive the unwitting, so could disingenuous human beings. The problem of creating networks of trust pressed hard upon Americans of the antebellum frontier. In its new towns and cities, large numbers of strangers encountered each other without the luxury of shared history. In many cases they had not grown up near each other, did not know each other's parents and grandparents. Neither secular nor religious associations were immune. Itinerant and loosely organized faiths like the Baptists suffered particularly from people they characterized as false preachers and frauds.[116] Similar concerns arose over business transactions, amid an expanding economy and marked geographic instability. These problems came close to early Mormonism. Smith's father had lost the family's savings to a ginseng export scheme in 1802 because his business associates proved untrustworthy. For some, extended family networks proved the key to the problem of trust on the frontier.[117] For many others, either certificates from known church bodies (easily forged) or Masonic secrets (potentially decoded from exposés) served as safeguards for reliability. With a growing reputation for debauchery and immunity to legal prosecution (unmerited according to the Saints but still widely believed) superimposed on the sheer demographics of a region exploding in population, Mormon Nauvoo suffered from the problem of interpersonal unreliability to a significant degree. Smith served as a magnet for opportunists; a seeming multitude of them hitched wagons to the rising star of the church, before turning away in fury. In the Nauvoo Temple cultus Smith finally had a reliable, ritual way to distinguish friend from foe, one that merged the strengths of Masonry with the structure of his ecclesiastical organization.[118]

The Names of Things

Central to the process of discernment was the development within the temple cultus of ritual names for participants. Reflecting the quest for primal language (chapter 5), the power of seer stones (chapter 3), the seal of Christ (chapter 6), and the act of adoption into the family of Christ (chapter 8), Mormon participants in the temple liturgy received "new names." Such names evolved from the general sense of bearing Christ's name to an emblem of the cosmic familialization of the temple cultus.[119]

As with all of the Nauvoo cultus, new names had antecedents in broader Christianity. In earliest Mormonism such names bore the plain sense of Isaiah 62:2, which announced that the followers of Jehovah "will have a new name."[120] Mormons sang of the new name from their first hymnal and praised it in published essays.[121] Mormons expected God to call his people by a new name, something the Book of Mormon proposed as part of their baptismal and Eucharistic rites.[122] The name Protestants and Latter-day Saints acquired was the name of Christ, a mark that they belonged to him.

By 1836 the Saints had begun to identify special names with Smith's interpreter stones via creative exegesis of Revelation (2:17 and 3:12). Such was the import of Joseph Sr.'s blessing that Lewis Robbins would receive "a white stone with a new name written thereon."[123] These passages, understood by Adam Clarke to refer to tesserae, small stones proving one's rights to inclusion in a pagan festival, yielded to a variety of interpretations across Christianity.[124] Though Clarke, a Methodist, did not make the comparison, the communion tokens of Presbyterian holy fairs were a modern version of this stone, and one of the possible proximate exemplars of the white Mormon stones.[125] In Nauvoo, the association between stones, names, and tokens became firmer still. By the 1840s Smith had made clear that he had a stone, *gazelem*, that probably contained his own sacred name (see chapter 5).

In the Egyptian project, names were clearly central to the ancient, holy language. The ancient pictographic glyphs Smith invested such energy in were not simply words; they were, in their very essence, names. Language, after all, began for antebellum Christians with Adam's naming of the animal creation. The pursuit of such names animated the Egyptian scripture. In those hieroglyphs the Saints discovered exotic names no one else knew, names like Ahman, Phah Eh, or Ki Ahbroam. Smith had shared with his Saints names like Laman, Moriancumer, and Deseret for years, relics of ancient Hebrew or even Adamic gleaned from the pages of the Book of Mormon. More traditionally, Smith took special pleasure as a translator in decoding the Hebrew names of figures in the Bible, finding the deeper meanings of names like Adam, Cain, and Abel.[126] In the early movement, some leading Saints applied these names directly to themselves. To protect their communalist property covenant in Kirtland, Church leaders used code names in published revelations. These were dramatic biblical and biblical-sounding names, including Barauch Ale, Enoch, Mahalaleel, Shalemanasseh, and several others.[127] By the Nauvoo period the Saints had spent over a decade experimenting with the names of the ancients, trying them on, feeling pride at their mastery, savoring their ancient or hidden meanings. In Nauvoo such names became much more personal.

The Nauvoo Temple rites concerned themselves intimately with names and holy language. Beyond a petitionary prayer uttered in Adamic, the temple gave Latter-day Saints access to sacred names as old as the world, perhaps older. In ongoing exegesis of Revelation, Smith returned to the theme of the white stones for believers, preaching that in these stones a "new name" would be revealed symbolically, if not literally.[128] These names proved to be continuous with the sacred seals Mormons had been pursuing for years. Through them the Saints knew how they would be addressed in the eternities and how in turn they would address the eternities. The new name of the temple connected believers to ancestors as well as to the heaven from which they sprang and to which they would return.

Over time Smith clarified that new names were to be the conduits through which revelation came. In 1840 Smith preached that the Melchizedek priesthood, closely associated with temple liturgy, holds "the keys of the Kingdom of God in all ages of the world to the latest posterity on the Earth and is the channel through which all knowledge . . . is revealed from heaven."[129] Five months later Smith explained that the names of certain patriarchs were central to this process of seeking revelation. He explained in a spring sermon: "In asking have Referance to a personage Like Adam for God made Adam Just in his own Image [.] Now this [is] a key for you to know how to ask & obtain."[130]

Through the Mormon Chain of Belonging (see chapter 8) Smith proposed, believers could gain access to God via sacred ancestors. Names were central to the process of such revelation. Smith's followers stayed true to this vision of the names of ancient patriarchs as conduits for revelation. According to Brigham Young, "Adam['s] name was more Ancient than he was it was the name of a man long before him, who enjoyed the priesthood. New name should be after some Ancient Man whereby you are enabled to ask for present future & past."[131] These names, personal connections with the ancient dead, functioned like supernatural communion tokens to bestow access to the paschal table of the Lord's Supper. Instead of the initials of the minister or church, or even a scriptural passage, the figurative Mormon tokens contained the eternal names of the believers. Adam, archetypically, learned his own name through a *gazelem* stone.[132] Brigham Young, a careful student of Smith's metaphysics, preached that believers "should want to address the th[ro]ne to enquire after Ancient things which transpired on to plannets that roled away before this Plannet came into existence—I should use my New Name which is Ancient & refered to Ancient things."[133] Young's claim followed Smith's 1840 teachings on the meaning of priesthood keys as "channels" by which God revealed the mysteries. Early patriarch Isaac Morley (1786–1865) told Lorenzo Snow (1814–1901): "Ask and thou shalt receive the gift and blessing of a white stone in that stone a new name written that no man knoweth save him to whom it is given. And thro' & by that blessing thou shallt attain to the faith once delivered to the Saints."[134] Through the ancient names vouchsafed by seer stones, the Saints could participate in the experience of Adam and the creation of the cosmos, a history stretching eons before the creation stories told in Genesis. The names by which they came to be called in the temple liturgy were names that antedated the entire Bible.

In his 1844 King Follett Discourse, Smith emphasized the power of names rightly understood. Though the transcripts of the sermon are somewhat muddled on this point, Smith's beliefs are reasonably clear. Flaunting his linguistic knowledge, Smith announced that the Greek New Testament "talks about Yachaubon the son of Zebedee—means Jacob." By comparison, the King James Version of "the N[ew] T[estament] says James—now if Jacob had the keys you might talk about James and never get the keys." Keys were potent words—sacred names—obtained through temple rites. These names were crucial to the order of the universe; failure to use them correctly risked the loss of salvation. Another transcript of the sermon has Smith asking, "How can we escape the damnation of hell unless God be with us—Men bind us with chains—Read from the Hebrew Yingacoub—Jacob. Greek Ichobon—Jacob."[135] In the phrasing of another sermon transcript, "you may talk about James thro all Eternity" and still not "escape the d[amnatio]n. of hell."[136] Simply put, if the patriarch's name was Jacob, he could never provide keys to someone calling him James.[137] Conversely, someone who did know a patriarch's ancient name might gain access to his keys. Just as calling God Baal was idolatry, so was calling Jacob James. Even God, greatest and most ancient of the patriarchs, had a name in this language. According to Smith, years earlier, "Great God has a name by which he will be called which is Ahman."[138]

To outsiders the King Follett Discourse demonstrated Smith's confidence in his abilities as a translator, the glorying of an autodidact at his superficial knowledge of foreign languages. To those within the inner circle, though, Smith was alluding to his temple and its holy use of language, Adamic as refracted through biblical Hebrew. By knowing the true names of things, the Saints gained access to true worship. The hieroglyphic quest of the 1830s had come to fruition in the new names of the Nauvoo liturgy.[139] For the Anointed Saints, the secret of Jacob and James was a secret for the eternities, an appropriation of the cosmos, past and future.

The Final Conquest of Death

Names, discernment, and induction into a celestial kindred all pointed toward a mystical capacity to negotiate the afterlife safely. According to a posthumous entry in Smith's official diary, he called the Nauvoo endowment the "principles and order of the priesthood." This "order pertaining to the Ancient of days" represented "all those plans & principles by which any one is enabled to secure the fulness of those blessings [to] come up and abide in the presence of the Eloheim in the eternal worlds."[140] The act of "coming up" referred to passage through a series of angels, gatekeepers of the celestial kingdom of Elohim, the mighty God of the Old Testament.[141] Much as Masons traversed a gauntlet of fellow Masons in their inductions, Mormons prepared to traverse a gauntlet of angels en route to their final integration into the society of heaven.

The end goal of the cosmic catechism of the Nauvoo Temple was the ritual transformation of believers into immortal members of the society of heaven. Brigham Young encapsulated Smith's view of the temple in an 1853 sermon: "Your endowment is, to receive all those ordinances in the House of the Lord, which are necessary for you, after you have departed this life, to enable you to walk back to the presence of the Father, passing the angels who stand as sentinels, being enabled to give them the key words, the signs and tokens, pertaining to the Holy Priesthood, and gain your eternal exaltation in spite of earth and hell."[142] This end was what Smith and his followers had been moving toward for years.

Each time assured salvation appeared close at hand, it seemed that a new rite was required. For the Nauvoo liturgy, Smith returned to the purification and anointing of Kirtland. Answering the Protestant concept of sanctification as the stage beyond regeneration, Smith reconceived anointing in Nauvoo. Smith's Nauvoo reappropriation of the Kirtland anointing was the sacramental parallel of the higher life promised to Protestants through the "second blessing."[143] The power of the Nauvoo anointing lay in its ability to resolve doubts that naturally arose for those who had been sealed or anointed in Kirtland. Sometimes it seems to a modern observer that it was hard for participants to be certain that the Kirtland sacraments could save, that their effect could be permanent. A lot had changed in the years since Kirtland. The Nauvoo anointing confirmed that original assurance. The crowning Nauvoo rite prepared the body for its great transition, as believers "annointed" spouses for "burial" in order to "have claim upon" each other "in the morning of the first Reserrection."[144]

This amplification and revision of the Kirtland anointings drew from the New Testament story of the woman (traditionally Mary Magdalene) who anoints Jesus's feet with spikenard in Mark 14:6–9 ("she is come aforehand to anoint my body to the burying"), one that Latter-day Saints merged with other New Testament narratives.[145] Smith took Jesus at his word, as did his brother Hyrum, who blessed Addison Pratt, heading to the South Pacific as an evangelist in 1843, "you shall receive the anointing and the endowment...and your body prepared for the burial."[146] Brigham Young perpetuated Smith's teaching and practice after his death.[147]

While it is tempting to attribute the funerary overtones of this rite to idiosyncratic exegesis of the spikenard story by Mormon primitivists, Smith and his followers did not simply echo the New Testament text. They integrated the image of a woman anointing Jesus's feet into their broader system of seals, covenants, anointing, and the conquest of death. In the images of ancient embalming (the Marcan narrative prefigured Mary's visit to the empty tomb with embalming herbs) the Saints seem also to have recalled the sweet oils of Old Testament priestly rites, the chrisms they had physically mimicked with cinnamon-flavored whiskey and lavender-scented oil. Physical and metaphysical touching, augmented by sacred liquids, prepared the Saints, as their Savior before them, for the temporary grave of the righteous. The association between temple liturgy and death was so close that anointing for burial actually occasionally occurred on deathbeds.[148]

The Nauvoo rites promised participants power over their own election. In these rites the Mormon seer had finally and fully conquered election and banished the specter of backsliding. While immensely reassuring, this power could be dangerous, as evangelical critics observed. To describe the Saints, critics at times employed a timeworn phrase of opprobrium, "antinomianism," the doctrine that saved believers were beyond the law and could safely ignore it.[149] In the American debates over antinomianism, the question of knowing one's election status prospectively and the ramifications of such knowledge were never far from the surface.[150] In practice antinomianism became a term of derision applied to those who sought greater certainty of salvation and sanctification or who rejected ecclesiastical or creedal strictures. Mainstream Calvinism had maintained the Perseverance of the Saints for centuries. In practice the theological construct of Perseverance was unreliable for believers, never certain of their own election to begin with. Because election could not be known beforehand, gross sins after entering a church covenant were proof that claims to regeneration had been illusory all along, rather than being lost through sin. For many of those branded antinomian, this fragile uncertainty negated the promise of Perseverance and gave the lie to the experience of regeneration.[151]

By most contemporary definitions, antinomianism opposed both orthodox Protestantism and the sacramentalism usually associated with Catholicism. In practice, though, groups characterized as antinomian occasionally emphasized the power of certain observances. Most often they chose the Lord's Supper, the sacrament associated with holy seasons and camp meetings. Smith's temple was a complex fusion of sacramentalism, sanctification, and antinomianism, what historian John Brooke has called "institutionalized antinomianism."[152] In Nauvoo, Mormons secured the certainty of salvation not so much in the internal states of sanctification or second blessing as in the external rites of the temple, a heavenly future vouchsafed by a sacramental present. The confusion over when exactly the endowment had occurred in Kirtland, reflecting the affective regeneration of the 1830s rites, was largely absent in Nauvoo. Though participants were deeply moved spiritually by their new endowments, the Nauvoo Temple liturgy represented an actual sacrament, a rite determining salvation. The final attainment of election came with the physical ritual of the Nauvoo anointing. The clean water and oil, now set within the Nauvoo cultus and explicitly binding people across the chasm of death, actually assured their salvation. As opposed to the extreme unction of Catholicism, the Mormon unction sealed the believer to heaven long before she lay on her deathbed.

Smith worked up to the sacrament of certain election over the course of the last decade of his life. The relevant kernel was present in the earliest church. The Book of Mormon and New Translation of the Bible both investigated the possibility of special believers possessing either certain election or the supernatural capacity to bind heaven. Around 100 BCE, God said to Alma, a high priest who had resisted the execution of a martyr named Abinadi, "I covenant with thee, that thou shalt have eternal life."[153] A late namesake of Nephi, living around the time of Christ, pronounced

several unpopular prophecies and stood by them despite rancor and persecution on the part of the society he criticized. In response God blessed
this later Nephi with the promise that "all things shall be done unto thee
according to thy word." Specifically and pregnantly, this power was
phrased as part of the power to "seal on earth" people and connections
such that they "shall be sealed in heaven."[154] The same was true of Enoch
and Moses in the New Translation.[155] Enoch was so powerful that he
commanded the mountains and rivers in a battle to defend his people
and then led his entire city through the process of "translation," a merger
of election and the immediate conquest of death in which participants
were mystically transformed from mortal to immortal.[156]

Anointing in Nauvoo served as a synecdoche for the salvational power
of the entire temple liturgy. In the 1843 amplification of the new and
everlasting covenant that authorized polygamy, Smith privately explained
that the seals of the temple were sufficient to finally guarantee one's place
in "the Lamb's Book of Life." Only "murder, whereby to shed innocent
blood" and recanting the temple covenant could imperil salvation for
those who had been anointed and sealed. Using the language he elsewhere used to describe the postmortal force of the Nauvoo endowment,
Smith informed the Anointed Quorum through the 1843 polygamy revelation that those who participate in polygamy "shall pass by the angels,
and the gods, which are set there, to their exaltation and glory in all
things."[157] Some have proposed that this emphasis in the revelation was
an intentional salve to the conscience of participants in polygamy, but
this account ignores the substantial history of the pursuit of certain
election long before the implementation of polygamy.[158]

Though the polygamy revelation was not widely disseminated
before Smith's death, he further explained his vision of salvational
surety in a March 1844 sermon on Elijah. Charting "a road between" the
"Presbyterian" (Calvinism) and the "Methodist" (Arminianism), Smith
described the nature of sin after sealing: murder or rejecting the covenant would leave no chance for complete repentance—though, like King
David, such sinners would be spared an eternity in hell.[159]

Mormon antinomianism had parallels in Methodist sanctification, a
set of beliefs and practices advocated by Wesley that receded as
Methodism moved into the mainstream. For early Methodists, sanctification was the stage beyond conversion, often the result of the
constant introspection and piety of weekly class meetings and
occasional revivals that brought the regenerated believer to a holy

perfection through the visitation of the Spirit. Smith's antinomianism differed from the Protestant phenomena that preceded him. Rather than a protest against the empty formalism of law, Smith expressed both a visceral yearning for a secure death and a reliance on sacraments. During rising controversies over polygamy and ongoing criticism that he was not pious enough to be a prophet, Smith told his followers "he would take us there [to heaven] as his backload." In telling his people he would carry them to heaven on his back, he meant that the sacraments he was revealing would be adequate to ensure their place in heaven in a way that Victorian piety and the endless flight from backsliding never could. In the context of such a sacramental relationship, there was no room for small-minded criticisms of impious behaviors. He promised his followers that "if we would not accuse him he would not accuse us."[160]

As with the rest of the temple cultus, the individual and social coexisted in the culminating rite and its sacramental security against sin. The Nauvoo anointing of the body for burial was specifically to allow people to "have claim on" their loved ones at the time of the resurrection, rather than merely an individualistic preparation for death. The early Saints, under Smith's direction, literalized and expanded a figurative reference in the New Testament, integrating it into their temple experience. This rite maintained family relationships: spouses prepared each other for burial so that death could not separate them. Just as they were sealed as Christ's to eternal life, so were they sealed as each other's to rise in the resurrection. Instead of raising Hiram Abiff from the grave, Mormons practiced raising each other; the mystical names they learned included their own, names that situated them in the cosmic past and heavenly future. The Mormon tokens were supernaturalized sureties of their participation in the celestial fraternity of angels. The power of these rites remained with Smith to the very end. According to one visitor to Smith's jail cell in Carthage, Illinois (see chapter 10), the night before his death Smith described "the secret of godliness," a coded reference to temple rites, to a select group of followers in preparation for the Smith brothers "to go to their joy." In the phrase of a member of that group, the cell in the county jail became "the gate of paradise for" those Latter-day Saints.[161]

Even with salvation assured, though, the Saints were not eager to die. With rare exceptions, the conquest of death is no rush to die; it is an attempt to live without fear. The immortalism of the 1830s persisted as a hope that not only was salvation secured but also death would not even temporarily disrupt community. The Nauvoo cultus provided concrete, often specific, reassurances to Latter-day Saints hoping for long life. The prospect of immortality was never very far away. Assembling in the temple, the Saints prayed that they would live "three score years and ten," a reference to the Psalmist's prayer for longevity (90:10), what many Christians understood as the divinely decreed human life span, "the common age of man."[162] In June 1842 Smith promised the Psalmist's seventy years to "that soul that has righteousness enough to ask God in the secret place for life every day of their lives."[163] As for many of their peers, such a life span represented a promise of God's satisfaction with their efforts, a major theme in the patriarchal blessings of the 1830s. The Anointed Quorum continued the theme, as in its group prayer of June 26, 1842, when its members pleaded with God that "His chosen might be blessed and live to man's appointed age."[164] In their negotiations with Providence, the Latter-day Saints, like many Protestants, held out a hopeful insistence that God would respect their earnest desire to die at an advanced age.

As in Kirtland, the physical rites of the temple proved difficult to disentangle from faith healing; by the time of Nauvoo, healings with anointing oil had come into their own, an ongoing merger of power from on high with the physical rites of temporal and eternal salvation. In Nauvoo both anointing and faith healing continued to expand.[165] The sacred bathing of the Kirtland rites found a home in the multivalent and metaphysically potent font that stood in the temple basement on the backs of biblical oxen, emblems of the tribes of Israel. The font, dedicated long before the rest of the temple, was to be the liquid grave that allowed the Saints to seal their dead to themselves and to exaltation, the rite they called baptism for the dead (see chapter 8). The font's power extended to mortals in their negotiation with their own deaths as well. Into the waters that sealed their ancestors to heaven came the Latter-day Saints to be healed in body as they were restored in spirit. For the Saints the font was a modern pool at Bethsaida, one whose waters the ever-proximate angels troubled, filling them with miraculous power.[166] Such healing baptisms were meant to occur only within the departments of the temple.[167] Even the sacred vestments of the temple liturgy, the clothing of heaven, was felt by many to have special powers to prolong life, as if dressing as angels could bestow angelic invulnerability.[168] As ill-informed as John C. Bennett could be about Mormonism, he rightly appreciated the connection between the temple and the death conquest. In Bennett's phrase, Mormons "believe that the shirts will preserve them from death, and secure to them an earthly immortality."[169] After Joseph and Hyrum's June 1844 murder, some Saints wondered whether the brothers might have survived had they worn their temple clothing; Willard Richards credited his lack of wounds to wearing his garment.[170] Once again, aspects of ritual Mormonism proved crucial both to the death conquest and to their vulnerability to criticism when, inevitably, one of their number fell prey to the King of Terrors.

After Smith died in 1844, the completion of the temple became the raison d'être for the main body of the church under Brigham Young. Smith had not lived to see the new rites performed there, or to codify them. That work he left to the Anointed Quorum led by Brigham Young and his allies. The apostles' control of the temple rites gave them great power in dealing with other potential successors in the aftermath of Smith's murder.[171] Smith had required the temple's construction by revelation, and in the temple Latter-day Saints sealed their heritage from Smith. Performance of temple rites kept the Saints in the United States longer than they should have remained, but the faithful felt they had no choice.[172] During their last winter in Nauvoo, Latter-day Saints performed endowment and related ceremonies for up to twenty hours a day, posting twenty-four-hour guards and hiding from vigilante groups and lawmen. The temple rites steeled their resolve for the migration ahead, bound them as a society on earth and in heaven, and made their calling and election certain. Even as they faced vigilante violence in their City of Joseph (the Mormon name for Nauvoo after Smith's death), the Saints loyal to the apostles clung to the ground where their martyrs lay until they could seal themselves into the heaven family. The memory of those rites carried them through the twenty-year hiatus between functioning temples and cemented the associations that proved central to the persistence of the church that Young led.

How best to understand the Mormon temple is a matter of some controversy. Latter-day Saints maintain that the temple liturgy is the order of heaven, rituals observed by Father Adam himself, and the culminating sacrament of Christ's church. In this view they have stayed true to Smith's animating vision. For outsiders this sort of confessional explanation will prove unsatisfactory. Regardless of the provenance of this liturgy, though, there is much to be learned from understanding how these rites unfolded contextually, and what problems they addressed for participants. Some scholars, most notably Richard Bushman, have argued that the temple was the codification of early Mormon enthusiastic impulses, the ritual and symbolic canon that allowed energetic spirituality to be constrained into a persisting church body.[173] The temple almost certainly played such a role, allowing a church organization to accommodate strong spiritual and mystical impulses. The cultus was also, though, an infrastructure to overcome death and the vagaries of election. A variety of voices in early Mormonism, most visibly the Prophet and his father (before his death from consumption in 1840) hoped urgently for long life and secure salvation. In the temple Latter-day Saints had not just fervent hopes and prayerful promises; they possessed a set of instructions and a collection of physical and metaphysical acts that assured them of the desired result. In a manner of speaking, the Saints participated in a heavily biblicized mystery religion. Negotiating the space between Calvinists and Arminians, speaking to issues of vital importance in the history of Christianity, they saw their way clear to a society on the other side of the gulf of death.

Translating Masonry in 1842 as he had previously translated hieroglyphs, metal plates, the Authorized Bible, and Protestant theology, Joseph Smith developed a ritual framework for immortality and eternal life. In this system Smith came full circle back to a revelation in his preface to the Pentateuch, in which God announced: "this is my work [and] my glory, to [bring to pass] the immortality & the eternal life of man."[174] In the temple, the Latter-day Saints were inducted—adopted—into a cosmological fraternity, a family of humans, angels, and Gods, a group of beings with ancient names belonging to the species "Ahman" (see chapters 8 and 9). As they performed the rites of their temple the Saints joined the society of heaven by creating a chapter on earth.

8

The "Lineage of My Preasthood" and the Chain of Belonging

A well-born son of Pennsylvania landowners, John Milton Bernhisel (1799–1881) was an elegant gentleman, a graduate of the University of Pennsylvania practicing medicine in New York City, when itinerant elders preached him the Latter-day Saint Gospel in the late 1830s. The middle-aged doctor converted and rapidly rose through church leadership ranks. After a brief stint as the New York church's presiding elder, Bernhisel moved to Nauvoo in 1843. A confirmed bachelor, he boarded with Joseph Smith's family, providing political and medical advice, even delivering Smith's child. The same year, eight months before Smith's death, Bernhisel, still unmarried at the age of forty-four, participated in a distinctive ritual that changed his kinship forever.[1] An affidavit-like note in Smith's official journal reports:

> The following named deceased persons were sealed to me (John M. Bernhisel) on Oct[ober] 26th 1843, by President Joseph Smith: Maria Bernhisel, sister; Brother Samuel's wife, Catherine Kremer; Mary Shatto, (Aunt); Madalena Lupferd, (distant relative); Catherine Bernhisel, Aunt; Hannah Bower, Aunt; Elizabeth Sheively, Aunt; Hannah Bower, cousin; Maria Lawrence, (intimate friend); Sarah Crosby, intimate friend, / died May 11th 1839/; Mary Ann Bloom, cousin.[2]

In this curious transaction, Bernhisel became eternal husband (or brother or father) to eleven deceased friends and relatives, including his sister, his brother's wife, and four aunts. The seals of the Kirtland Temple cultus had broadened and deepened from assured salvation to a metaphysical cement for relationships imperiled by death.

Bernhisel's family continued to expand in Nauvoo. On February 3, 1846, Bernhisel "came to the sacred Alt[a]r in the upper room of the 'House of the Lord'... and there upon gave himself to Prest. Joseph Smith (martyred) to become his son by the law of adoption and to become a legal heir to all the blessings bestowed upon Joseph Smith pertaining to exaltations even unto the eternal Godhead."[3] In this rite the now-dead prophet became Bernhisel's ritual father. The final phrase of the description of this adoption ceremony made clear the ultimate destination of these familial connections—"exaltations" that extended all the way to the "eternal Godhead," terms Latter-day Saints understood differently from Protestants. By the power of Smith's priesthood, this adoptive ritual integrated Bernhisel into a sacred scale of exaltation that ultimately encompassed God himself (see chapter 9).

Armed with this holy sonship, the doctor took his adopted father's widow, Melissa Lott (1824–1898), as a levirate wife (the widow of a kinsman married for religious or cultural reasons) in 1846, briefly engaging in polygamy with living spouses before settling in Utah on the youngest of his wives.[4] In the 1860s, by then an earthly monogamist and prominent Utah politician, Bernhisel took another 106 deceased women as plural wives.[5] Chained to Smith's sacerdotal family even as he was the patriarch of his own kindred, Bernhisel had the assurance of glory and security in the life to come. When he finally died, Bernhisel was the first-degree celestial relative of hundreds of people. In the strikingly communal idiom of Mormon salvation, heaven for the loyal doctor had begun well before he closed his eyes in death.

Bernhisel's story emblematizes the distinctive family system that Smith elaborated over the last decade of his life. The doctor was one of hundreds, then thousands, who entered Smith's celestial kindred through temple-associated rites. This heaven family, a sacerdotal genealogy extending backward past the Garden of Eden and forward to a glorious future, became the doctrinal and ritual core of Smith's legacy. Through this heaven family, all of humanity could be interconnected in indissoluble bonds—the broad kinship group was the actual structure of heaven. Drawing on antecedents in evangelicalism, the diluted Swedenborgianism that contributed to the domestic heaven, the Neoplatonic Chain of Being, and metaphysical Israelitism, the Mormon heaven family provided a network of eternal belonging for the Latter-day Saints. This heaven family became the organizational implementation of Smith's soteriological assault on the opposing poles of antebellum Protestantism: Calvinism and Arminianism. In place of election or conversion of the will without backsliding, Smith proposed a sacramental guarantee of salvation that was in its essence communal.

As Smith refracted, reformed, and translated several interwoven ritual and theological systems, his heaven family developed in step with his temple liturgy, both of them situated firmly within other aspects of early Mormonism. Beginning in the early 1830s with a "patriarchal" priesthood and associated patriarchal blessings, the heaven family incorporated a new mode of Christian adoption, baptism for the dead, and eternal and plural marriage, all in a novel genealogical reformation of the Great Chain of Being. Fundamentally, Smith was dealing with certain basic questions: How big was the society of heaven? Who could and would join it—what did election mean? How would it be entered—what were the mechanics of salvation? What did the afterlife society have to do with salvation? What happened to one's offspring in the afterlife; could their salvation be guaranteed? What role did one's ancestors play in the salvation community? These questions proved to have multiple, complex, interwoven answers. Together, these answers constituted a sacerdotal kindred, a heaven protected from loneliness and heartache by the restoration of the divine family.

The Domestic Heaven

Smith's heaven family entered active debates within American Protestantism about the shape and nature of heaven. Though closely related to holy death culture, these debates extended beyond it. For orthodox Calvinists—particularly the clergy—the heaven of Augustine, dubbed "theocentric" by scholars, ruled the day. This theocentric model of the afterlife emphasized the majesty of God at the expense of human relationships. Worthy believers would in the afterlife pay no attention to other humans, as all creatures and their creaturely associations paled in comparison with God's divine glory. The strict division proposed by some between theocentrism and other models is not entirely secure, and there are justifiable questions over whether theocentrism ever represented the religious belief of nonelites: for example, individuals as orthodox as Jonathan Edwards and his family occasionally expressed sentiments related to afterlife reunions seemingly incompatible with theocentrism.[6] Scholarly reservations regarding the nature of the division between domestic and theocentric traditions should not push too far in the other direction, though. Tendencies clearly compatible with theocentrism are demonstrably present in Reformed Christianity, and although frank Calvinism was on the wane, Presbyterians and Congregationalists continued to wield considerable intellectual influence in nineteenth-century America.[7]

Never entirely without critics and holdouts, theocentrism had a formidable adversary in the early republic. With the rise of the populist evangelical movements—primarily the Methodists and Baptists, though all traditions were affected—came much greater attention to human relationships in the afterlife. Although some details of its history remain controversial, a rising sentimentalism, combined with Romanticism, populism, and centrifugal social pressures, provided support for what has been called the domestic heaven. With roots in the secular lovers' gardens of the Renaissance and Swedenborg's highly physical vision of afterlife, the rising heaven of American Protestantism was a place of happy reunions of believers and the persistence of family associations, the sacred land where "parting is no more."[8] God remained supreme, but kith and kin could recognize each other and potentially resume their relationships after death had curtailed them.

Though the flowering of the domestic heaven is often dated to the postbellum period and America's attempt to come to terms with the mass death of the Civil War, domestic sensibilities about death and afterlife figured prominently in antebellum culture as well.[9] The domestic heaven reflected and affected theological and social trends even as it ordered Protestant responses to death. This new heaven was compatible with a much more egalitarian view of religion than arbitrary election of the saved, even as the Arminianism that often accompanied it left open the ominous possibility of backsliding.[10]

In the perceived social disruption of massive migration, increasing religious voluntarism, the rise of democratic ideals, and limited and unreliable lines of communication, older models of integrated societies strained and often broke. The individual mattered more in this new world, felt more equal to religious and political leaders. Young men left their fathers' farms to make new lives on the frontier.[11] For participants in the culture of the early American republic, old cultural precepts gave way to new, and heaven itself accommodated and responded to them.[12] Whereas theocentrism hewed to traditional hierarchies, proponents of the domestic heaven tended to be much more egalitarian. Rather than being subservient to patriarchs or angels, these believers answered only to their own families.

Despite a generally antihierarchical spirit, the domestic heaven still contained the possibility of graded rewards familiar from older models of heaven, though such degrees of glory were a relatively weak echo of prior celestial hierarchies of archangels, angels, and assorted other supernatural beings.[13] More often, Protestants emphasized that heaven was where parting is no more, as they envisioned heavenly meetings with family and friends in eulogies and diaries. By the postbellum period, the complex balance between the glory of God and the perseverance of human relationships had blossomed into a full-fledged domestic heaven whose proponents saw themselves as rebels against Calvinist orthodoxy.[14] Proponents of the domestic heaven anticipated the seamless continuity of family life before and after death. They would sit together beside the hearth, smiling, conversing, and worshipping God.

Those most exposed to the social stresses of migration and poor communication may have taken particular solace in the promise of relational persistence. Nancy Towle represents many other traveling evangelicals. As she traversed the American republic, drawing souls into the community of the blessed, she often fretted over the uncertainty of contact and communication—both letters and people could disappear into the vast times and spaces of early national America. A single woman on Christ's errand, Towle frequently reflected on the mandate to sacrifice family for the evangelization of many souls. She justified long absences from her family with the promise of a heavenly society of the saved. Her rhetoric notwithstanding, it was the death of her stoic father and vaguely deistic brother Philip that mattered most to her religious and emotional stability. She spent months attempting to sort out the final details of Philip's last days and placed his tomb marker prominently at the beginning of her published memoir. She openly confessed that Philip's death drove her to doubt Providence and even her own sanity. However strong and insistent her commitment to God's excellence and the community of the saved, what nearly drove her insane was the thought that her biological brother was forever lost.[15]

Joseph Smith appears at first glance to have been an unembarrassed proponent of the domestic heaven, but this impression is misleading. On purely sentimental grounds, he hoped to have his loved ones with him after death, a point he made repeatedly and emphatically. In public pronouncements that irritated estranged followers and Protestant neighbors,

Smith announced publicly that he preferred hell with his friends to heaven alone (see chapter 6). The preservation of human ties represented the core of his preaching, what he defended with a revelation announcing that the "sociality which exists amongst us here will exist among us [in the afterlife]."[16] In a meeting during the buildup to the Kirtland holy season, Smith announced his fervent hope to earn "a crown, to enjoy the society of father mother Alvin Hyrum Sophron[i]a Samuel Catharine Carloss Lucy the Saints and all the sanctify[ie]d in peace forever."[17] In this personal prophecy, Smith merged the community of the blessed with his own family; he did not believe he would recognize only his family in the afterlife. This act of straddling the theocentric and domestic heavens pointed toward the future course of Smith's teachings. In a complex variety of interlocking rites and doctrines, Smith revealed an answer to both prevalent models of heaven: family would indeed last forever, but not in the form proposed by what became Victorian society.

Over time, Smith developed a genealogical reformation of the Neoplatonic Chain of Being. This Mormon Chain of Belonging incorporated all the different strands of his heaven family, including the closely related systems of spiritual adoption, patriarchal blessings, baptism for the dead, and celestial marriage. A new reading of the Christian theology of adoption stood at the center of this set of doctrines.

Adoption Theology

The rites by which Dr. John Bernhisel became Joseph Smith's son in the eternities began simply, as a reinterpretation of the Protestant image of a believer's adoption to Christ.[18] What Latter-day Saints called the Law of Adoption after Smith's death became a belief that worthy Latter-day Saints could personally recapitulate Christ's role in the adoption of the New Testament. Just as God could adopt a person, so could other believers, whether an evangelist preaching the message to a receptive convert, a patriarch bestowing a ceremonial blessing, or an apostle adopting people close to him. The early Mormon theology of adoption held that the creation of new sacerdotal relationships could result in the salvation of the people entering these new relationships. This distinctive belief began as a sort of exposition of biblical and Protestant ideas about the process of the new birth in Christ. With time, adoption began to show the marks of Smith's sacerdotal genealogy, culminating in a ritual shortly after the Prophet's death with few if any equivalents in antebellum America, whereby adult believers formally became celestial parents to unrelated adults. More than anything, ritual adoption is a testament to the extent to which the Church of Jesus Christ of Latter-day Saints was meant to be the society of heaven and full membership in it the sign of and pathway to exaltation.

Theological Roots of Adoption

The language of adoption in antebellum Protestantism explicitly and self-consciously derived from the New Testament, in which the term generally refers to a Christian spiritualization of the Israelite covenant in the Pauline writings. Thus in the inspiring and potent language of Romans 8, "as many as are led by the Spirit of God, they are the sons of God. For ye have not received the spirit of bondage again to fear; but ye have received the Spirit of adoption, whereby we cry, Abba, Father."[19] In this passage Paul promised early Christians that they could come to call God "father." The plainest sense of adoption in antebellum Protestant practice was the notion of membership in the community of Christians, the family of God, which—depending on one's ecclesiastical affiliation—took place at the moment of conversion, baptism, proselytization, formal acceptance into a church covenant, or perhaps Final Judgment at the world's end. In each of these transitions, adoption represented a gateway into a particular community of believers. From Puritans and their Reformed heirs to Methodists and Baptists, to Anglicans and Episcopalians, adoption had a secure place in early American Protestantism.

For Puritans salvation was inescapably corporate, merging church and society in federal covenants. These Puritan covenants cast a long shadow over the communities that derived from them, including the frontier societies in which Mormonism arose. Unfortunately, the assurance that God would save the regenerate in church covenants did not mean that biological families would stay together after death. Children often, notoriously, failed to live up to parental and societal expectations; typical transgressions excluded them from membership in the community of the saved. From the Puritans' deep hunger to keep their offspring safe arose, temporarily and intermittently, the Halfway Covenant, a system to allow children and grandchildren to derive at least some protection from the regenerate status of their parents.[20] By the time of Joseph Smith, formal covenant theology, as well as its

Halfway Covenant, had largely receded, both as Congregationalism became increasingly peripheral during the Second Great Awakening and as new theological approaches emerged in the changing religious landscape.[21] Still, the general sense of adoption as election remained.

Some learned commentators situated adoption within the culture in which Paul lived. Charles Buck argued for precedent in Roman law (whereby childless patrons could choose a legal heir for their name and wealth) as the source of Paul's comparison in the New Testament. Buck described the early Christian practice of seeing Christ as the parent, giving his name, the "new name," to the believer undergoing adoption. In Buck's account, adoption as conversion represented an "eternal glory" that was "perpetual as to its duration," a reminder of the Perseverance he endorsed as a committed Calvinist.[22] The Roman precedent proved crucial to the Mormon interpretation of adoption.

The populist denominations that overran Calvinist orthodoxies in the early American republic tended to emphasize a community of believers as distinct from Puritan church covenants.[23] The newer Protestantisms focused less on covenant or election and more on the individual experience of conversion. The meaning of adoption as the experience of regeneration was probably most prominent among Methodists.[24] In a pair of sermons entitled "Witness of the Spirit," John Wesley laid out his thinking on adoption and Christian experience. Wesley spoke of the "spirit of adoption" of Romans 8 as the personal witness of God's love, "proof that [the believer] is a child of God."[25] He distinguished it, as Paul had, from the "spirit of bondage," the state of unregeneration. Among the Reformed Methodists, many believers claimed adoption as a "child of God" as synonymous with regeneration and distinct from the sanctification of the Holy Spirit or baptism per se.[26] With many Mormon founders coming from the Methodist tradition, the spirit of adoption as the experience of regeneration is an important precedent for the later Mormon practice.[27]

Wary of excessive ecclesiastical power, many evangelicals saw adoption more as entry into the body of Christ than into a Puritan covenant. While it is tempting to see this later view as much more individualistic than the Puritans' covenant theology, evangelicals and revivalists also acutely perceived the community of such believers, both in life and in death. By receiving regenerating grace and the converting promise of God's adoption, these Protestant believers knew their souls were saved, and that they would thereby be reunited with their saved friends after the Final Judgment.[28] This shift in adoption rhetoric within the populist denominations more than anything pushed the clergy from the scene. No minister oversaw the formation of a covenant; instead a preacher or itinerant revivalist guided believers to their own membership in the family of God.

When Joseph Smith began his religious career, adoption referred to the dual nature of conversion, the sense of an individual experiencing salvific regeneration through communion with God coupled with the resulting community of the saved. Smith sacramentalized adoption, first with patriarchal blessings and baptism for the dead, complementary impulses of connection and salvation, then with family sealings within the Nauvoo Temple cultus. Mormonism sharply rejected both the individualism and the anticlericalism of Methodist or Baptist adoption, restoring a sacerdotal organization to the concept.

The first Mormon discussion of adoption came in the Book of Mormon, which equated adoption with being "born again; yea, born of God."[29] Such rebirth came because the people made a "covenant" to "be called the children of Christ, his sons, and his daughters." Through this process believers took upon themselves "the name of Christ."[30] Throughout, the Book of Mormon highlighted the view of adoption as conversion, often effected through evangelism. Early Mormon preaching followed the Book of Mormon on this point. Adoption was the act of assuming the name of Christ through conversion, often associated with baptism. Protestants argued over whether baptism represented the moment of adoption or was merely the duty of those who had already been adopted, but the Saints largely elided such theological controversies. Though they ultimately endorsed a thoroughly sacramental view of baptism and adoption, in the beginning this distinction mattered relatively little.

Images of seals, covenants, and baptism clustered together around adoption without definitive resolution through the 1830s. In 1837, Parley Pratt touched on adoption in his influential *Voice of Warning*. Describing the activity of the apostles in establishing God's "organized government on the earth,"[31] Pratt announced that the apostles "prepared to unlock the door of the kingdom, and to adopt strangers and foreigners into it as legal citizens, by administering certain laws and ordinances, which were invariably the laws of adoption; without which no man could ever become a citizen."[32] Simultaneously emphasizing regeneration, Pratt taught that "there were no natural born subjects of that kingdom . . . none could be citizens without the law of adoption, and all that believed on the name of the king, had power to be adopted; but there was but one invariable rule or plan by which they were adopted," a state that straddled basic church membership and receipt of "the Holy Spirit of promise," which was "the seal of their adoption."[33] In this last line, Pratt combined the threads of sealing, the "spirit of promise," and adoption as membership in the kingdom. Brief editorials in the *Millennial Star* perpetuated this traditional reading of "the glorious law of adoption into the kingdom of God."[34]

An evangelistic sect from the beginning, Mormonism employed the image of adopting one's proselytes into the family of God, an extension of prevalent Protestant beliefs. The relationship of evangelist and convert represented a family relationship, one imbued with the power to save. Thus Wilford Woodruff claimed of his British proselytes that "the first fruits of my ministry...are bound to me closer than the ties of consanguinity," and Addison Pratt wrote from Tubuai in the South Pacific to tell his wife of "the six first persons I have adopted into the kingdom by baptism."[35] According to an 1841 proselytizing statement made by missionaries near Boston, believers "must be adopted in order to become citizens of his kingdom. Baptism of course then is the ordinance of adoption."[36] By the 1840s Mormon sacramentalism had confirmed adoption as a ritual, one inextricably tied to the work of evangelizing the world.[37]

Smith's Egyptian scripture taught that the precedent for this glorious evangelizing power was God's covenant with Abraham. In the published scripture, God told Abraham that he would be patriarch to an innumerable seed in part through the proselytization of unbelievers. "As many as receive this Gospel shall be called after thy name, and shall be accounted thy seed, and shall rise up and bless thee, as their father."[38] Abraham, through evangelism, became the father to the faithful.

Joseph Smith continued to use the traditional definition of adoption as late as 1841. In early May he preached an exegesis of Romans 9 in two sermons that counterposed "the adoption, and the covenants" to the "election of individuals." In strong if uncertain terms, Smith preached that "all the election that can be found in the scripture is according to the flesh and pertaining to the priesthood."[39] By 1843, Smith was making the sacramental view of adoption clear—believers would need to "subscribe [to] the articles of adoption to enter" the kingdom of God.[40]

Patriarchs and Orphans

Smith often integrated strands from varied traditions within and without Christianity. In this vein, he preached in 1839 that "an Evangelist is a patriarch even the oldest man of the Blood of Joseph or of the seed of Abraham, wherever the Church of Christ is established in the earth, there should be a patriarch for the benefit of the posterity of the Saints as it was with Jacob in giving his patriarchal blessing unto his Sons."[41] Though on its face the definition sounds like an idiosyncratic attempt to place an early Mormon priesthood office, "patriarch," into the Pauline litany of Ephesians 4, Smith was making a statement about the meaning of adoption. Evangelists brought souls to adoption and thereby gained a claim on those they converted. Converts became the children of their evangelists similar to the way they became the children of Jesus. Patriarchs, patterned on the biblical Jacob and led by Joseph Sr., first operationalized this role of human adoptive parents.

Joseph Jr. made his father the first patriarch, the modern Father Israel for the Church of Christ. Though he never integrated it consistently into his broader sacerdotal system, Smith made clear that his father exercised a patriarchal priesthood on behalf of the church. In a self-conscious imitation of Jacob's deathbed blessings, Joseph Sr. began to impart words of wisdom and promises of power to believing Mormons.[42] These blessings reflected a combination of hopeful prayers directed at fellow worshippers and an idiosyncratic exercise of metaphysical fatherhood. With time, after the patriarch's own death and his transfer of the patriarchal power to his oldest living son, Hyrum, Joseph Jr. clarified that the patriarchal priesthood represented the sealing power of the New Testament apostles, a power central to the sacerdotal genealogy.[43] Through his blessings and his priesthood, the patriarch adopted believers into the family of God.

Smith's patriarchal system was not without antecedents. Many American Protestants cherished opportunities to bless one another, particularly during spiritual gatherings. Blessings from venerable old men were particularly prized, gentle echoes of Old Testament exemplars. In the hands of the elder and younger Joseph Smiths, this usually informal practice became a highly specific ritual embedded in a richly contoured conceptual system. In many early cases the blessings were bestowed in communal meetings apparently patterned on Methodist love feasts.[44] This aspect of Mormon ecclesiology became widely known and derided outside the church, with critics maintaining that Joseph Sr. "mumble[d], with his eyes shut, over the heads of the orphan children of the church."[45] Seceders reprinted their blessings as signs of the credulity of Mormons.[46]

The scoffing of critics and seceders is unsurprising—Joseph Sr.'s blessings promised amazing powers to recipients, from gifts of tongues to supernatural translocations, from willed immortality to interplanetary travel.[47] Often Joseph Sr. told recipients that they were sealed to eternal life or their names were written in the Lamb's Book of Life. In these spectacular patriarchal blessings, the image of sacerdotal fatherhood wove in and out of the process of adoption into the sacerdotal lineage—through these blessings the large majority of recipients, even in the early years, discovered themselves adopted into the family of Israel, most often as the children God promised Abraham would be as numerous as the sands of the sea.

In a highly literal adaptation of American Israelitism, the early Mormon patriarch revealed to recipients their place in the Israelite lineage, generally as descendants of Joseph of Egypt through either of his sons Ephraim or Manasseh. Essentially all of the major themes understood under the rubric of ritual adoption were present in the early patriarchal blessings. The blessings framed the problem as spiritual orphanhood and the solution as adoption into the family of God. In parallel with and perhaps motivating specific aspects of the system of adoption, the patriarchal system also proposed men as fathers within Israel. Patriarchs adopted certain believers in parallel to their adoption to Christ.

The Egyptian scripture of the 1830s provided theological foundation for the patriarchal system. In the published scripture, God promised Abraham that he would "put upon thee my name; even the Priesthood of thy father." This short phrase united the various strands of the patriarchal priesthood—the assumption of God's name was the basic definition of adoption, the priesthood was a lineal one taken from Abraham's father, and in this act, God himself provided an example of the grand patriarchal blessing, concluding with the promise "my power shall be over thee."[48] Abraham learned that he was "a rightful heir" possessing the "right belonging to the fathers." The prefatory paragraphs for the Book of Abraham state that the patriarchal priesthood "came down from the fathers, from the beginning of time," before "the foundation of the earth." Father Adam, densely intertwined with astral hierarchy and lineal priesthood in the Egyptian project, was the source for Abraham's power. As an heir, Abraham learned that he would become "a father of many nations."[49] The Mormon patriarchs that followed in Abraham's footsteps would in turn become fathers to nations of their own.

The group best understood as requiring an ecclesial father were bona fide orphans. Many recipients received patriarchal blessings specifically "that thou mayest no longer be an orphan."[50] Joseph Sr. made clear to such orphans that the church would provide the family structure they lacked. New Saints would thereby "have Fathers and Mothers in israel."[51] Joseph Sr.'s role as father to the fatherless was one the Saints embraced enthusiastically. The official eulogy for Father Smith recalled that "the widow and the orphan have received his Patriarchal blessing."[52] This view did not die with Joseph Sr. In 1840 apostle Heber Kimball continued to worry about the fatherless, ensuring the presence of a duly ordained patriarch to bestow the required blessings.[53]

Orphans came in various shapes and sizes. For a controversial sect like the Latter-day Saints, conversion often meant estrangement from biological family. The practice of gathering to consecrated lands in Missouri and Illinois only intensified the threat that Mormonism represented to traditional kinship ties. The patriarchal priesthood and its blessings presented an important solution to the problem, a central one for the fledgling church. Joseph Sr. and others revealed that a natural father, if "an idolator" (an allusion to Abraham, whose father worshipped idols), would need to be replaced by a spiritual father to ensure the recipient's place in the kingdom of heaven. Stephen Post (1810–1879) learned that he was "an orphan as to the things of the kingdom, for thy natural father hath no power to bless thee."[54] Joseph Sr. recognized that his son was constructing an ecclesial family that could come into sharp conflict with biological kin (his own brother ostracized him angrily in the wake of Joseph Jr.'s revelations), and in his blessings he reminded the Latter-day Saints of their sacrifices and rewards. He reminded Mary Smith that "thou hast left thy father's house, and thy near relatives for the gospel's sake."[55] To others Smith asserted that "thou hast been united to Kindred blood," an attempt to minimize the social fracture of conversion and establish the church community, with him as its lineal head.[56]

Orphanhood could even extend to those whose parents were Latter-day Saints. Joseph Sr. told David Elliot (1799–1855) that his father was "not as yet perfected in the faith, yet if he will seal this blessing upon thy head it shall be well, and it shall be called in his name." Joseph Sr.'s replacement for Elliot's inadequate father used the language of sacred adoption: "I seal a father's blessing that thou mayest not be an orphan, but call God, thy father."[57] This practice provided flexibility for a natural father to become sufficiently righteous to be able to take over the spiritual blessing bestowed by the Mormon patriarch. Even as the patriarch held open the possibility of a natural father's integration into the process, the tension between spiritual and natural relationships intruded. At times Father Smith urged evangelism to solve the problem, as when he instructed Emanuel Murphy (1809–1871) to "preach to thy father and mother and bring them into the kingdom."[58] Such proselytism represented the ultimate goal, generating a seamless overlap of biological and sacerdotal families.

Employing the language of evangelism as the adoption of converts, Joseph Sr. blessed Martha Knowlton (1822–1881) "by the consent of thy Father and the request of Br Page thy Spiritual Father."[59] Three father figures hovered over the head of Miss Knowlton that day. The patriarch stood physically beside the figurative presence of her biological father and of Elder John Page (1799–1867), the apostle who converted her. Each of these men had a claim on Martha, the first and last making their claims through the patriarchal and evangelistic interpretation of spiritual adoption.[60] Through their access to Latter-day Saint teachings and priesthood, these men had the capacity to adopt others into the family of heaven. Indeed at times Joseph Sr. employed language generally reserved to Jesus to describe his duties to those he blessed as patriarch. To Margaret Johnstun (1818–1883) Joseph Sr. announced: "I will be wil[l]ing to acknowle[d]ge the[e] in the great day of the lord."[61] This was the language Jesus had used, the idea that taking Christ's name meant that the believer would be acknowledged by him at the Final Judgment. The patriarch's claim in this blessing framed a central component of the early patriarchal priesthood, an act of creating relationships that mirrored the relationship between Christ and believers. The patriarch, the paradigmatic human adoptive father, stood in for Jesus in an act of sacred mimesis.

Though roots in New Testament evangelism are clear, patriarchal blessings placed themselves in an Old Testament setting as well. In fact the biblical language of the genealogy of Israel provided precedent for the interposition of adoptive fathers in the Latter-day Saint system. Who was father to whom seemed inextricably linked to entry into the saving covenant of Jehovah with his people. The seemingly endless "begats" of the Table of Nations (and similar genealogies) in the Hebrew Bible were pregnant with meaning for the Latter-day Saints. Assuming a Hebraic language of genealogy and covenantal ethnicity, the Mormon patriarchs began to adopt people into the nation of Israel. Joseph Sr. advised Roswell Blood (1803–1867): "thou art not of gentile blood but of the seed of Israel yet thy companion is a Gentile and goeth in the way of the Gentiles. But if she will repent and obey the gospel she shall become the seed of Abraham through the law of adoption."[62] Even as Blood's bloodline was declared spiritually, his wife's proved susceptible to correction. This was not merely absorption into the body of Christ, the way many Protestants understood adoption; the early patriarchal priesthood contained the contours of the heaven family and a distinctive ethnic identification.[63] As one example among many, Hyrum Smith blessed Susanna White (b. 1819) in 1841 in order, his blessing affirmed, "that you might have a Name in Israel, as Daughter of Abraham in the lineage of Joseph, in the tribe of Ephraim."[64] Soon nearly every blessing included such an assignment to one of the tribes of Israel.

Despite rhetoric about the community of the blessed, and much like Nancy Towle or the originators of the Halfway Covenant, Mormon elders generally preferred their biological kin. Alongside evangelistic power, the patriarchal priesthood served to assure Mormons of the integrity of their bonds with their physical offspring. Amos Fuller (1810–1853) learned from Joseph Sr. that his was "a blessing which shall rest on thee and on thy seed," while Clarissa Perry (b. 1807) learned that she would "have children in the covenant with thee."[65] In several cases men received from this patriarchal priesthood the ability to save their own children. Joseph Bosworth (1790–1850) thus received "power to save thy family, even all so that none of them shall be lost."[66] Joseph Cooper (b. 1787) learned that he would "be a patriarch in thy family to seal blessings on thy children to the latest generation."[67] In these cases men became capable, potentially, of effecting the salvation of their own offspring. This theme became so prominent that critics remembered Joseph Sr. as an automaton issuing promises of plenteous and righteous offspring.[68] The patriarchal blessings did not just face backward to the tribes of Israel, defining each believer as an heir of a given tribe. They also anticipated the end of time, a future ordered by generations of Latter-day Saints interconnected by the blessings of the patriarchal priesthood. Adoption was the key to both past and future.

Since adoption and the seal of Christ were the metaphor for the process by which converts secured salvation, images of sealing appeared in the early patriarchal blessings. Joseph Sr. told Emanuel Murphy: "I seal the seal of God upon thy forehead, and seal thee up unto eternal life."[69] To Marcellus McKown (b. 1807) Joseph Sr. provided "many blessings upon thy family, even to the sealing of them up unto eternal life."[70] The new relationships established in the evangelizing adoption served the purpose of preparing kindreds for the Second Coming of Christ. Jonathan Crosby (1807–1892) learned that he would rise to meet Jesus at the Second Coming, "and thy thousands shall be with thee."[71] Emphasizing the extent to which participation in the holy lineage could save kindreds intact, Joseph Sr. promised Lorenzo Snow that "all thy kindred shall be brought into the kingdom and have a Celestial Glory."[72] Kith combined with kin in that world: Joseph Sr. promised Latter-day Saints that their friends would join them in heaven. He informed Wilford Woodruff's wife, Phebe Carter (1807–1885), that "if thou wilt keep the commandments thou shalt have all of thy friends. They shall be members of the covenant."[73] The blessing of Jacob Chapman (b. 1803) demonstrates the ways that patriarchal blessings filled the space once occupied by the Halfway Covenant. Chapman learned that "great grace shall flow unto thee through the covenant which thou hast received, and by which thy blessings shall descend down and reach thy posterity that they may be numbered with the children of Abraham and receive an inheritance with their brethren and enjoy all the privileges of the kingdom on earth."[74] The vast and local coexisted in this practice—patriarchal adoption saved Chapman's grandchildren even as it bound them all to Abraham himself. The theological and the emotional also coexisted in these blessings, as when Joseph Sr. told Gad Yale (1790–1870): "God will not suffer that thou shalt always mourn for thy companion, for God shall give thee power to save thy family in the celestial kingdom."[75]

Through their patriarchal priesthood the Latter-day Saints could save almost anyone into the family of heaven; the early patriarchal blessings were often about the creation of a durable community that would survive death and damnation. At an early patriarchal blessing meeting, participants pledged "to enjoy each others society forever more even all the blessings of heaven and earth."[76] Though the intensity of the apocalyptic, immortalist rhetoric of patriarchal blessings cooled somewhat by the 1840s, another ritual system arose to continue the work of establishing the heaven family. The Christian sacrament of adoption supplemented, expanded, and reinterpreted the patriarchal priesthood, restoring an ancient practice in a new context.

Baptism for the Dead

Entering long-standing debates about the fate of the unbaptized dead, Smith revealed in a funeral sermon for Seymour Brunson (1798–1840) in August 1840 that Mormons could perform baptism—what the Saints understood as the New Testament rite of adoption—for their deceased ancestors.[77] To the general debate Smith added an intensely personal element: not only did Mormons solve the Protestant "scandal of particularity," Mormons claimed their ancestors as their own, not just to identify themselves as ethnic Israelites but to craft permanent associations with their dead. During the sermon, the dead actively mingled with the living: observers described the apostle David Patten, dead for almost two years, among Brunson's angelic escort to heaven.[78] Smith's brother Alvin was also present conceptually at the beginning of baptism for the dead, as the restored rite rejected the insinuation that Alvin had died unbaptized and would not merit heaven.[79] Hyrum, the oldest brother, was immediately baptized for Alvin on revelation of the practice.[80]

The Saints embraced the opportunity of baptism for the dead with great gusto. Some accounts describe hundreds of baptisms occurring in a single day, turning the Mississippi into a spirited froth.[81] Descending beneath the earth into the waters of baptism, the Latter-day Saints were adopted into the family of God for their dead loved ones. With baptism for the dead, Smith's theology of adoption reached into the proximate and remote pasts. Whereas the patriarchal blessings identified a lineage among the Hebrew patriarchs, a tie to one of the original tribes of Israel, baptism for the dead began to assemble the individual links in the chain back to Adam, the first human.

In part Mormons were rejecting Calvinism; in part they delighted in such a ritual assurance of the salvation of their ancestors. Though Smith rapidly constrained the holy melee in the Mississippi River that ensued on his revelation of the practice, the urgency among Latter-day Saints to perform this ritual led to the separate dedication of the baptismal font in the Nauvoo Temple years before the temple itself was completed.[82] Latter-day Saints came to this sacred pool to renew their covenant with God, to heal their bodies, and to adopt their dead into the heaven family.[83] This baptism for the dead was a major doctrine for Latter-day Saints, one they tied to ancient Christianity (via the Marcionites) and advertised proudly throughout the world.[84] By 1845, even the Finnish press was commenting on the practice.[85] In this act of lineal reversal, Latter-day Saints served as surrogates—"Saviors on Mount Zion" according to Smith's distinctive exegesis of Obadiah—of their dead kin.[86] This view of themselves as secondary saviors invigorated and expanded the notion of surrogate fathers present within the patriarchal priesthood.[87]

In a sermon six weeks before his death, Smith reiterated his view of baptism for the dead as adoption. He preached that believers could obey "the Law of the Gospel" for their friends, performing baptism, the act of "belong[ing] to the Kingdom," on their behalf.[88] Smith anticipated that his followers would come to Nauvoo at least once in their lives to perform this rite of adoption (and its amplification into temple ritual) for their kith and kin.

As the promise of Abraham and the power of the covenant secured sure salvation for a believer's posterity, baptism for the dead established links in the chain connecting present believers to past patriarchs. In baptism for the dead, the Mormon covenantal system, its patriarchal priesthood, became potently bidirectional. Not only did dead ancestors have a claim on the living through their bloodlines, the living had claim on the dead through their performance of the adopting ritual of baptism.[89] Mormons were to "save themselves and their progenitors, as well as secure their posterity."[90]

Baptism for the dead merged the patriarchal priesthood and its associated blessings with the anointing and sealings of the Kirtland Temple and the perfecting rites of the Nauvoo Temple. Smith is remembered to have preached in the 1840s: "those who are baptised for their dead are the Saviours on mount Zion & they must receave their washings and their anointings for their dead, the same as for themselvs, till they are connected to the ones in the dispensation before us and trace their leniage to connect the priesthood again."[91] These acts of adoption and sealing into a covenantal relationship created sentimental and sacred attachments to the dead that Davies has called the "soteriological lineage," a subset of what I term the sacerdotal genealogy.[92] In the canonized revelation on the practice, Smith revealed, in a distinctive exegesis of Hebrews 11:40, that "we [the living] without them [the dead] cannot be made perfect; neither can they without us be made perfect."[93] Perfection, the state of endless progression Smith called exaltation, was available only if the living bound themselves to the dead, and vice versa, without a single missing link. Mere genetic connections were insufficient: Smith's new system was sacerdotal rather than biological, created rather than inborn.[94]

In his swan song sermon in April 1844, Smith asked the graphic and rhetorical question "What kind of characters are those who can be saved, although their bodies are moldering and decaying in the grave?" He answered that the ancients who could be saved from the grave were the deceased kin of Smith's followers, the recipients of his ordinance for the dead.[95]

Baptism for the dead brought living initiates into closer proximity with the dead through their descent into the "liquid grave."[96] It also explained the New Testament image of Christ "preaching to the spirits in prison," a topic the Saints had wrestled with since the 1830s.[97] Each participant assumed the name of the dead as she entered the watery grave to redeem them, to adopt them into the heavenly family. "The ordinance of baptism by water, to be immers'd therein in order to answer to the likeness of the dead," Smith explained, "this ordinance was instituted to form a relationship with the ordinance of baptism for the dead."[98] In other words, the sacrament of adoption, water baptism, necessarily entailed its application to the dead. Through metaphysical correspondence, a familiar Christian ordinance held the clue to the radical Mormon rite. Because baptism mimicked death, it had to be performed for the dead.

In fact, the fonts in which this practice would take place in sanctified Mormon temples as a "similitude of the grave" were required by divine mandate to be located "underneath where the living are wont to assemble," a physically emphatic expansion of the traditional Christian view of dying to sin and being born again in Christ.[99] Smith would not let his followers forget that the dead remained where their families left them, in the grave, awaiting the redemptive intervention of the living.

Mormons were not the only ones to seek out the dead in this period. Shakers were famous during their Era of Manifestations for visions of the dead, while by the 1850s spiritualist visitations were occurring throughout America.[100] Visions of the dead demonstrated the reality of the supernatural world and imparted power to the living, often in a quest to convert the living.

In their effort to save those who had gone before, the Latter-day Saints moved beyond such visions of the dead. The Mormons were seeking out and converting the dead rather than being converted by them. In the words of Brigham Young, the Latter-day Saints intended to "go forth and officiate for my fathers, for my mothers, and for my ancestors, of the earliest generation."[101] Almost no one besides the Latter-day Saints chose the ordinance of salvation and adoption to connect with their dead as a direct attack on the Protestant war against Catholic works for the dead.[102] The ritual and sometimes rapturous union effected by baptism for the dead supported a sacramentalism strong enough to defy death. This new adoption represented by baptism for the dead allowed creation of links in a chain that stretched from the Latter-day Saints to their Father Adam and beyond. The use of that image, a chain, pointed to the central infrastructure of the heaven family.

The Mormon Chain of Belonging

Patriarchal blessings, adoption, and baptism for the dead developed within a distinctive reformation of an ancient and prevalent philosophical construct, the Great Chain of Being.[103] This Chain of Being, also known as the Scale of Creation (or *Scala Naturae*), is generally attributed to Plato as interpreted by Aristotle. In Aristotle's formulation, three key features, plenitude, continuity, and gradation, mattered most. These principles maintained that all things that could exist do exist, and they do so in an infinite hierarchy of being. Early philosophers used the construct to explain biological diversity and the relation of the Divine to Creation. Christian Neoplatonists employed the Chain to explain mystical hierarchies and relationships with angels, well exemplified by Robert Fludd's depiction (figure 8.1) in his famous "Integra Naturae Speculum Artisque imago." During the long eighteenth century, the Chain's insistence on hierarchy at the center of existence wedded it to increasingly obsolescent aristocracies. Even as it came under attack for aristocratic associations, the Chain still supported natural theology, the rise of popular astronomy, and commonsense musings about the harmony and complexity of nature.[104]

Smith employed the Chain in this traditional way even as he set about creating a genealogical permutation of it, what I term his Chain of Belonging. This Smithian Chain drew on his encounters with Egyptian papyri, astronomical natural theology in the spirit of Thomas Dick, the metaphysical law of correspondence, and religious inspiration.[105] Smith's system represented both a redaction and a contestation of the traditional Chain. Smith's genealogical reformation—in opposition to the traditional Chain, based in static hierarchies—was dynamic, able to embrace the possibility of progress. In Smith's genealogical revision the hierarchy of glories that had encompassed demigods, angels, and humans became

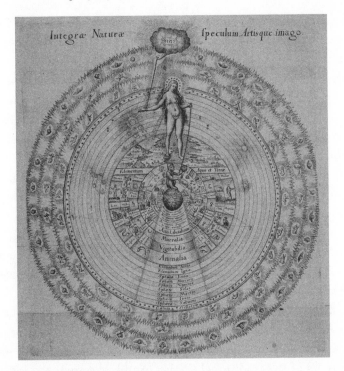

Figure 8.1 Robert Fludd illustrated his 1617–1619 *Utriusque cosmi, maioris scilicet et minoris, metaphysica*...with this image, "Integra Naturae Speculum Artisque imago" ("The Mirror of the Whole of Nature, and the Image of Art"), which depicts the Great Chain of Being in its late medieval/early modern splendor. Notice particularly the integration of humanity and cosmos and the incorporation of astral imagery into the body. Image courtesy of the Library of Congress.

instead a family tree, a sacerdotal genealogy. As Mormons exercised the rites of adoption, they expanded their glory within the Chain. The new types of family relationships they created integrated them directly into the cosmos.

The first hint of Smith's Chain of Belonging came in the 1830s, as he sketched the contours of afterlife glory. As the 1830 Book of Mormon provided little insight on the afterlife beyond a general affirmation of physical resurrection and a traditional heaven and hell, Smith's initial description of the topic came in 1832, in a visionary experience he shared with Sidney Rigdon.[106] Soon canonized as the Vision, this revelation sought to resolve the question of degrees of blessedness in the afterlife.[107] Using images familiar from Thomas Dick's astronomical Chain of Being,

Smith's assistants introduced the revelation as "the economy of God and his vast creation throughout all eternity."[108] In the revelation Smith explained that "if God rewarded every one according to the deeds done in the body, the term 'heaven,' as intended for the saint's eternal home, must include more kingdoms than one."[109] To explain the gradations in this system, Smith appropriated the scripture traditionally most used to support the Chain of Being.[110] In his famous treatise on resurrection (1 Corinthians 15), Paul employed a cosmic simile. As the dim stars deferred to the moon, and the moon in turn to the bright sun, so did humans enter a hierarchical glory after death. In his letter, Paul mentioned only heavenly and earthly beings ("celestial" and "terrestrial" in the KJV), while Smith disclosed a third kingdom named "telestial," apparently a composite of the first two, corresponding to stars. Although with time the Saints saw this revelation as describing a tripartite heaven, initially Smith described many more gradations than three.

Almost a year later Smith returned to the theme in his Olive Leaf revelation. After emphasizing that particular laws governed particular glories, Smith proposed afterlife glories as a cosmic map that met the requirements of the traditional Chain: "And there are many kingdoms; for there is no space in which there is no kingdom; and there is no kingdom in which there is no space, either a greater or a lesser kingdom."[111] Moving in and out of several loosely related proof texts, Smith praised the perfect order of heavenly bodies, the type of religious astronomy that carried the Chain into the nineteenth century. Smith then reappropriated Christ's parable of the twelve laborers in the vineyard to confirm his 1832 Vision. Contrary to received interpretations of the parable, in which day laborers received the same wage no matter when they started their work, Smith revealed that the twelve laborers received different glories, according to the time they began to labor in the vineyard. With received interpretations, Smith acknowledged that each laborer would enter into the heavenly hierarchy and be saved; against Protestant interpretations, Smith saw the duration of their labor as the marker of the glory they would inherit in that heavenly afterlife.[112]

Several authors have commented that, despite the Vision, early Latter-day Saints largely appeared to be dualistic believers in heaven and hell.[113] Functional dualism, as much as the apparently tripartite model of the Vision, hid the real extent of Smith's heaven, which resided entirely within the celestial kingdom reserved for those who had "enter[ed] into

this order of the priesthood." Using code words for his sacerdotal genealogy, Smith promised that outside his celestial heaven the dead "cannot
have increase."[114] He meant that the infinite gradations of the sacerdotal
genealogy occurred only in the celestial kingdom. That family structure
was the harmonizing "economy" that the 1832 Vision only hinted at.

In 1842 Smith had Phelps revisit the 1832 Vision in verse—a poem
published in *Times and Seasons* over Smith's signature.[115] According to
this poem, the three kingdoms "all harmonize like the parts of a tune,"
emphasizing the harmony standing at the heart of the Chain.[116] In a sermon in 1844, Smith explicitly associated the Vision with his postmortal
Chain. In his Sermon in the Grove, he announced that "Paul—says there
is one Glory of the Sun the moon & the Stars—& as the Star differs
&C—They are exalted far above princ[ipalities]. thrones dom[inions]. &
angels—& are expressly decl[are]d. to be heirs of God."[117] The worthy
believers compared in the Vision to astral bodies were, as heirs of God,
greater than the angels within the calculus of the Chain of Belonging,
according to this sermon. By 1844 the association between the Vision
and the Chain had matured, integrating the language of adoption and the
divine heirship of Christ, which served as the basis for the *imitatio Christi*
that underlay Smith's divine anthropology, in which humans claimed a
place above angels in the Chain (see chapter 9).

Smith's celestial kingdom occupied a conceptual space outside the traditional theocentric or domestic heavens. The Mormon heaven was
emphatically not a heavenly garden of nuclear families jointly worshipping God. In place of the many families of the domestic heaven, there was
one boundless family of intelligences, "a perfect chane from Father Adam
to his latest posterity."[118] Nor was it a heaven of unaffiliated humans worshipping God from their place at the midpoint of the ontological Chain of
Being. Smith's genealogical chain extended from church members to
their file leaders to the Prophet himself, then through the biblical patriarchs, ultimately to Adam. At the Second Coming, Adam, in the valley of
Adam-ondi-Ahman, would seal all humanity to God.[119] In 1841 Smith
described his ecclesial hierarchy in precisely the terms of the Chain of
Being as "a principle of order or gradation."[120] The priesthood was based
on the Chain, and this priesthood in turn supported the genealogical
Chain. This lineage provided the infrastructure of salvation, as in Smith's
revelation to Newel Whitney, promising "honor and immortality and
eternal life to all your house both old and young because of the lineage
of my Preasthood."[121] Every "link in the chain of priesthood" had to

participate, just as each type of being had been required for the integrity of the traditional Chain of Being.[122] A single link missing or unworthy of the priesthood could break the entire Chain.[123] Brigham Young followed Smith in this regard, promising in an 1847 sermon to "extend the Chain of the Pristhood back through the apostolic dispensation to Father Adam."[124]

In Smith's Chain, relationships were the essence of ontological glory. Postmortal glory derived from the scope of one's location within the family tree. In a brother-in-law's paraphrase, "Dominion & powr in the great Future" was "Commensurate with the no of 'Wives Childin & Friends' that we inherit here."[125] In the language of Hyrum's brother-in-law, "a Man's Dominion will be as God's is, over his own Creatures and the more numerous the greater his Dominion."[126] The degrees of heaven reflected no mere statement of merit or ontological superiority: they were an index of one's placement in the genealogy of eternal "intelligences."[127] Status in the Mormon Chain of Belonging echoed the "crowns of many stars" of Protestant evangelists and the number-less offspring God promised to Abraham. Reflecting such evangelistic themes, Sally Randall exclaimed that "the more I do [for the dead] the greater will be the crown."[128]

The distinctively sacerdotal genealogy of the Latter-day Saints pointed more than anything to what intellectual historian Arthur Lovejoy called the "temporal" Chain of Being, a hierarchy that evolved through time.[129] By merging the chain's hierarchy with familial images, Smith made the chain relationally dynamic. Those adopted by the patriarchal priesthood into the genealogical chain progressed forever as a family hierarchy. In Brigham Young's 1847 explication:

> I will show you a rule by which you may Comprehend the exhal-tation of the faithful. I will use myself as A figure, & say that I am ruling over 10 sons or subjects ownly & soon each one of them would have 10 men sealed to them & they would be ruler over them & that would make me ruler over 10 Presidents or Kings whareas I was ruler over 10 subjects ownly or in other words I ruled over one Kingdom but now I rule over 10. Then let each one get 10 more. Then I would be ruler over 100 Kingdoms & so on continued to all eternity & the more honor & glory that I could bestow upon my sons the more it would add to my exhaltations.[130]

There could be no end to progress in this system. This was a model of God as progenitor as well as God as King. It was one, via the *imitatio Christi*, that Latter-day Saints employed to understand the shape of their after-life (see chapter 9).

Perhaps the best visual depiction of Smith's sacerdotal genealogy is the distinctive "DIAGRAM OF THE KINGDOM OF GOD" attributed to first-generation apostle Orson Hyde. The diagram (figure 8.2) depicts

> the order and unity of the kingdom of God. The eternal Father sits at the head, crowned King of kings and Lord of lords. Wherever the other lines meet, there sits a king and a priest unto God, bearing rule, authority, and dominion under the Father.... The most eminent and distinguished prophets who have laid down their lives for their testimony ... will be crowned at the head of the largest kingdoms under the Father, and will be one with Christ as Christ is one with his Father; for their king-doms are all joined together ... and to every man will be given a

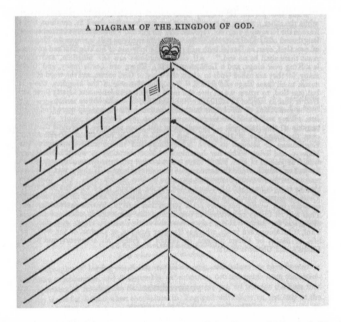

Figure 8.2 "Diagram of the Kingdom of God" (*Millennial Star* 9:2 [January 15, 1847]: 23) depicts the early Mormon Chain of Belonging as a sacerdotal family tree, converting the ontological connections of the Chain of Being into genealogical ties. Image courtesy of the Church History Library, The Church of Jesus Christ of Latter-day Saints.

kingdom and a dominion, according to his merit, powers, and
abilities...there are kingdoms of all sizes, an infinite variety to
suit all grades of merit and ability.[131]

The "infinite variety" and "grades" of the final phrase are typical references to the Chain of Being, and the diagram itself demonstrates in two
dimensions the Mormon Chain of Belonging.[132] In the Mormon depiction, the branching lines are the essence of the celestial hierarchy, the
priesthood seals able to interconnect all humanity rather than classifying
nodes to segregate distinct kinds of beings, as they are in Fludd's "Integra
Naturae Speculum Artisque imago." Smith's Chain was no taxonomy, no
classification of the orders of existence—it was a family tree.

Polygamy

Smith's genealogized Chain of Belonging served as the conceptual basis
for a radical revision of marriage, the relationship most closely associated with reproduction. Smith's novel marital system, termed variously
celestial marriage, plural marriage, or polygamy, brought the Chain into
famous and controversial reality. Practiced at some point in the 1830s,
given a theoretical foundation in the early 1840s, and confessed publicly
in 1852, polygamy became synonymous with Mormonism, a well-known
story that continues to unfold in the twenty-first century. The story of
Utah polygamy has been told in great detail and need not detain us
here.[133] In its beginnings, though, what historian Kathryn Daynes has
called "proto-polygamy," the practice looked rather different and remains
relatively poorly characterized. Proto-polygamy involved around thirty
wives for Smith and encompassed approximately two hundred men and
seven hundred women in the practice in Nauvoo.[134] Shrouded in secrecy
and controversy, the prurient drama of polygamy has largely overwhelmed its conceptual antecedents and contexts within Smith's religious system. Careful attention to these contexts, though, disambiguates
the heaven family from polygamy per se and provides a theoretical basis
for understanding how early participants accommodated polygamy into
their belief system. Celestial marriage made the sacerdotal genealogy
generative, strenuously protested the shrinking nucleus of the Victorian
family, and attempted to overcome the social alienation of death.
Polygamy was an attempt to answer a vital question: How could mortal

affections integrate into the limitless scope, both in time and in extent, of the love of divine beings?

The phrase "celestial marriage" emphasized two interrelated facets of Smith's heaven family, its eternal duration and its situation within the cosmic Chain of Belonging. Smith's marital system developed in tandem with his theology of adoption and patriarchal priesthood. Proto-polygamy sounded like nothing so much as spousal adoption. Rather than integrating a convert or a child into the genealogical infrastructure, this time it was a spouse, with whom many more children could come. As they entered plural marriage, Mormons integrated spouses into their Chain of Belonging, thereby increasing their dynastic gravity in the kingdom of celestial glory. Through priesthood power and with close integration into the temple cultus, Latter-day Saints established temporally limitless relationships with each other, their prophet, and their God.

Mormon proto-polygamy did not arise in a cultural vacuum. The early national and antebellum period witnessed a great deal of sexual experimentation; marriage was a natural locus for social contest. From John Humphrey Noyes (1811–1886) at Oneida to the Shakers, to Fanny Wright (1795–1852) and Robert Owen (1801–1877), to the Cochranites of Maine, a broad spectrum of critics assaulted marriage as evangelicals advocated it, hoping to liberate men, women, and society from the strictures of nuclear monogamy.[135] Independent of the reformers, the facts of life also resisted proto-Victorian marriage. Premature death, both legal and informal divorce, infidelity, geographical dislocations, communication failures, and prolonged absences all contributed to fluidity in marriage practice. Death was the best known and most respected threat to marital stability. Many Americans lived substantial portions of their lives as widows or widowers. Serial monogamy was common as a result. Bereavement was not the only way that antebellum Americans could find marriages disrupted, though. As they moved across the open frontiers of the new republic, men often separated from their wives. Travel and communication were slow and uncertain. The frontier also called to men eager to abandon their wives—advertisements in newspapers requesting knowledge of a husband's whereabouts are a testament to this social fluidity.[136] Once they had settled in a new location or been disconnected from communication with their spouses for a prolonged period, people felt themselves free to engage in new marital relationships, with or without a legal divorce.

In the antebellum period many Protestants saw marriage primarily as a way to control sexuality. Marriage constrained the physical appetites and prevented sexual dissolution. Though companionate models had begun to gain currency in the early republic, for strict believers in the theocentric heaven, marriage was sufficiently impersonal that they anticipated that they would worship Christ for millennia before they ever realized a spouse was standing beside them.[137] According to long-standing Christian tradition dating to Paul, it was "better to marry than to burn."[138] Whereas Paul had intended to honor celibacy, American clergy instead emphasized the necessity of marriage.[139] Joseph Smith was as hostile to abstinence as the New England clergy were, even defaming Shaker celibacy as antibiblical in an 1831 revelation.[140]

The marriage Smith sought to reform was sexually and religiously charged, ever-threatened by death, and more mutable than evangelicals were comfortable admitting. Though he was a harsh critic of the Victorian model, Joseph Smith believed himself to be a powerful advocate of family. Where the Bible appeared to argue against the centrality of marriage, Smith took pains to correct it. Most centrally and famously, the Bible had announced in an encounter between Jesus and the Sadducees that there was no marriage in the resurrection, an account present in all three synoptic gospels.[141] Using the Mosaic practice of levirate marriage to frame the question, these priestly interlocutors asked Jesus what would happen to a woman whose husband-brothers died and remarried her serially. In this thought experiment, a total of six husbands tried and failed to produce offspring on behalf of their dead brother. The Sadducees, nonbelievers in resurrection, used levirate marriage to prove the absurdity of Jesus's claim to an afterlife. Jesus dismissed their argument by stating that there would be no marriage in heaven, even as, particularly in the Lucan account, he strongly affirmed the reality of resurrection. Although Smith left Matthew unrevised, his New Translation of Mark shared the resurrection emphasis of the Lucan narrative. Where the KJV reported that God is not "the God of the dead, but the God of the living," Smith explained the latter clause in a way that returned attention to the problem of life after death—"for he raiseth them up out of their graves."[142] Contrary to almost every other exegete and in defense of the social resurrection, Smith saw this scriptural narrative as a key to a lost doctrine.[143] In the Sadducean thought experiment Smith found evidence that marriage, performed correctly, could defy death. Reading the Sadducees' taunt as literally true, Smith saw in eternal marriage an endorsement of polygamy.

Smith's interpretation rejected traditional exegesis, a school of thought exemplified by Adam Clarke, who described rabbinical arguments about postmortal reunions. Some rabbis solved the Sadducean puzzle, according to Clarke, by maintaining that a widow belonged only to the first husband. For his part, Clarke sharply criticized models of postmortal marriage as "libertin[ism]," offended by the implication that marital relationships would support sexual intercourse in the afterlife. The Methodist divine interpreted language from scripture by arguing that all humans would be angels, which meant that they would be immortal and bereft of all human passions and affections.[144] Smith's inversion of the Sadducean encounter became central to the Mormon explanation of polygamy. Phelps discussed the story with his wife in 1835, and Smith continued the same line of reasoning in his 1843 revelation sanctioning polygamy.[145] When forced to justify polygamy publicly in Nauvoo in 1844, Smith explained that this scripture specifically pushed him to consider polygamy during his work on the New Translation.[146]

Smith grappled with another passage in his New Translation that pointed toward the paradox at the center of his redefinition of marriage as a celestial relationship. In 1 Corinthians 7, Paul advocated celibacy but settled for a halfhearted endorsement of marriage, emphasizing the imminent dissolution of all marriages by noting that "they who have wives, shall be as though they had none." To this Smith added a crucial explanation: "for ye are called and chosen to do the Lords work." Families were not permanently threatened; they would need to defer, though, to the needs of evangelism and church community.[147] This rule applied to Mormon itinerants who often left family for months or years.

Smith's sacerdotal family competed with individual nuclear families. Being connected to many sometimes threatened the connection to the few. The key to understanding Smith's apparently contradictory approach to marriage is his incorporation of the marital relationship into the communal heaven family. While it is true that early Latter-day Saints dissembled to protect their practices from outsiders, Smith's support of marriage as he understood it appears genuine. Marriage allowed believers to create relationships of eternal durability. Most controversially, Smith's notions of exclusivity and sexual piety were subjugated to his broader goal of establishing the heaven family. Comments he made in response to a vehement temperance sermon in 1841, "what many people called sin was not sin & he did many things to break down superstition & he would break it down,"[148] might as easily have been applied to his assault on Victorian sexual piety as to his rejection of teetotalism. Smith was not, as he saw it, advocating libertinism.[149] He was proposing that a human soul could seal itself to myriad others in tender intimacy, bringing the limitless affections of the heavens into relationships on earth.

Celestial Marriage

When Smith first realized that he would teach the eternal durability of marriage is not certain. He grew up among people who, ignoring the protestations of their ministers, looked forward to family reunions in the afterlife.[150] In revealing how families could persist into the eternities, Smith was sketching out methods whereby the aspirations of many lay believers could be fulfilled. Though he preceded the postbellum efflorescence of the domestic heaven, Smith put into doctrine and ritual the beliefs of many of his peers, entering a divide between clergy and laiety in American Protestantism. Many if not most of the Protestant clergy stuck with Charles Buck in declaiming that marriage is a "very near and strict [union], and indeed indissoluble but by death."[151] However adamantly these conservative believers emphasized the earthly sanctity of marriage, they would not fall into the Sadducees' trap. Beyond the generic sense of the community of the blessed, few clergy or theologians endorsed the possibility of eternal marriage. If pushed, some might have admitted that a spouse would be one face among many they recognized and loved in the afterlife.

Long before they heard of the plurality of marriage, Smith's followers embraced his promise that they could be with their spouses forever. Even in the debacle over the "Fanny Alger affair" (an apparently polygamous relationship with a servant girl in the early 1830s, often considered Smith's first plural marriage),[152] the notion of permanent marriage covenants circulated publicly. In response to what he saw as Smith's adultery with Alger (1816–1889), Oliver Cowdery drafted and forced publication of the Latter-day Saints' "Articles of Marriage," a sternly Victorian document. After maintaining the necessity of strict monogamy, though, the regulations encouraged couples to "fulfill your covenants from henceforth and forever."[153] That "forever" came into increasingly clear view with the passage of time; the Latter-day Saints recycled the phrase to describe marriage in 1842 as they dealt with John C. Bennett, who tested the limits of proto-polygamy with disastrous results.[154]

During the Kirtland holy season, the Saints emphasized the durable society they were building as a church community. In one particularly powerful patriarchal blessing meeting already mentioned, the attendees pledged "to enjoy each others society forever more even all the blessings of heaven and earth."[155] Around this time, Mormons applied similar language to the marriage relationship. According to Phelps, the durability of marriage was "one of the most glorious consolations we can have in the flesh."[156] Later that year Phelps described the postmortal scope of marriage for the Latter-day Saints, explaining to his wife that "you will be mine in this world and in the world to come; and so long as you can remain on earth as you desire, I think you may as well use the word 'forever,' as 'till death.'"[157] In conjunction with immortalism, these private letters reflected an exegesis of 1 Corinthians: the Mormon heaven was the place "where the man is neither without the woman, nor the woman without the man in the Lord."[158] Mormons would live to the coming of Christ and would then continue in their marital relationships.

The earliest Latter-day Saint weddings were not superficially different from those of surrounding Protestants, though they were already pointing toward radical distinction.[159] The first wedding Smith performed, uniting Newell Knight (1800–1847) and Lydia Bailey (1812–1884) in 1835, demonstrates the shape of early Mormon marriage.[160] The couple were blessed, in typical Protestant style, "with the addition of long life and prosperity" for their union. Simultaneously, Smith taught that "marriage was an institution of h[e]aven institude in the Garden of Eden." Smith clarified that he was "conferring" the gifts of "Adam and Eve" on the conjugals. He then defined matrimony as "the blessings that the Lord confered upon Adam and Eve in the Garden of Eden," imagery confirmed in a Mormon hymn.[161] Evangelicals generally saw Adam and Eve as model monogamists and the proof of the validity of Protestant marriage.[162] Though it is tempting to see Smith's reference as basically Protestant, he took the Eden trope and turned it on its head. Even in 1835, as evidenced by his work on the Egyptian project, Joseph Smith was attributing great sacerdotal, covenantal, and mystical powers to the first parents in humanity's first garden and its occupants (see chapters 4 and 5).[163] Adam was a mighty patriarchal king, Eve his queen. When Smith said, "that it was necessary that it [marriage] should be Solemnized by the authority of the everlasting priesthood" during this wedding, he was referring to Adam and his patriarchal priesthood, not to a general Christian image. Knight's and Bailey's marriage in similitude of Eden suggested that their marriage would involve them in the sacerdotal genealogy of Mormonism.

As the Garden turned attention to Smith's lineal priesthood, it also pointed toward eternity: what had existed in the earth's first paradise would also exist in its last paradise. Celestial marriage combined the family backward through time, tying those wed within Mormonism to the first family, Adam and Eve, and to their magnificent genealogical power. Though Smith's radical distinction of celestial marriage from Protestant marriage only increased with time, he always returned to the primal garden. (As a harbinger of future developments, Lydia Bailey was legally still married to an abusive husband who had abandoned her; she agreed to violate local bigamy laws only at Smith's urging.)[164]

In January 1836, Smith supervised a wedding in which guests celebrated as had participants in the New Testament wedding at Cana. Recalling the setting of Christ's first miracle as he pointed cryptically toward the future, Smith announced that the weddings he performed were "conducted after the order of heaven," following the precedent of Abraham, Isaac, and Jacob.[165] Still using innocuous language, Smith referred to the patriarchal priesthood undergirding his sacerdotal genealogy. Over the next half decade, Smith continued to elaborate the doctrinal and ritual basis for such a heavenly order. By 1842–1843, as formal polygamy developed, the integration of marriage into patriarchal priesthood became explicit and inescapable. In 1842, Smith instructed Newell Whitney (1795–1850) to marry Smith to Newell's daughter Sarah (1825–1873). Their vows emphasized that the marriage was performed "in the name of my holy progenitors," based on the "right of birth which is of priesthood," one "obtained by the Holy Melchisedeck[,] Gethrow [Jethro,] and other of the Holy Fathers," emphasizing the men that had given authority to Abraham and Moses.[166] Echoing the language of patriarchal adoption, these powers would "concentrate" in Newell, the father of the plural bride, and through him to his "posterity forever." The wedding rites closed with the phrase "let immortality and eternal life hereafter be sealed upon your heads forever and ever."[167] The Whitney wedding made clear that the patriarchal authority was vested in newlyweds who took vows sanctioned by the priesthood, as it incorporated rhetoric from Smith's covenant and adoption theology.

With its integration into the corporate seals of Elijah's temple, marriage itself became a sacrament, an innovation in American

Protestantism.[168] Smith preached in 1843 that "we have no claim in our eternal comfort in relation to Eternal things unless our actions & contracts & all things tend to this end."[169] He made the same statement in his official revelation, announcing that "no one can reject this covenant and be permitted to enter my glory."[170] There was no way to participate in an eternally durable relationship unintentionally, just as, for many Protestants, there was no way to be saved without knowing it. In a funeral sermon in August 1843 Smith warned again that failure to anticipate the Mormon afterlife would prevent heavenly reunions, in another exegesis of the Lucan account of the Sadducean interrogation.[171] It would also, he informed William Clayton, mean that "they will cease to have increase when they died."[172] The urgency that this risk imparted meant that at least in one recorded case, celestial marriage was performed on a deathbed.[173]

Joseph Kingsbury (1798–1898) provides an emotionally powerful view into the heaven family as it intermingled with marriage. An early convert to Mormonism, Kingsbury married Caroline Whitney (1816–1842) in 1836. Caroline died in the fall of 1842 in childbirth after a three-month illness, perhaps eclampsia, leaving Kingsbury a devastated widower. When Joseph Smith Jr. laid his hands on Kingsbury on March 23, 1843, he gave a blessing that clearly demonstrated the interrelationships of the myriad aspects of the heaven family. Framing it as the second of Kingsbury's patriarchal blessings, Joseph Smith sealed Kingsbury and his wife up to their personal salvations. In the process he made clear that their marriage was eternal, and that as they were sealed to salvation they were sealed to each other. On that March day, Kingsbury's yearnings for his lost wife gained clear form. In Smith's phrase,

> I Seal the[e] up to Come forth in the first reserection unto Eternal Life—And thy Companion Caroline who is now dead thou shalt have in the first Reserection for I seal thee up for and in her behalf to Come forth in the first Reserection unto Eternal lives (and it Shall be as though She was present herself) and thou Shalt hail her and She Shall be thine and no one Shall have power to take her from thee. And you both Shall be Crowned and enthroned to dwell together in a Kingdom in the Celestial Glory in the presents of God, And you Shall Enjoy each other['s] Society & Embraces in all the fulness of the Gospell of Jesus Christ wourl[d]s with out End.[174]

Though Kingsbury completed a formal temple sealing in 1845 with a female proxy representing Caroline, the die was cast in 1843 through this multipotent blessing.[175] The Kingsbury blessing serves to clarify the development of the term "seal" from assured salvation to a bond between people. As we have seen in chapter 7, this sealing power contained several integrated meanings, whose foundation was the capacity to make human associations invulnerable to death by assuring salvation. Through the adoption theology, a surrogate could bear the seal of salvation for another, could be a channel through which salvation came. The image of "seal" as a specific bond between people reflects this intermediate understanding. Though some have argued for a sharp distinction between the different modes of sealing, polygamy makes clear the extent to which they are inseparable.[176] Through celestial marriage, participants were simultaneously sealed to salvation and thereby sealed to each other. The 1840s use of "seal" to refer to cemented interpersonal relationships was conventional language catching up to an established concept.

By the time the Latter-day Saints made polygamy public, the wedding rites had achieved stable form. In this canonized form, the system merged marital sealings into the temple cultus. Orson Pratt published the rites in the East Coast church organ the *Seer*, followed by republication in the *Millennial Star*. The ceremony specifically had a groom promise "with a covenant and promise" to "fulfill all the laws, rites, and ordinances, pertaining to this holy matrimony, in the new and everlasting covenant." Participants did so with a specifically celestial audience in mind. The marital commitment was made "in the presence of God, angels, and these witnesses."[177] The merger of personal commitment, the church covenant, and angelic community, present since the 1830s, had come to a final form.

Plurality

In the early 1840s, through the Anointed Quorum of the Nauvoo Temple, Smith began to reveal the full extent of his rejection of Protestant marriage both in heaven, and—much to the alarm of enemies and neighbors—on earth. Mormons would have their spouses for eternity. They would also hold them polygamously. His exegesis of the Sadducean interrogation always held eternity and plurality in a bold but uneasy equilibrium. Mormon references to "celestial" marriage are often seen as a smoke screen, a euphemism for the "spiritual wifery" of other reformers and critics of Victorian marriage, to make polygamy sound more respectable.[178] Such a view is incorrect: the celestial nature of Smith's family was central from the beginning.

The eternity of marriage pointed to plurality in at least two ways. The temporal flattening of eternal marriage made any act of remarriage after bereavement clear evidence of polygamy. Images of eternity also invoked cosmic time and cosmic order. The human family was the microcosm of an astronomical macrocosm. The plurality of worlds explained the plurality of family.

The continuities of eternity and plurality, readily apparent in retrospect, did not come naturally to early Latter-day Saints. Though it was an outgrowth of the heaven family, plural marriage represented to participants and observers a radical departure. In its distinctions from the rest of the heaven family, polygamy drew on, contested, and amplified various contexts in American culture and Christian history. Understanding proto-polygamy requires awareness of contexts both internal and external to Mormonism.

First and foremost, plural marriage grappled with death. The Sadducees had taunted Jesus with a thought experiment meant to subvert patriarchal marriage patterns. A literal resurrection, they teased, threatened strange permutations on marital arrangements. Although no Jew would endorse polyandry, most expressed reverence for the levirate duty. What happened, exactly, when a widower remarried? What about a widow? Behind the taunting stood the age-old cultural problem of remarriage after bereavement. To answer the Sadducees' question, the early Latter-day Saints responded that all marriages could be saved from the clutches of death, albeit in a new form. Polygamy provided reassurance that no ties would be severed, even in a society where widows and widowers multiplied seemingly without limit. Indeed, Hyrum's loss of his first wife, Jerusha, and subsequent marriage to Mary Fielding (1801–1852) brought this point forcefully to bear, as various authors have noted, including Hyrum himself.[179] Explaining and resolving this problem for family and followers alike, Joseph Smith offered a solution that preserved human relationships even as it radically revised the image of marital intimacy. Whereas other Protestants were beginning to anticipate heavenly reunions with spouses and children, Smith had the audacity to take the Sadducean thought experiment to its hyperlogical conclusion—not even serial remarriage could be abrogated by death.

Polygamy was also a radical act of biblical exegesis.[180] In the same general sense that charismata or early Christian communism shattered the uncomfortable and fragile truce that Bible-believing Christians made with scripture's supernatural content, so did polygamy point to the paradox at the center of Protestantism. Most American denominations were based on a book, commonsensically understood, written by and for a culture so radically different as to defy common sense. The biblical narrative reported and endorsed a variety of alien practices, a public secret that vexed the Protestant clergy. Within a bibliocentric worldview in which Scripture was the last word, the onus was on those who did not practice polygamy to explain why Abraham, Father Israel, and the Davidic dynasts, from whose consecrated seed came the Messiah, had wives and concubines.[181]

Mormon exegesis of biblical precedents for polygamy began with the Book of Mormon. In a much-quoted denunciation of polygamy and libertinism, a prophet named Jacob allowed God to "raise up seed unto" himself by polygamy if necessary.[182] This disclaimer alluded to Abraham, whom Jehovah allowed to impregnate Hagar, one of Abraham's servant girls, after his wife Sarai proved barren. This particular image persisted through the course of polygamy; Smith made specific mention of this Old Testament precedent in his 1843 revelation.[183] Other patriarchs followed Abraham's lead, and the Latter-day Saints in turn followed the lead of the patriarchs. When the Saints referred to polygamy as "patriarchal marriage," they had two meanings in mind. First, they meant marriage performed by their patriarchal priesthood, the power that created permanent sacerdotal relationships. Second, they meant marriage as practiced by the Bible's patriarchs.

The references to polygamy in Smith's preferred theological dictionary made clear polygamy's ancient roots and its persistent attraction for groups on Christianity's fringes. Attributed to a variety of heretical groups like the Anabaptists (and the derivative Knipperdolings), Abyssinians, and Nicolaitans, polygamy was a sign of enthusiasm and depravity for mainstream Protestants.[184] To many observers, Mormon polygamy sounded like nothing so much as a return to the notorious Munster of the sixteenth-century Anabaptists, the most famous fruits of the Radical Reformation. When John C. Bennett—for whom the experiment with polygamy had erupted into scandal, ostracism, and defection—embarked on a defamation tour, he compared his former coreligionists to ancient fanatics, the Anabaptists first among them.[185]

Another observer, writing before polygamy's revelation, correctly predicted plural marriage on the basis of other similarities to the Anabaptists.[186]

With his practice of polygamy, Smith was declaring sides in an ancient battle between visionaries and orthodoxers, between religious anomie and the established order. Just as he found reassurance in accounts of Marcionite baptism for the dead, so it appears that Smith gained confidence in his belief that he was restoring an ancient rite from polygamy's frequent recurrence throughout Christian history.

From its early inception, polygamy affirmed the eternity of every marital relationship in the face of serial bereavement and remarriage. Polygamy also integrated into Smith's restoration of biblical practices. Polygamy meant power, a power that would see its full expression when life unfolded on the broader stage of the universe, a power encompassed by Smith's priesthood.

The New and Everlasting Covenant of Marriage

Celestial marriage represented an extension of and elaboration upon Smith's covenant theology. Although it has been tempting, on the basis of later practice, to equate Mormonism's "new and everlasting covenant" solely with plural marriage, this equation elides important features of its development. Celestial marriage did not exhaust the scope of Mormonism's covenant.[187] What is striking is that Smith chose the phrase he used to describe his church and its priesthood ("new and everlasting covenant") as the title for his reform of the marriage system. The appropriation of covenantal language by celestial marriage demonstrated that family was the template for all relating and that Smith merged into his system the sometimes contradictory impulses of biological and ecclesial relationships. His covenant sought an outward focus. Whereas monogamy was exclusive and inwardly focused, polygamy was inclusive and outwardly focused. Smith's heaven family project constituted whole villages and kindreds around a paterfamilias rather than domestic hearths around a single couple.[188]

In the first decades of the nineteenth century, the patriarchal family of colonial New England gave way to mobile, individualized family units competing in and moving around the new republic. The storied, solemn coherence of New England towns was yielding to the free-for-all of life in new communities.[189] Though a skeptic could protest that the Puritans never achieved the patriarchal model or that societal norms surrounding the family are always in the midst of change, antebellum Americans underwent dramatic social change, and they believed that a traditional family model was on the decline.

Smith, who often sent his closest disciples on prolonged missions far from home, was acutely aware of the potential need to sacrifice the domestic hearth for the purposes of evangelism. In an 1840 letter to his apostles, he announced that "a man filled with the love of God, is not content with blessing his family alone but ranges through the world, anxious to bless the whole of the human family."[190] Polygamy, as a subset of Smith's family system, represented a marriage contract to encompass all of humanity. To the constricting hearth of Victorian piety, Smith responded with an ever-enlarging sacerdotal family. To situate Smith within Western political philosophy, polygamy was more Rousseau than Locke, more community than individual, more cosmopolitan than national. Smith's communal, sacerdotal system replaced the affectionate marriage of the Romantics and the isolated hearth of the Victorians. The way to survive the degradation of the world, Smith believed, was not to hide in a pious home but to band together in an ever-enlarging community sanctified by priesthood.

Some authors have argued for an irony in the Mormon system, that Smith believed in smaller families in the afterlife than those his Protestant peers anticipated, but that is not true.[191] Smith's eternal family was far vaster than the nuclear models of proto-Victorianism—every human being could join the Mormon heaven family. Faithful Latter-day Saints would see to that, even if they had to finish the work of sealing during Christ's millennial reign. Through adoption into the heaven family, all who did not refuse would eventually join that celestial society. One marker of the magnitude of Smith's family was his mother's anticipation, as she addressed the assembled church body shortly after his death, that church conferences were a preparation for the "millions" she would address in "celestial Glory."[192] The distinctions between the Mormon heaven family and the typical Protestant society of the blessed in the afterlife are more subtle than is often appreciated. What Smith and his followers were emphasizing, though, was the relevance of individual humans and the intensity of the individual relationships among humans, even in the presence of God's glory. There was something about the human capacity to relate to other humans that had to persist into eternity.

Tensions and Conflicts

Many authors have rightly emphasized the extent to which Smith's family system imposed order in the face of disorder. These accounts, though, risk missing just how disruptive Smith's eternal family was to the order advocated by Protestants. All antebellum Americans were struggling with changes in family life in one way or another. Evangelicals encouraged regeneration, seeing personal conversion and piety as the building blocks of a new world. Secularists welcomed changes in social structure as liberation from outmoded religion, while conservatives battled to strengthen their theologies in the face of religious voluntarism. Masons and other fraternal organizations worked to establish extraecclesial ties. What set Smith and his followers apart was not their struggle against social disorder. It was their intense otherworldliness, their fierce rejection of Protestant theologies, their potent sacramentalism, their simultaneously domestic and hierarchical model.

In his complex negotiations between domestic unity and membership in the sacerdotal kindred, Smith confronted a tension present in Christianity since its origins. In the New Testament, Jesus instructed his followers to "hate" their families in order to be worthy of discipleship, a hard teaching for two millennia of Christians and one that Smith explicitly invoked at times.[193] Particularly during periods of change, reform, or sectarian activity (what are often different faces of the same phenomenon), accepting Christ meant abandoning the comfort of home and family. The populist itinerants of the Second Great Awakening routinely eschewed domestic comforts to spread the good word of Christ. Mormonism forced the same trade-off. Early Mormonism was not easy for anyone. Smith was estranged from his in-laws and often absent from home, a dramatic and continuous stress on his first wife, Emma Hale. Though new religions grow through networks of kith and kin, this expansion is as likely to split as to unite any specific family group. The Latter-day Saint gospel broke genetic kindreds even as it relied upon such networks for proselytizing. Many narratives of conversion emphasized abandonment of natal families for the embrace of the new covenant; the church had been dealing with broken biological families from the beginning.

Domestic loyalties had a way of preventing a more glorious work in the views of many. Historian Whitney Cross proposed something like

this insight in his explanation of sexual experimentation on the antebellum New York frontier. "Intensely spiritual people discovered an
incompatibility between absolute good will among all regenerate beings
and the exclusive attachments of a man and a woman legally bound
together."[194] In the cruder phrase of William Phelps, monogamy represented the "gordian knot of bastard matrimony."[195] The new and
everlasting covenant, representing a pan-human allegiance, superseded
the mere love of any one man for any one woman. Smith seemed to be
making an analogy between the Latter-day Saints and God the Father,
whose love was boundless. God's love only grew with each additional
beloved soul. As the heaven family rejected exclusivity, it did so with an
eye toward a love that knew no bounds. As Latter-day Saints experimented with an eternally expanded hearth, they were in effect trying
out the relationships God and Christ promised to every righteous human
being. And there was something about creating those relationships that
mattered.

Understanding Smith as a harsh critic of the proto-Victorian family
sheds light on his practice of asking followers for their first wives.[196] In
about a dozen instances, Smith wedded women who were legally married
to other men. This practice, generally but inaccurately termed polyandry,
represented about a third of Smith's marriages.[197] His request for these
dual wives represented an Abrahamic test for these women and their
legal husbands. In marrying these women, Smith declared that the new
and everlasting covenant overwhelmed all prior social systems.[198]

Critics have tended to see Smith's dual wives as evidence of the
Prophet's overwhelming libido and/or his appetite for power. But Smith
seems to have been making a point with his creation of dual wives—the
established spousal relationships that held sway in decent society could
never block the grand project of Mormonism: the creation of an immortal
family that implemented these relationships in wider and wider circles of
kinship. Whereas John Humphrey Noyes practiced complex marriage
and Emanuel Swedenborg reshuffled (postmortally) marital associations
for love, Smith adjusted relationships as needed to establish the sacerdotal genealogy. In the calculus of the early Mormon heaven family, civil
marriages were as meaningless as unauthorized baptisms. No special dispensation was required to annul a civil marriage. The romance of affectionate couplings was simultaneously unstable and constricting as it
collapsed into an isolated nuclear island, separated from the continent of
humanity.[199] Following the uncomfortable phrase of Jesus in the New

Testament, God might require believers to hate their spouses in order to love the Kingdom.

The melancholy experience of Smith's dual wife Zina Diantha Huntington (1821–1901) and her young husband, Henry Jacobs, exemplifies the fracture between domestic romance and Smith's new system of celestial marriage. Huntington married Smith in 1842, though she continued to cohabit with Jacobs and bear him children. After Smith's death, Brigham Young required Huntington as a levirate wife, and the heartbroken Jacobs tried unsuccessfully to start again with a new companion.[200] Writing to his dual wife, Jacobs lamented, "Zina my mind never will change from Worlds without Ends, no never, the same affection is there and never can be moved I do not murmur nor complain of the handlings of God no verily, no but I feel alone and no one to speak to, to call my own."[201] Huntington, by then a powerful matriarch in Utah Mormonism, spoke for many Mormon women when she reflected that polygamy had made "love" a "false sentiment" when it was applied romantically to the institution of marriage.[202] The constriction of devotion to two individuals violated the expansive scope of the heaven family: the doubled lives of Smith's dual wives served as a strong reminder that marriage was not primarily to protect exclusive pairings but to create a heavenly network of belonging.

Even in the complexity of his protest against Victorianism, Smith's family covenant concerned itself repeatedly, incessantly, with death. Smith spent his entire religious career creating a space for secure salvation before death independent of both Arminianism and Calvinism. The seals of Kirtland and endowments of Nauvoo, the patriarchal blessings and Books of Life, the proxy baptisms and sacred anointings, all sought to make the Saints invulnerable to death and damnation. It bears repeating that what mattered most about death in Calvinism and Arminianism was the risk that salvation could be lost before death and never recovered. To secure his followers against death, Smith revealed an array of rites, beliefs, and practices to guarantee salvation. Celestial marriage took its rightful place in the Mormon cultus. Through the patriarchal priesthood and the sacerdotal genealogy that it created, the Latter-day Saints believed that they were already living in the heavenly society.[203]

Smith's heaven family expressed a theology that assaulted deeply held views of all the major Protestantisms surrounding the Latter-day Saints. In place of the individual elected to Calvinist regeneration or the

converted Arminian who chose not to reject God's grace, Smith revealed
a sacramentalism grounded in his patriarchal system that could save
anyone. In the 1840s, Smith assured mourning parents that even their
backsliding children could be saved by the strength of the covenant. It
was the power of the priesthood of the patriarchs, the merger of lineal
affinity and sacerdotal authority, that could perhaps save even the
unworthy.

The possibility that children could be saved by the covenant of their
parents took shape as Smith clarified the meaning of Elijah and election.
In the Elias Higbee funeral sermon Smith preached that the

> Doctrine [of] Election.—sealing of the servants of God on the
> top of their heads. tis not the cross as the catholics would have it.
> doctrine of Election to Abraham was in the relation to the Lord,
> a man wishes to be embraced in the covenant of Abraham. A man
> Judge Higby—in world of spirits, is sealed unto the throne, &
> doctrine of Election sealing the father & children together.[204]

Two weeks later Smith returned to the topic, preaching to his followers:
God "shall reveal the covenants to seal the hearts of the fathers to the
children and the children to the fathers.—anointing & sealing—called
elected and made sure."[205] The sealing power seemed strong enough to
save offspring. Puritans had allowed baptism as a placeholder for unre-
generated parents who were themselves children of regenerate parents.
Their children, the grandchildren of the pious, covenanted generation, could still be included in the covenant. The covenants of early
Mormonism always contained this genealogical aspect. In many cases
Latter-day Saints understood the "everlasting covenant" as the promise
God made to Abraham in Genesis 17, a perpetual guarantee regarding
his offspring. Similarly the rainbow of Genesis 9 was seen as the marker
of that covenant carried forward, God's promise to protect the offspring
of the righteous from harm. In the early 1830s, Smith preached that
"the Lord hath redeemed his people Israel, according to the election of
grace which was brought to pass by the faith and covenant of the[i]r
fathers."[206] Generic preaching on the Israelite covenant had become the
specific power of the sacerdotal genealogy over the course of Smith's
career.

The 1843 Higbee funeral sermon further clarified the potency of
Smith's family sealing rituals. Smith claimed that through sacerdotal

sealings, his followers would join the immortal prophet and bind their children to themselves so strongly that nothing could break them apart. "A measure of this sealing is to confirm upon their head in common with Elijah the doctrine of election or the covenant with Abraham—which when a Father & mother of a family have entered into their children who have not transgressed are secured by the seal where with the Parents have been sealed."[207] William Clayton's account of the funeral sermon confirmed that when parents make "their calling and election sure...a seal is put upon the father and mother [securing] their posterity so that they cannot be lost but will be saved by virtue of the covenant of their father."[208] This power answered both Calvinists and Arminians. Against the Arminians, children could be saved without ever experiencing regeneration and conversion. Against the Calvinists, it was the employment of Elijah's patriarchal priesthood, rather than the sovereign will of God, that saved kindreds together.

Such a view easily degenerates into the type of anomie that the opponents of antinomianism routinely decried, and after Smith's death, the Latter-day Saints had to grapple with the implications of a system that their founding prophet had only sketched out. They debated what adoption meant, who God was exactly and how he related to the human family, and what free will meant if a covenant could save even the unworthy.[209] By the twentieth century, the distinctive belief that relationships could save even the unworthy had largely receded, with modern Mormons emphasizing the centrality of individual will and Arminian views of salvation. Had he lived longer Smith might have emphasized that his was a corporate vision of grace, that just as the God of Calvinism could save unworthy souls, so could the patriarchal covenant. He might have spent more time clarifying his marvelously literal reading of Obadiah in which the Saints became "saviors on Mount Zion." He might have emphasized how his was another view of sacramentalism, that it was not just the anointings and temple catechisms that saved the Latter-day Saints, it was the sacred communion they created as they suffused their relationships with a priesthood power that came through Christ. In the event, Smith revealed a power to save his followers but did not systematize its theological implications.

In addition to the assurance of salvation, polygamy also contained the promise of endless glory as a function of expansion of the family in the afterlife. Employing the infrastructure of the Chain of Belonging, polygamy promised that a couple's glory would rise endlessly with their celestial offspring. The size of one's family was, in the calculus of the Mormon Chain, the measure of one's actual glory.[210] This hope for generative glory, rather than Swedenborg's sensually "conjugial" love, seems to be the foundation for Smith's anticipation that procreation would persist in the afterlife.[211] Smith's Latter-day Chain grew with each new relationship he and his followers created.[212]

The notion that afterlife glory derived from the size of one's family underlay a dynastic explanation of the need for polygamy. Several young women agreed to participate in the practice in hopes of bringing afterlife glory to themselves, their offspring, and their natal families.[213] In the merger of the sacerdotal genealogy with marital practices, increasingly Mormons saw themselves as royalty in the next life. With time, the claim to queenhood and kinghood became quite prominent—this appropriation of royal titles was shorthand for the promise of high status in the postmortal Chain of Belonging as a result of the families they created within the temple.

Joseph Smith's family system, however controversial and socially disruptive, was not simply the sexual experimentation of a communitarian mystic from New York's Burned-Over District. Nor was it simply a cloak for the overflowing libido of a charismatic prophet, however physically satisfying plural marriage might have been for husbands. Smith spent years developing a ritual and theological system that recast community and the relationship to God as a binding and saving pedigree. Polygamy negotiated the extremes of atomistic families in a fractured world and generated coherent community in the face of death, creating in the process a heaven on earth.

The excitement associated with Smith's heaven family will be difficult for a modern audience to appreciate. William Phelps, preaching Joseph Smith's eulogy in 1844, proclaimed,

> when the temple is made ready for the holy work; so we can go on from birth to age; from life to death; and from life to lives; and from world to heaven; and from heaven to eternity; and from eternity to ceaseless progression; and in the midst of all these changes; we can pass from scene to scene; from joy to joy; from glory to glory; from wisdom to wisdom; from system to system; from god to god, and from one perfection to another, while eternities go and eternities come, and yet there is room—for the

curtains of endless progression are stretched out still and a god is there to go ahead with improvements.[214]

Smith's sacerdotal genealogy brought the universe's powers to bear in defense of extended human associations, even as they gave the universe a decidedly familial face. In the words of Parley Pratt, "the celestial [family] order is an order of eternal life; it knows no death."[215]

9

Divine Anthropology

Translating the Suprahuman Chain

In 1845 William Phelps published a short story to celebrate the revelations of his martyred prophet. Having just written a hymn, "Come to Me," in which a postmortal Joseph beckoned to his followers across the veil of death, Phelps turned to fiction to express the ontological infrastructure that permitted and gave order to such reunions.[1] Serialized in the *Times and Seasons*, "Paracletes" tells the story of a vast kindred of divine beings, their name derived from a New Testament title (*parakletos*) understood by many antebellum Christians to represent the Holy Spirit.[2] In this idiosyncratic and often spectacular fiction, Phelps situated the earth's history within a grand cosmic order of creation, progression, and exaltation. In "Paracletes," a "head" God oversees a boundless dynasty of divine beings with angelic-sounding Hebrew names. These paracletes become embodied as humans according to a "plan of salvation," thereby acquiring the experience necessary to develop the status of "head" of their own offspring. Paracletes create worlds, develop in metaphysical maturity and power, and reproduce after their own kind. The story begins as a figure named Milauleph, the first paraclete (as reflected by the Hebrew letter aleph in his name), undertakes to create and people a world.[3] He does so and is then exalted with his offspring. His brothers, named for each of the first seven letters of the Hebrew alphabet, implicitly follow a similar course, including a fall into a mortal state. Situating his story in Idumia, a scriptural code word for Earth, Phelps wanted the reader to believe that he fictionalized only minor portions of this distinctive cosmology.[4] The story and its underlying cosmology proposed the absolute equivalence of humans, Gods, and angels—these beings, his story afffirmed, are different developmental stages rather than distinct types of beings. They are all paracletes.

Though there is room to contest aspects of the fidelity of Phelps's depiction of Smith's worldview, "Paracletes" provides an important early and comprehensive account of Smith's divine anthropology, a term I have proposed to capture the sense in which Smith saw God and humans as conspecific.[5] Phelps and Smith differed primarily in the name they gave to such beings. Whereas Phelps borrowed from New Testament Greek, Smith acquired the name Ahman from the pure language of Adam.[6] As Smith sketched out the life cycle of the species Ahman, he further reformed the Chain of Being, collapsing its upper expanses into the sacerdotal genealogy. Instead of demigods and nine degrees of angels, in Smith's reading there were only divine-human beings—members of a family—in the highest echelons of the Chain. The ontological collapse within the Mormon Chain demonstrates that the distinctive Mormon beliefs in divine humanity and human divinity are inextricably connected to the seals of the sacerdotal genealogy within the Mormon Chain of Belonging. The intense universal anthropomorphization of Smith's divine anthropology broadcast human relationships onto the cosmos, establishing their permanence in both time and space. This divine anthropology became Smith's ritual and theological swan song, the culminating volley in his battle against death. In this anthropology, supported by a distinctively Mormon *imitatio Christi*, the Latter-day Saints saw their own safe passage to a heaven so inseparable from the good things of earth as to deny completely the power of death.

Pre-existent Intelligences

"Paracletes" began, as did the divine anthropology, in a time before beginnings, before Eve and Adam entered the Garden. Early in his career, Smith announced that just as Christ had an existence before mortality, so did all humanity.[7] Human pre-existence combined several conceptual strands to frame the remainder of the divine anthropology. In the New Translation of Genesis, Smith announced that a spiritual creation anteceded the physical creation, an exegetical solution to the competing creation accounts of the received text.[8] An incidental reference in an 1831 denunciation of Shakers alluded to this claim, a human "creation before the world was made."[9] Within the New Translation, Smith introduced a version of the New Testament "war in heaven," in which Lucifer drew unfaithful spirits from heaven to become demons.[10] These events before the physical creation of the world pointed toward a central element of divine anthropology—humans followed Jesus much like Moses, who existed "in similitude to mine only begotten."[11] In 1833 Smith adopted Jesus's voice in an inspired reworking of the Gospel of John. Introducing a theme that persisted throughout the divine anthropology, Jesus announced: "I was in the beginning with the Father," and "all those who are begotten through me are partakers of the glory of the same." Addressing Mormons directly, Jesus told them "ye were also in the beginning with the Father." In this syllogism, Smith revealed an *imitatio Christi* to animate the divine anthropology. While Americans have famously recast Christ in their own image for centuries, in this case Mormons radically recast themselves in the image of Christ, "the great prototype of all saved beings."[12] In place of the pietistic tradition generally traced to Thomas à Kempis's fifteenth-century *Imitation of Christ*, in which believers strove to pattern their moral lives after the example of Jesus, Mormons saw the secrets of their past and future in the scriptural record of Christ's life and the promises of his glorious afterlife. Christ showed humans the way. In his Incarnation, Christ obliterated the distance between God and humans. If Christ had pre-existence, so did humans.[13] Through Christ, humans experienced a birth that obliterated all births—they had no beginning. In the phrase of the Mormon revelation, "Man was also in the beginning with God. Intelligence, or the light of truth, was not created or made, neither indeed can be."[14]

Even at this early stage, the doctrine of human pre-existence circulated inside and outside the church. In early 1833, the Saints composed a hymn devoted to Enoch, one of the central figures of the New Translation's restoration of lost texts, in which they proclaimed:

> With God he saw his race began,
> And from him emanated man,
> And with him did in glory dwell,
> Before there was an earth or hell.[15]

The Egyptian project expanded and refined this teaching. In a pregnant correction of the KJV, the Abraham creation account clarified that what entered Adam's nostrils at the time of his mortal birth was not the divine *ruakh*, but "the man's spirit."[16] That spirit, just as Christ's, existed before Eden. In June 1835, cryptically describing the contents of the papyrus translation, Phelps announced: "we shall by and bye learn that we were with God in another world, before the foundation of the world, and had our agency: that we came into this world and have our agency, in order that we may prepare ourselves for a kingdom of glory; become archangels, even the sons of God."[17] The funerary papyri proved an excellent platform to explain the details of human preexistence. In the ultimately canonized Book of Abraham (c. 1842), Smith saw Abraham's vision of the world's history as beginning with a divine council of "the intelligences that were organized before the world was." These divine-human intelligences participated with God in the creation of the earth.[18] Smith continued to reveal details of this life before life throughout his career.[19]

Human pre-existence dovetailed nicely for Smith with the eternal nature of matter, a doctrine he worked on in parallel (see chapter 2). Some thinkers of antiquity argued for the eternity of matter, the probability that, in the phrase of Justin Martyr, God "formed the world out of unfashioned matter."[20] With linguistic training Smith would, as some other observers, find in the Hebrew verbal root *BR' the proof that God "organized" the world rather than willed it into existence ex nihilo.[21] Such a notion had pre-Christian precedent: Lucretius, the famous Epicurean poet, had maintained that "naught from nothing springs," an idea that circulated in a variety of learned sources at the time of Smith. In an interesting sense, Smith was responding to Lucretius's famous "argument from symmetry." Discouraging what he saw as an irrational fear of death (while rejecting the eternity of human souls), Lucretius had argued that human indifference to the period of "eternal time" in which humans did not exist before birth should result in an equal indifference to the period of time after they ceased to exist. Smith agreed that these periods were symmetrical and not to be mourned. The reason, though, was that there was no nonexistence on either side of mortal life. For the Mormon prophet, the fact that humans existed before they were born proved that they would exist after they died.[22]

Human pre-existence proved heady material for the Latter-day Saints. In the phrase of Parley Pratt shortly before Smith's death, they were told to "learn what man was before this life and what he will be in the worlds to come. Or seated high on a throne celestial surrounded with the chaotic mass of unorganized existence; search out the origin of matter and of mind."[23] Smith was solving problems both human and cosmic in scope when he extended preexistence from Christ to all humanity.

The notion of preexistence was not unique to Smith. Many Christians historically and contemporarily believed in the pre-existence of Christ;

some, following Origen and Plato in their own complex ways, even believed in the pre-existence of human souls. The Gnostics particularly preached that angels had pre-existed alongside Christ.[24] Believers had a variety of scriptural texts to draw on for a belief in human preexistence, most famously Job's account of "morning stars" that "sang together" at the time of creation, a group that paralleled "all the sons of God" who "shouted for joy" in the presence of the Creator (38:7).[25] For the Latter-day Saints, scriptures traditionally understood to refer to predestination confirmed human pre-existence.[26] What distinguished Smith from most other voices was his ontological *imitatio Christi*. Smith's humans were like Christ; they were Job's "sons of God" beside the "morning stars" in the time and space before the world was.

Rather than the devotional, pietistic *imitatio Christi* of other Protestants, for Smith's followers the imitation of Christ was a way to understand themselves, their origins and endings, or more properly, the fact that they had neither. The rest of the divine anthropology in many respects explained how it was that humans came to be present with God, Jesus, and the angels before the world was. Human pre-existence launched the Latter-day Saints on a sustained exploration of what it meant for angels and humans to be the same kind of being.

Angels

Angels, the sons of the morning whose shouts for joy confirmed at least limited pre-existence for many Christians, played a central role in Smith's divine anthropology. Encounters with and explanations of angels were present with Smith from the beginning of his religious career to its end, and over the course of that career, angels became a potent medium for rephrasing and reinterpreting the nature of humans and the nature of God. Situated between God and humanity in biblical, metaphysical, Neoplatonic, and folk traditions, angels played complex, variable, and controversial roles in the construction of cosmology, human identity, and the nature of God. As in other traditions, angels explained a great deal for the Latter-day Saints. Because angels proved so central to the divine anthropology, understanding the conceptual context of angels in Western religion is important before considering Smith's distinctive views.

Of the many varied angelologies in Western traditions, the ones most relevant to Smith include those that left an imprint in biblical narratives, those of elite Anglo-American Protestants in the late eighteenth and early nineteenth centuries, and those of lay believers contemporary with the Latter-day Saints. The complexity of ancient angelologies need not detain us long. Sometimes bearing the marks of antecedent polytheisms, angels in the Hebrew Bible generally either represented humanlike manifestations of Divinity (the "angel of Yahweh's presence") or a multiplicative hierarchy of suprahuman beings.[27] Whatever these angels were—and they meant different things to different groups—they were generally not human.

Within early Christianity, these multivalent beings served different groups in different ways. Several New Testament authors were comfortable with Hebrew traditions. With the interposition of Greek philosophy, a hierarchical multiplicity of angels, from the archangel(s) through cherubim, principalities, thrones, dominions, and other angelic orders proved the essential harmony and complexity of the Great Chain of Being. Despite such Hellenic borrowings, popular devotion began with time to shift more toward the saints, Christianity's "holy dead."[28] The image of Jacob's ladder, a trope for the potential of the Chain and the capacity to be connected to the heavens, was a perfect emblem of angelic intercourse with humanity.[29] Sometimes the border between resurrected beings and angels was permeable. The New Testament, particularly in its account of Jesus's Transfiguration, supported speculation about angels as patriarchs returning to earth. In this story Elijah and Moses met Jesus on a mountain, traditionally Mt. Hermon, a visitation his disciples witnessed.[30] Such an equation of angels and at least certain humans had been a recurring, if highly controversial, theme for the entire history of the Hebrew Bible.[31]

Early Christian ideas about angels evolved through the medieval period. Though there was never a single normative view of angels, they were often seen as forces for good to counterbalance demons. They also continued to constitute hierarchies that confirmed human social structures and played into Neoplatonic and related ideas about how the universe operated under the hands of an all-wise and all-powerful Creator.[32]

In the early modern period, the major Protestant groups held mixed views of angels. Martin Luther turned a tolerant eye, allowing lay beliefs to persist.[33] Second-generation Reformers, Jean Calvin being the best known example, were not eager to incorporate angels into worship and theology, seeing them as superstitions or dangerous distractions from

Christ. They argued against perceived excesses of belief. Reformers were not entirely successful at keeping angels to a low profile, however. The epic poem *Paradise Lost*, by John Milton (1608–1674), solidified and perpetuated a traditional angelology that still influenced conservative evangelicals in the early nineteenth century.[34] Increase Mather (1639–1723) wrote an entire tome on angels at the end of the seventeenth century, while across the Atlantic, the Anglican divine John Reynolds (1667–1727) published a speculative set of "queries" about angels with answers drawn from biblical texts, although he did not expect to see angels roaming eighteenth-century England.[35] Two generations later, Jonathan Edwards did not worry about angels much, despite his astounding revivalistic experiences and strong support for New Light Calvinism.[36]

As Western Protestants slowly absorbed Enlightenment principles, the role of angels diminished further.[37] Enlightenment rationality and religious conservatism left less room for angels, particularly as physical beings, in the worldview of educated believers.[38] Still, many Protestants continued to affirm belief in the higher orders of angels and saw them as the subdivine pinnacle of the Chain of Being; some saw in angelic encounters a kind of democratic power.[39]

However uncomfortable Reformed theologians and clergy became with interventionist angels, the biblical witness required them to maintain the view that angels were present at least in heaven.[40] Buck's treatment of angels for his *Theological Dictionary* is emblematic of the complex role angels played for Protestants in the early nineteenth century. Buck began his entry by claiming angels as "a spiritual intelligent substance, the first in rank and dignity among created beings," a recognizable if diluted invocation of the tenets of the Chain of Being. He admitted that angels were probably created before humans but was unwilling to take a firm stand. After toying with the various orders of angels both good and bad and the biblical proof texts for graded orders of angels, Buck avoided committing to any particular angelology. He was satisfied, quoting Hebrews 1:14, "to know that they are all ministering spirits, sent forth to minister to them who are heirs of Salvation." Citing Reynolds in his suggested readings, Buck refrained from even the relatively mild speculation of his eighteenth-century predecessor. Whatever the specifics, in most conservative treatments, angels remained distant from human experience.[41]

Outside conservative circles, though, angels continued to stir believers. Although the tenor of visits changed with time, in Smith's day visionaries still reported direct encounters with angels. Generally these were luminous supernatural beings with a message from God; however, particularly in the eighteenth century, they might as easily have been a dead friend or relative come with a warning.[42] The varied individuals by the early nineteenth century who claimed visits from angels were almost invariably outside the mainstream. Swedenborg was a sort of prototype for these encounters, with his decades spent in near-daily communion with angels who were former humans. Given more credit than others, probably because of his scientific training and social prominence, Swedenborg's accounts of angels circulated in the first decades of the nineteenth century.[43] Even someone as learned and conservative as Jonathan B. Turner could praise Swedenborg in comparison with less educated fanatics.[44] By the 1840s Swedenborg's *Heaven and Hell*, packed tight with accounts of conversations with angels, was an American bestseller.

Most lay Protestants stood between the extremes of conservative Calvinists and visionaries. Many continued to wonder about the nature and proximity of angels without claiming to have seen them. Though little can parallel the complexity of medieval angelology, even America under the spell of Enlightenment thought supported a variety of quite specific discourses about angels. In fact, one reason for Buck's pronouncements on the insolubility of ongoing controversies—over topics from angels' corporality to their mission to their access to the earth and its inhabitants—was because these debates continued to rage among believers. A sentimentalism not yet divorced from the supernatural wonders of the seventeenth century continued to allow that angels might still play a role in human lives, particularly at deathbeds as heavenly escorts or in times of peril as supernatural guardians.[45] Some interpreted natural sounds in the environment as an angelic choir preparing to welcome a dying man to heaven.[46] Heard but not seen, such hosts were allowed near human beings only when the veil separating heaven and earth was already thin.

Lay believers did, however, embrace angels as guardians, protectors assigned to specific individuals. These beings personalized the interest of the Divine in human fate, a belief even Luther had maintained despite the later Protestant resistance to the teaching (Calvin particularly disliked the notion of guardian angels).[47] These protectors in desperate times could be understood metaphorically, as ways to keep God and the sacred in human lives without the frank supernaturalism required to explain physical encounters between humans and supernatural beings.[48] The clergy generally resisted even such diluted invocations of angelic power. Buck confronted the ongoing controversy over guardian angels by quoting Matthew Henry's Bible commentary: "What need we dispute...whether every particular saint has a *guardian* angel, when we are sure he has a *guard* of angels about him?"[49] Still, lay believers could not be persuaded to abandon such beliefs entirely.[50]

Mormon Angels

Into this milieu came the young Joseph Smith. Early in his religious career he announced, to the bemusement of critics and the adulation of followers, that he experienced sustained direct encounters with scores of angels, promising the same privileges to all who embraced his priesthood. Probably beginning with Moroni, the lost prophet of American prehistory, Smith reported having audiences with myriad supernatural beings after his First Vision.[51] More than anything, these figures were holy men resurrected from the pages of ancient scripture. Smith derived his authority from them, used them as external evidences of his gold plates, shook their hands, and revealed their ancient identities. He also, through his genealogized Chain, forced a reconsideration of the upper echelons of the celestial hierarchy in direct antagonism to theocentric tradition. In simplest terms, his angels were the human dead, from the most glorious patriarch to the humblest of the dearly departed.

Smith posited the equivalence of humans and angels as early as the spring of 1832. As part of his ongoing efforts to recover the lost language of Eden (see chapter 5), Smith shared with his inner circle a "Sample of Pure Language." In it he made clear that *Awman* (spelled "Ahman" in publications) represented divinity, the divine species, "the being which made all things in all its parts." Jesus, humans, and angels all received names in this revelation—*Son Ahman, Sons Ahman,* and *Angls-man,* respectively. Even in this early statement stood the hint that humans would be superior to angels—humans were "the greatest parts of Awman," whereas angels were to "minister for or to" humans.[52]

The Bible also served to ground Smith's encounters with angels. The Lucan account of the Sadducean interrogation of Christ that figured so prominently in support of the plurality of wives provided further support for the equivalence of humans and angels. According to the New

Translation, Jesus answered the Sadducees by teaching that the resurrected are "equal unto the angels; and are the chil[dren] of God, being the children of the resurection."[53] During the Kirtland holy season, Smith reported an almost perfect recapitulation of the Transfiguration encounter—the same patriarchs who had visited Mt. Hermon to see Jesus came to Latter-day Saint Kirtland. Whereas other contemporary Protestants saw in the Transfiguration account support for "heavenly recognition" of deceased loved ones, Smith saw Elijah and Moses as evidence that angels were fundamentally human.[54]

The heroes of scriptural narratives proved to be the crucial link between humans and angels for the early Latter-day Saints. These figures cemented for the Latter-day Saints the possible equivalence of humans and angels. By the early 1830s, Smith had proposed specific angelic identities for key patriarchs. The chief archangels of Christian traditions, Michael and Gabriel, Smith announced, were in fact the fathers of humanity's two foundations, Adam and Noah.[55] Adam had been important to a variety of metaphysical and religious traditions, and some have suggested that Smith drew upon hermetic ideas about Adam. Smith seems more than anything, though, to have understood Adam in familial context, as the first human parent, the exemplary patriarch of the human race. Michael-Adam, "who acts under the direction of Christ," directed a network of patriarchal angels, who figured in a variety of settings in early Mormonism.[56]

The humanized angels cared passionately about the living. Not only did the Latter-day Saints care for angels, the angels looked after them. According to an 1839 sermon, "These men are in heaven, but their children are on Earth. Their bowels yearn over us."[57] In the same sermon, Smith employed a distinctive exegesis of Matthew 13:31–32 to make the same point. "The fowls are the Angels," and "these Angels come down combined together to gather their children."[58] Caring within the family of Ahman extended in both directions.

Though Adam-Michael as the Ancient of Days was the most famous of the humanized angels, he and Noah-Gabriel were not alone in the Mormon angelology. In an application of his characteristic exegesis, Smith revealed in the fall of 1840 that when the Book of Hebrews announced that Abel, "being dead, yet speaketh" (a famous martyrological and vaguely necromantic phrase for many Protestants), it meant that Abel had appeared to Paul as an angel.[59] Abel, Smith informed his followers, had been resurrected, had "become a righteous man an angel of God by receiving his body from the dead."[60] So had Enoch, who visited the New Testament Jude. "He is a ministring Angel to minister to those who shall be heirs of Salvation and appered unto Jude as Abel did unto Paul, therefore Jude spoke of him 14 & 15 verses in Jude."[61] Such a reading of Christian scripture integrated with Smith's own religious experience and scriptural tradition. Visiting angels brought scripture, Abel visiting Paul and Enoch Jude, the way Moroni visited Smith.[62]

Biblical patriarchs pointed the way for the rank and file. In 1839 Joseph Smith taught that angels, as opposed to demons, were "Saints with there resurrected Bodies."[63] A year later he announced: "Angels are beings who have bodies and appear to men in the form of man."[64] This was an elaboration of the Abraham theogony, in which what Lucifer and his minions lost was the opportunity to be embodied. Disembodied angels, according to Smith's theogony, were in fact demons. But if angels had bodies, how could they be different from resurrected humans? The answer for Smith was simple: they were the same. This earthly intimacy portended a community to come. Don Carlos Smith followed his brother Joseph's lead, preaching that if the Latter-day Saints "keep his word shall all be actuated By the same principles be as one man; & as angels are obedient to the same word we shall have Concorse to them & also to all the Heavnly throng."[65] There was a promise of the society of angels for those who obeyed. "If you live up to these principles how great and glorious—if you live up to your privilege the angels cannot be restrain'd from being your associates."[66] In Hebrews 12:22–23, Latter-day Saints found reassurance that they could expect a community of Saints and "the innumerable company of angels."[67] In 1843 Smith described the afterlife glory in which Latter-day Saints come to "mount Sion," "the city of the living God," filled with angels, a communion made possible by Elijah and his temple.[68]

Smith's understanding of angels as advanced humans resonated with his followers. They took great pride in knowing angels' secrets and in seeing in angelic identities their own eternal prospects. Phelps seized on these humanized angels in the *Messenger and Advocate* in 1835. There he answered his rhetorical "Are the angels in glory the former prophets and servants of God?" with an emphatic yes, an image he confirmed in a Eucharistic hymn.[69] Sidney Rigdon reiterated this claim in the same venue two months later.[70] This conviction only increased under the power of Smith's continued audiences with the dead as angels.

Ultimately, Smith and his colleagues took the identity of humans and angels to its logical conclusion. Joseph Smith Jr., the patriarch of the last phase of human history, was himself an archangel. One reminiscent account of the Kirtland holy season recalled: "At the close of the fore noon meeting Apostle Erastus Snow Said when they were convened in the Kirtland Temple there was a young man wrought upon by the Spirit of prophecy & foretold that the prophet Jos Smith would be the Sixth Angel."[71] Smith went on record to that effect in 1840, during a "fast & Prayer Meeting." The Prophet preached "that inasmuch as the Saints will leav[e] of[f] Speaking evil of one another & not Speaking evil of the Seer which Speaking evil of the archangel or the holy Keys which he held" they would receive their requested blessings.[72] In this strongly worded prohibition of criticism, Smith employed the image of angel as a sort of priesthood office, a designation that persisted after his death (see chapter 10).

As he made angels human, Smith flattened the ontologies of prior angelic hierarchies. Though he made passing rhetorical reference to the "dominions" and "principalities" of prior angelologies, he radically minimized the explanatory power of the traditional Chain of Being. The hierarchy of Smith's Chain was genealogical rather than ontological: it had no room for dominions and principalities as distinct orders of angels. Whereas someone like John Reynolds had proposed that certain righteous individuals might potentially join the angelic hierarchies, Smith claimed that angels would be incorporated into the human family hierarchies.[73]

The flattening was not entirely complete: Smith did endorse one important hierarchical subdivision within the hosts of angelic beings. In exegesis of passages in the first chapters of Hebrews, Smith revealed that ministering spirits were a lesser stage of maturity than angels per se.[74] In 1839 he preached that "the Spirits of Just men made perfect are those without bodies."[75] In 1841 he "explained a difference between an angel and a ministering spirit; the one a resurrected or translated body, with its spirit, ministering to embodied spirits—the other a disembodied spirit, visiting and ministering to disembodied spirits."[76] In a funeral sermon in 1843 Smith again stressed "the importance of understanding the distinction between the spirits of the just, and angels." According to Smith, "Spirits can only be revealed in flaming fire, or glory. Angels have advanced farther—their light and glory being tabernacled, and hence appear in bodily shape."[77] Swedenborg, too, had divided spirits from angels in his taxonomy of the supernatural world, though his taxonomy differed some from its early Mormon counterpart.[78] An editorial in *Times and Seasons* shortly after Smith's death proposed a belief in multiple orders of angels, minimally archangels, resurrected angels, and ministering spirits, which may represent "two distinct races in the heavenly world." The middle group comprised "the angels, which are resurrected bodies." This editorial went further than Smith, using correspondence to assign to particular beings particular guides: "the angels who minister to men in the flesh, are resurrected beings, so that flesh administers to flesh; and spirits to spirits."[79] This was following Smith's own view that correspondence explained pairings between spirit and spirit and flesh and flesh. This odd taxonomy meant essentially that angels could interact with humans as physical guardians, while the recently human, awaiting resurrection, could minister to spirits in prison (Smith even distinguished two separate postmortal ministries of Christ, before and after his resurrection).[80] Even this hierarchy, though, was compatible with the ontological flattening, as the status of ministering spirits was merely a way station for those who would soon achieve the higher status. These ministering spirits would one day be reembodied.

The promotion of human beings reached such a remarkable extent that Smith finally proposed that the term *angel* could refer to an inferior class of beings, an extended exegesis of the Lucan account of the Sadducees' interrogation of Christ. Those *Sons Ahman* who could not be integrated into the family tree (along with those humans unfit for "exaltation") would be retained as servants to their more exalted cousins, an inversion of the Augustinian teaching.[81] They would be "appointed angels in heaven, which angels are ministering Servants to minister for those who are worthy of a far more, and an exceeding, and an eternal weight of glory."[82] Stripped of family, these "angels" fell below the hierarchy of heaven. This bold claim, made clearest in expositions of plural marriage, drew on another exegetical line. Following an earlier sermon by Smith, the Nauvoo High Council asked rhetorically "Know ye not that we shall judge Angels?" and then confirmed explicitly that "the saints are to judge angels."[83] In this marvelously literal reading of Paul, the Latter-day Saints would not just distinguish angel from demon in mortality, as they learned through the Nauvoo Temple cultus, but would command angels in the afterlife.[84] The name of the supernatural beings who had been critical to the upward reach of the traditional Chain of Being became instead a name for the *Sons Ahman* who had fallen short.

They would find only a place of subservience in the Mormon Chain of Belonging.

Orson Pratt, recalling and interpreting Smith's "Sample of Pure Language" in the early 1850s, invoked the Chain of Being to show angels their place below humans.

> Sons Ahman [humans] are the greatest of all the parts of God excepting Son Ahman [Jesus] and Ahman [God the Father], and that Anglo-man [angels] are the greatest of all the parts of God excepting Sons Ahman, Son Ahman, and Ahman, showing that the angels are a little lower than man. What is the conclusion to be drawn from this? It is, that these intelligent beings are all parts of God, and that those who have the most of the parts of God are the greatest, or next to God, and those who have the next greatest portions of the parts of God, are the next greatest, or nearest to the fulness of God; and so we might go on to trace the scale of intelligences from the highest to the lowest.[85]

Pratt was notorious for an idiosyncratic animism that differed somewhat from his prophet's views, but the core of his sentiment is clear: Smith inverted the suprahuman Chain as he familiarized the old hierarchy. Smith revealed a system in which, by token of genealogical scope, humans superseded angels within the classification of the species Ahman. Although Pratt had strayed from Smith's genealogical interpretation, he nevertheless remembered the species Ahman and the displacement of angels from their once proud thrones. In any event, neither Smith nor Pratt stopped with angels. Early Latter-day Saints radically reconceptualized both God and humans.

That God in Yonder Heavens

With time, Smith's angelology led toward elaborations that forever marked Mormonism as Christian heresy. The elimination of a separate ontology for angels and exaltation of humans in Smith's Chain of Belonging collapsed the space separating humanity from God. By eliminating this ontological space Smith also opened up the possibility of recasting the role of God and his place in the Chain in a direct assault on the theocentric worldview. Though Protestants called God Father, Smith's sacerdotal system understood this relationship in a stunningly literal way. Just as God had stood above the hierarchically arranged pulpits at the Kirtland Temple during the 1836 holy season, so would he stand at the head of the eternalized human family hierarchy. This is the great mystery that Smith publicized in his most famous sermon, an address to the April 1844 church conference inspired by the death of King Follett a month earlier. In a broad-ranging sermon that fed into the bitter theological conflicts culminating in his death, Smith crystallized the themes of his divine anthropology, a decade in formation. He announced to the assembled church the "secret" that "God himself who sits in yonder Heavens is a man like unto one of yourselves."[86] Smith's God was not the ontologically distinct Creator of the Chain of Being, but the founding parent of its genealogical hierarchy (see figure 9.1).

Such radical claims became possible with a particular view of Christ's incarnation, Mormonism's ontological *imitatio Christi*. If Jesus was like God, and the Latter-day Saints were like Jesus, then human lives and relationships illuminated God's life and relationships. Responding to criticism from seceders after his King Follett Discourse, Smith delivered his Sermon in the Grove to clarify and defend his views in June 1844. In another marvelously literal interpretation of the New Testament, Smith proclaimed that Jesus did only "what he seeth the Father do."[87] To Smith, this meant that God, as Christ, had once been a mortal being; they both had passed through the same stage in the life cycle of Ahman.[88] Jesus provided the model, according to Smith's exegesis, for understanding God's nature.

The equation of humans and God as beings correspondent to Christ pushed toward another commonsensical but heretical conclusion. God, the Father of all Sons Ahman, was a resurrected being with skin and bone. Just as the resurrected Christ had touched and been touched by his disciples, so could God the Father embrace his followers. This physical God was the exemplar of the Mormon afterlife. Persistent embodiment had been central to Smith's account of death and afterlife, to his solution to the problems death posed, since the beginning of his career (see chapter 2), though some Mormons like Parley Pratt did not fully realize this in the 1830s.[89] Protestant neighbors in Kirtland, on the other hand, were aware of the doctrine by 1836, when Reverend Coe commented that Mormons believed in "a material being, composed of body and parts," rather than the "wooden God" of orthodox American Protestantism.[90] For God, the perfect exemplar of humanity and the grand patriarch of

Figure 9.1 This image from John Hafen's illustrated edition of Eliza R. Snow, *O My Father* (New York: Ben E. Rich, 1916), celebrates the Mormon image of God as an embodied parent. Image courtesy of the Church History Library, The Church of Jesus Christ of Latter-day Saints.

the genealogical Chain, to lack a body was absurd and blasphemous to the Latter-day Saints. In instructions to followers entitled "Observations of the Sectarian God," Smith preached: "That which is without body or parts is nothing. There is no other God in heaven but that God who has flesh + bones."[91] In this pronouncement stood both the necessity of bodily resurrection and the potency of the *imitatio Christi*. If God had no immortal body, then neither could Christ or the *Sons Ahman*. But Christ manifestly had a body; therefore, God did, too. Though scattered biblical proof texts confirmed the fact of God's corporality, it was the imitation of Christ that provided the logical infrastructure for Mormons.

Nauvoo in the 1840s buzzed with Smith's rejection of the "sectarian" God of Protestantism. A pseudonymous editorial in *Times and Seasons* argued strongly for a corporeal God.[92] Centuries of theology underlying orthodox views of God's nature fell on mostly deaf ears in the Mormon Zion. The Anglican visitor Henry Caswall found himself unable to satisfy Nauvooans during his 1842 visit. In fact, the Latter-day Saints seemed to defame the God of Protestantism as, in Caswall's paraphrase, "a God worthy only of hatred; in fact, 'the greatest devil in the universe.'"[93] By 1845, the Latter-day Saints had openly parodied a popular hymn by Thomas Bayly (1797–1839), "The Rose That All Are Praising," in a biting celebration of theologial superiority. In the parody's opening stanza, the Saints exult:

> The God that others worship is not the God for me;
> He has no parts nor body and cannot hear nor see;—
> But I've a God that lives above—
> A God of power and of love.[94]

The Mormon God, the argument ran, proved the limitless potential of human futures. Though Protestants complained that Mormons had degraded God with their anthropomorphism, for Smith and the Saints this insight was fully compatible with God's supreme excellence, understood within their genealogical Chain.

The Saints' commitment to permanent corporality proved so strong that it ultimately encompassed all of the Mormon Godhead. Whereas their Protestant neighbors saw Christ's Incarnation as the only time Deity became corporeal, the Latter-day Saints believed that even the Holy Ghost (in many other Christian traditions representing the mind, love, or influence of the Father and Son) would acquire a body. In 1844, Smith announced that "the holy ghost is yet a Spiritual body and waiting to take to himself a body."[95] This image of the New Testament Paraclete as an early stage in human development may well be the source of Phelps's title for his 1845 short story. While some Protestants endorsed the Holy Ghost's distinct personhood within the Trinity, almost none predicted his corporality.[96] For Latter-day Saints, the calculus of the divine anthropology required it.

Capturing divine anthropomorphism in other American religious traditions is not easy. For creedal Christians a humanized God was the sort of absurdity only Gnostics and fanatics would endorse. Those, like

Emerson, who rejected the God of the Reformed tradition generally replaced him with something spiritual like the Transcendental Oversoul. Even the famously physical Emanuel Swedenborg distinguished an immaterial God from his Incarnation as Jesus.[97] Preaching an idiosyncratic modalism, Swedenborg came much closer to the Protestant mainstream than the Mormons did. There were occasional dissenting voices, like the liberal Congregationalist Horace Bushnell, who proposed a complexly anthropomorphic God, though with relatively little resonance among his learned peers.[98] Despite the lack of official support from churches or clergy, it seems likely that a significant proportion of Protestant believers envisioned an embodied God at some level of imagination. Indeed, the reason for the strenuous commitment to preaching on divine immateriality was probably the persistence of images of a corporeal God in folk imagination. Whether, if pressed, lay Protestants would confess that they understood embodiment metaphorically is not entirely clear. For Smith, though, persistent divine embodiment was crucial to the *imitatio Christi*. God's body, as the bodies of all the constituents of Ahman, would never go away. Christ incarnate and resurrected was witness to that fact.

Theosis: Exaltations and Perfections

A persistently embodied God, the *imitatio Christi*, and human preexistence pointed toward a state the Latter-day Saints called "exaltation." As Smith unveiled his priesthood, his temple rites, and his heaven family through the 1840s, he made it increasingly clear that humans had a magnificent potential as *Sons Ahman*. The Saints would rise, through the relationships they created and sealed, to a status beyond their wildest imaginings, a state scholars often call apotheosis or deification. When Smith first decided that human destiny was divine, when he realized that he would teach apotheosis to his followers, is not certain. From the early 1830s, within the overarching context of the Mormon *imitatio Christi*, several related threads supported theosis: the temporal Chain of Being, the conspecificity of humans and angels as children of God, the Abraham theogony with its divine council of future patriarchs, the heaven family, and the temple cultus.

Though there is a hint in the Book of Mormon (Alma 12:31), the doctrine of theosis appears to have begun with the 1832 revelations known as the Olive Leaf and the Vision, and the rising theology of the Kirtland Temple. In the Vision, Smith revealed that the saved Saints "are gods, even the sons of God."[99] In the Olive Leaf, Smith introduced a "light of Christ" that filled the "immencity of space," "giveth life to all things," drove the planets in their orbits, and filled the minds of seekers with truth. Explaining that each human soul would be "sanctified from all unrighteousness that it may be prepared for the Celestial glory," Smith foresaw that each soul would be "crowned with glory." These souls, as resurrected bodies "quickened by a portion of the Celestial glory," would "receive of the Same even a fulness." Smith then invoked images from the astronomical Chain of Being and juxtaposed them with Jesus's Parable of the Laborers. Each different worker had a specific "time" or "season," echoes of the planetary orbits, to receive the light of Christ. Smith then suggested that the seven angels and seals of Revelation were the times and seasons of his reinterpretation of the Parable of the Laborers. At the appearance of the seventh and final angel, Smith declared, "the saints shall be filled with his glory & receive their inheritanc[e] & be made equal with him [God]."[100]

Parley Pratt reprinted the Olive Leaf with its promise of "equality" in his *Voice of Warning*.[101] This view that humans could become "equal" with Christ scandalized Protestants, as well as some Latter-day Saints.[102] When Methodist polemicist La Roy Sunderland (1804–1885) called the Olive Leaf "nonsense and blasphemy," Pratt responded in strident defense, identifying a variety of proof texts to suggest that scriptural promises to know "all truth" or to be able to "do all things" required eventual human "equality" with God.[103]

The logic of the Olive Leaf appealed broadly. Smith's brother-in-law, Lorenzo Snow, reported that the Olive Leaf's exegesis of the parable merged in his mind with a promise made by Joseph Sr. "at a blessing meeting in the Kirtland Temple." From this flash of "inspiration," Snow recorded a couplet that now summarizes the divine anthropology for most observers. "As man now is, God once was; / As God now is, man may be."[104] According to Snow, no matter where a believer joined the genealogical Chain of Belonging, she would eventually, through the progress of the entire Chain, achieve the status of Godhood. Joseph Smith returned to this point strongly in a sermon in 1843, asking rhetorically, "What was the design of the Almighty in making man, it was to exalt him to be as God, the scripture says ye are Gods and it cannot be broken, heirs of God and joint heirs with Jesus Christ equal with him possesing all power &c."[105]

While the Olive Leaf was the beginning, the Latter-day Saints drew on a variety of conceptual foundations in advancing theosis. Probably most important over the course of theosis was the Mormon *imitatio Christi*. The divine anthropology was a stunningly literal interpretation of Jesus's injunction at the Sermon on the Mount to "be ye therefore perfect, even as I am perfect."[106] Jesus showed the Latter-day Saints the pathway to human perfection. That Christ was equal to God was a surprise to no one—such a claim was central to Trinitarianism.[107] Although Mormonism had new scripture to support this—Christ was the foremost among the pre-existent, intelligent beings called Ahman, "the one like unto God" in the theogony of the Egyptian project—most Christians were comfortable with Christ's equivalence to God in some important sense. This connection was enough to support the reach of the Mormon *imitatio Christi*. Shortly after Smith's death, an editorialist used precisely this image in laying out Mormon apotheosis and the centrality to it of the conquest of death. The Latter-day Saints, according to the editorial, "are like Christ, and he is like God; then, O, then, they are all 'Living Gods,' having passed from Death unto Life, and possess the power of eternal lives!"[108] This was the Mormon *imitatio Christi* writ large.

The possibility that humans could be like Christ was more real because Mormons had established an equivalence of angels and humans. Recognizing the logical implications of angels as resurrected patriarchs, Phelps announced in 1833 to fellow Saints: "You are independent above all the creatures under the celestial kingdom, if you are faithful."[109] When Hebrews 1 announced that Jesus was "so much better than the angels," the Saints saw themselves in the same state. They also returned to Luke 20 and its language of angelic identity, as in Phelps's 1835 assurance that believing Mormons would "become angels, even Sons of God, for an eternity of glory."[110] A few months later Phelps foresaw that the faithful would inherit "a kingdom of glory; become archangels, even the sons of God."[111] In each of these cases, distinctive exegeses of Christian scripture confirmed the radical implications of Smith's reformed Chain: the fluid identity of angels, humans, and Christ.

Smith's sustained *imitatio Christi* relied centrally on his genealogical revision of the temporal Chain of Being, which provided a means to understanding how entities as vastly inferior as humans could become entities as vastly superior as Christ or God. The Chain established hierarchical relationships among its members. As the constituents of the Chain progressed in unity, individual members came to occupy a station previously held by a superior member.[112] It is difficult to read the King Follett Discourse except as an application of the temporal Chain of Being to the Mormon afterlife. Smith explained that to be "joint heirs with Christ" (Romans 8:17) meant "to inherit the same glory power & exaltation" and to "ascend [to] a throne as those who have gone before." Speaking for Christ, Joseph continued: "when I get my K[ingdom] workfed [sic] out I will present to the father & it will exalt his glory" so that "he will take a Higher exhaltation & I will take his place and am also exhalted." Thus the Father "obt[ai]ns K[ingdom] rollg. upon K[ingdom]. so that J[esus] treads in his tracks as he had gone before."[113] Observer George Laub's account of the sermon is even more typical of the temporal chain: "we are to goe from glory to glory & as one is raised the Next may be raised to his place or Sphere and so take their Exaltation through a regular channel. And when we get to where Jesus is he will be as far ahe[a]d of us in exaltation as when we started."[114] Once again, Christ showed the way for the Latter-day Saints. In the Sermon in the Grove, Smith returned to the topic. Employing the language of human potential and the power of education, Smith explained, "You have got to learn how to be Gods yourselves; to be kings and priests to God, the same as all Gods have done; by going from a small degree to another, from grace to grace, from exaltation to exaltation, until you are able to sit in glory as doth those who sit enthroned in everlasting power."[115] This reformed Chain encompassed a heavenly kindred of divine beings.[116]

The temple cultus represented the methods by which the Latter-day Saints would enter the Chain of Belonging. By the 1840s Smith's temple rites clearly promised priesthood kingship for the faithful as a euphemism for divinization. In 1843 Smith was preaching that "Gods have an ascendency over the angels angels remain angels.—some are resurrected to become god. by such revelations as god gives in the most holy place.— in his temple."[117] In May 1844 Smith reported that his temple rites allowed his followers to "assend above principalities."[118] Employing traditional names for hierarchies of angels, Smith strongly emphasized his inversion of the Chain. Even this phraseology invoked the *imitatio Christi*, appropriating language Peter had reserved for Christ, who would make the "angels and authorities and powers...subject unto him" (1 Peter 3:22).[119] In the Sermon in the Grove, Smith preached: "Every man who reigns is a God," and would be "exalted far above princ[ipalities]. thrones dom[inions]. & angels."[120] While Masons also saw themselves as present and future priests and kings, Smith was not just donning bishops' miters and dreaming of royal conquest in the afterlife. He was proposing a divine anthropology, an equation of all human personages that organized the vast expanses of space and the anonymizing admixture of the grave.

The contextual and cultural touchstones of Mormon theosis are diverse. Smith may have drawn license from fragments of prior Christianities available to him in Buck's *Theological Dictionary*. Normatively Buck used apotheosis to discredit the Catholic practice of canonization (which he believed mimicked earlier pagan practices), though he mentioned obliquely Christian heresies and pre-Christian religions that hinted at or preached a divine potential for believers.[121] He also mentioned Jakob Böhme's claim that he could "make fallen man rise to the glory of angels."[122] Buck's dictionary probably did little more than help Smith situate himself vis-à-vis Protestantism and the ancient church. Smith did not specifically invoke these antecedents in promulgating the doctrine.

The Bible also served to ground Mormon belief. Smith's followers discovered fragments as early as the Garden of Eden narratives, seeing the serpent's promise that the first humans would become "as gods" as evidence that Eve and Adam were destined for Godhood.[123] The premortal council, a reflex of much older Canaanite traditions, also served to ground claims to a divine anthropology.[124] The Book of Abraham clearly equated premortal patriarchs with the "Gods" of the divine council.[125] The proof text Mormons most preferred was Psalm 82, in which the Psalmist addresses Israel with the potent but confusing claim "Ye are Gods." The Mormons were in good company on this point: Jesus used this text in a verbal joust with priestly critics.[126] Mainstream interpreters like Adam Clarke stumbled over the language, "probably the only place" in scripture where the term was "applied to any but the true God."[127] Whatever the textual difficulties, mainstream interpreters explicitly rejected the polytheistic reading, preferring instead the metaphorical reading that believers are "like God," as in "ye are my *representatives*; and are clothed with my power and authority to dispense judgment and justice."[128]

Mormon exegesis could become extreme. In the 1845 editorial, God's name sealed in the foreheads of believers in John's Revelation (14:1)—an echo of the temple rites of anointing and sealing—confirmed the divine future for humanity. In homespun and unanswerable logic, the editorialist wrote "'Their Father's name,' bless me! That is GOD!" Continuing in the simultaneously idiosyncratic and commonsensical vein that marked much early Mormon exegesis, the editorialist continued, explaining that "'his name in their foreheads,' undoubtedly means *'God'* on the front of their crowns."[129] As they bore the name of the Father, it became their own. The inevitable march to eternal progression of those adopted into the genealogical Chain of Belonging had reached its glorious conclusion.

Many believers found these teachings heady and irresistible. Parley Pratt, who had a penchant for advertising Smith's radical theologies to outsiders, included in an 1844 pamphlet a call for readers to "soar with me amid unnumbered worlds which roll in majesty on high [to] explore the lengths and breadths of organized existence." Those who would come to learn from Smith would discover the "future destiny, of things and beings...of the organizations of angels, of spirits, of men and animals; of worlds and their fullness; of thrones and dominions, principalities and powers."[130] Mormonism, as Pratt broadcasted it, promised the potential to comprehend the Chain of Belonging and assume one's rightful place. This excerpt from his new pamphlet made it into the Nauvoo church newspaper.[131]

Outsiders found Mormon theosis ridiculous. Newspaper editor and critic Thomas Sharp, summarizing material from a seceder, wrote that Mormons "believe that they will have power to create worlds, and that these worlds will transgress the law given," a reference to the fortunate fall of Adam and Eve, an event meant to be repeated anew for each divine royal couple.[132] The Congregationalist critic Jonathan B. Turner summarized Mormon belief in an 1842 diatribe: "Every Mormon is not only to be a god hereafter; he has, in his own belief, been a demigod from all eternity, or at least an angel heretofore."[133] One Latter-day Saint reportedly told an Anglican professor "that the Mormons believed that departed saints become a portion of the Deity, and may be properly denominated 'Gods.'"[134] While critics saw mere fanaticism, the Latter-day Saints saw the secret to human nature in a radical but commonsensical approach to the Incarnation.

Other, mostly later, practitioners of American metaphysical religion believed in something similar to Mormon apotheosis, mixing ideas about metaphysical correspondence with a cheery perfectionism and something resembling panpsychism, the idea that all matter is sentient. Warren Felt Evans (1817–1889) wrote: "It has ever been a doctrine of the esoteric philosophy and a religion of all ages and nations that each immortal spirit is a direct emanation from the 'Unknown God.'...Each individual spirit is not God, but a god, and is possessed of all the attributes of its parent source, among which are omniscience and omnipotence."[135] The noted spiritualist Judge John W. Edmonds (1816–1874), writing a decade or so after Smith, had a "message [that] announced humans as minor deities, divinities in the making." Swedenborg held a somewhat similar view in which the Divine spirit filled the universe, though for Swedenborg these angelized humans taken together constituted a vast zodiacal body, his *Maximus Homo*.[136] Instead of a zodiacal body or the union with Christ, though, Smith saw humans as conspecific with God. It was God's family they shared rather than his mystical substance. This family relationship pointed the way to the conquest of death. In the Elias Higbee funeral sermon, Smith referred to heaven as "a resurection and glory beyond the grave which God and angels had secured."[137]

The Plurality of Gods

The divine anthropology pointed toward a radical view of the afterlife supporting a distinctively Mormon polytheism. Two main elements supported Smith's view of a "plurality of Gods." First, fragments of Mesopotamian polytheism in the Hebrew Bible, coupled with the royal plural "Elohim," provided biblical proof for a plurality of Gods, according to Smith's marvelously literal exegesis. Second, according to the logic of apotheosis, if humans became gods, then every righteous human would add to the number of gods. The Chain of Belonging could never end, so divinities would never end either.

The Bible's Gods

As Smith read and revised the Christian canon, he found evidence for a plurality of Gods from beginning to end. In Genesis he saw a council of Gods creating the earth; in Paul's letters he saw "Lords many"; and in Revelation he saw a kingdom of "kings and priests" to God. Smith's belief, complex and equivocal during the 1830s, came into certain form in the context of the Egyptian project. An 1832 revision in the New Translation pushed away from polytheism, while the 1832 Vision and Olive Leaf revelations suggested that righteous humans could themselves be gods.[138] In the 1830s, Smith seems to have been struggling to decide whether the term "god" could be used to describe all divine beings or might be restricted to the name of the divine parent of human beings (who would themselves become divine). By March 1839, Smith began making public possible connections between the "many gods" of the divine anthropology and the cosmic hierarchies of the Egyptian project, an association that became unequivocal with the publication of the Book of Abraham in 1842.[139] Smith emphasized both distinctive grammatical constructions and obscure passages in the Bible to support his biblical view of polytheism.

Smith probably discovered in early 1836 that the Hebrew name for God, Elohim, was a plural form, a grammatical observation to which Mormons frequently returned.[140] The grammar documents of the Egyptian project that arose at the same time gave hints of the existence of multiple divine beings; the published scripture strongly interpreted Elohim as "the Gods" of the divine council.[141] (Modern scholarship suggests the possibility that Mormons correctly identified polytheism in the Hebrew Bible, though with radically different implications.)[142] Mormons saw the nominal superlative, often used to refer to God's glory, as further evidence of polytheism. When the Bible called the Israelite God the "God of Gods" or "Lord of Lords," the Latter-day Saints saw an ancient reference to divine plurality.[143] In the same vein, Smith's followers translated Yahweh Elohim (rendered "LORD GOD" in the KJV) as "the Lord of the Gods."[144] Further outside the grammatical mainstream, Mormons found references to God's Father in the cryptic, fraught reference to "God and his Father" of Revelation 1:6 or the apposed genitives of 2 Peter 1:17.[145] With these confirmations from the sacred Hebrew and the guidance of their prophet, the Saints stood ready to restore to the world what they believed had been common knowledge in the biblical epochs, for "'the Gods,' in old times, was common intelligence."[146]

The KJV often—more than two hundred times—ceded the existence of foreign gods, though always with the stern warning that they must not be worshipped. For Smith and his followers, these were complex clues to the existence of gods beyond God. One editorialist for the *Times and Seasons* proposed "to treat the subject of the 'Living God,' in contradistinction to a *dead God*, or, one that has, 'no body, parts, or passions,' and perhaps it may be well enough to say at the out set, that Mormonism embraces a plurality of Gods," using the "Lords many" of 1 Corinthians 8:4–5 (a Pauline reference to paganism) to provide further biblical support for his argument.[147]

Eternal Progressions

The possibility of divine plurality, what critics called polytheism, arose in Mormonism at the confluence of several currents in the early to middle 1830s. The plural gods of the Hebrew Bible provided biblical support for this belief. More important, though, human theosis, expressed within the Chain of Belonging, forced the point logically, since if humans became gods postmortally then there were necessarily more gods than one. With subtle indications in the latter 1830s, Smith became quite public with this teaching in the 1840s. After clarifying that the members of his Chain of Belonging were the "kings and priests" of Revelation, Smith quoted from and amplified his Book of Abraham in his 1844 Sermon in the Grove. Hearkening back to the cosmology of the Egyptian project, in which all celestial bodies obeyed a strict hierarchy of influence and orbits, Smith announced that the fact that there "may exist two men on the earth—one wiser than the other—wo[ul]d. shew that an[o]t[he]r. who is wiser than the wisest may exist—intelligences exist one above anot[he]r. that there is no end to it."[148] To Smith, in a way he never worked out entirely, the familial chain of divinities had no end, could have none, whatever that prospect of endless deities meant. Critically, though, eternity was organized as an eternal family—in the paraphrase of one loyal follower, "the work of *generation* is not to cease forever."[149]

Projecting the plural Mormon Godhead onto the cosmos, an editorialist in February 1845 described the vast compass of plurality, tracing the flow of God's power "from world to world; from system to system; from universe to universe; and from eternity to eternity, where, in each, and all, there is a presidency of Gods." The editorialist grounded his claim in Smith's exegesis of Genesis 1:1 from his King Follett Discourse.[150]

Beyond the occasional Unitarian mocking Calvinists for the illogic of Trinity and rather dim memories of ancient heresies, there was very little cultural support for polytheism in Smith's milieu.[151] There were occasional voices in favor of polytheism in the early American republic, most famously Benjamin Franklin in his deistic and idiosyncratically Neoplatonic "Articles of Belief."[152] This was not a common belief by any stretch; published examples are hard to find in the early nineteenth century. Despite this evident distinction from most of their peers, the way to divine plurality was clear to the Latter-day Saints. Not only were there fragments of ancient religion to support it both inside and outside the Bible, polytheism made a certain kind of sense within a church charged with a glorious future of royal priesthood power. Plurality of Gods became inevitable at the confluence of the Chain of Belonging and the ontological identity of the species Ahman.

The Queens of Heaven

The Elohim of early Mormonism stood as the "head" God of the heaven family. He was the Father of the *Sons Ahman*, the figure they would imitate in the eternal progress of the Chain of Belonging. The familialized Chain pushed Mormonism into one more radical doctrine. The God of early Mormonism was no holy bachelor, existing in the cosmos outside family entanglements. He participated in a recognizable family structure, bound not only to offspring but to a spouse. Distinct from the dyadic divine feminine of other esoteric traditions, the Heavenly Mother of Mormonism, preached perhaps as early as 1835, was God's wife. Such was the inexorable logic of Smith's heaven family: God could be no father without a mother at his side. The logic of the divine anthropology required it. If humans, angels, and gods were all stages in the life span of a single species, then there could be no male god without a divine wife. She was the exemplar for the women being anointed queens and priestesses in Smith's temple.

In the 1830s Smith and Phelps provided a template for female divine power in their treatment of a royal mummy they named Katouhmun and her progenitor Egyptus. This mummy, one of the four that Mormons purchased from Michael Chandler, demonstrated the confluence of royalty, priesthood, women, and power. (She may have figured in the Book of Abraham as a victim of human sacrifice.)[153] In the KEP, Phelps and Smith linked priestesses and queens to the founding of Egypt, the creation of scripture, and the secrets of hieroglyphs. It was Egyptus, the daughter of Ham, who discovered Egypt and bestowed upon it her name.[154] The published Book of Abraham situated women in the theogony, as "the Gods" created humans "male and female," which dual state was "in the image of the Gods."[155] One of the first announcements of the Egyptian project made veiled reference to this future doctrine. After summarizing the outlines of the divine anthropology, including theosis, Phelps projected gender onto that heavenly space, "where the man is neither without the woman, nor the woman without the man in the Lord."[156] Attempting to demonstrate the eternity of marriage in a reappropriation of Paul, Phelps pointed toward the presence of divine women in the heavenly world.

In addition to the Egyptian papyri, Smith found precedent for a female heavenly being in an amplification of the gendered promises of Revelation (1:6; 5:10). In a phrase he employed in the 1832 Vision to describe the state of exaltation, Smith dubbed devout Latter-day Saint men "Kings & Priests."[157] As the Nauvoo Temple rites and celestial marriage unfolded, it became clear that such kings and priests were marrying "queens" and "priestesses" for the eternities. There could be no king without a queen, no priest without a priestess. This was the sort of assiduous familialization that Smith referred to in sermons to the newly founded Nauvoo Female Relief Society. In an innovation that scandalized the fraternal Masons, Smith's translation of Masonic ritual encompassed women as well as men in the familial power of the patriarchal priesthood. Such priestly wives required, in the logic of the divine anthropology, an exemplar in heaven.

In many respects, God's wife was a secret doctrine, one of the mysteries of early Mormonism, and she remained largely implicit before Smith's death. Shortly after his death, though, his lieutenants, perhaps emboldened by their leader's radical frankness on the divine anthropology in spring and summer 1844 and seeking to honor their martyred prophet, made the existence of a heavenly mother or queen of heaven public to a remarkable degree.

Phelps's "Come to Me" of the fall of 1844 had the martyred prophet calling to his followers to join him in heaven. There Phelps put in Smith's mouth the invitation to "Come to me; here's the myst'ry that man hath not seen; / Here's our Father in heaven, and Mother, the Queen."[158] Around Christmas the same year Phelps exclaimed in a melodramatic letter to Joseph's younger brother William: "O Mormonism! Thy father is God, thy mother is the Queen of heaven." Phelps further wrote regarding Jesus's premortal anointing that "his mother stood with approving virtue, and smiled upon a Son that kept the faith as the heir of all things," then argued that the Jews "thought so much of this coronation among Gods and Goddesses; Kings and Queens of heaven, that they broke over all restraints and actually began to worship the 'Queen of heaven,' according to Jeremiah."[159] Rereading a biblical indictment of matriolatry in light of Smith's divine anthropology, Phelps discovered fragments of the eternal Gospel. Around the same time, Phelps repeated belief in mother-queens in his "Paracletes." There the protagonist Milauleph began the story as "a child with his father and mother in heaven."[160] Leaving his celestial nest, Milauleph came to earth to found a kindred all his own.

Although Phelps, Smith's intellectual companion and linguistic coach, provided the earliest clear documentation of the belief, others soon corroborated his observations. Eliza Roxcy Snow, Smith's best known plural wife and one of the most powerful women in early Mormonism, confirmed the Heavenly Mother in a poetic apostrophe to the God Smith revealed, occasioned by the death of her mortal father in October 1845. Entitled "My Father in Heaven," her poem entered Mormon hymnody as "O My Father," ultimately achieving semicanonical status.[161] Playing with Protestant death poetry that occasionally addressed a deceased parent as a father or mother in heaven, Snow moved to a radical question to which Smith's divine anthropology propelled her.[162]

> In the heav'ns are parents single?
> No, the thought makes reason stare;
> Truth is reason—truth eternal
> Tells me I've a mother [t]here.[163]

Such was the logic of later reminiscences of this teaching, emblematically the paraphrase of Smith's dual wife Zina Huntington, who remembered the Prophet asking rhetorically "how could a Father claim his title unless there were also a Mother to share that parenthood?" This being was the "eternal Mother, the wife of your Father in Heaven."[164] Orson Pratt made the more staid announcement in the *Seer* in 1853 that "the father of our spirits is the head of his household."[165] Though later versions of this doctrine pushed in new directions, the fundamentals were a necessary corollary of the divine anthropology.

Nineteenth-century America witnessed new opportunities for women and new solutions to traditional limitations on their power (with the most strides early and late in the century). Within mainline Protestantism, women and clergy were waging a campaign of feminization that would have far-reaching effects, as historian Ann Douglas has carefully described (though not without critics).[166] Despite an expanding view of female potential, almost no one proposed a female deity within mainstream Protestantism. At the metaphysical periphery, on the other hand, the feminine often joined the masculine. Swedenborg preached a complex, composite gendering of God, while European metaphysicians had long preached a feminine divine aspect (for Jakob Böhme, this was the divine "Virgin"), a yin-yang dyad that encompassed both male and female in a single entity.[167] For the Shakers, founder Ann Lee (1736–1784) as Mother Wisdom completed such a dyad,[168] while thinkers as far apart as Mary Baker Eddy (1821–1910) and Elizabeth Cady Stanton (1815–1902) preached a dyadic God.[169] Often the dyadic rhetoric returned to ancient stories about Eve split from Adam in the Creation story, a disruption to sexual unity forever in need of resolution. Josiah Priest, among others, adopted this view that humans in their pure state were both male and female, in the image of a bigendered God.[170] These dyadic teachings of the metaphysicians have led some to see Smith's Mother in Heaven as an expression of just such a composite deity.[171]

Despite such predecessors and peers, Smith preached a female deity who was the married companion of the male God rather than the Shaker dyad or Swedenborg's essential unity or Böhme's Virgin.[172] This entity was a humanized divine wife, the eternal consort of an immortal family man.[173] Adam was no split dyad as the metaphysicians taught; he was a full-fledged man married to Eve, a physically distinct entity and queen of heaven. What seems to have mattered most to Smith and his early followers is that God the Mother placed God the Father into the family context. Both were fully integrated into the heaven family tree, a married spousal unit. Together they were the parents of Jesus and the *Sons Ahman*.[174]

Though Smith was never explicit on this point (he barely admitted his own polygamy in public), his followers tended to believe that the Divine Mother was one of many wives, reflecting God's involvement in the family structure of polygamy. Indeed God's mimetic son, Jesus, was preached as polygamous, probably married to the sisters Mary and Martha, as well as Mary Magdalene.[175] Ultimately God's plural marital status is not critical. Even as a monogamist, Smith's Elohim/Ahman, a physicospiritual parent rather than a Creator ex nihilo, was sufficient to have scandalized Smith's evangelical peers and their heirs. This scandalous God was the apex of Smith's new and everlasting covenant of belonging, the patriarch of Smith's heaven family, the "head" of the Gods.

In the divine anthropology stand many of early Mormonism's most startling departures from American Protestantism. Knowing who the early Mormons were and what they were seeking requires coming to terms with this radical set of beliefs. Despite its obvious distinction, the divine anthropology sounded surprisingly familiar to many listeners. There were proof texts and ancient threads of Christian or Hebrew religion to support every one of the beliefs Smith advanced. The scattered clues in the scriptural and parascriptural legacy of Judaism and historic Christianity were only props, though, tools Smith used to communicate his overarching vision of the conquest of death and hell through an assiduous familialization of the cosmos. Where other Christians understood a metaphorical kinship, the adoption of regeneration, Smith described an ontological identity, the literal family connectedness of humans and God. When Jesus told his audience to "be ye therefore perfect, even as your father in heaven is perfect," the Latter-day Saints took him at his word. In a sustained if implicit exegesis of John 14:6, the Latter-day Saints saw Jesus as the way not just to God but to Godhood, their guide to maturity as members of the species Ahman. This was the *imitatio Christi*, the meaning of the genealogized Chain of Belonging.

In the divine anthropology, Smith's death conquest came to its mighty fruition. Death could have no sting when the eternity of human relationships was written into the very fabric of the universe. By placing humanity into God's literal family, Smith reassured his followers that they could be "Saved from all [their] enemies even [their] last enemy which is death."[176] In the boundless divine anthropology of early Mormonism stood the great promise of death conquered. The pleasure of Smith's followers in his revelations comes through clearly in Phelps's popular hymn "There Is No End," a paean to the divine anthropology and the Chain of Belonging heavily influenced by the Egyptian project. Asking believers "if you could hie to Kolob, / in th' twinkling of an eye," Phelps painted a picture of the grand scope of Smith's familialized afterlife. In the closing phrase:

> There is no end to glory;
> There is no end to love;
> There is no end to being:
> Grim Death sleeps not above.[177]

10

"Death Cannot Conquer the Hero Again"

The Death and Afterlife of a Martyr

Crossing the Mississippi after midnight in a leaking skiff in June 1844, Joseph Smith Jr. fled toward the comparative safety of the Rocky Mountains. The morning of his final departure, however, Smith crossed back over the river into Illinois instead of continuing his flight from an arrest warrant. As he crossed this Rubicon, he reportedly said, "I am going like a lamb to the slaughter, but I am calm as a summer's morning. I have a conscience void of offense toward God and toward all men. If they take my life I shall die an innocent man, and my blood shall cry from the ground for vengeance, and it shall be said of me 'He was murdered in cold blood!'"[1] He then reportedly reassured several loyal militiamen that they need not fight to protect him because "they cannot do more to you than the enemies of truth did to the ancient Saints—they can only kill the body."[2] The Mormon prophet then proceeded to Carthage, the Hancock County seat, for trial.

What brought Smith back to certain imprisonment and ultimately his death at the hands of a vigilante mob was the plea of his followers. His flight from the law imperiled the city of Nauvoo, and several prominent Nauvooans complained that "when the wolves came the shepherd ran from the flock, and left the sheep to be devoured." In the main account of the incident, Smith responded to their complaints: "If my life is of no value to my friends it is of none to myself."[3] In the paraphrase of eyewitness Dan Jones (1810–1862), Smith exclaimed: "it is better for your brother, Joseph, to die for his brothers and sisters, for I am willing to die for them."[4] There is reasonable evidence that Smith felt he was acting against his own self-interest and his understanding of God's will, but the accusation of betrayal was too real for him to ignore.[5] He could not bear the thought that he had abandoned his friends.

Joseph Smith seems, in the accounts that have survived, to have recognized a trade-off. He could remain alive while his people saw him as a traitor, or he could become their dead martyr. Betrayal was a transgression that could not be forgiven.[6] Smith had promised his people as much in 1843: "if I do not stand with those who will stand by me in the hour of trouble and danger, without faltering I give you leave to shoot me."[7] Though he very much wanted to live and believed he had a workable solution to his legal difficulties, Joseph could not bear such an accusation from his followers. Although a relatively early tradition had Joseph ask "Brother Hyrum, you are the oldest, what shall we do?" (to which Hyrum reportedly answered, "Let us go back and give ourselves up, and see the thing out"), contextually Joseph appears to have asked his brother whether flight represented betrayal. When Hyrum confirmed the feared interpretation, Smith accepted a martyr's fate.[8] Less than a week later, the brothers were dead.

A Martyr's Death

As he stood at the height of his powers—a candidate for the U.S. presidency, a military officer technically (if idiosyncratically) outranking George Washington and commanding a militia larger than that belonging to the state of Illinois, mayor of a thriving town that rivaled Chicago in size and activity, prophet of a burgeoning religious movement—Smith was executed by a vigilante mob while being held without bail in the county jail. Though his supporters and even some enemies were shocked by the outcome, storm clouds had been gathering for years. The details are complex, but in brief, a group of prominent Mormons seceded in protest against Smith's teachings and practices, publishing an opposition periodical called the *Nauvoo Expositor*. When Smith's municipal government destroyed the *Expositor*'s press, conflict spiraled out of control, resulting in the Smith brothers' imprisonment in Carthage Jail—after Smith's decision to return and face the law— on accusation of inciting a riot. On June 27, 1844, a mob comprised largely of local militia, their faces painted black, stormed the jail. After a futile attempt at self-defense with a smuggled pistol, Smith rose to a window, issued the first words of the Masonic cry of distress, and fell to his death, his body riddled with bullets.[9] Even at this late stage, Joseph had lived to lose another sibling: Hyrum was shot to death moments before his prophet-brother.

As he breathed his last that bloody afternoon, Smith became in the minds of his followers the most important martyr since Jesus. Smith's death and martyrdom performed several functions for Latter-day Saints. His martyrdom defined their outsider status and, as it had for early Christians, helped them imagine their own deaths. Importantly, martyrdom also represented a solution to the problem of Providence for early Mormons.[10] Martyrdom pushed responsibility for death onto an enemy rather than God and assured salvation for the deceased. It helped to answer the vexing question: Why does God let good people die before their time?

Beyond the general work of martyrdom, Joseph Smith's martyrdom specifically exemplified several aspects of the Mormon death conquest— through martyrdom, his people could begin to imagine what it meant to be a postmortal divine being, a "Savior on Mount Zion." Smith's death was the test of his theology par excellence. Beyond theology, Smith's martyrdom highlighted and reified tensions within the movement, particularly conflicts over the proper model of kinship and the role of human agency in the commission of divine vengeance.

Martyrdom, War, and Power

For many Christians, martyrdom has represented an assault on a more powerful foe. The earliest Christians employed martyrdom in their fight against pagan Rome; later Protestants employed martyrdom in their struggle against Catholic Rome. Martyrdom imparted sacred power to the weaker or less numerous side in social, theological, and military conflicts.

Mormons accrued several memorable experiences with conflict and marginalization in their first two decades; most of their martyrdom narratives ultimately derived from the long conflict with Missourians. In 1833–1834, earlier settlers displaced Mormons from their lands in Jackson County. Smith responded by forming the impromptu militia force called Zion's Camp, which disbanded amid a dozen Mormon deaths from cholera. After the resettlement of Smith's followers in a new county in Missouri, conflict again escalated, ultimately erupting into the small-scale civil war that ended in Smith's incarceration in Liberty, Missouri, in the fall of 1838.

Two events stand out as focusing the narrative of martyrdom during 1838: a battle at Crooked River in which an apostle died, and a lopsided battle at Haun's Mill that was termed a massacre by the Latter-day Saints. David Patten, a prominent church leader, participated in a skirmish with Missouri militia at Crooked River in October, receiving fatal musket wounds. Latter-day Saints immediately mourned what they saw as an incontestable martyrdom—the death of an apostle at the hands of the enemies of the church. According to a eulogist, Patten "died that evening in the triumphs of faith; having laid down his life as a martyr in the cause of his country and his God."[11] Parley Pratt, recalling Patten's funeral, commented that "a whole people, as it were followed them to the grave. All wept whose feelings were not too intense to find vent in tears. He was the only member of the Quorum of the Twelve who had as yet found a martyr's grave."[12] Five days later, a group of thirty Mormons were ambushed at Haun's Mill by vigilantes, who killed eighteen men and boys.[13] Haun's Mill and Crooked River became central signposts in the history of Mormon martyrdom.

The men who died in the Mormon War in Missouri were the vanguard of an ever-expanding mass of Mormon martyrs in this period. The majority of still-committed Latter-day Saints had to flee Missouri, often under duress. Winter treks, without adequate footwear, became the stuff of poems, hymns, and legend. Those who fell were "murdered, or rather martyred!"[14] Mormons estimated that they lost three hundred souls in the Missouri conflict, perhaps 5 percent of the core church population, but this was an overestimation.[15] (Early Christians tended similarly to overestimate the number of actual martyrs.)[16] Some observers have suggested that the primary death toll from the Missouri debacle was under fifty, that frontierspeople died prematurely even without forceful displacement, and much of the mortality in the immediate aftermath of the Missouri conflict could be attributed to poor living conditions in Nauvoo. Independent of the actual numbers involved, Mormons sometimes claimed to be "the only sect in Christendom, who in this nineteenth century can exhibit the irresistible evidence of martyrdom, in support of its cause."[17]

Once they arrived in Illinois, the Saints turned significant resources toward a rhetorical, political, and financial battle with Missouri. They lobbied the U.S. president, petitioned state legislatures, and waged a war of words in the press, employing the language of martyrdom. Their claims resonated with many outsiders.[18] Mormon rhetoric became so marked that some new converts doubted their merit as untried Latter-day Saints. Church leaders had to persuade these converts that the martyrdom of the few protected the many.[19]

Martyrdom allowed Mormons to establish identity with two crucial groups—the "Revolutionary Patriots" and ancient Christians. The blood of the "Patriots of 76" was almost universally hallowed in the new American republic. Most Americans used language about spilled blood to describe the lasting authority of the Revolutionary War, dramatizing the strength of the republic on the basis of the patriots whose blood had made America.[20] Still further in the past, ancient Christians represented for many Protestants the purity of Christianity in their struggle against pagan Rome.

In a memorial for "Stephen Jones, an old Revolutionary soldier, who died in Quincy Illinois," a Mormon poet accused Missouri of trying to "sprinkle" its "soil with the old soldier's blood." Although his heart finally stopped in Illinois, Jones nevertheless received the martyr's promise that he would "dwell with the blest in their holiest home." An editorial footnote to the Jones eulogy specified that "two old revolutionary soldiers, met their fate in Missouri under these circumstances; one was literally cut to pieces by an old corn knife, the other was whipped, if not to death nearly so."[21] The goriest of those references is to the elderly Thomas McBride, killed at Haun's Mill. By report, McBride was dismembered with "an old corn cutter or scythe" after being shot. As he begged for mercy, McBride invoked his silver hair and, according to the later account, his revolutionary credentials, but the Missouri vigilante instead "lay[ed] open the skull and behead[ed] the body of the poor sufferer who had fought and spilt his blood for the privileges enjoyed by his murderer."[22] Though McBride had been born in March 1776, the Mormons nevertheless seized on his rumored participation in the War of Independence to make their point.[23] While there is no particular reason to assume intentional deception—Mormons were probably including the War of 1812 in the broader struggle for independence, as many other Americans did— this was a powerful rhetorical strategy.

Mormons also used martyrdom to establish an identity with ancient Christians. According to an official editorial early in the Nauvoo period, "many, very many, have suffered death in its most horrid forms" as a result of persecution, just as "the saints of old." In fact, "the saints could not, without bartering their religion, and their hopes of eternal life, expect to escape [persecution]."[24] The Saints wore it as a badge of pride— Edward Partridge (1793–1840), a Mormon convert from the Society of Friends who played a prominent role in the 1830s, wrote to his brother, asking rhetorically, "Who, among all the professors of religion throughout Christendom except Latter day Saints, can say that they have had to pass through great tribulation?" before comparing the Saints to the New Testament martyrs.[25]

Drawing rhetorical power from the identities martyrdom allowed them to claim, Mormons turned the tables on their Protestant critics and enemies. According to a statement Smith published in the *Times and Seasons* in 1839,

> some of our beloved brethren, have had to seal their testimony with
>   their blood; and have died martyrs to the cause of truth; yet,
> Short, though bitter was their pain,
> Everlasting is their joy.[26]

As he reused the final lines of Hannah More's (1745–1833) hymn "The True Heroes: or, the Noble Army of Martyrs," Smith pushed himself and his followers into previously Protestant space, appropriating from his critics and enemies the traditional Protestant identity with the men and women slain by Catholics.[27] This became a recurrent theme among the Latter-day Saints. Even before Smith's murder, Eliza Snow accused Protestant clergy in no uncertain terms: "Thou art already associated with Herod, Nero and the 'bloody Inquisition.'"[28] In that neat trio of comparisons Snow invoked the Jewish king who murdered Christ, the pagan Roman who persecuted Christians, and the Spanish Inquisition, which tortured the innocent. The language of martyrdom allowed Mormons to portray the mainstream of American Christianity as kindred to inquisitors or pagan Romans. Whereas Protestants used Foxe's *Book of Martyrs* to paint Catholics as enemies to God, the Latter-day Saints turned the same rhetoric back on Protestants.[29]

The Problem of Providence

Martyrdom helped Mormons situate themselves vis-à-vis their neighbors even as it generated justifications for group membership and self-fulfilling prophecies of cultural distinction. But martyrdom served another important function for the Saints by helping them work through the tension within the Providential worldview.[30] Martyrdom meant that the cause of death did not need to be sought in God's anger with the decedent or her family. Recovery from illness or reprieve from a deathbed were easy to attribute to God, but interpreting unwanted misery or premature death required substantially more emotional energy. Was death a sign of God's punishment—an afflicting providence meant to weaken psychological ties to life on earth—or was it a reprieve from further suffering? Neither explanation was particularly comforting for bereaved survivors. Martyrdom allowed believers to displace the cause of death onto another party and to anticipate secure salvation for the decedent.

Given the explanatory power of martyrdom, it is no surprise that the term came to refer to many more than those who died in battle. To describe premature or unwelcome deaths—from the deaths of the members of the Smith family to many, if not most, Mormon deaths in the 1830s and 1840s, to the deaths of many "thousands" of Latter-day Saints throughout the nineteenth century—Mormons used the term "martyrdom."[31]

The Smith family narratives display a strong tendency to attribute martyrdom to deaths not caused by direct physical violence. In the closing paragraphs of her memoir, Lucy attributed her daughter-in-law's death from natural causes to the Missouri persecutions, then announced that "the sum of martyrs in our family [is] no less than six in number."[32] This claim mixed sadness with proud defiance and optimism for heavenly reunions. While Hyrum and Joseph were the only family members murdered by enemies, Lucy and her family saw the other deceased Smiths as martyrs. Joseph Sr.'s death from probable tuberculosis—the omnipresent scourge of the era—was "brought upon him through suffering by the hands of ruthless mobs."[33] (The official obituary suggested that the emotional shock of watching Joseph Jr. being carried off to possible execution in 1838 was Joseph Sr.'s death blow.)[34] Son Don Carlos died in 1841 from a probable pneumonia, but Lucy believed he contracted his fatal disease because persecutions forced him to recover the church's printing press in unhealthy conditions ("an underground room through which a spring was constantly flowing") to publish the *Times and Seasons*.[35] Samuel died from an uncertain illness, perhaps pneumonia, approximately a month after his brothers' murder in 1844. Lucy reported that "his spirit forsook its earthly tabernacle, and went to join his brothers, and the ancient martyrs, in the Paradise of God."[36] Lucy appears to have thought of Alvin differently, perhaps because his death preceded the founding of the church. Though she did not explicitly apply the title of martyr to Alvin, she was nevertheless adamant that his death was not from natural causes. In her words, "Alvin was murdered by a quack physician."[37] William Phelps publicly concurred with Lucy that essentially all the Smith deaths qualified as martyrdom.[38]

Rank-and-file Saints used the same rhetoric to describe deaths in their own families. John E. Page in his autobiography remembered the death of his wife and two children "as martyrs to our holy religion, who died through extreme suffering for the want of the common comforts of life."[39] Page did not pretend that his family members had been assassinated by musket fire or burned to death—their suffering in the misery of the early nineteenth-century frontier was enough of a sacrifice for their faith. Often the corporate and the personal intertwined, as when Phineas Richards (1788–1874) assured his wife after they lost a son at Haun's Mill that "George is gone an early martyr to the cause of Zion, strong in the faith (through Babylon's Rage). Lay not this thing too much at heart, but trust in Christ alone, and realize that God is right."[40] Edward Partridge died of natural causes shortly after the move to Illinois. According to his official obituary, "he lost his life in consequence of the Missouri persecutions, and he is one of that number whose blood will be required at their hands."[41] Others, like Caroline Whitney Kingsbury, who died of an uncertain illness later, were similarly accounted to Missouri.[42]

The endemic malaria at Nauvoo was attributed to "broken constitutions, that often terminate in martyrdom, by premature deaths," which were "brought on by sufferings and cruelties from a ruthless banditry."[43] An official editorial, describing the deaths from malaria, noted that "all this [is] in consequence of the above named exposures, brought upon them by the State of Missouri, by their unhallowed proceedings against an innocent people."[44] Even outsiders were willing to concur that the forced migrations took their toll. Daniel Kidder (1815–1892), a critical Methodist writer, commented that "several women and children perished in their dreary flight, too feeble to sustain such cruel exposure."[45]

Martyrdom not only pushed iniquity from the deceased to her enemy, it promised the deceased a holy future, a state often conjured by reference to the "crown" that would adorn the head of the dead martyr in heaven.[46] William Phelps, in his funeral oration for the Smith brothers, emphasized this fact with his "corrected" translation of Revelation

14:13—"congratulate the dead who die in the Lord," he said, for theirs was a martyr's glory.[47] In Smith's sermon shortly before his death, he announced "those saints who have been murdered in the persecution shall triumph in the celestial world."[48] There was no uncertainty about their salvation.

Living and dying in the shadow of their scattered war martyrs, the Latter-day Saints were able to make sense of premature death, confident that their enemies, rather than God, stood behind the multitude of their deaths. They were not just maintaining outsider status or exhibiting a persecution complex, though these also played a role in Mormon martyrdom. The Saints were coming to terms with Providence.

Death Must Not Conquer the Hero

However prepared they seemed for martyrdom, Smith's death came as a painful shock to the Latter-day Saints. Neither he nor his followers expected that he would actually die in Carthage, no matter how melodramatic the rhetoric. At times it seemed that Smith was invulnerable. He dodged execution after his surrender in November 1838 when a state militia officer stepped forward to stop an illegal court-martial. He then avoided what his followers feared would be a death sentence in Liberty, Missouri, when his jailers allowed him to escape. In Nauvoo this pattern continued, with frequent episodes of hiding from the law or finding lawyers or politicians who could free him from possible extradition back to Missouri, where Mormons believed he would be killed. Despite these successes, or perhaps because of them, Smith began in the early 1840s to describe intimations of his own death. His people did not believe him, but he told several individuals he thought that God would not protect him further (some understood him to be confessing problems with polygamy, while others understood him to be announcing that he had prepared the church to persist in his absence).[49]

The fact that Smith died, so brutally and for most Latter-day Saints so unexpectedly, was a wrenching trial for his church. He had been professing power over death for over a decade, had brought them scriptures from mummies and ancient burial grounds, and had unveiled a death-defying temple cultus. For Smith to die at the hands of a mob threatened the entire edifice of Mormonism. The charismatic prophet who had revealed an all-encompassing plan of death conquest had been killed by a band of possibly inebriated vigilantes in a frontier jail. No echelon of angels had intervened; no act of nature had interfered. The Prophet had died.

The Saints mourned Smith's loss profoundly. Beyond public and private mourning, the Latter-day Saints transformed and reinterpreted the death of their leader. Most impressively, Mormons imagined Smith's ongoing involvement with the work of the church and employed the concepts of his *imitatio Christi* to define him as a savior to the church.

Mormons mourned as if for a king, their entire society reflecting the magnitude of his death. In the phrase of an official announcement echoing Psalm 137, the Saints "felt [called] also to mourn over the bodies of their martyred chiefs, to hang their harps upon the willows, and in their overwhelming grief to cease for a while from the common avocations of life."[50] Dan Jones described the scene in Nauvoo—"everyone sad along the streets, all the shops closed and every business forgotten."[51] Some worried that their grief, however intense, was inadequate to the gravity of the event.[52] Other Saints employed the language of Providential mourning and Romantic sentimentality to see Nature itself pause to recognize the passing of the Prophet. In the words of one, "the elements had stilled, as if in surprise."[53] Two of Smith's plural wives recalled that "all creation was astir" as they remained awake the entire night "with our arms around each other, untill the dawn."[54]

Mormons across America mourned the passing of their leader. Parley Pratt in the New York *Messenger* published a martyrdom broadside to bring East Coast Mormons into intellectual and emotional communion with Nauvoo.[55] Some branches in the diaspora preached their own local funeral sermons for the fallen leader. A month after Smith's death, conference president William Burton of Chautauqua County, New York, "preach[ed] Joseph's and Hyrum's funeral sermon, on the Sabbath at 11 o'clock," using Revelation 14:12–13 ("Blessed are the dead which die in the Lord") as his text. As a result "a deep solemnity rested upon the congregation," and a visiting minister apparently converted to Mormonism on the spot.[56]

In Smith's death Mormons again found themselves in close proximity to ancient precedent. Early Mormonism's Jewish proselyte, Alexander Neibaur (1808–1883), penned a poem called "LAMENTATION Of a Jew among the afflicted and mourning Sons and Daughters of Zion, at the assassination of the Two Chieftains in Israel, JOSEPH AND HYRUM SMITH," with Psalm 79 invoked in the Hebrew epigraph. In Neibaur's phrase:

They have rejected and slain our leaders
Thine anointed ones
Our eyes are dim, our hearts heavy
No place of refuge being left.[57]

Appropriating the language of the Hebrew Bible, Neibaur returned to the ancient struggle to understand and accept the will of God as the force behind history. As they ached at the loss of their beloved leader, Mormon believers imagined themselves anew as part of ancient Israel.

Vengeance and Blood Crying from the Earth

Martyrdom did not entirely solve the problem of Providence. Mourners yearned for justice. Martyrdom did not fully sublimate the anger felt by the bereaved; images of blood feud often lurked nearby.[58] The tension in the Providential worldview again reared its head in the apocalyptic images of martyrs' blood inciting God to vengeance and the oaths many Saints took to avenge Smith's death.

In the immediate aftermath of Smith's murder, the Latter-day Saints did not rise up in civil war as Governor Thomas Ford feared. The Nauvoo Legion (the Mormon militia force) did not muster. Instead the Saints pleaded that the "murderers" not be allowed to "cumber the earth," urging outsiders to help "wash off the blood of these two innocent men, from Hancock county" by requiring that the guilty "atone for the innocent blood of Joseph and Hyrum Smith," apparently through lawful execution.[59] When the brothers' bodies first arrived in Nauvoo, Phelps preached a sermon on Revelation 6, apparently following Smith's antemortem instructions.[60] In this apocalyptic text (especially verse 9), "the souls of them that were slain for the word of God" cried from beneath an altar, "How long, O Lord, holy and true, dost thou not judge and avenge our blood on them that dwell on the earth." In 1839, Smith had preached that "the blood of those whose souls were under the alter, could not be avenged on them that dwell on the earth, until their brethren should be slain, as they were," a point Brigham Young echoed the same month.[61] Each Mormon death brought the destruction of Mormons' enemies closer to realization.

Intense, conflicting emotions saturated the Mormon response to Smith's death. According to the reminiscent report of an eyewitness, one of the men who unloaded the corpses from the wagon in Nauvoo, "Jurking up the coat and hat of Brother Joseph mingled with blood and dirt [said], 'Vengence and death awate the perpetrators of this deed.'"[62] Simultaneously, church authorities rushed to head off further violence. The original report from Carthage blamed Missourians for the murder and urged peace from the stunned faithful.[63] Governor Ford, embarrassed at his failure to protect Smith and fearing the escalation of violence, urged the Saints to allow the rule of law to punish the vigilantes. The church's pacific response to the murders did not indicate resignation or powerlessness. (Although Nauvoo had been officially disarmed days earlier, weapons remained among the Nauvoo Legion, and some Mormons had already begun building new ones.)[64] John Loveless, seeing a crowd celebrate the news of the Smiths' death, wished to be strong enough to have "sent them to their congenial spirits, howling devils of the infernal regions."[65] Jacob Gibson said that "the first murmurs, were revenge from almost every quarter."[66]

The Saints were able to maintain peace only because they were confident that God would exact vengeance himself. In Dan Jones's phrase, "the only comfort that kept them from sinking under the oppression and the loss was knowing that a day of swift reckoning would come also before long and that he who has the correct scales in his hand perceives the whole."[67]

Harsh realities soon dashed hopes for justice. Outside the state, onlookers decried the mode of Smith's execution but not generally the fact of his death. This tepid protest did little to encourage the dispensation of justice within Hancock County. Some of the ringleaders were arrested but were soon acquitted of all charges. By Mormon report, friendly witnesses were bullied and threatened with death, and the jury excluded Mormon sympathizers. Human government had betrayed the Saints, first in the person of Governor Ford, then in the failure to convict any of the Smiths' murderers.[68]

Mormon anger at times took the form of oaths of vengeance. Allen Joseph Stout (1815–1889) recalled: "I there and then resolved in my mind that I would never let an opportunity slip unimproved of avenging their blood upon the enemies of the church of Jesus Christ. I felt as though I could not live; I knew not how to contain myself, and when I see one of the men who persuaded them to give up to be tried, I feel like cutting their throats."[69] Another man announced: "I have covenanted, and never will rest nor my posterity after me until those men who killed Joseph & Hyrum have been wiped out of the earth."[70] Reuben Hedlock

(1805–1869), in a statement published in an August 1844 broadside, proclaimed: "my hand shall be raised to avenge the wrongs and death of the innocent."[71] William Phelps made the distinctive but intriguing proposal that Smith himself would take direct vengeance on his murderers as a destroying angel.

> [Smith] is where he can use the treasury of snow and hail; he can now direct the lion from the thicket to lay the gentile cities waste; and cause the young lion to go forth among the herds and tread down and tear in pieces and none can deliver. Wo to the drun[k]-ards with Ephraim! and the great whore of Babylon! for their destruction is sure, and their end near.[72]

The early Saints knew that their desire to assist God in his work would evoke claims of murder (or treason, if they attacked militia members).[73] This concern may have led to the grisly language—extensions of Masonic terminology—that kept vengeance oaths a secret. "If any of you betray us you are traitors of course you must expect the penalties put in force," explained one church leader in explication of these penalties. "I should not cut your throats but pray God to intervene to cut your own throat."[74] Even in the grisly image of a Masonic punishment executed, the Latter-day Saints hesitated between righteous fury and the patience to wait on God's wrath.

Such violent declarations supported the integrity of a community as they demonstrated the centrality of the figure that had passed. The Mormon cry for vengeance, while ritually more complex, differed little from later calls made by mainstream Americans after the assassination of Abraham Lincoln, when the entire North yearned for the death of the man who stole their hero from them.[75]

Spilled blood and its capacity to mark or accurse a particular place became a sustained metaphor in Mormon discussions about the meaning of martyrdom and God's response to it. When John C. Bennett first courted Smith, he said of the Missouri conflict: "the blood of the slain is crying from the ground for condign vengeance."[76] To claim that blood has stained the earth is to describe a disruption of cosmic order that cannot persist. Rather than decomposing with the rest of the body, blood alters the composition of the earth, creating a permanent mark of a life stolen prematurely. The blood within the ground had a voice for Mormons, and it cried from the dust with great urgency.

With blood as a witness, the bereaved hoped that their cries for Providential intervention would meet with success. In the phrase of Smith's dual wife Zina Huntington, "O God how long before thou wilt avenge the innosent blood that has ben shed?" But she did not stop there: "How long," she wondered, "before thou wilt avenge the Earth."[77] Following the lead of Revelation 6, Mormons believed Smith's death would finally tip the scales of justice and bring down God's wrath.[78] Wilford Woodruff said that "the world is sheding the blood of prophets Patriarch & Saints in order to fill up their cup."[79] When the cup finally filled, God would exact vengeance.

The lived Mormon exegesis of Revelation 6 provided an infrastructure for mediating the tension between the desire for justice and the need for vengeance. It called for God to act but admitted that he might not. It provided a place to retreat to when exacting personal vengeance seemed impossible.[80] Zina Huntington captured the sentiment in her diary: "Remember Thy People in mercy O Lord of hosts and avenge innocent Blood in thine own way."[81] The Bible was not the only literary reference the Saints made in situating their desire for justice. Sarah Richards (1802–1892), for example, invoked Milton's poem "On the Late Massacre in Piedmont," calling out: "Avenge, O Lord, thy slaughtered saints, whose bones / Lie scattered on the Alpine mountains cold."[82]

The language of spilled blood as a stain on the land allowed the Saints to vilify their opponents in the press. The *Times and Seasons* extra reporting the murders proclaimed: "the state of Illinois [is] stained with innocent blood."[83] Eliza Snow made the point clear in her poetic eulogy:

> Once lov'd America! what can atone
> For the pure blood of innocence thou'st sown?
> Were all thy streams in teary torrents shed,
> To mourn the fate of those illustrious dead,
> How vain the tribute for the noblest worth
> That grac'd thy surface, O degraded earth! . . .
> O, wretched murd'rers! fierce for human blood!
> You've slain the Prophets of the living God;
> Who've borne oppression from their early youth
> To plant on earth the principles of Truth.
> Shades of our patriotic fathers!
> Can it be, Beneath your blood-stain'd flag of liberty
> The firm supporters of our country's cause,
> Are butcher'd while submissive to her laws?[84]

Phelps's popular poem "Praise to the Man" concurred with Snow's assessment. "Long may his blood, which was shed by assassins / Stain Illinois while the earth lauds his fame."[85] Even survivor John Taylor's blood was thus sanctified to "cry to heaven for vengeance."[86]

Images of bloodstains were dramatically tangible for the mourning Saints. In the summer heat the bullet-riddled bodies leaked dark fluids onto the floor of the Mansion House, the visible mark of a martyr's blood seeping into the ground of Illinois. Whereas the bones of the dead marked ancestral ground (see chapter 4), the blood of the dead marked a disruption of community.[87]

The idea of blood's power to stain is present in the Book of Mormon narrative of the once bellicose Ammonite people who turned to pacifism. These converts took a vow to "stain our swords no more with the blood of our brethren . . . for perhaps, if we should stain our swords again they can no more be washed" clean.[88] Elsewhere in the Book of Mormon, God explained that he destroyed wicked cities "to hide their iniquities and their abominations from before my face, that the blood of the prophets and the saints shall not come any more unto me against them," a phrase repeated through several destructive iterations.[89] Mormon explained in an apostrophe to the nineteenth-century reader that there shall come "a day when the blood of saints shall cry unto the Lord, because of secret combinations and the works of darkness."[90]

Both Smith and the Book of Mormon followed biblical precedent. The blood of the very first martyr had "crie[d] unto [God] from the ground" to curse his murderous brother Cain "from the earth, which hath opened her mouth to receive [Abel's] blood."[91] Later Hebrew law claimed that "blood defileth the land, and the land cannot be cleansed of the blood that is shed therein," and Jehovah ordered an attack on King Ahab "that I may avenge the blood of my servants the prophets, and the blood of all the servants of the Lord."[92] The Christian New Testament employed the same rhetoric. Those who threatened early Christians risked incurring a wrath that had been building for centuries. According to the Christian appropriation of Old Testament tradition, "the blood of all the prophets, which was shed from the foundation of the world, may be required of this generation."[93]

Though sacred beliefs about the body and its life force likely played a role, there is in the language of bloodstains calling out to God an image of blood feud sublimated. The stained earth recalled the tit for tat of retributive execution familiar to anthropologists of many human societies. Placing the vengeance of the blood feud in God's hands may have

allowed expression of great pathos without the obligatory counter-
murder characteristic of actual blood feuds.

A Prophet's Afterlife

One central way the Latter-day Saints came to terms with the death of
Smith was by seeing him as actively involved in the work of the church
and the lives of its members, death notwithstanding. Smith's death made
the afterlife community more real, as his people imagined him alive and
involved from beyond the veil of death.[94] This belief in Smith as caring for
the Saints after his death merged with their beliefs about secondary saviors. While Latter-day Saint ideas mirrored the Catholic veneration of
saints, Mormons situated these beliefs firmly within the particularities
of their own tradition.

In June 1845, Zina Huntington mused, "Behold they rest in
peace.... But Joseph and Hirum are not here. Yet we belive they are doing
a great work in our favour behind the Vale."[95] Apostle Wilford Woodruff
repeatedly preached that the Smith brothers were "mingling with the
Gods, where they can plead for their brethren," language he borrowed
from Phelps's panegyric hymn.[96] According to one patriarch, "Joseph the
Martered Prophet... has gone to prepare the way for us, and can do more
for us than He could do if He was here."[97]

As the Saints imagined their Prophet's afterlife activities, they
employed images and language Smith had preached for years. Joseph was
one of the dead whose bowels yearned over the living. Phelps preached in
his funeral sermon that "Joseph has gone to his royal kindred in paradise,
from whom the keys, the power, and the mystery came, for the use and
benefit of mortal and immortal beings."[98] In the words of Samuel Richards
(1824–1909), Joseph deceased was a minister "not only on earth but in
heaven, and under the earth," the latter an allusion to Jesus's descent
into hell.[99] Because Smith had long taught that the dead looked after the
living, his people easily imagined the dead Joseph looking after them.
Rather than a fallen prophet of immortality, Smith was a divine being: he
and Hyrum were "like demi-gods."[100]

As they imagined Smith's afterlife glory, the Latter-day Saints found
ways to believe in their own. In death as in life, Smith guided his followers to heaven. In the words of Heber Kimball: "We want to get the
same exaltation; the same glory; the same kingdom, and mansions of our
Father, where Joseph has gone, and Hyrum has gone."[101]

Early Mormons had clear, literal images of Smith orchestrating the work of the church from beyond the veil. Phelps's hymn "Come to Me" imagined Smith inviting his people to join him in heaven.[102] Phelps also preached in late 1844: "I want you all to recollect that Joseph and Hyrum have only been removed from the earth, and they now counsel and converse with the Gods beyond the reach of powder and ball."[103] Lucy Mack, representing Smith's biological family, maintained a similar belief, preaching to the assembled church in 1845 that her son had died "to take the case [of the persecuted church] up himself" before the Divine Judge.[104] As he had in life, Joseph Smith represented in death a conduit to heaven for his followers.

Beliefs about Smith's postmortal fate ranged from the abstract and metaphorical to the highly tangible. Phelps preached: "God, man, and Mormonism, are not only material, but eternal, and therefore, like Jesus, when martyred they come to life again."[105] How soon Smith would come to life was controversial. There is some evidence that the Saints expected their prophet to visit them physically as soon as they completed the Nauvoo Temple. Parley Pratt, reflecting that the Smiths "though ded yet they live," encouraged completion of the temple so "that when done we might meet Hour beloved Prophets at the time of the inducment of the faithful."[106] A few days after Christmas in 1845, during the height of activity in the temple, the assembled Saints sang Phelps's "Come to Me" as if to effect a reunion with the Prophet.[107] There is in that hymn and its performance inside the temple something of the yearning in Pratt's sermon, Mormons' hunger to be reunited with their prophet through the rites of his temple. Outside observers repeatedly claimed that Mormons anticipated a visit from the resurrected Smith at the dedication of the temple.[108] Whether the Saints believed that the martyred brothers had redefined the nature (or timing) of the Second Coming or that they would return in glory before the great resurrection, dramatic power was imputed to the fallen prophets, priests, and kings of Mormonism. They were far from dead in the minds of their people.

Many Latter-day Saints seized on the image of Joseph returned from the dead to describe an August 1844 meeting in which many present felt that God sanctioned Young as Smith's ecclesiastical successor.[109] On reflection many attendees believed that Young had been overcome by Smith's spirit to such an extent that Smith himself was speaking through Young. Many Saints took this supernatural association to mean that Smith would remain with the church over which Young had assumed control.[110] While the story of Smith's spiritual presence anointing Young expanded with time, the event fit well within the culture of Nauvoo after Smith's death. Visions of Smith in Nauvoo during this period were not uncommon. One of Smith's plural widows emblematically noted that she "Dreamed of seeing Joseph Smith" the first winter after his death.[111] The August 1844 meeting merged the general sense of Smith's involvement in church affairs with the expectation that the Saints would see their prophet again.

Afterlife and the Imitatio Christi

Language about blood that would force God to intervene merged with images of Smith as sacrificing his life for his people to point toward a bold comparison that scandalously united various strands of Mormon thought. In death, according to the divine anthropology, Smith became a divine being, and within the framework of his patriarchal priesthood, a secondary savior.

In his last few years, Smith experimented with the title of angel as a special priesthood office, calling himself the "archangel" of the church (see chapter 9). With his death, there was no obstacle to his ascent to such a status. The sermon preached at his funeral explicitly bestowed this title on the Mormon prophet, and some Saints called Smith the "Angel of the Church."[112] Within the divine anthropology, "angel" referred to a particular type of divine being, a stepping-stone between humanity and divinity. As a deceased martyr, Smith occupied such a place by right.

The Saints were careful to distinguish Smith from Jesus even as they employed Jesus's martyrdom as the antecedent for the Prophet's death. Eliza Snow, referring to "blood so noble," claimed that Smith was the martyr second to Jesus in importance.[113] The official eulogy proclaimed that Smith had "done more, save Jesus only," than anyone else for human salvation.[114] Even as they were careful to distinguish Smith from Jesus, the Saints used rhetoric that collapsed the distance between the two.

Language about Smith as a sacrifice furthered the comparison between him and Christ. Of the many memorial poems to the Prophet in the Nauvoo newspapers in the first year after his death, almost all of them focused on his role as a holy sacrifice.[115] Such memorials followed Smith's lead, as he compared himself to a lamb "prepared for the slaughter" both in 1838 and again in 1844, a reference to the "suffering servant" of Isaiah (53:7) understood by Christians to refer to Jesus.[116] In the words of Joseph Fielding, the Prophet "die[d] for this People." Fielding explicitly situated Joseph's experience within the martyrdom of Jesus: "Is this an Earnest of what has to take Place in this Last Dispensation, is the Blood of the Sheep again to be shed like that of the Shepherd as in former Days, Father if it be possible let this Cup pass from us, but if not let thy Will be done and let us be strengthened to endure to the End."[117] Smith as a sacrificial lamb led to a sort of culmination for the adoption theology. One published account of Smith's murder had him live just long enough on the ground beneath the jail window to exclaim Jesus's words from the cross, "O, Father, forgive them, for they know not what they do."[118] According to Dan Jones, Smith had spilled "atoneing blood" on the Illinois soil.[119] Various followers soon compared Smith's death to Jesus's crucifixion.[120] There was a sense in which Smith had extended salvation to his followers as a savior on Mount Zion, secondary to Christ. Smith's widow Zina Huntington prayed "through the worthiness of Thy Sons I may be able to enter through the Gate into the Selestial City and dwell with the Sactified."[121] John Taylor's paean to Smith, "The Seer," made explicit how important Joseph's *imitatio Christi* was to the Saints:

> Unchanged in death, with a Saviors love
> He pleads their cause, in the courts above....
> His home's in the sky;—
> he dwells with the Gods....
> He died; he died—for those he lov'd.[122]

We should be clear—the Latter-day Saints never claimed that Smith was Jesus or a replacement for Jesus. He was a sheep, while Christ was the shepherd. What the Mormons did appear to be claiming was that Smith was foremost among secondary saviors. The *imitatio Christi* was more than just a theological construct; it was a tool for grieving and explaining. Brigham Young communicated this theme in August 1844:

> Joseph has always been preserved from his enemies, until now, but he has sealed his testimony with his blood, and his testament is now in force. While the testator lived it was all in his hands, but now he is dead. There is no remission of sins without the shedding of blood. You will soon wake up and know things as they are—there has been a great debt paid; there will be no need

of more blood of the saints being shed at present, by and by you
will understand and see that all is right.[123]

Young's speech combined the soteriology of secondary saviors with the
Book of Revelation language of the martyrs who finally forced God's
hand. Young was telling his people that Smith had saved them by offering
his own blood to complete the long line of martyrs. With the death of the
Smith brothers, the loss of Mormon lives would cease.

A Prophet's Relics

While Smith as an angel protected his followers in heaven, Smith as a
corpse both guided the mourning of his followers and pointed out unre-
solved tension within his legacy. An amplification and outgrowth of the
culture of holy dying, the story of the postmortem journey of Smith's
body ties various threads together, including the sacred power of the
body and blood and Smith's imitation of Christ. Simultaneously, strife
over Smith's body points out the ongoing conflict between the individual
and the corporate, between the rising Victorian model of family and
Smith's sacerdotal protest against it.

The story of the martyr's remains began even before Smith's followers
recovered his body. According to one heavily embellished account (see
figure 10.1):

> The ruffian . . . who set him against the well-curb, now gathered a
> bowie knife for the purpose of severing his head from his body.
> He raised the knife and was in the attitude of striking, when a
> light, so sudden and powerful, burst from the heavens upon the
> bloody scene, (passing its vivid chain between Joseph and his
> murderers,) that they were struck with terrified awe and filled
> with consternation. This light, in its appearance and potency,
> baffles all powers of description. The arm of the ruffian, that held
> the knife, fell powerless; the muskets of the four, who fired, fell
> to the ground, and they all stood like marble statues, not having
> the power to move a single limb of their bodies.[124]

God, this story suggested, would preserve Joseph's body for a holy burial.
He would not let the mob steal a proper burial from the bereaved Latter-
day Saints. While the story is fictitious, it is no surprise that John Taylor

Figure 10.1 An early, embellished account of Smith's murder had a ruffian threatening to desecrate his corpse through decapitation. A supernatural light prevented the desecration. Image courtesy of the Church History Library, The Church of Jesus Christ of Latter-day Saints.

and many other Saints readily accepted its accuracy.[125] Mormons went to great lengths to prevent desecration of those hallowed remains.

The intact but bloody bodies of the Smith brothers returned to Nauvoo in a straw-packed wagon, greeted by "crowds of mourners" who were "lamenting the great loss of our Prophet and our Patriarch."[126] At the Mansion House, close friends and family prepared the brothers for burial, filling their bullet wounds with camphor-soaked cotton. The bodies were then displayed for intimates. By at least one firsthand account, "gore" and "the blood of the two godly martyrs mingling in one pool in the middle of the floor" were visible during the initial viewing.[127] A visiting physician reported that the stench during the viewing required the burning of tar, vinegar, and sugar to allow visitors to tolerate their encounter with the bodies.[128]

Two days after his murder, Smith's body was exhibited in a public viewing in the parlor of the Mansion House. From 8:00 a.m. to 5:00 p.m., thousands of Latter-day Saints visited the Prophet's remains, encased in a wood coffin with a movable glass window protecting his face. His body was enclosed in white cloth, which was attached to the coffin with black velvet tabs. According to a firsthand account, "the thousands made their way forward, sad and desirous of having the last look at their dear brethren whose solemn counsels and heavenly teachings had been music in their ears, lighting their paths and bringing joy to their hearts."[129] In the late evening, the faithful followed a funeral procession toward the Nauvoo cemetery, pausing at the preaching ground beside the temple to hear William Phelps offer a funeral oration.[130] Fearing the theft of the revered remains, the funeral procession carried sand-filled coffins to burial in the city cemetery, apparently without a grave marker.[131] Late that night, the bodies were removed from their actual hiding place in the Mansion House to a makeshift burial in the foundation of the Nauvoo House, during a violent storm that frightened the nervous buriers but protected the bodies from enemies.[132]

The Prophet's remains were reportedly sought after by many, from vigilantes eager to receive some reward for bringing Smith to justice, to anti-Mormons eager to desecrate the relics of Mormonism's founder, to opportunists hoping to make great profit from selling them to a phrenological museum.[133] There was precedent for worries about desecration, as was clear in the offensive treatment of the body of Chief Blackhawk (1767–1838) a few years previously in nearby Burlington, Iowa, a sad event memorialized by Mormons in the Nauvoo newspaper.[134] Recognizing the potency of the sacred remains of a martyr, Smith's family and followers worked strenuously to protect the dead brothers from their enemies. The nearly completed Tomb of Joseph would not do. Nor would a marked grave.

In retrospect, such worries may represent more the sacred concerns of the Saints than an objective threat, much like anti-Mormons' fear of the power of the Nauvoo Legion. The more important conflict over the martyrs' relics actually took place among the Saints. Joseph's body quickly became a point of contention between Brigham Young, representing the ecclesial family, and Emma Smith, representing the biological family. With her husband buried in the foundation of their home, Emma controlled the Prophet's remains. Young found this intolerable. Less than two months after the false interment, Brigham Young announced to the Nauvoo Saints the necessity of removing the remains to the Tomb of Joseph, invoking a promise to the martyr.

Perhaps in response to Young's desire to have the martyr's remains interred in the tomb beside the temple, Emma transferred the corpses in great secrecy to the foundation of an outbuilding on the Smith family property, apparently hiding her decision even from Hyrum's widow, who had sided with Young. During her transfer of the remains, it is reported that Hyrum's corpse was carefully inspected and a lock of Joseph's hair was removed for Emma's safekeeping.[135] With this secret reinterment, Emma secured permanent control of her husband's body.[136]

Employing the familiar language of communal resurrection in phrases drawn directly from Smith's preaching, Young used astonishingly harsh words to contest Emma's control over her husband's body by claiming that Joseph would condemn her at the resurrection for failing to place his corpse in the Tomb of Joseph (see chapter 2). The harshness underscores the urgency with which Young sought the martyrs' bodies, reflecting and shaping the concern of lay Mormons over the fate of Smith's bones.[137] John C. Bennett—by then aligned with James Strang, another possible successor to Joseph Smith—argued strongly in 1846 for the need to seize "the bodies of *Joseph and Hyrum*" along with "the *mummies* and *papyrus*" to improve the success of the Strangite offshoot.[138] At least three of the possible successor groups sought control of the Smith relics.

Despite the objections of the Apostles and their followers (including Hyrum's family), Emma kept the brothers' location secret. Emma would die with the location untold and probably misremembered, asking to be buried beside Joseph though she missed the spot by a few yards. Her oldest son and others of his family claimed that they knew the location but never disclosed it.[139] Evidence suggests they did not know as much as they claimed. The poetic and mentally imbalanced David Hyrum Smith (1844–1904), the son born some months after Joseph Jr.'s death, pined for many decades for the location of his father's body in a plaintive hymn sung by the Reorganized Church of Jesus Christ of Latter Day Saints (RLDS)—a competing church led by Joseph Smith's widow, Emma, and his oldest son, Joseph III (1832–1914), and renamed Community of Christ in 2001.[140]

Finally and fortuitously, utility projects on the Mississippi in the 1910s threatened the Smith family land on the riverbanks, necessitating the location and transfer of all mortal remains for their protection from flooding. W. O. Hands, an RLDS engineer hired to find the bodies, reported that God guided him, after considerable toil, to the location of the martyrs' relics on January 16, 1928.[141] When they were removed, members of the RLDS church inspected the bodies, photographed the skulls, and reinterred them within a monument in a significant ceremony on January

20. They did not alert the Utah church, now run by their cousins, to this project until it was complete.

The Utah cousins were not pleased. The anger of Joseph Fielding Smith (1876–1972)—Hyrum's grandson and future president of the Utah church—at the disinterment represents his reverence for the martyrs' remains and his concern that they were out of the hands of his church. "These remains should not have been disturbed, and such a despicable act could only be performed by those who are lacking in all the finer feelings."[142] He claimed that his cousin had "debased himself in the sight of all honorable men as well as in the sight of God, in this unholy and sacrilegious act." Fielding Smith and his colleagues even transiently considered bringing suit against their midwestern kin. The Utah group claimed to have known the location of the remains all along, despite a lack of evidence to support their claim. The Nauvooans replied that they were responding in part to rumors that the relics had been stolen and installed in the Salt Lake Temple.[143] One feels their satisfaction in disproving the rumors running through the war of words waged in regional newspapers.

Tensions and Fault Lines

Emma Smith and the church her son came to lead had every right to her husband's corpse. The fact that Brigham Young also attempted to make a claim on the corpse points to the radical nature of Smith's redefinition of family. Because Smith had simultaneously amplified both an ecclesiastical and a biological approach to family, his death introduced the critical threat of schism. Though Mormonism had generated its share of sects during Smith's life, at his death the fundamental tension was between ecclesial and biological communities. The most important rift was between the Apostles, who had spent the last several years at the center of Smith's church community, and Smith's own family, led by his widow. The verbal battles over Smith's remains represented a much deeper divide.[144]

Probably because the idea of biological family was more powerful, Young fought an uphill battle against those who followed Smith's widow and children. On the one hand, Smith's teachings about the power of a lineal priesthood suggested that Smith's sons would of necessity come to lead the church when they reached adulthood. This line of reasoning had enough support that Young left open for some years the possibility that one of Joseph Smith's sons could take the helm of the Utah church.[145] On the other hand, Smith's teachings suggested that patriarchal priesthood could create novel ties that trumped genetics. Emblematic of this tension was the highly publicized late 1844 letter from William Phelps, self-consciously representing the Apostles, to William Smith, the last of Joseph Smith's brothers, who came into frequent conflict with the Apostles. "I respect you and the 'Twelve,' and all their kin, as my own blood relations," Phelps explained to William, employing the language of consanguinity to describe the relationships that existed among the Latter-day Saints.[146]

In April 1847, as he was superintending a mass exodus to the Rockies, Brigham Young paused to write a plaintive missive to Lucy Mack Smith, "A Mother in Israel." In attempting to woo her into membership in his church, Young used strong language to combine the biological and ecclesiastical definitions of family. Young called his followers "her children in the Gospel," then made reference to "your dear husband, our Father in Israel." He continued, writing that God "has given you a family to increase without number, which shall continue worlds without end; & we rejoice that we are of that number." He then made specific reference to the temple, the mechanism by which he had established control of the ecclesial family. He wrote Mother Smith that he intended to "build a house unto the Most High" in the Rockies to perform "ordinances...that shall bring back again the Children of Adam & Eve, Abraham & Sarah, Joseph & Lucy into the presence of the Most High God, even the places that they were destined for from before the foundation of the world." If Lucy would agree to join with Young and the main body of the church, "there is no Sacrifice we will count too great to bring [you] forward."[147] Lucy had long considered herself the matriarch of the church, an assumption Joseph Jr. had supported wholeheartedly. Even as Young failed to persuade her (Lucy died a decade later, under the care of her daughter-in-law Emma, in Nauvoo), he made clear just how strongly her son had revised the meaning of family.

Although most of Smith's biological family refused him, Young managed to assume control of the ecclesial family. In his supervision and codification of the Nauvoo Temple rites and sealings, and particularly in the rites of adoption that evolved shortly after Smith's death, Young strongly asserted his role as conservator of the church family. As far back as the 1830s, patriarchal blessings had dealt specifically with the strains that existed between church and biological families. In the controversies after Smith's death, the temple rites and associated sealings overwhelmed other forms of attachment.

For the Latter-day Saints, who had staked their reputations and their lives on the career of their death-vanquishing hero, the death of the Prophet both illuminated and modified their pursuit of the conquest of death. As an undead martyr and divine being, Smith has continued to leave his mark in the lives of the churches that derive from his prophetic ministry. With the commonsense, supernatural logic of his preaching, Smith proved to his followers the possibility that death could truly be conquered. From his near-fatal bout with typhoid and Alvin's death in his youth, Smith grew into a potent critic and reformer of the culture of antebellum America, revising the culture of holy dying and proposing a dramatic reformulation of family. In his life and in his death, Smith struggled to resolve the painful tensions within the religious worldview of antebellum America. In the eyes of many of his followers, this struggle ultimately yielded the utter conquest of death.

AFTERWORD

This book began as an attempt to make sense of two observations, one academic and one highly personal. Academically, I noticed that Mormon angels are not like the angels of most other traditions: Mormon angels are humans at a different developmental stage. On a personal level, as a physician treating the sickest of the sick I was deeply moved by the human urgency of the deathbed and struck by the relative lack of guidance for people facing this most difficult transition (or terminus, depending on one's belief). As I grappled with the meanings of these two observations, I immersed myself in the documentary record of earliest Mormonism and its cultural contexts. I carried the questions of how humans relate to suprahuman beings and confront their possible demise with me throughout this research. What I found—a new account of earliest Mormonism—induced in me the "salutary vertigo" enjoined on readers by the historian Peter Brown.

Many early Mormon beliefs—polygamy/adoption, the divine anthropology, temples—sound strange to most modern readers. They should. Such beliefs are more Antique than modern. As alien as they are to modern readers, the beliefs of Smith's early Mormons display a stunning ambition and coherence. Based on a handful of central assumptions, Smith and his colleagues described a complex and dramatic set of beliefs and rituals. Even so, not all of these beliefs will bear translation to modern sensibilities. I agree with the early Latter-day Saints that excessive emphasis on a nuclear family can limit our ability to function as a society and constrain our religious sensibilities, but I do not support polygamy as the solution to the problems of the Victorian nucleus. While I appreciate the grand scope of a system that urges us to treat all humans as potential kin, I feel blessed to have just one spouse and a small handful of children. Understanding early Mormons on their own terms, though, allows modern readers, including perhaps practicing Mormons, to imagine ways to carry forward the communal vision of Mormonism's founding prophet without requiring a return to the polygamy that the Latter-day Saints abandoned at the turn of the twentieth century.

The approach I took in this book—as an intensive care unit physician whose soul is deeply stirred by the courage with which his patients face the possibility that they may not survive—participates in what I believe is a healthy direction for Mormon studies and American religious history. This approach requires, in my view, a willingness to separate ourselves from the subjects of our inquiry long enough for their voices to be heard but to do so in a way that respects our shared humanity. This approach is paradoxical, making the subjects of research both foreign and familiar in a complex web of interactions. This approach must also confess the effects of time. Religious traditions and their host cultures change significantly over time—modern Mormons believe that this process occurs through God's guidance to their current prophetic leaders, while outsiders descry the relentless nature of cultural change. Twenty-first-century images and ideas come easily to hand to explain antebellum terms, concepts, and phrases, but they generally do so by clouding our view of how these women and men actually behaved and believed. For this reason, I have limited my scope of inquiry to documents from the Nauvoo period and before, with few exceptions. I have tried not to measure early Mormonism against modern Mormon or Protestant or rationalist viewpoints. I have also framed questions in a way that I hope makes the answers interesting regardless of one's beliefs about the relevance or verity of supernatural experiences. My work fits broadly within the "lived religion" school of religious history, but it does so with the caveats that ideas do matter and that, particularly for religions on social fringes, boundaries between clergy and laity are highly permeable.

I apologize that I have not been entirely fair to the Protestantisms that Mormonism protested against. I have tried to acknowledge where the Mormon caricature of Protestantism poorly described actual beliefs and practice, but I have also attempted to allow the Mormon narrative its own space. Mormons were reacting to particular understandings of Protestant religion, however inaccurate. American Protestantism in the early nineteenth century was notoriously and marvelously diverse; to also capture Protestantism in its richness would require a treatment twice the length of this book. Because my goal was to clarify what early

Mormonism meant to participants, I allowed Mormon caricatures to stand more than I would have in a history devoted to American Protestantism. In addition, while Mormons saw what they understood as serious deficiencies in antebellum Protestantism and sought to solve them, there is more to Mormonism than its protest against Protestantism. Giving early Mormons space enabled a more focused and coherent account of what Mormons did and believed.

Allowing Mormonism a freer rein also makes clear the complexity of early Mormon theology and philosophy. Theirs was a visionary and potent eclecticism that can cause trouble for intellectual historians. Academic training often persuades historians of the importance of respecting the scholarly work that has preceded them, allowing that work to have a coherence, even an authority, of its own. The more academic view has led to prior attempts to see Mormonism as clearly deriving from specific traditions, whether Protestant millenarianism or Renaissance hermeticism or Restorationism. But Smith and other early Mormons were drawing "fragments" of other traditions and concatenating them in novel ways unauthorized by those prior traditions. As one example among many, Smith's assiduous "materialism" (minimally an account of and protest against the risks of physical dissolution that attend death) is compatible, within Mormonism, with elements of an otherwise antimaterialist Neoplatonism. The sources from which Mormons could engage such ideas are similarly eclectic: theological dictionaries, poems, hymns, stray quotations in the exchange papers, school primers, brief essays in newspapers, distinctive biblical proof-texting, or superficial reading of some versions of the original arguments. These diverse, nonspecialist sources have been underappreciated and underexplored, perhaps in part because they are hard to bring into an academically satisfying account of a worldview. This book has attempted to rectify this deficiency.

The personal has never been far from the subject matter of this book for me. There is something like a community of people who have suffered the death of a loved one. Those of us who have lost a parent or a lover or a friend or a child know something that no one else does. It is not a language, really, but a shared awareness that is difficult to communicate to someone who has not experienced such grief. I have come to appreciate through this research how fully early Mormons took part in the community of souls who have known the wordless but not noiseless agony of bereavement.

It would be easy today, in a culture still often in utter denial of the possibility of death, to see elements of the lost worldview described in this book as possible ways forward, to view their solutions with nostalgic reverence. There is some truth in this claim: this lost worldview has enriched my own strenuous negotiations with Fate and physiology as a physician. But it would be wrong to discount the gift of life prolonged through applications of advanced medical technologies. In sleepless nights at bedsides in the intensive care unit, my colleagues and I have coaxed years, even decades from acutely diseased bodies, and we should not be embarrassed at the objectives our technologies and attention have achieved. We should not seek a return to nineteenth-century medicine and its associated high mortality merely because our modern death culture suffers from serious defects and distortions. Nor should we assume that older approaches to death are flawless. Early Mormons still suffered when loved ones died and were devastated at the frequency of their losses. Still, I believe that elements of the older death culture, particularly its emphasis on the deathbed as a place of healing, community, and vision, could improve our experiences when, despite our best efforts, we, too, confront the end of our mortal sojourn.

Ultimately, my impression of the legacy of Joseph Smith is that what matters is who we see beside us when we discover that we are in the precincts of death. Whether mortal or immortal, whether living or dead, what matters is who our companions are, to whom we have committed ourselves. While it is true that we each die alone in a physiological sense, death is more than the moment that circulation permanently ceases; it is also the human drama that surrounds that cosmos-rending moment. And in the borderlands between life and death, we need not be alone. There is an inescapable paradox here. We should love deeply and durably. But we are to love beings who will necessarily and inevitably die. Entering relationships, loving, building lives together, always brooks the risk of bereavement. Early Mormons, as so many humans before and since, recognized those risks but chose repeatedly to commit to each other, to covenant a loyalty that could withstand death. To borrow once more Peter Berger's justly famous phrase, religion for Joseph Smith and his followers did not just provide "banners" for believers to carry as they "walk, inevitably, toward" death, it provided a company of Saints who could walk toward, and—earnestly, anxiously—*through* death with each other. The journey, hopefully extending through the breadth of cosmic space and time, mattered to the extent that it was undertaken with others.

NOTES

Introduction

1. Peter Berger, *The Sacred Canopy: Elements of a Sociological Theory of Religion* (New York: Doubleday), 51.
2. Geoffrey Gorer is widely credited with drawing attention to the problems of modern death culture in "The Pornography of Death." See his *Death, Grief, and Mourning* (New York: Doubleday, 1965), esp. 192–99. See also Philippe Ariès, *The Hour of Our Death* (New York: Knopf, 1981).
3. See, e.g., Klaus Hansen, *Quest for Empire: The Political Kingdom of God and the Council of Fifty in Mormon History* (East Lansing: Michigan State University Press, 1967); John Brooke, *The Refiner's Fire: The Making of Mormon Cosmology, 1644–1844* (Cambridge: Cambridge University Press, 1994); Fawn M. Brodie, *No Man Knows My History: The Life of Joseph Smith, the Mormon Prophet*, 2nd. ed. rev. and enl. (New York: Knopf, 1971); Richard Hughes and Leonard Allen, *Illusions of Innocence: Protestant Primitivism, 1630–1875* (Chicago: University of Chicago Press, 1988), 133–52; and Marvin Hill, *Quest for Refuge: The Mormon Flight from American Pluralism* (Salt Lake City: Signature Books, 1989).
4. *WJS*, 352.
5. See, e.g., Douglas Davies, *The Mormon Culture of Salvation* (Aldershot, England: Ashgate, 2000); Klaus Hansen, *Mormonism and the American Experience* (Chicago: University of Chicago Press, 1981), chapter 3; Lester E. Bush, *Health and Medicine Among the Latter-day Saints* (New York: Crossroad, 1993), chapter 1; and Mary Ann Meyers, "Gates Ajar," in *Death in America*, ed. David Stannard (Philadelphia: University of Pennsylvania Press, 1977), 112–33.
6. Robert Orsi, *Between Heaven and Earth: The Religious Worlds People Make and the Scholars Who Study Them* (Princeton: Princeton University Press, 2005).
7. I concur with the approach outlined in Caroline Walker Bynum, *Resurrection of the Body in Western Christianity, 200–1336* (New York: Columbia University Press, 1995), xv–xvi.
8. Jane Tompkins, *Sensational Designs: The Cultural Work of American Fiction, 1790–1860* (New York: Oxford University Press, 1986), popularized this use of the phrase "cultural work."

9. Peter R. L. Brown, *The Body and Society: Men, Women, and Sexual Renunciation in Early Christianity* (New York: Columbia University Press, 1988), xvii.

10. In this study I report early Mormon beliefs rather than taking sides in a debate among Mormon scholars regarding the possibility that the migrant families of the Book of Mormon narrative affected only a small part of the Americas, both geographically and genetically.

11. I chose this over, e.g., the "creative literalism" described by Richard Cummings, "Quintessential Mormonism: Literal-Mindedness as a Way of Life," *Dialogue* 15:4 (winter 1982): 92–102, to emphasize the supernatural bent of Mormon exegesis.

12. I thank Jane Barnes and Jonathon Penny for helping me summarize in this paragraph this book's view of Joseph Smith.

Chapter 1

1. *APR*, 418. Compare the Providentialist revision of his death in *HC* 6:50.

2. *WWJ* 2:229; compare 1 Corinthians 15:26.

3. *WJS*, 353.

4. *APR*, 404.

5. L***** S*****, *"The fool hath said in his heart, there is no God,"* *Wasp* 1:35 (December 31, 1842): 4, emphasis in original.

6. E. R. Snow, "Apostrophe to Death," *T&S* 4:3 (December 15, 1842): 48.

7. [Jacques] Saurin, "Comparison Between Heathenism and Christianity," *EMS* 1:6 (November 1832): 43. Saurin (1677–1730) was a noted Huguenot preacher. See also Charles Buck, *Theological Dictionary* (Philadelphia: Edwin T. Scott, 1823), 93, which proclaimed that through Christianity "death itself, the king of terrors, has lost its sting."

8. Philippe Ariès, *Western Attitudes Toward Death* (Baltimore: Johns Hopkins University Press, 1974), 55, proposed and popularized the "beautiful" death. His *The Hour of Our Death* (New York: Knopf, 1981) is a foundational text. Pat Jalland, *Death in the Victorian Family* (Oxford: Oxford University Press, 1996), 8, prefers "good," the most accepted term among Anglo-American scholars. See, e.g., Drew Gilpin Faust, *This Republic of Suffering: Death and the American Civil War* (New York: Knopf, 2008). Methodists often called it "happy": A. Gregory Schneider, "The Ritual of Happy Dying Among Early American Methodists," *Church History* 56:3 (September 1987): 348–49. For "triumphant," see Randy J. Sparks, "The Southern Way of Death: The Meaning of Death in Antebellum White Evangelical Culture," *Southern Quarterly* 44:1 (fall 2006): 35–36, and Nancy Towle, *Vicissitudes Illustrated in the Experience of Nancy Towle, in Europe and America*, 2d ed. (Portsmouth, N.H.: John Caldwell, 1833), 34–35.

9. John Greenleaf Whittier, *The Supernaturalism of New England* (New York: Wiley & Putnam, 1847), 103. See also Jeremy Taylor, *The Rule and Exercise of Holy Dying* (London: J. Heptinstall, 1703).

10. Stephen Stein, *The Shaker Experience in America* (New Haven: Yale University Press, 1994), 81, and Faust, *Republic of Suffering*, 7. On the Southern experience see Scott Stephan, *Redeeming the Southern Family: Evangelical Women*

and Domestic Devotion in the Antebellum South (Athens: University of Georgia Press, 2008), 183–220. On the African-American view see Mark S. Schantz, *Awaiting the Heavenly Country: The Civil War and America's Culture of Death* (Ithaca: Cornell University Press, 2008), 137.

11. Standard accounts like Gary Laderman, *The Sacred Remains: American Attitudes Toward Death, 1799–1883* (New Haven: Yale University Press, 1996); Faust, *Republic of Suffering*; and Schantz, *Culture of Death*, have failed to engage this problem. Lewis Saum, *The Popular Mood of Pre–Civil War America* (Westport, Conn.: Greenwood Press, 1980), and Stephan, *Southern Family*, 220, have done a better job.

12. Keith Thomas, *Religion and the Decline of Magic* (New York: Oxford University Press, 1997), and Eamon Duffy, *The Stripping of the Altars: Traditional Religion in England, 1400–1580* (New Haven: Yale University Press, 2002).

13. On Puritans, see David Hall, *Worlds of Wonder: Days of Judgment* (New York: Knopf, 1989), 197, 210. For antebellum Protestants, see Buck, *Theological Dictionary*, 82, 180, 185, 193–94, 235, 307, 465, 520–21, 581.

14. Ann Douglas, *The Feminization of American Culture* (New York: Knopf, 1977), 202–3.

15. Alan MacFarlane, "Death and the Demographic Transition: A Note on English Evidence on Death 1500–1750," in *Mortality and Immortality: The Anthropology and Archeology of Death*, ed. S. C. Humphreys and Helen King (London: Academic Press, 1981), 249–50; Daniel Walker Howe, *What Hath God Wrought: The Transformation of America, 1815–1848* (New York: Oxford University Press, 2007), 473, 530; Robert William Fogel, *The Escape from Hunger and Death, 1700–2100* (Cambridge: Cambridge University Press, 2004), 1–2.

16. *Wasp* 1:19 (August 27, 1842): 2. This appears to be a popularization of the work of Berliner Johann Ludwig Casper (1796–1864). On statistics in early America, see Patricia Cohen, *A Calculating People: The Spread of Numeracy in Early America* (New York: Routledge, 1999).

17. Nicholas Marshall, "In the Midst of Life We Are in Death: Affliction and Religion in Antebellum New York," in *Mortal Remains: Death in Early America*, ed. Nancy Isenberg and Andrew Burstein (Philadelphia: University of Pennsylvania Press, 2003), 177. I have included the adopted Murdock twins for Joseph Jr. and all stillborn children for both.

18. Fred Woods, "The Cemetery Record of William D. Huntington, Nauvoo Sexton," *Mormon Historical Studies* 3:1 (spring 2002): 131–63; M. Guy Bishop et al., "Death at Mormon Nauvoo, 1843–1845," *Western Illinois Regional Studies* 9:2 (fall 1986): 70–83; and H. Dean Garrett, "Disease and Sickness in Nauvoo," in *Regional Studies in Latter-day Church History*, ed. H. Dean Garrett (Provo, Utah: Department of Church History and Doctrine, Brigham Young University, 1995), 169–82.

19. Data drawn from sexton reports published in the *Wasp* and the *Nauvoo Neighbor*, database in my possession.

20. John Greenhow, "To the Editor," *T&S* 5:2 (January 15, 1844): 412.

21. See, e.g., Towle, *Vicissitudes*, 119.

22. See, e.g., Towle, *Vicissitudes*, 61, 63, and letter to William Phelps, December 1, 1837, HBLL.

23. Peter Metcalf and Richard Huntington, *Celebrations of Death: The Anthropology of Mortuary Ritual*, 2d ed., rev. (Cambridge: Cambridge University Press, 1991).

24. On the book's impact, see Jalland, *Death in the Victorian Family*, 18–19.

25. Buck, *Theological Dictionary*, 70, 143, confirms the popularity of Hervey among Anglo-Americans. On Smith's ownership, see Christopher Jones, "The Complete Record of the Nauvoo Library and Literary Institute," *Mormon Historical Studies* 10:1 (spring 2009): 193.

26. Funeral sermons were often appended to collections of sermons by noted clergy.

27. See, e.g., Buck, *Theological Dictionary*, 137–38, and John Robinson, *A Theological, Biblical, and Ecclesiastical Dictionary* (London: Longman et al., 1815), s.v. "Death."

28. James Hervey, *Meditations and Contemplations* (New York: Richard Scott, 1824), 17–22.

29. "Thoughtful," *Wasp* 1:28 (October 29, 1842): 3; see also *Wasp* 1:52 (April 26, 1843): 2.

30. See, e.g., "The Burial of Little Nell," *Wasp* 1:7 (May 28, 1842): 1; Mrs. C.M. Sawyer, "The Young Mother," *Wasp* 1:29 (November 5, 1842): 1; "Home, Sweet Home," *Wasp* 1:2 (April 23, 1842): 1; and Douglas, *Feminization*, 200.

31. Little Eva is the daughter of the family that owns Uncle Tom in Harriet Beecher Stowe's novel *Uncle Tom's Cabin*. See Laderman, *Sacred Remains*, 55–56. See also T. S. Arthur's *Ten Nights in a Bar Room and What I Saw There* (Philadelphia: J. W. Bradley, 1858); Ariès, *Western Attitudes*, 61, 67; James Farrell, *Inventing the American Way of Death, 1830–1920* (Philadelphia: Temple University Press, 1980), 40; and Faust, *Republic of Suffering*, 7, 277. That children were often the exemplars of holy dying in fiction emphasizes a significant cultural change from prior epochs.

32. Sparks, "Southern Way of Death," 39–40.

33. Laderman, *Sacred Remains*, and Douglas, *Feminization*.

34. On the similarly holy deathbed of Joseph Sr., see Samuel M. Brown, "The 'Beautiful Death' in the Smith Family," *BYU Studies* 45:4 (2006): 129–39.

35. Brown, "Beautiful Death."

36. *EMD* 2:103, 139, 156.

37. On the surgeries, see LeRoy S. Wirthlin, "Joseph Smith's Boyhood Operation: An 1813 Surgical Success," *BYU Studies* 21:2 (spring 1981): 135. On Smith's memory, see *EMD* 1:140–41.

38. See, e.g., *EMD* 1:158, 168, 171, 185.

39. *EMD* 1:60. This account of deathlike conversion mirrored one in the Book of Mormon hero (Alma 36). On revivalists, see Ann Taves, *Fits, Trances and Visions: Experiencing Religion and Explaining Experience from Wesley to James* (Princeton: Princeton University Press, 1999).

40. James B. Allen, "The Significance of Joseph Smith's 'First Vision' in Mormon Thought," *Dialogue* 1:3 (autumn 1966): 29–46.

41. Joseph Smith, "Brother O. Cowdery," *M&A* 1:3 (December 1834): 40.

42. *EMD* 1:576, 578, 469 (including n5).

43. Richard L. Bushman, *Joseph Smith: Rough Stone Rolling* (New York: Knopf, 2005), 42; *EMD* 2:194; and Douglas Davies, *The Mormon Culture of Salvation* (Aldershot, England: Ashgate, 2000), 86–87.

44. Dan Vogel, *Joseph Smith: The Making of a Prophet* (Salt Lake City: Signature Books, 2004), unnecessarily pathologizes the Smiths' relationships.

45. *LB*, 351. Heroic medicine used toxic and purgative insults to battle against disease. Though in the nineteenth century it was more dangerous than helpful, heroic medicine served as the basis for the allopathic tradition, which came to dominate Western medicine in the twentieth century.

46. It is impossible to distinguish appendicitis from calomel ingestion at this remove. Fear of calomel was culturally appropriate and medically reasonable: Guenter B. Risse, "Calomel and the American Medical Sects During the Nineteenth Century," *Mayo Clinic Proceedings* 48 (1973): 57–64.

47. *LB*, 351–52.

48. Hervey, *Meditations*, 45–46, with context in Ariès, *Hour of Our Death*, 394; Schneider, "Happy Dying"; and Robert Wells, *Facing the "King of Terrors": Death and Society in an American Community, 1750–1990* (Cambridge: Cambridge University Press, 2000), 45.

49. *LB*, 354.

50. Farrell, *Way of Death*, 11, 18–19.

51. Hervey, *Meditations*, 21, emphasis in original; see also Robinson, *Dictionary*, s.v. "Death."

52. Whites judged Indian converts by their compliance with holy dying: Laura Stevens, "The Christian Origins of the Vanishing Indian," in Isenberg and Burstein, *Mortal Remains*, 25; Erik R. Seeman, "Reading Indians' Deathbed Scenes: Ethnohistorical and Representational Approaches," *Journal of American History* 88:1 (June 2001): 17–47; and John Peck and John Lawton, *An Historical Sketch of the Baptist Missionary Convention of the State of New York* (Utica: Bennett and Bright, 1837), 127.

53. Douglas, *Feminization*, 200–201, fails to appreciate this important motif.

54. Schneider, "Happy Dying."

55. Saum, *Pre–Civil War America*, 99–101.

56. Schantz, *Culture of Death*, 30, 33, misunderstands this phenomenon. While classicist ideas were important in early national America, the problem of salvation dominated the prescribed calm of the holy deathbed.

57. *JSPR1*, 95, 101 [*D&C 42*].

58. John 8:52.

59. "Obituary," *T&S* 1:8 (June 1840): 128.

60. Saum, *Pre–Civil War America*, 92–94.

61. *LB*, 352–53.

62. See, e.g., "Closing Scene of Life," *Wasp* 1:8 (June 4, 1842): 2.

63. Schneider, "Happy Dying," 360–61.

64. Jarena Lee, *Religious Experience and Journal of Mrs. Jarena Lee, Giving an Account of her Call to Preach the Gospel* (Philadelphia: n.p., 1849), 15–17, and Towle, *Vicissitudes*, 32.

65. "Obituary," *EMS* 2:15 (December 1833): 117. The editor revised his account of William Hobert's deathbed, confessing that he later received information that Hobert had been more delirious than originally supposed.

66. See, e.g., Wilford Woodruff, "Br. Taylor," *T&S* 6:9 (May 15, 1845): 908.

67. See, e.g., "Obituary," *EJ* 1:3 (July 1838): 48; and "Payson, Ill. February 4th, 1840," *T&S* 1:5 (March 1840): 80; "Obituary," *T&S* 1:8 (June 1840): 128;

and "Death of Elias Higbee," *T&S* 4:15 (June 15, 1843): 233. For Anglo-American Protestantism, see Hervey, *Meditations*, 14; Saum, *Pre–Civil War America*, 98–99; and Wells, *King of Terrors*, 45–47, 84, 102.

68. See, e.g., Wilford Woodruff, "Br. Taylor," *T&S* 6:9 (May 15, 1845): 907; Eli Gilbert, "Huntington, Ct, September 24, 1834," *M&A* 1:1 (October 1834): 9–10; and "Dear Brother Pratt," *T&S* 3:11 (April 1, 1842): 739, 742.

69. Schantz, *Culture of Death*, 182, and Jay Ruby, *Secure the Shadow* (Cambridge: MIT Press, 1996).

70. *APR*, 250, line breaks added. See Michael Hicks, "Joseph Smith, W. W. Phelps, and the Poetic Paraphrase of 'The Vision,'" *Journal of Mormon History* 20:2 (fall 1994): 63–84.

71. Farrell, *Way of Death*, 38–39; Sheila Rothman, *Living in the Shadow of Death: Tuberculosis and the Social Experience of Illness in American History* (New York: Basic Books, 1994), 94; David Stannard, *The Puritan Way of Death: A Study of Religion, Culture, and Social Change* (New York: Oxford University Press, 1977), 65.

72. See, e.g., Peck and Lawton, *Historical Sketch*, 124.

73. Hervey, *Meditations*, 24.

74. Robert B. Thompson used this poem in his eulogy for Joseph Smith Sr., "An Address Delivered," *T&S* 1:11 (September 1840): 173.

75. Deborah Smith, "'The Visage Once So Dear': Interpreting Memorial Photographs," in *Painting and Portrait Making in the American Northeast: Dublin Seminar for New England Folklife: Proceedings 1994*, ed. Peter Benes (Boston: Boston University, 1994), 265. Faust, *Republic of Suffering*, describes this phenomenon during the Civil War.

76. *APR*, 367, and *EJ* 1:1 (October 1837): 16.

77. On Puritans, see Gordon Geddes, *Welcome Joy: Death in Puritan New England* (Ann Arbor: UMI Research Press, 1981), and Stannard, *Puritan Way of Death*. On Methodists, see Schneider, "Happy Dying," 363.

78. *LB*, 354, and *APR*, 250.

79. Children could also summon a parent home: Saum, *Pre–Civil War America*, 103; Ariès, *Western Attitudes*, 16, 34; Schantz, *Culture of Death*, 103; "Obituary," *EMS* 2:15 (December 1833): 238. Such images are common cross-culturally: Peter Metcalf and Richard Huntington, *Celebrations of Death: The Anthropology of Mortuary Ritual*, 2d ed., rev. (Cambridge: Cambridge University Press, 1991), 85–90, 104.

80. James Montgomery, "Parting Words," *T&S* 3:8 (February 15, 1842): 701; compare James Montgomery, *Sacred Poems and Hymns* (New York: D. Appleton, 1854), 134–35.

81. Peter Marshall, "Angels around the Deathbed: Variations on a Theme in the English Art of Dying," in *Angels in the Early Modern World*, ed. Peter Marshall and Alexandra Walsham (Cambridge: Cambridge University Press, 2006), 83–103.

82. Susan Juster, *Doomsayers: Anglo-American Prophecy in the Age of Revolution* (Philadelphia: University of Pennsylvania Press, 2003), 57–59, 65, 82, 114, 116; Elizabeth Reis, "Immortal Messengers: Angels, Gender, and Power in Early America," in Isenberg and Burstein, *Mortal Remains*, 164, 167; and Jon Butler, *Awash in a Sea of Faith: Christianizing the American People* (Cambridge, Mass.: Harvard University Press, 1990), 182.

83. Leigh Eric Schmidt, *Hearing Things: Religion, Illusion, and the American Enlightenment* (Cambridge, Mass.: Harvard University Press, 2000), 203, 220–21; Elizabeth Reis, "Otherworldly Visions: Angels, Devils and Gender in Puritan New England," in Marshall and Walsham, *Angels in the Early Modern World*, 295–96; and Sparks, "Southern Way of Death," 41.

84. Rothman, *Shadow of Death*; 126–27, Wells, *King of Terrors*, 74; *EMS* 2:18 (March 1834): 139.

85. Robinson, *Dictionary*, s.v. "Elijah."

86. *LB*, 238.

87. See, e.g., Fred C. Collier and William Harwell, eds., *Kirtland Council Minute Book*, 2d ed. rev. (Salt Lake City: Collier's, 2002), 126, and *EMS* 2:15 (December 1833): 117.

88. Letter of Heber Kimball to John Taylor, November 9, 1840, reprinted in *WJS*, 49n1.

89. Colleen McDannell and Bernhard Lang, *Heaven: A History*, 2d ed. (New Haven: Yale University Press, 2001), esp. xiv, 257–86. See, e.g., Towle, *Vicissitudes*, 39; *LB*, 714, 727; L[yman] O. L[ittlefield], "Died," *Wasp* 1:28 (October 29, 1842): 3.

90. George Kimball, "Origin of the John Brown Song," *New England Magazine*, new ser., 1 (1890): 372, and American Sunday-School Union, *Union Hymns* (Philadelphia, 1835), 527.

91. Schantz, *Culture of Death*, 62.

92. *LB*, 356.

93. Dean C. Jessee, *Personal Writings of Joseph Smith*, rev. ed. (Salt Lake City: Deseret Book, 2002), 531; compare *LB*, 612.

94. *WJS*, 112, April 9, 1842.

95. *EMD* 1:55, and Dean C. Jessee, *The Papers of Joseph Smith: Autobiographical and Historical Writings* (Salt Lake City: Deseret Book, 1989), 265.

96. *JSPR1*, 101 [*D&C* 42:45]. Meyers, "Gates Ajar," 124, is incorrect.

97. Mosiah 18:9.

98. "Obituary," *EMS* 2:16 (January 1834): 127.

99. *WJS*, 112.

100. Douglas, "Consolation Literature," and Marshall, "Midst of Life," 182, 185.

101. Saum, *Pre–Civil War America*, and *The Popular Mood of America, 1860–1890* (Lincoln: University of Nebraska Press, 1990), and Farrell, *Way of Death*, 37–38.

102. See, e.g., Rothman, *Shadow of Death*, 228.

103. An early Protestant example is quoted in "Persecution," *M&A* 1:9 (June 1835): 175. For a Mormon example, see Littlefield, "Funeral of Ephraim Marks," *Wasp* 1:1 (April 16, 1842): 4.

104. [Joseph Smith], "Sidney Rigdon, &c.," *T&S* 3:22 (September 15, 1842): 922–23.

105. The fight was over polygamy: Todd Compton, *In Sacred Loneliness: The Plural Wives of Joseph Smith* (Salt Lake City: Signature Books, 1997), 239–40.

106. Sadly, Eliza later died in Pittsburgh after Rigdon had lost his bid to gain control of the church after Smith's death: Richard S. Van Wagoner and Steven Walker, *A Book of Mormons* (Salt Lake City: Signature Books, 1982), 237.

107. On *avaritia* in Christianity, see Ariès, *Hour of Our Death*, 130–31, 308–9.

108. Philip Greven, *The Protestant Temperament* (New York: Knopf, 1977), 30–34.

109. Sparks, "Southern Way of Death," 39–40.

110. Towle, *Vicissitudes*, 41, 62; see also William Pitts, *The Gospel Witness* (Catskill, N.Y.: Junius Lewis and Co., 1818), 103.

111. Schantz, *Culture of Death*, 28.

112. *HC* 4:587; compare *WWJ* 2:168.

113. Jessee, *Personal Writings*, 264, June 6, 1832.

114. George M. Marsden, *Jonathan Edwards: A Life* (New Haven: Yale University Press, 2004), 69.

115. "Obituary," *EJ* 1:3 (July 1838): 48.

116. "Obituary," *T&S* 3:6 (January 15, 1842): 669.

117. Montgomery, "Parting Words," 701.

118. Douglas, *Feminization*, 209.

119. Noah Webster, *The American Spelling Book* [1783] (Boston: John West, 1807), 168; Milton V. Backman, *Joseph Smith's First Vision* (Salt Lake City: Bookcraft, 1980), 50.

120. L[ittlefield], "Communicated," *Nauvoo Neighbor* 1:47 (March 20, 1844): 2, and "Be Happy," *Wasp* 1:32 (December 10, 1842): 3.

121. *JSPR1*, 101 [*D&C* 42:45].

122. "Payson, Ill. February 4th, 1840," *T&S* 1:5 (March 1840): 80.

123. *WJS*, 107, March 20, 1842; see also Wilford Woodruff, "Sabbath Scene in Nauvoo," *T&S* 3:12 (April 15, 1842): 751.

124. "Obituary," *EMS* 2:15 (December 1833): 117.

125. *WWJ* 2:161–62.

126. David Fischer, *Albion's Seed: Four British Folkways in America* (Oxford: Oxford University Press, 1989), 113, sees this death culture as more malevolent than it was. Vogel, *Joseph Smith*, xx, 4, misapprehends the specific case of Lucy Mack Smith.

127. *APR*, 419.

128. Marshall, "Midst of Life," 176, 182.

129. Frances Trollope, *Domestic Manners of the Americans*, New York reprint, 4th ed. (London: Whittaker, Treacher & Co., 1832), 144.

130. On First Great Awakening, see Marsden, *Edwards*, 429, 496; on antebellum period, Schantz, *Culture of Death*, 112.

131. See also Davies, *Culture of Salvation*, 86.

132. Brown, "Beautiful Death," 135–36.

Chapter 2

1. *FWR*, 3.

2. 2 Corinthians 5:1–4 and John 5:28–29.

3. On similar early Christian and rabbinic uses of Ezekiel's dream, see Caroline Walker Bynum, *Resurrection of the Body in Western Christianity, 200–1336* (New York: Columbia University Press, 1995), 54.

4. *JSPR1*, 44–47 [*D&C* 29:18–20].

5. See, e.g., Frances Trollope, *Domestic Manners of the Americans*, New York reprint, 4th ed. (London: Whittaker, Treacher & Co., 1832), 78.

6. William Morain, *The Sword of Laban: Joseph Smith, Jr. and the Dissociated Mind* (Washington, D.C.: American Psychiatric Press, 1998), 109–10, incorrectly ties this prophecy to Smith's osteomyelitis. Smith may be alluding to Moses's curse of the Egyptians (Exodus 8:21; compare Psalm 78:45).

7. *JSPR1*, 246–47 [D&C 76:44].

8. Orson Hyde, "A Prophetic Warning," *M&A* 2:10 (July 1836): 345.

9. *JSPJ1*, 75.

10. E. R. Snow, "Missouri," *T&S* 5:3 (February 1, 1844): 430.

11. Early patristic authors had similar ideas: Caroline Walker Bynum, "Material Continuity, Personal Survival, and the Resurrection of the Body: A Scholastic Discussion in Its Medieval and Modern Contexts," *History of Religions* 30:1 (August 1990): 83.

12. Charles Buck, *Theological Dictionary* (Philadelphia: Edwin T. Scott, 1823), 282. These traditions ultimately derive from Josephus, Eusebius, and Lactantius, *De Mortibus Persecutorium*, in which, for example, Galerius's "body, with intolerable anguish, was dissolved into one mass of corruption." A. Cleveland Coxe, ed., *The Ante-Nicene Fathers* [1885], 10 vols., reprint ed. (Peabody, Mass.: Hendrickson, 1999), 7:314.

13. Stephen Reed Cattley, ed., *The Acts and Monuments of John Foxe*, 8 vols. (London: R. B. Seeley and W. Burnside, 1837–41), 8:656–57.

14. "Persecution," *M&A* 1:11 (August 1835): 171–75, esp. 175.

15. On Smith's use of Buck's *Theological Dictionary* see Matthew Bowman and Samuel M. Brown, "The Reverend Buck's *Theological Dictionary* and the Struggle to Define American Evangelicalism, 1802–1851," *Journal of the Early Republic* 29:3 (fall 2009): 441–73, esp. 469. On Foxe, see Edward Stevenson, *Reminiscences of Joseph the Prophet* (Salt Lake City: by the author, 1893), 6.

16. *LB*, 354. The entire passage has been crossed out in the original manuscript. The published version deletes this material, admitting only that Lucy "manifest[ed] such mingled feelings of both terror and affection at the scene before her, as are seldom witnessed."

17. "Burial of the Mormon Girl," *Wasp* 1:1 (April 16, 1842): 1–2.

18. A. Gregory Schneider, "The Ritual of Happy Dying Among Early American Methodists," *Church History* 56:3 (September 1987): 353.

19. "Home, Sweet Home," *Wasp* 1:2 (April 23, 1842): 1.

20. Mrs. C. M. Sawyer, "The Young Mother," *Wasp* 1:29 (November 5, 1842): 1, and "Home, Sweet Home," *Wasp* 1:2 (April 23, 1842): 1.

21. Stephen Prothero, *Purified by Fire: A History of Cremation in America* (Berkeley: University of California Press, 2001), 71–72.

22. Robert Wells, *Facing the "King of Terrors": Death and Society in an American Community, 1750–1990* (Cambridge: Cambridge University Press, 2000), 67.

23. *APR*, 403.

24. Wells, *King of Terrors*, 58.

25. Prothero, *Purified by Fire*, and Michael Sappol, *A Traffic of Dead Bodies: Anatomy and Embodied Social Identity in Nineteenth-Century America* (Princeton, N.J.: Princeton University Press, 2002). Liminality is prominent in the anthropological literature and has been expounded by Arnold van

Gennep, *The Rites of Passage* [1909] (Chicago: University of Chicago Press, 1960), and later expanded by Victor Turner and Edmund Leach. See Peter Metcalf and Richard Huntington, *Celebrations of Death: The Anthropology of Mortuary Ritual*, 2d ed., rev. (Cambridge: Cambridge University Press, 1991), 115, and Mary Douglas, *Purity and Danger: An Analysis of Concepts of Pollution and Taboo* [1966], Routledge Classics Edition (London: Routledge, 2002).

26. Alma 19:1–10; compare John 11:39.

27. See also John Wigger, *Taking Heaven by Storm: Methodism and the Rise of Popular Christianity in America* (New York: Oxford University Press, 1998), 108.

28. Ward may have meant the "Hosannah Shout," a threefold repetition of "Hosannah, to God and the Lamb, Amen," used extensively during the 1836 Kirtland holy season (see chapter 6 herein). This shout makes no reference to raising the dead.

29. Maria Ward, *Female Life Among the Mormons; A Narrative of Many Years' Personal Experience* (New York: J. C. Derby, 1855), 19–25; compare Mark 5:39–43.

30. Gregory Prince, *Power from On High: The Development of Mormon Priesthood* (Salt Lake City: Signature Books, 1995), 149–52, and Matthew Bowman, "Raising the Dead: Mormons, Evangelicals, and Miracles in America," *John Whitmer Historical Association Journal* 27 (2007): 75–97.

31. 1 Kings 17:17–24, John 11:39, Matthew 10:8, Acts 26:8, 3 Nephi 7:19, 4 Nephi 1:5.

32. "History of Joseph Smith," *T&S* 6:7 (April 15, 1845): 868.

33. See *EPB*, esp. 95, 105, 183, 186, 193.

34. *EPB*, 177.

35. On Quakers, see David Fischer, *Albion's Seed: Four British Folkways in America* (Oxford: Oxford University Press, 1989), 529; on Lacy, see Susan Juster, *Doomsayers: Anglo-American Prophecy in the Age of Revolution* (Philadelphia: University of Pennsylvania Press, 2003), 25.

36. Buck, *Theological Dictionary*, 587–88; Juster, *Doomsayers*, 65, 225; and Bowman, "Raising the Dead."

37. J. B. Turner, *Mormonism in All Ages: or the Rise, Progress, and Causes of Mormonism* (New York: Platt & Peters, 1842), 94, 98.

38. John Wesley, *The Works of the Rev. John Wesley*, 15 vols. (London: Thomas Cordeux, 1812), 13:213–15.

39. Bowman, "Raising the Dead."

40. Paul Johnson and Sean Wilentz, *The Kingdom of Matthias* (New York: Oxford University Press, 1994), 38–43.

41. Methodist Daniel Kidder (*Mormonism and the Mormons: A Historical View of the Rise and Progress of the Sect of Self-styled Latter-day Saints* [New York: Land & Standford for the Methodist Episcopal Church, 1842], 219–20) attempts to discount Mormon claims to miraculous healings, while allowing Methodists similar claims. See also Walter Norton, "Comparative Images: Mormonism and Contemporary Religions as Seen by Village Newspapermen in Western New York and Northeastern Ohio, 1820–1833" (Ph.D. diss., Brigham Young University, 1991), 289.

42. John C. Bennett, *The History of the Saints; or, An Expose of Joe Smith and Mormonism* (Boston: Leland and Whiting, 1842), 176–79, quoting the "Rev. Mr. Tucker" (see Tucker's biography in *EMD* 3:34–35).

43. Mark 16:18.

44. Benjamin F. Johnson, *My Life's Review* (Independence, Mo.: Zion's, 1979), 13.

45. *HC* 7:523. The claim of D. Michael Quinn, *The Mormon Hierarchy: Origins of Power* (Salt Lake City: Signature Books, 1994), 618, and Prince, *Power*, 150–51, that church historian and apostle George A. Smith (in a letter of August 29, 1855, to Brackenbury's widow) confirmed the Mormon resuscitation attempt appears to rest on a misapprehension of the dual meaning of "resurrection." See *Wayne Sentinel* 9:22 (February 14, 1832), *Burlington [Vermont] Sentinel* 31:12 (March 23, 1832), *Ohio Star* (April 12, 1832), and the erroneous repeat publication of the article in *Wayne Sentinel* 9:30 (April 11, 1832); Dale R. Broadhurst clarified these newspaper sources.

46. *WWJ* 1:70.

47. "An Address to the Citizens of Salem," *T&S* 3:1 (November 15, 1841): 580.

48. [Oliver Cowdery], "The 'Atlas' Article," *M&A* 2:19 (April 1836): 303.

49. *EJ* 1:3 (July 1838): 43.

50. "Sidney Rigdon, &c.," *T&S* 3:22 (September 15, 1842): 922–23.

51. "The 'Atlas' Article," 303.

52. Oliver B. Huntington, "Spirit Experiences," *Young Woman's Journal* 6:8 (1895): 376–81, and Todd Compton, *In Sacred Loneliness: The Plural Wives of Joseph Smith* (Salt Lake City: Signature Books, 1997), 75.

53. Bowman, "Raising the Dead," presents exemplary twentieth-century Mormon folklore.

54. Philippe Ariès, *The Hour of Our Death* (New York: Knopf, 1981), and Bynum, *Resurrection*.

55. "Venezuela," *EMS* 1:12 (May 1833): 96.

56. See, e.g., Thomas Hartwell Horne, *Introduction to the Critical Study and Knowledge of the Holy Scriptures*, 4 vols. (Philadelphia: E. Littell, 1825), 3:500 (Smith's copy is in the Community of Christ Library-Archive, Independence, Missouri). On rural cemeteries, see Mark S. Schantz, *Awaiting the Heavenly Country: The Civil War and America's Culture of Death* (Ithaca: Cornell University Press, 2008), 70–86.

57. [Jacques Saurin], "Comparison between Heathenism and Christianity," *EMS* 1:5 (October 1832): 35.

58. Alma 16:9–11.

59. Mormon 6:15.

60. A. B. Cole, "My Mother's Grave," *Nauvoo Neighbor* 1:37 (January 10, 1844): 3.

61. *EMD* 1:513.

62. "To the Public," *Wayne Sentinel*, September 29–November 3, 1824, *EMD* 2:217–18.

63. Dan Vogel, *Joseph Smith: The Making of a Prophet* (Salt Lake City: Signature Books, 2004), 49, and Morain, *Sword of Laban*, 147, erroneously argue that ten months after burial the Smiths could have determined the integrity of

the burial plot without disinterring Alvin. Anatomists rejected bodies more than a few days past death. Joseph Sr.'s advertisement assumed that Alvin's remains had been stolen shortly after his burial, a crime undetectable in the dirt at ten months' remove.

64. *LB*, 493.

65. Dean C. Jessee, *Personal Writings of Joseph Smith,* rev. ed. (Salt Lake City: Deseret Book, 2002), 431.

66. On Gideon Carter, see Alexander Baugh, "A Call to Arms: The 1838 Mormon Defense of Northern Missouri" (Ph.D. diss., Brigham Young University, 1996), 238–39, and Beth Shumway Moore, *Bones in the Well: The Haun's Mill Massacre, 1838; A Documentary History* (Norman, Okla.: Arthur H. Clarke, 2007), 34–35. On McBride, see *Wasp* 1:11 (June 25, 1842): 4.

67. Joseph Smith et al., "Liberty Jail, Clay Co. Mo.," *T&S* 1:7 (May 1840): 100.

68. Norton, "Comparative Images," 260–61.

69. E. D. Howe, *Mormonism Unvailed* (Painesville, Ohio: by the author, 1834). D. Michael Quinn, *Early Mormonism and the Magic World View* (Salt Lake City: Signature Books, 1987), 136–37, erroneously sees Howe's references to Smith's expertise "in the arts of necromancy" (*Mormonism Unvailed*, 12, 31–32, 43, 94) as reference to the disinterment.

70. Buck, *Theological Dictionary*, 520–21, calls relics "a stupid veneration." See also Gary Laderman, *The Sacred Remains: American Attitudes Toward Death, 1799–1883* (New Haven: Yale University Press, 1996), 68, 74.

71. In parallel, sadistic whites mutilated the bodies of dead slaves to threaten a group that at the time considered suicide a reasonable exit from slavery: Schantz, *Culture of Death*, 154.

72. Ruth Richardson, *Death, Dissection, and the Destitute*, 2d ed. (Chicago: University of Chicago Press, 2001), 131–58.

73. Sappol, *Traffic*, 108; see also Richardson, *Death*, 78, 84.

74. Sappol, *Traffic*, 5.

75. Ronald D. Dennis, ed., "The Martyrdom of Joseph Smith and His Brother Hyrum by Dan Jones," *BYU Studies* 24:1 (winter 1984), 95.

76. Sappol, *Traffic*, 36. On pre-Christian antecedents, see Mike Parker Pearson, *The Archaeology of Death and Burial* (College Station: Texas A&M University Press, 2000), 6.

77. Sappol, *Traffic*, 322.

78. *LB*, 352, 356, 362, 465; Dean C. Jessee, "Joseph Knight's Recollection of Early Mormon History," *BYU Studies* 17:1 (autumn 1976): 31.

79. *LB*, 356.

80. I assume that Palmyra weather was similar to neighboring Utica in 1823–24 (data obtained from the University of Maine's Historical Climatology of New England website, www.umaine.edu/oldweather) and that Alvin's grave was deeper than approximately two feet, applying standard calculations from modern forensic anthropology: William Rodriguez and William Bass, "Decomposition of Buried Bodies and Methods That May Aid in Their Location," *Journal of Forensic Sciences* 30:3 (July 1985): 836–52. The effluvia of decay would almost certainly have leached into the ground through what was probably a simple wooden coffin.

81. Laderman, *Sacred Remains*, 76.

82. Critical sources suggest that Joseph Jr. believed that his son would assume Alvin's mantle: John A. Clark, *Gleanings by the Way* (Philadelphia: WJ & JK Simon, 1842), 226; *EMD* 2:264, 4:286, 347.

83. *EMD* 4:298, 320.

84. *LB*, 411–19, Prince, *Power*, 193.

85. On monstrous births in colonial New England, see David Hall, *Worlds of Wonder: Days of Judgment* (New York: Knopf, 1989), 176.

86. James Henretta, "Families and Farms: *Mentalité* in Pre-industrial America," *William and Mary Quarterly* 35:1 (January 1978): 29, maintains that the use of necronyms, prevalent until the 1840s in Massachusetts, signified a lack of individualism. Joseph Smith's use modulates this position. See also Catherine Albanese, *A Republic of Mind and Spirit: A Cultural History of American Metaphysical Religion* (New Haven: Yale University Press, 2007), 74, and Vogel, *Joseph Smith*, 125.

87. David Paulsen, "The Doctrine of Divine Embodiment: Restoration, Judeo-Christian, and Philosophical Perspectives," *BYU Studies* 35:4 (1995–96): 6–94.

88. Parley P. Pratt, *The Millennium and Other Poems: To Which is Annexed a Treatise on the Regeneration and Eternal Duration of Matter* (New York: W. Molineux, 1840), iv, explicitly affirmed the power of Mormon materialism to "comfort and console myself and friends when death stared me in the face."

89. Bynum, *Resurrection*.

90. Robert Boyle, *Some Physico-Theological Considerations about the Possibility of the Resurrection* (London: H. Herringman, 1675), esp. 198. On cannibalism, see Bynum, *Resurrection*, 31, 40–41, 55, 103, 111–12, 127.

91. John Locke, *An Essay Concerning Human Understanding*, 40th ed. rev. (London: William Tegg and Co., 1877), 264 (Book II, Chapter xxvii).

92. Dick and Smith have something in common with Tertullian and Athenagoras: Alan Segal, *Life After Death: The Afterlife in Western Religions* (New York: Doubleday, 2004), 567–69.

93. *M&A* 3:2 (November 1836): 423, reprinting Thomas Dick, *Philosophy of a Future State* (New York: R. Schoyer, 1831), 89–90.

94. James Hervey, *Meditations and Contemplations* (New York: Richard Scott, 1824), 27.

95. Schantz, *Culture of Death*, 52–54.

96. Sappol, *Traffic*, 260, and Laderman, *Sacred Remains*, 54.

97. Prothero, *Purified by Fire*, 83.

98. Laderman, *Sacred Remains*, 54.

99. Buck, *Theological Dictionary*, 525.

100. Samuel Drew contributed importantly to this discussion with his *Essay on the Identity and General Resurrection of the Human Body* (London: R. Edwards, 1809): Schantz, *Culture of Death*, 52–53. Smith was diametrically opposed to the view Drew propounded.

101. Nauvoo Mormons owned Locke's *Essay*: Jones, "Nauvoo Library," 200.

102. Parley Pratt, "Philosophy of the Resurrection," *MS* 2:7 (November 1841): 97–100.

103. *APR*, 353; compare *JD* 16:356.

104. *APR*, 355. Another transcript reads "No fundamental principle of one creature can be changed to another Creature": *WJS*, 182.

105. Schantz, *Culture of Death*, 54.

106. Bynum, *Resurrection*.

107. Alma 11:44; compare Luke 21:18.

108. Howe, *Mormonism Unvailed*, 72. Edward Stillingfleet, bishop of Worcester, famously criticized Locke's *Essay*, resulting in a public exchange of letters that only ended with Stillingfleet's untimely death.

109. *JSPR1*, 294–95 [*D&C* 88:26].

110. "Death of Elias Higbee," *T&S* 4:15 (June 15, 1843): 232–33.

111. *JSPR1*, 334–35 [*D&C* 93:33–35].

112. *APR*, 466.

113. *JD* 18:334.

114. "Try the Spirits," *T&S* 3:11 (April 1, 1842): 745, and George D. Smith, ed., *An Intimate Chronicle: The Journals of William Clayton* (Salt Lake City: Signature Books, 1995), 103 [*D&C* 131:7–8].

115. These emanations (see Albanese, *Mind and Spirit*, 51, 178, 347, 260, 464) are an important component of the Olive Leaf revelation (*D&C* 88) and *D&C* 93. See discussion in chapter 9 herein.

116. *APR*, 419; compare 1 Corinthians 15:50.

117. *WJS*, 370–71; see also *JD* 7:163–64, 12:68–69, 21:229.

118. Bynum, *Resurrection*.

119. See, e.g., William Penn and George Whitehead, *The Christian Quaker* (Philadelphia: Joseph Rakestraw, 1824), 329–32, 510–13, or the Shaker view espoused in Calvin Green and Seth Wells, *A Summary View of the Millennial Church* (Albany: Packard and Van Benthuysen, 1823), 302–5, or the measured view of Adam Clarke, *The New Testament of our Lord and Saviour Jesus Christ* (Philadelphia: Thomas Cowperthwait and Co., 1838), 153.

120. See also Pratt, *Millennium*, 128.

121. See, e.g., Bettina Bildhauer, *Medieval Blood* (Cardiff: University of Wales Press, 2006), and Caroline Walker Bynum, *Wonderful Blood: Theology and Practice in Late Medieval Germany and Beyond* (Philadelphia: University of Pennsylvania Press, 2007).

122. Susan Lederer, *Flesh and Blood: A Cultural History of Transplantation and Transfusion in Twentieth-Century America* (New York: Oxford University Press, 2008), 33–36.

123. [Jacques Saurin], "Comparison between Heathenism and Christianity," *EMS* 1:5 (October 1832): 35; [Sidney Rigdon], "Faith of the Church," *M&A* 1:11 (August 1835): 165; and *D&C* 58:53, 63:28, 101:80, Genesis 9:4, Leviticus 17:14; compare William Phelps, "Letter No. 9," *M&A* 1:10 (July 1835): 146, and Orson Pratt, "The Pre-existence of Man," *Seer* 1:5 (May 1853): 70; *NewT*, 102 [Moses 6:59]; compare 1 John 5:6–8.

124. Bynum, *Resurrection*.

125. See also Pratt, *Millennium*, 131–32.

126. Orson Pratt, "The Pre-Existence of Man," *Seer* 1:3 (March 1853): 37.

127. *APR*, 339 [*D&C* 130:2].

128. William H. Gilman et al., eds., *The Journals and Miscellaneous Notebooks of Ralph Waldo Emerson*, 16 vols. (Cambridge, Mass.: Harvard University Press, 1960–82), 4:7.

129. Jon Butler, *Awash in a Sea of Faith: Christianizing the American People* (Cambridge, Mass.: Harvard University Press, 1990), 188; Joseph A. Conforti, *Jonathan Edwards: Religious Tradition and American Culture* (Chapel Hill: University of North Carolina Press, 1995), 62–63.

130. Laderman, *Sacred Remains*, 74–76.

131. Ariès, *Hour of Our Death*, 388.

132. Laderman, *Sacred Remains*, 76, 132, and Lewis Saum, *The Popular Mood of Pre–Civil War America* (Westport, Conn.: Greenwood Press, 1980), 101.

133. *WWJ* 2:483 and Compton, *Sacred Loneliness*, 371. On Emma, see Richard L. Bushman, *Joseph Smith: Rough Stone Rolling* (New York: Knopf, 2005), 554.

134. *WWJ* 3:3.

135. *WWJ* 2:450.

136. Deborah Smith, "'The Visage Once So Dear': Interpreting Memorial Photographs," in *Painting and Portrait Making in the American Northeast: Dublin Seminar for New England Folklife: Proceedings 1994*, ed. Peter Benes (Boston: Boston University, 1994), 259.

137. Philippe Ariès, *Western Attitudes Toward Death* (Baltimore: Johns Hopkins University Press, 1974), 80, and Schantz, *Culture of Death*, 167.

138. On the Smith death masks, see Ephraim Hatch, *Joseph Smith's Portraits: A Search for the Prophet's Likeness* (Provo, Utah: Religious Studies Center, Brigham Young University, 1998).

139. Jay Ruby, *Secure the Shadow* (Cambridge: MIT Press, 1996), and Smith, "Visage."

140. Schantz, *Culture of Death*, 180–81.

141. Steven G. Barnett, "The Canes of the Martyrdom," *BYU Studies* 21:2 (spring 1981): 205–11.

142. Barnett, "Canes"; Glen Leonard, *Nauvoo: A Place of Peace, a People of Promise* (Salt Lake City: Deseret Book, 2002), 403; and Jennifer Reeder, "Eliza R. Snow and the Prophet's Gold Watch: Time Keeper as Relic," *Journal of Mormon History* 31:1 (spring 2005): 120–21. On Woodruff, see *WWJ* 2:450.

143. *JD* 4:294.

144. On relics, see, e.g., Buck, *Theological Dictionary*, 520.

145. Jonathan A. Stapley and Kristine Wright, "The Forms and the Power: The Development of Mormon Ritual Healing to 1847," *Journal of Mormon History* 35:3 (summer 2009): 65–66, 78, and Wilford Woodruff, *Leaves from My Journal* (Salt Lake City: Juvenile Instructor Office, 1881), 75–79; compare *WWJ* 1:347.

Chapter 3

1. *EMD* 2:61, 197, and Rodger I. Anderson, *Joseph Smith's New York Reputation Reexamined* (Salt Lake City: Signature Books, 1990), 49–53.

2. Whitney Cross, *The Burned-over District: The Social and Intellectual History of Enthusiastic Religion in Western New York, 1800–1850* (Ithaca: Cornell University Press, 1950), 80. Smith suggested the restoration of biblical animal sacrifice in his temple: *WJS*, 42–43, and Wandle Mace,

"Autobiography 1809–1890" (MSS 921, HBLL), 29. Though animal sacrifice has been deeply stigmatized, these performances are important to many ritual traditions (Jonathan Z. Smith, *Relating Religion: Essays in the Study of Religion* [Chicago: University of Chicago Press, 2004], 145–59), and the slaughter of animals was a familiar process for antebellum America's rural inhabitants.

3. Keith Thomas, *Religion and the Decline of Magic* (New York: Oxford University Press, 1997); David Hall, *Worlds of Wonder: Days of Judgment* (New York: Knopf, 1989); Charles H. Lippy, *Being Religious, American Style: A History of Popular Religiosity in the United States* (Westport, Conn.: Greenwood Press, 1994).

4. Jon Butler, *Awash in a Sea of Faith: Christianizing the American People* (Cambridge, Mass.: Harvard University Press, 1990).

5. Butler, *Sea of Faith*, 185–86. See, e.g., D. Michael Quinn, *Early Mormonism and the Magic World View* (Salt Lake City: Signature Books, 1987), 26, and Herbert Leventhal, *In the Shadow of the Enlightenment: Occultism and Renaissance Science in Eighteenth-century America* (New York: New York University Press, 1976).

6. Leventhal, *Shadow of the Enlightenment*, 110, 113–14; Alan Taylor, "The Early Republic's Supernatural Economy," *American Quarterly* 38:1 (spring 1986): 6–34.

7. Mark Ashurst-McGee, "A Pathway to Prophethood: Joseph Smith as Rodsman, Village Seer, and Judeo-Christian Prophet" (M.A. thesis, Utah State University, 2000), 82. E. D. Howe, *Mormonism Unvailed* (Painesville, Ohio: by the author, 1834), makes several references to Smith's necromancy, as does Daniel Kidder, *Mormonism and the Mormons: A Historical View of the Rise and Progress of the Sect of Self-styled Latter-day Saints* (New York: Land & Standford for the Methodist Episcopal Church, 1842, 29.

8. Thus a confession-cum-repudiation in *EJ* 1:3 (July 1838): 43, and his mother's complex and generally misunderstood disavowal in *LB*, 323.

9. See, e.g., Quinn, *Magic*; Mark Ashurst-McGee, "Moroni: Angel or Treasure Guardian," *Mormon Historical Studies* 2:2 (2001): 39–75, and the fall 1984 (24:4) issue of *BYU Studies*. For historical context, see Taylor, "Supernatural Economy," and "Rediscovering the Context of Joseph Smith's Treasure Seeking," *Dialogue* 19:4 (winter 1986): 18–28.

10. *WJS*, 366.

11. Recent historiography of early modern Europe, on the other hand, emphasizes these themes. See, e.g., Edward Bever, *The Realities of Witchcraft and Popular Magic in Early Modern Europe: Culture, Cognition and Everyday Life* (Basingstoke, England: Palgrave Macmillan, 2008).

12. John Greenleaf Whittier, *The Supernaturalism of New England* (New York: Wiley & Putnam, 1847), 57–59, and Taylor, "Supernatural Economy," 16.

13. Taylor, "Supernatural Economy," 19.

14. Ashurst-McGee, "Moroni," 44.

15. Taylor, "Supernatural Economy," 8, 22–23. Johannes Dillinger, *Magical Treasure Hunting in Europe and North America* (Basingstoke, England: Palgrave, forthcoming), similarly emphasizes economic over religious meanings.

16. *EMD* 4:249–50. Oliver Cowdery refers to the same "hidden treasures of the earth" in *M&A* 2:1 (October 1835): 198. Compare Quinn, *Magic*, 35.

17. *LB*, 414.

18. Robert Pogue Harrison, *Dominion of the Dead* (Chicago: University of Chicago Press, 2003), xi. The root indicates "earth"-dwellers as opposed to gods, who were "sky"-dwellers. Those who came of the earth would return to the earth, as Harrison suggests.

19. Roger Kennedy, *Hidden Cities: The Discovery and Loss of Ancient North American Civilization* (New York: Free Press, 1994).

20. Thaddeus Mason Harris, *The Journal of a Tour into the Territory Northwest of the Alleghany Mountains; Made in the Spring of the Year 1803* (Boston: Manning & Loring, 1805), 62, 147–48; Kennedy, *Hidden Cities*, 85; and Dan Vogel, *Indian Origins and the Book of Mormon: Religious Solutions from Columbus to Joseph Smith* (Salt Lake City: Signature Books, 1986), 24.

21. Josiah Priest, *American Antiquities, and Discoveries in the West*, 2d ed., rev. (Albany: Hoffman and White, 1833), 53. On Priest, see De Villo Sloan, "The Crimsoned Hills of Onondaga: Josiah Priest's Hallucinatory Epic," *Journal of Popular Culture* 36:1 (August 2002): 86–104.

22. Fawn M. Brodie, *No Man Knows My History: The Life of Joseph Smith, the Mormon Prophet*, 2d ed. rev. and enl. (New York: Knopf, 1971), 19, and Rich Troll, "Samuel Tyler Lawrence: A Significant Figure in Joseph Smith's Palmyra Past," *Journal of Mormon History* 32:2 (summer 2006): 58.

23. Caleb Atwater, "Description of the Antiquities Discovered in the State of Ohio and Other Western States," *Archaeologia Americana: Transactions and Collections of the American Antiquarian Society* 1:5 (1820): 5, 179–80.

24. "Grave Yards in Cities," *T&S* 6:10 (June 1, 1845): 923.

25. "The Indian's Death Song," *Wasp* 1:16 (August 4, 1842): 3.

26. *JSPJ1*, 273; compare *HC* 3:36.

27. *EPB*, 5; see also Dean C. Jessee, *Personal Writings of Joseph Smith*, rev. ed. (Salt Lake City: Deseret Book, 2002), 24, and Genesis 49:25.

28. On treasure caves, see Ronald Walker, "The Persisting Idea of American Treasure Hunting," *BYU Studies* 24:4 (fall 1984): 435–36, and Ashurst-McGee, "Prophethood," 237.

29. *EMD* 2:60.

30. *EMD* 2:130, 152–54. See also Dan Vogel, "The Locations of Joseph Smith's Early Treasure Quests," *Dialogue* 27:3 (fall 1994): 204–7.

31. Henry Caswall, *The City of the Mormons; or, Three Days at Nauvoo, in 1842* (London: J. G. & F. Rivington, 1842), 26–27; *WWJ* 6:508–9; *JD* 4:105, 14:331, 15:183, 17:30, 281–82, 19:37–38; Alexander Baugh, "Parting the Veil: Joseph Smith's Seventy-six Documented Visionary Experiences," in *Opening the Heavens: Accounts of Divine Manifestations, 1820–1844*, ed. John W. Welch (Salt Lake City: Deseret Book, 2004), 279, 301–2, and *EMD* 2:41–42, 97–98, 4:227.

32. Elias Higbee and Parley Pratt, "An Address," *T&S* 1:5 (March 1840): 69.

33. Kidd actually had buried treasure at Gardiner's Island. Walker, "Persisting Idea," 436, 438. See also John Welch, "The Miraculous Translation of the Book of Mormon," in Welch, *Opening the Heavens*, 184; and Quinn, *Magic*, 42, 62. Noted treasure hunter Joseph Stafford (ancestor of Joseph Smith's Palmyra neighbors) recorded in a 1767 receipt for services rendered a

quest for "treasures hid by Indians," John Brooke, *The Refiner's Fire: The Making of Mormon Cosmology, 1644–1844* (Cambridge: Cambridge University Press, 1994), 118 (figure 5).

34. Gerard Hurley, "Buried Treasure Tales in America," *Western Folklore* 10:3 (July 1951): 200–201; Walker, "Persisting Idea," 443; and Taylor, "Supernatural Economy," 11. On European antecedents, see Bever, *Popular Magic*. I thank Steve Fleming for his input.

35. *EMD* 4:254.

36. Ashurst-McGee, "Moroni," 44–45.

37. R. C. Finucane, *Ghosts: Appearances of the Dead and Cultural Transformation* (Amherst, N.Y.: Prometheus Books, 1996), 12, 101, and Taylor, "Supernatural Economy," 12.

38. *EMD* 4:411–12.

39. *JSR*, 281 [*D&C* 111:9–10].

40. H. Michael Marquardt and Wesley Walter, *Inventing Mormonism: Tradition and the Historical Record* (Salt Lake City: Smith Research Associates, 1994), 73n44.

41. Jessee, *Personal Writings*, 13. See also a renunciation of interest in "filthy lucre" in *EMD* 4:135.

42. *LB*, 347; Jessee, *Personal Writings*, 13. Oliver Cowdery, "Letter VIII," *M&A* 2:1 (October 1835): 297–98.

43. According to Smith, both Moroni (through Lehi) and Joseph Smith (through Joseph, son of Jacob/Israel) were actual Israelites with the same Hebrew blood in their veins.

44. Oliver Cowdery, "Letter VIII," *M&A* 2:1 (October 1835): 298. See also Richard L. Bushman, *Joseph Smith: Rough Stone Rolling* (New York: Knopf, 2005), 51.

45. Mormon 8:14.

46. Richard S. Van Wagoner and Steven Walker, "The Joseph/Hyrum Smith Funeral Sermon," *BYU Studies* 23:1 (winter 1983): 14.

47. *EMD* 1:552, *EPB*, 8.

48. Walker, "Persisting Idea," 435–36.

49. W. W. Phelps, "Letter No 12," *M&A* 2:2 (November 1835): 221–23, and *EMS* 1 (January 1833): 8.

50. Sources are not entirely clear on how much of the hill's size and shape was related to burials—the Book of Mormon suggests that a hill antedated the Jaredite battle (Ether 15:11) but the hill was expanded by the burials in or beside it.

51. Mormon 6:2; spelling corrected in the 1837 edition.

52. Mormon 6:15.

53. Oliver Cowdery, "Letter VII," *M&A* 1:10 (July 1835): 159.

54. Ether 15:1–4, 11–12, 18; Mormon 6:15, 8:2; compare J. B. Turner, *Mormonism in All Ages: or the Rise, Progress, and Causes of Mormonism* (New York: Platt & Peters, 1842), 207.

55. Ether 13:21; compare Isaiah 14:20 and 1 Kings 13:22.

56. Mosiah 8:9–11.

57. Mosiah 8:8, 12, 19; Mosiah 21:27; 22: 14.

58. Omni; Mosiah 8 and 21–22; Ether.

59. Mormon 6:6.

60. Mormon 8:16.
61. 1 Nephi 4.
62. *JD* 19:38; compare *D&C* 17.
63. Richard L. Bushman, *Believing History: Latter-day Saint Essays* (New York: Columbia University Press, 2004), 242.
64. Gorgets are crescent-shaped neck armor, but in reference to Native relics, gorget has referred to presumed arm guards for archery or other objects with central holes: Orville H. Peets, "What, Really, Were Gorgets?," *American Antiquity* 31:1 (July 1965): 113–16, Ashurst-McGee, "Prophethood," 168.
65. Ashurst-McGee, "Prophethood," 157, 163, 172–73, and Quinn, *Magic*, 252.
66. Ashurst-McGee, "Prophethood," 164–65, 230, 247–48.
67. Ashurst-McGee, "Prophethood," chap. 4, esp. 321–29.
68. *WWJ* 5:382–83, 8:500.
69. According to Michael Marquardt (personal communication), Mormons first publicly referred to Urim and Thummim in 1832: "Questions proposed to the Mormonite Preachers," *Boston Investigator* 2 (August 10, 1832), 2.
70. Phelps, "Despise Not Prophesyings," *T&S* 2:7 (February 1, 1841): 298.
71. Richard S. Van Wagoner and Steven Walker, "Joseph Smith: 'The Gift of Seeing,'" *Dialogue* 15:2 (summer 1982): 53, 61.
72. Van Wagoner and Walker, "Seeing," 49–53; see also *EMD* 4:320.
73. George D. Smith, ed., *An Intimate Chronicle: The Journals of William Clayton* (Salt Lake City: Signature Books, 1995), 96 [*D&C* 130:10].
74. *MS* 26 (February 20, 1864): 118–19.
75. *WJS*, 169.
76. Smith, *Intimate Chronicle*, 96, and *APR*, 339; compare *D&C* 130 and Revelation 4:6.
77. See, e.g., Charles Buck, *Theological Dictionary* (Philadelphia: Edwin T. Scott, 1823), 417.
78. *Saints' Herald* (October 1, 1879): 289–90, and Van Wagoner and Walker, "Seeing."
79. Jasmine Day, *The Mummy's Curse: Mummymania in the English-speaking World* (London: Routledge, 2006), 3, and Scott Trafton, *Egypt Land: Race and Nineteenth-century American Egyptomania* (Durham, N.C.: Duke University Press, 2004).
80. See John Lloyd Stephens, *Incidents of Travel in Egypt, Arabia Petraea, and the Holy Land* (New York: Harper, 1837); James Ewing Cooley, *The American in Egypt: with Rambles through Arabia Petraea and the Holy Land* (New York: D. Appleton & Co., 1843), from which Mormons reprinted "Egyptian Mummies," *Wasp* 1:21 (September 10, 1842): 4. See also "Egyptian Antiquities," *T&S* 3:13 (May 2, 1842): 774.
81. On Egyptians in early America, see Robert Wauchope, *Lost Tribes and Sunken Continents: Myth and Method in the Study of American Indians* (Chicago: University of Chicago Press, 1962), 7–27; Frances Trollope, *Domestic Manners of the Americans,* New York reprint, 4th ed. (London: Whittaker, Treacher & Co., 1832), 219; Priest, *American Antiquities*, 125.
82. Stanley French, "The Cemetery as Cultural Institution: The Establishment of Mount Auburn and the 'Rural Cemetery' Movement," in *Death in*

America, ed. David Stannard (Philadelphia: University of Pennsylvania Press, 1977), 83.

83. Smith called the Book of Mormon characters "hieroglyphics" in *T&S* 4:24 (November 5, 1843): 373. The Book of Mormon calls its language reformed Egyptian in Mormon 9:32, and Nephi claims fluency in 1 Nephi 1:2. Abner Cole, a contemporary parodist, said that the Indian who visited Smith was dressed like an Egyptian: Richard L. Bushman, *Joseph Smith and the Beginnings of Mormonism* (Urbana: University of Illinois Press, 1981), 120. Kirtland Congregationalist Truman Coe described "plates of the color of gold inscribed with hieroglyphics" in August 1836: Milton Backman, "Truman Coe's 1836 Description of Mormonism," *BYU Studies* 17:3 (spring 1977): 350. On ethnic identities, see Jessee, *Personal Writings*, 297, and Oliver Cowdery, "Letter IV," *M&A* 1:5 (February 1835): 80.

84. See "A Catacomb of Mummies Found in Kentucky," *T&S* 3:13 (May 2, 1842): 781–82, which followed Priest (*American Antiquities*, 125) in believing that "the authors of the embalmed Mummies found in the cave of Lexington, were of Egyptian origin." See also Angelo George, *Mummies, Catacombs, and Mammoth Cave* (Louisville, Ky.: George, 1994).

85. On the Ohio period, see Mark L. Staker, *Hearken O Ye People: The Historical Setting of Joseph Smith's Ohio Revelations* (Salt Lake City: Kofford Books, 2009). H. Donl Peterson, *The Story of the Book of Abraham: Mummies, Manuscripts, and Mormonism* (Salt Lake City: Deseret Book, 1995), details the mummies' provenance. The reference to "posthumous travelers" (from the *Cleveland Daily Advertiser* of March 26, 1835) is on p. 111. On farm income, Marvin Hill et al., "The Kirtland Economy Revisited: A Market Critique of Sectarian Economics," *BYU Studies* 17:4 (summer 1977): 396.

86. Jessee, *Personal Writings*, 360.

87. *WWJ* 1:143; compare Deuteronomy 33:19.

88. Stanley B. Kimball, "New Light on Old Egyptiana: Mormon Mummies 1848–71," *Dialogue* 16:4 (winter 1983): 84.

89. *JSPJ1*, 68, 73, 76, 105, 109, 113, 117, 120, 122–24, 135, 147, 178, 180, 184, 186.

90. Bruce Van Orden, "Writing to Zion: The William W. Phelps Kirtland Letters (1835–1836)," *BYU Studies* 33:3 (1993): 553–56.

91. Oliver Cowdery, "Egyptian Mummies—Ancient Records," *M&A* 2:3 (December 1835): 235; compare *HC* 2:348.

92. Willard Richards, Journal, July 11, 1846, *SelCol* 1:31.

93. "Who these ancient inhabitants of Egypt were, we do not at present say." Cowdery, "Egyptian Mummies," 233. This was edited in *HC* 2:348, placing the disavowal in the first person singular instead of the plural.

94. Glen Wade, "The Facsimile Found: The Recovery of Joseph Smith's Papyrus Manuscripts," *Dialogue* 2:4 (winter 1967): 52; Peterson, *Story of the Book of Abraham*, 192, 198; Charlotte Haven, "A Girl's Letters from Nauvoo," *Overland Monthly* 16 (December 1890): 623–24; Kidder, *Mormonism and the Mormons*, 120, and "A Glance at the Mormons," [New York] Sun, July 28, 1840, reprinted at www.sidneyrigdon.com/dbroadhu/NY/miscNYC2.htm, accessed December 9, 2007.

95. Samuel M. Brown, "Joseph (Smith) in Egypt: Babel, Hieroglyphs, and the Pure Language of Eden," *Church History* 78:1 (March 2009): 26–65; GAEL, 3–4, 21; and Abraham 1:11.

96. *Nauvoo Neighbor* 1:2 (May 10, 1843); compare *HC* 5:374–76.
97. Stanley Kimball, "Kinderhook Plates Brought to Joseph Smith Appear to Be a Nineteenth-Century Hoax," *Ensign* 11 (August 1981): 66–74; *T&S* 4:12 (May 1, 1843): 186–87. *HC* 5:372, reworking Smith, *Intimate Chronicle*, 100.
98. *Nauvoo Neighbor* 1:10 (July 5, 1843)–1:40 (January 31, 1844).
99. "Ancient Records," *Nauvoo Neighbor* 1:2 (May 10, 1843).
100. Bushman, *Rough Stone*, 69.

Chapter 4

1. Dean C. Jessee, *Personal Writings of Joseph Smith*, rev. ed. (Salt Lake City: Deseret Book, 2002), 345–46.
2. "Extracts from H. C. Kimball's Journal," *T&S* 6:1 (February 4, 1845): 787–88.
3. *WWJ* 1:10.
4. Kenneth Godfrey, "The Zelph Story," *BYU Studies* 29:2 (spring 1989): 31–56. Smith probably intended Onandagus as eponymous for the Onondaga tribes: Lori Taylor, "Telling Stories about Mormons and Indians" (Ph.D. diss., State University of New York, Buffalo, 2000), 177–78.
5. See, e.g., Michael Coe, "Mormons and Archaeology: An Outside View," *Dialogue* 8:2 (summer 1973): 46–47.
6. Godfrey, "Zelph," 35.
7. Wilford Woodruff retained some of Zelph's bones: *WWJ* 1:10, and Wilford Woodruff, *Leaves from My Journal* (Salt Lake City: Juvenile Instructor Office, 1881), 11. The Mormon Church owns Zelph's arrowhead: Richard S. Van Wagoner and Steven Walker, "Joseph Smith: 'The Gift of Seeing,'" *Dialogue* 15:2 (summer 1982): 66n53.
8. I thank Brad Kramer for this insight.
9. Smith compared Alvin to another mythic figure in 1843: *APR*, 291.
10. On Missouri's mounds, see Alphonso Wetmore, *Gazetteer of the State of Missouri* (St. Louis: C. Keemle, 1837), 254.
11. Robert Pogue Harrison, *Dominion of the Dead* (Chicago: University of Chicago Press, 2003), treats these themes in Western culture generally.
12. David Stannard, *The Puritan Way of Death: A Study of Religion, Culture, and Social Change* (New York: Oxford University Press, 1977), 180.
13. Wilford Woodruff, "Br. Taylor," *T&S* 6:9 (May 15, 1845): 907.
14. *APR*, 365–66. Smith may be alluding to Ether's curse of Coriantumr in Ether 13:21, discussed below.
15. George D. Smith, ed., *An Intimate Chronicle: The Journals of William Clayton* (Salt Lake City: Signature Books, 1995), 99.
16. On raising the dead, see Juanita Brooks, ed., *On the Mormon Frontier: The Diary of Hosea Stout*, 2 vols. (Salt Lake City: University of Utah Press, 1964), 1:171; Heber Kimball, "Resurrection," *JD* 4:294–95; Maurine Carr Ward, ed., *Winter Quarters: The 1846–1848 Life Writings of Mary Haskin Parker Richards* (Logan: Utah State University Press, 1996), 105–106; *WWJ* 3:301 and 3:325. The Saints were not clear on details, even in 1852: Smith, *Intimate Chronicle*, 430–31.
17. The lack of a "decent grave" was often highlighted in Missouri war memorials. See, e.g., Eliza R. Snow, "The Slaughter on Shoal Creek, Caldwell County Missouri," *T&S* 1:2 (December 1839): 32.

18. Biblical precedents include Genesis 50:25–26; Exodus 13:19; Joshua 24:32; though in Hebrew culture corpses were separated from the temple as ritually unclean. I thank Kevin Barney for this insight.
19. Jessee, *Personal Writings*, 563.
20. *APR*, 366.
21. Heeding the message of this sermon, Smith's followers ultimately transported Barnes's remains to Salt Lake City in 1852: *WWJ* 4:145–48.
22. Jessee, *Personal Writings*, 563.
23. Drew Gilpin Faust, *This Republic of Suffering: Death and the American Civil War* (New York: Knopf, 2008).
24. William Smith proudly noted in 1875 that "all of my fathers family that are dead, accept one [Alvin], are now Sleeping" together in Nauvoo: *EMD* 1:488.
25. Joseph Johnstun, "'To Lay in Yonder Tomb': The Tomb and Burial of Joseph Smith," *Mormon Historical Studies* 5:2 (fall 2005): 163–80.
26. Henry Caswall, *The City of the Mormons; or, Three Days at Nauvoo, in 1842* (London: J. G. & F. Rivington, 1842), 54. See the similar treatment of Americans generally in Frances Trollope, *Domestic Manners of the Americans,* New York reprint, 4th ed. (London: Whittaker, Treacher & Co., 1832), 60.
27. A.B. Child, "DIED—," *Wasp* 1:3 (April 30, 1842): 3. On burial *ad sanctos,* near a saint's relics, see Philippe Ariès, *The Hour of Our Death* (New York: Knopf, 1981), 31–33, 41.
28. Nancy Towle, *Vicissitudes Illustrated in the Experience of Nancy Towle, in Europe and America,* 2d ed. (Portsmouth, N.H.: John Caldwell, 1833), 138–39, 201.
29. James Farrell, *Inventing the American Way of Death, 1830–1920* (Philadelphia: Temple University Press, 1980), 107; Ariès, *Hour of Our Death,* 63, 339; Scott Stephan, *Redeeming the Southern Family: Evangelical Women and Domestic Devotion in the Antebellum South* (Athens: University of Georgia Press, 2008), 215; and Mark S. Schantz, *Awaiting the Heavenly Country: The Civil War and America's Culture of Death* (Ithaca: Cornell University Press, 2008), 77–81.
30. A. B. Cole, "My Mother's Grave," *Nauvoo Neighbor* 1:37 (January 10, 1844): 3.
31. "Kingdom Come," *Wasp* 1:44 (March 1, 1843): 1; see also "Crusader's Return," *Wasp* 1:1 (April 16, 1842): 1.
32. 2 Nephi 9:7; Mosiah 2:26; Mormon 6:15.
33. On anthropological theories of cultural development that tie ancestral remains to land rights, see Mike Parker Pearson, *Archaeology of Death and Burial* (College Station: Texas A&M University Press, 2000), 30, 136n43, and Harrison, *Dominion,* esp. 25.
34. Sidney Rigdon, "To the Honorable, the Senate and House of Representatives of Pennsylvania," *T&S* 5:3 (February 1, 1844): 421.
35. Noah Packard, "To the Honorable the Governor, Senate and House of Representatives of Massachusetts," *T&S* 5:9 (May 1, 1844): 517.
36. D. Michael Quinn, "The Mormon Succession Crisis of 1844," *BYU Studies* 16:2 (winter 1976): 187–233.
37. *HC* 7:254.
38. *D&C* 135:3; compare 2 Samuel 1:23.

39. "Trial of Elder Rigdon," *T&S* 5:17 (September 15, 1844): 649, 653–54.

40. The October 6–8, 1845, conference is recorded in "Conference Minutes," *T&S* 6:16 (November 1, 1845), 1008–15, and a manuscript in CHL (hereafter "Manuscript Minutes"). Young's rebuke of Emma Smith is in "Manuscript Minutes," 15.

41. Linda King Newell and Valeen Tippetts Avery, *Mormon Enigma: Emma Hale Smith*, 2d ed. (Urbana: University of Illinois Press, 1994), 199–219.

42. "Manuscript Minutes," 13; compare *LB*, 61.

43. "Manuscript Minutes," 11.

44. "Manuscript Minutes," 14–15.

45. *WWJ* 2:610.

46. Robert Berkhofer Jr., *The White Man's Indian: Images of the American Indian from Columbus to the Present* (New York: Knopf, 1978), 87.

47. Josiah Priest, *American Antiquities, and Discoveries in the West*, 2d ed., rev. (Albany: Hoffman and White, 1833), 54. "Central America," *Wasp* 1:35 (December 31, 1842): 2. Even the disdainful Frances Trollope (*Domestic Manners*, 219) allowed that the Indians might be Egyptian.

48. Thaddeus Mason Harris, *The Journal of a Tour into the Territory Northwest of the Alleghany Mountains; Made in the Spring of the Year 1803* (Boston: Manning & Loring, 1805), 62; Roger Kennedy, *Hidden Cities: The Discovery and Loss of Ancient North American Civilization* (New York: Free Press, 1994), 85; and a similar poem in Schantz, *Culture of Death*, 119.

49. Priest, *American Antiquities*, 37–38, 53–54. He called the Grave Creek Mound "a place of general deposit of the dead for ages."

50. *FWR*, 22.

51. *WWJ* 1:334.

52. John C. Bennett, *The History of the Saints; or, An Expose of Joe Smith and Mormonism* (Boston: Leland and Whiting, 1842), 189.

53. Caswall, *City of the Mormons*, 30.

54. Smith, *Intimate Chronicle*, 244.

55. Catherine Albanese, *A Republic of Mind and Spirit: A Cultural History of American Metaphysical Religion* (New Haven: Yale University Press, 2007), 147.

56. Berkhofer, *White Man's Indian*, 149–50.

57. Mormons advertised their knowledge of this name, distinguishing it from the confusion surrounding the term "Indian." See particularly "Origin of the Name Indian," *Wasp* 1:18 (August 20, 1842), 1.

58. William Phelps, "Letter No. 2," *M&A* 1:3 (December 1834): 34.

59. A pair of late nineteenth-century maps (erroneously) attributed to Joseph Smith, the "chart, and descriptions of Moroni's travels through this country," track the sole Nephite survivor through all the Mormon settlements of note, including Missouri, Ohio, Illinois, and Utah, as he wound his way to the great hill "Commorre N.Y." H. Donl Peterson, "Moroni, the Last of the Nephite Prophets," in *Fourth Nephi Through Moroni: From Zion to Destruction*, ed. Monte S. Nyman and Charles D. Tate, Jr. (Provo, Utah: Brigham Young University, Religious Studies Center, 1995), 244–47.

60. Oliver Cowdery, "Letter VII," *M&A* 1:10 (July 1835): 158; compare Priest, *American Antiquities*, 54.

61. Priest, *American Antiquities*, 54.

62. Priest, *American Antiquities*, 37, 65–66.

63. *WWJ* 2:610.

64. *EMD* 1:64. The 1832 account clarified that they were "engraven by Maroni & his fathers the servants of the living God in ancient days." Jessee, *Personal Writings*, 12.

65. Marilla Marks, ed., *Memoirs of the Life of David Marks, Minister of the Gospel* (Dover, N.H.: Free-Will Baptist Printing Establishment, 1846), 341.

66. On Mormon awareness of competing traditions, see Joseph Smith, "To the elders of the church of the Latter Day Saints," *M&A* 2:2 (November 1835): 210.

67. William Phelps, "The Book of Ether," *EMS* 1:3 (August 1832): 22.

68. See, e.g., "Stephen's Works on Central America," *T&S* 4:22 (October 1, 1843): 346; Jessee, *Personal Writings*, 533–34, *EMS* 1 (June 1833): 99; Charles Wandell, "Dear Brethren," *T&S* 2:22 (September 15, 1841): 545; and Charles Thompson, "Evidences in Proof of the Book of Mormon," *T&S* 3:5 (January 1, 1842): 640–44. George Laub attributed his conversion to Mormonism to Priest's *American Antiquities*: Eugene England, ed., "George Laub's Nauvoo Journal," *BYU Studies* 18:2 (winter 1978): 155.

69. *APR*, 365; compare Alma 19:1. On Protestants see Paul Gutjahr, *An American Bible, A History of the Good Book in the United States, 1777–1880* (Stanford: Stanford University Press, 1999), 63–69.

70. Curtis Dahl, "Mound-builders, Mormons, and William Cullen Bryant," *New England Quarterly* 34:2 (June 1961): 178–90.

71. The Book of Mormon contains more than two hundred newly attested personal names: Grant Hardy, ed., *The Book of Mormon: A Reader's Edition* (Urbana: University of Illinois Press, 2003), 690–706.

72. "The Indians," *M&A* 2:4 (January 1836): 245.

73. *LB*, 345.

74. Smith differed from most other Americans by considering the Mound Builders relatives of current Native peoples. See Brian W. Dippie, *The Vanishing American: White Attitudes and the U.S. Indian Policy* (Lawrence: University Press of Kansas, 1991), 8, 17.

75. See, e.g., Dippie, *Vanishing American*, and Laura Stevens, "The Christian Origins of the Vanishing Indian," in *Mortal Remains: Death in Early America*, ed. Nancy Isenberg and Andrew Burstein (Philadelphia: University of Pennsylvania Press, 2003).

76. The Book of Mormon indicated that Indians combined Nephite and Lamanite blood: Joseph Smith, Jr., trans., *The Book of Mormon: An Account Written By the Hand of Mormon, Upon Plates Taken From the Plates of Nephi* (Palmyra, N.Y.: E. B. Grandin, 1830), 30, 36 [1 Nephi 13:30, 15:30].

77. Oliver Cowdery, "Letter VII," *M&A* 1:10 (July 1835): 158.

78. *FWR*, 66.

79. Cowdery, "Letter VII," 159.

80. "Moroni's Lamentation," *EMS* 2:16 (January 1834): 128, reprinted in *M&A* 2:23 (August 1836): 368. William Smith claims its provenance in *On Mormonism* (Lamoni, Iowa: Herald Steam Book and Job Office, 1883), 33–35. This hymn is reminiscent of passages in *The Last of the Mohicans*: Dippie, *Vanishing American*, 21.

81. Beth Shumway Moore, *Bones in the Well: The Haun's Mill Massacre, 1838; A Documentary History* (Norman, Okla.: Arthur H. Clarke, 2007), 36–37, 114.

82. D[aniel] M. Crandall, "The Western Fields," *EJ* 1:4 (August 1838): 64.

83. Kennedy, *Hidden Cities*, 225–28, and Alden Vaughan, *Roots of American Racism: Essays on the Colonial Experience* (Oxford: Oxford University Press, 1995), 35, 49–53, Robert Wauchope, *Lost Tribes and Sunken Continents: Myth and Method in the Study of American Indians* (Chicago: University of Chicago Press, 1962), 30–31. Berkhofer, *White Man's Indian*, 35.

84. Ethan Smith—especially *View of the Hebrews* (Poultney, Vt.: Smith & Shute, 1823)—and Josiah Priest—especially *American Antiquities*—depended on James Adair (c. 1709–1783). Fawn M. Brodie (*No Man Knows My History: The Life of Joseph Smith, the Mormon Prophet*, 2d ed. rev. and enl. [New York: Knopf, 1971], 46–47) popularized *View of the Hebrews* as the source of the Book of Mormon, following Mormon hierarch B. H. Roberts, *Studies of the Book of Mormon*, ed. Brigham Madsen (Urbana: University of Illinois Press, 1985), esp. 235. This position misapprehends the relationships between the two books.

85. Berkhofer, *White Man's Indian*, 46–47, 77–79, 86.

86. Joseph Smith revealed that the Bible mentioned the Indians, in exegesis of John 10:16 (see 3 Nephi 15:17–21 and *D&C* 10:59–60). Orson Pratt also tied Natives to Israel in his diary, June 23, 1833 (MS 587, CHL), 7. See also Parley P. Pratt, *The Millennium and Other Poems: To Which is Annexed a Treatise on the Regeneration and Eternal Duration of Matter* (New York: W. Molineux, 1840), 46; Emma Smith, *A Collection of Sacred Hymns, for the Church of Jesus Christ of Latter Day Saints* (Kirtland, OH: F.G. Williams, 1835), 83–84; and Walker, "Seeking the 'Remnant': The Native American During the Joseph Smith Period," *Journal of Mormon History* 19:1 (spring 1993): 1–33.

87. Daniel Walker Howe, *What Hath God Wrought: The Transformation of America, 1815–1848* (New York: Oxford University Press, 2007), esp. 414–23.

88. "The Elders in the Land of Zion to the Church of Christ Scattered Abroad," *EMS* 1:2 (July 1832): 13.

89. William Phelps, "Letter No. 11," *M&A* 2:1 (October 1835): 193, and Walker, "Seeking the 'Remnant.'"

90. "The Indians," *EMS* 1:9 (February 1833): 71.

91. Phelps, "Letter No. 11," 193.

92. "The Indians," *M&A* 2:4 (January 1836), 245–48; see also Phelps, "Letter No. 2," 33–34.

93. 1 Nephi 22:7–8.

94. Karim Tiro, "'We Wish to Do You Good': The Quaker Mission to the Oneida Nation, 1790–1840," *Journal of the Early Republic* 26:3 (fall 2006): 376. There were minor exceptions, primarily Jesuits and the rare Quaker or Presbyterian, who saw proselytizing as a mode of empowerment for Native peoples, but no religious group was so focused on a restoration of the Indians to glory as the Mormons. For a fascinating literary view of the Book of Mormon and Mormon Indianism, see Jared Hickman, "The Book of Mormon as Amerindian Apocalypse," unpublished manuscript.

95. *JSPR1*, 10–11 [*D&C* 3:16–20].

96. Mormon 7, esp. v. 5.

97. Taylor, "Telling Stories," 127–28; compare Mosiah 27–28 and Alma 17–26.

98. *D&C* 28:8–9; 30:5–6. On the Lamanite mission, see Taylor, "Telling Stories," 108–57, Walker, "Seeking the 'Remnant,'" and Keith Parry, "Joseph Smith and the Clash of Sacred Cultures," *Dialogue* 18 (winter 1985): 65–80.

99. E. D. Howe, *Mormonism Unvailed* (Painesville, Ohio: by the author, 1834), 213.

100. *T&S* 5 (February 15, 1844): 433.

101. Parley Pratt, *The Autobiography of Parley Parker Pratt* (New York: Russell Brothers, 1874), 49, 54.

102. Taylor, "Telling Stories," 173. Phelps believed this was the beginning of Mormon polygamy: Phelps to Brigham Young, August 12, 1861, CHL; see also Howe, *Mormonism Unvailed*, 220, and B. Carmon Hardy, *Doing the Works of Abraham: Mormon Polygamy, Its Origin, Practice, and Demise* (Norman, Okla.: Arthur H. Clark, 2007), 35.

103. *JSPR1*, 153 [*D&C* 54:8]; see also *JSPR1*, 55 [*D&C* 30:6].

104. Mark L. Staker, *Hearken O Ye People: The Historical Setting of Joseph Smith's Ohio Revelations* (Salt Lake City: Kofford Books, 2009), 49–69.

105. Staker, *Ohio Revelations*, 77.

106. Bruce N. Westergren, ed., *From Historian to Dissident: The Book of John Whitmer* (Salt Lake City: Signature Books, 1995), 57.

107. 1 Nephi 13:12–14.

108. John Corrill, *A Brief History of the Church of Christ of Latter Day Saints* (St. Louis: Printed for the Author, 1839), 9; Howe, *Mormonism Unvailed*, 104–5; "Extracts of Letters from a Mormonite," *Unitarian* 1:5 (May 1, 1834), 253, Lee Copeland, "Speaking in Tongues in the Restoration Churches," *Dialogue* 24:1 (spring 1991): 19, and Taylor, "Telling Stories," 121–22, 194–95. On tongues as Indian language, see Howe, *Mormonism Unvailed*, 184. On "sacred theater," see Clarke Garrett, *Spirit Possession and Popular Religion: From the Camisards to the Shakers* (Baltimore: Johns Hopkins University Press, 1987).

109. Howe, *Mormonism Unvailed*, 184, 194.

110. Josiah Jones, "History of the Mormonites, Kirtland, 1831," *Evangelist* 9 (June 1, 1831): 134–35.

111. The Kirtland Indian imitations were somewhat similar to powwow meetings, which included "strange Antick Gestures, and Actions even unto fainting." Albanese, *Mind and Spirit*, 102. On Shaker visions of Indians, see 246–49.

112. Staker, *Ohio Revelations*, 175–77.

113. On the enthusiasms at Kirtland, see Staker, *Ohio Revelations*, 71–91, 160–62.

114. See, e.g., *EPB*, 77, 83, 124, 128.

115. Phelps, "Letter No. 11," 193.

116. Jan Shipps and John W. Welch, eds., *The Journals of William E. McLellin: 1831–1836* (Provo, Utah: Brigham Young University Press, 1994), 179, 182.

117. Taylor, "Telling Stories," 229–33.
118. Smith received delegations from the Sauk and Fox as well as the Pottawatamies. Church historians merged these encounters: *APR*, 481–82, Walker, "Seeking the 'Remnant,'" 27; *WWJ* 2:246; *HC* 5:480; and the letter of August 28, 1843, from Joseph Smith to the Pottawatamies, CHL.
119. Parley P. Pratt, *Proclamation of the Twelve Apostles of the Church of Jesus Christ of Latter-day Saints* (Liverpool: Wilford Woodruff, 1845), 5.
120. David Whittaker, "Mormons and Native Americans: A Historical and Bibliographical Introduction," *Dialogue* 18:4 (winter 1985): 34–35.
121. Robert Campbell protested the treatment of Indians by Georgia using language identical to that the Mormons employed to protest their expulsion from Missouri: Howe, *What Hath God Wrought*, 350.
122. E. Robinson and D. C. Smith, "Address," *T&S* 1:1 (November 1839): 1.
123. Walker, "Seeking the 'Remnant,'" 3–4; compare *D&C* 130:12–13.
124. *WWJ* 3:505–6, corrected from original at CHL. (This chief was one inspiration for Longfellow's "Hiawatha.") See similar plea in Colin Calloway, *New Worlds for All: Indians, Europeans, and the Remaking of Early America* (Baltimore: Johns Hopkins University Press, 1997), 89.
125. Trollope, *Domestic Manners*, 181, Dippie, *Vanishing American*, 67, and Howe, *What Hath God Wrought*, 426.
126. *JSPR1*, 274–75, [*D&C* 84], Richard L. Bushman, *Joseph Smith: Rough Stone Rolling* (New York: Knopf, 2005), 628, and *JD* 10:235.
127. See also *Seer* 2:6 (June 1854): 284–85.
128. *JSPJ1*, 271 [*D&C* 116:1], *JSPR1*, 269 [*D&C* 78:15]; Robert J. Matthews, "Adam-ondi-Ahman," *BYU Studies* 13:1 (autumn 1972): 27–35; and Leland H. Gentry, "Adam-ondi-Ahman: A Brief Historical Survey," *BYU Studies* 13:4 (summer 1973): 553–76. See also William Swartzell, *Mormonism Exposed, being a Journal of a Residence in Missouri from the 28th of May to the 20th of August, 1838* (Pekin, Ohio: by the author, 1840), 11–12; compare *D&C* 117:8 and Reed Peck's untitled letter of September 18, 1839, generally known as the "Reed Peck Manuscript," copy in CHL, 19–20.
129. *JSR*, 270 [*D&C* 107:53–57].
130. Daniel 7; compare *D&C* 116. On uses of Daniel, see Alan Segal, *Life after Death: The Afterlife in Western Religions* (New York: Doubleday, 2004), 262.
131. *EPB*, 4, 8.
132. *WWJ* 8:172; see also *WWJ* 6:482.
133. *WWJ* 7:129; compare Oliver Huntington, *History of the Life of Oliver B. Huntington, Written by Himself* (n.p., n.d.), 52–53, and Priest, *American Antiquities*, 41.
134. John H. Wittorf, "An Historical Investigation of the Ruined 'Altars' at Adam-ondi-Ahman, Missouri," *Newsletter and Proceedings of the Society for Early Historic Archaeology* 113 (April 15, 1969): 1–8, presents and summarizes several late sources on the ruins. See also Gentry, "Adam-ondi-Ahman," 574–75, who favors the altar on Spring Hill and the foundations of a tower on Tower Hill. See also Edward Partridge, Diary, January 1835, CHL.
135. On altars, see Charles Buck, *Theological Dictionary* (Philadelphia: Edwin T. Scott, 1823), 18, and Paul K. Conkin, *The Uneasy Center: Reformed*

Christianity in Antebellum America (Chapel Hill: University of North Carolina Press, 1995), 47, 188, 190.

136. Reed Peck Manuscript, 19–20. Although Peck had seceded at the time, his evidence for this otherwise reasonably attested claim seems persuasive.

137. James H. Hunt, *Mormonism: Embracing the Origin, Rise and Progress of the Sect, With an Examination of the Book of Mormon* (St. Louis: Ustick and Davies, 1844), 164.

138. On the grave legend, see Matthews, "Adam-ondi-Ahman," 30–31, and Jean Bickmore White, ed., *Church, State, and Politics: The Diaries of John Henry Smith* (Salt Lake City: Signature Books, 1991), 606. On outside observers, see Gentry, "Adam-ondi-Ahman," 574–75.

139. Matthews, "Adam-ondi-Ahman," 30.

140. On Calvary, see Royal Robbins, *Outlines of Ancient and Modern History* 2 vols. (Hartford: Edward Hopkins, 1835), a book Woodruff read in 1837 (*WWJ* 1:127).

141. See Kathleen Flake, "Translating Time: The Nature and Function of Joseph Smith's Narrative Canon," *Journal of Religion* 87:4 (October 2007): 497–527, for a complementary view.

142. Burkhofer, *White Man's Indian*, 72–73.

143. Native groups had inhabited these areas for centuries, often with complex social and agricultural systems, contrary to European belief.

144. Ann Douglas, *The Feminization of American Culture* (New York: Knopf, 1977), 221, Richard Hughes and Leonard Allen, *Illusions of Innocence: Protestant Primitivism, 1630–1875* (Chicago: University of Chicago Press, 1988), 14–21, and Theodore Bozeman, *To Live Ancient Lives: The Primitivist Dimension in Puritanism* (Chapel Hill: University of North Carolina Press, 1988), 238–40.

145. Buck, *Theological Dictionary*, 425, s.v. "Paradise"; Priest, *American Antiquities*, 126.

146. On Mountain Cove, see Albanese, *Mind and Spirit*, 269.

Chapter 5

1. Mosiah 28:14–16.

2. The two accounts appear to refer to different relics. The simplest explanation is that both an engraved "stone" and "gold plates" were collected from the Jaredite battlefield graveyard.

3. Omni 1:14–23.

4. Joseph Smith, "To the Editor," *T&S* 4:13 (May 15, 1843): 194.

5. Richard L. Anderson *Joseph Smith's New England Heritage*, 2d ed. (Salt Lake City, Utah: Deseret Book, 2002), 160.

6. 2 Nephi 1:14.

7. "Kingdom Come," *Wasp* 1:44 (March 1, 1843): 1. See also "Reflections on the Grave," *Wasp* 1:6 (May 21, 1842): 3; Ann Douglas, *The Feminization of American Culture* (New York: Knopf, 1977), 207; and "Memory," *Wasp* 1:6 (May 21, 1842): 1.

8. Susan Juster, *Doomsayers: Anglo-American Prophecy in the Age of Revolution* (Philadelphia: University of Pennsylvania Press, 2003); 21, 112; Ann

Taves, *Fits, Trances & Visions: Experiencing Religion and Explaining Experience from Wesley to James* (Princeton: Princeton University Press, 1999); and Clarke Garrett, *Spirit Possession and Popular Religion: From the Camisards to the Shakers* (Baltimore: Johns Hopkins University Press, 1987).

9. See, e.g., Nancy Towle, *Vicissitudes Illustrated in the Experience of Nancy Towle, in Europe and America*, 2d ed. (Portsmouth, N.H.: John Caldwell, 1833), 177, and John Wigger, *Taking Heaven by Storm: Methodism and the Rise of Popular Christianity in America* (New York: Oxford University Press, 1998), 53, 108. See Taves, *Experiencing Religion*, 76–118, on the Methodist shout tradition.

10. *EMD* 1:60–62, 1:27–28. See also James B. Allen, "The Significance of Joseph Smith's 'First Vision' in Mormon Thought," *Dialogue* 1:3 (autumn 1966): 29–46.

11. Alma 36: esp. 10–23.

12. Alma 18:40–19:36, 27:17.

13. Leigh Eric Schmidt, *Hearing Things: Religion, Illusion, and the American Enlightenment* (Cambridge, Mass.: Harvard University Press, 2000), which is the best treatment of these themes.

14. R. C. Finucane, *Ghosts: Appearances of the Dead and Cultural Transformation* (Amherst, N.Y.: Prometheus Books, 1996), 126–29, 160–61, 178–79, 222.

15. Mosiah 8:15–16, 18.

16. *JSPR1*, 26–27 [*D&C* 21:1].

17. *JSPJ1*, 100.

18. Wilford Woodruff used this epithet 31 times in his journal, concentrating them in 1841–43. See also the John Taylor obsequies in *D&C* 135:3, "Prospectus," *Seer* 1:1 (January 1853): 1, and Towle, *Vicissitudes*, 153.

19. 2 Nephi 3: 6–7, 11. Smith expanded this prophecy in his New Translation of Genesis 50:26–27: *NewT*, 681–85.

20. Isaiah 29:10 and 2 Nephi 3:18–20; see also Emma Smith, *A Collection of Sacred Hymns, for the Church of Jesus Christ of Latter Day Saints* (Kirtland, Ohio: F. G. Williams, 1835), 95–96.

21. See Juster, *Doomsayers,* and Richard L. Bushman, "The Visionary World of Joseph Smith," *BYU Studies* 37:1 (1997): 183–204.

22. Mark Ashurst-McGee, "A Pathway to Prophethood: Joseph Smith as Rodsman, Village Seer, and Judeo-Christian Prophet" (M.A. thesis, Utah State University, 2000), esp. 82.

23. Matthew Henry, *An Exposition of the Old and New Testament*, 3 vols. (London: Joseph Ogle Roginson, 1928), 1:706, 899.

24. Dean C. Jessee, *Personal Writings of Joseph Smith*, rev. ed. (Salt Lake City: Deseret Book, 2002), 427.

25. 2 Nephi 18:19; compare Isaiah 8:19.

26. Mormon 8:15.

27. *WWJ* 2:155.

28. William Phelps, "Despise Not Prophesyings," *T&S* 2:7 (February 1, 1841): 298; see also William Phelps, "The Answer," *T&S* 5:24 (January 1, 1845): 758.

29. John Taylor, "The Seer," *T&S* 5:24 (January 1, 1845): 767.

30. Mosiah 8:17.

31. Juster, *Doomsayers*; see also Walter Brueggemann, *The Prophetic Imagination*, 2d ed. (Minneapolis: Fortress Press, 2001).

32. Contemporary biblical exegesis saw Isaiah 29 as a reference to the destruction of Jerusalem and the hope of regeneration in the future. Adam Clarke, *The Holy Bible Containing the Old and New Testaments*, 6 vols. (New York: T. Mason and G. Lane, 1837) 4:128–31. See Joseph Blenkinsopp, *Isaiah 1–39: A New Translation with Introduction and Commentary* (New Haven: Yale University Press, 2000), 398–402, for current exegesis.

33. See, e.g., David Wright, "Isaiah in the Book of Mormon: Or Joseph Smith in Isaiah," in *American Apocrypha: Essays on the Book of Mormon*, ed. Dan Vogel and Brent Lee Metcalfe (Salt Lake City: Signature Books, 2002), 157–234; Donald W. Parry and John W. Welch, eds., *Isaiah in the Book of Mormon* (Provo, Utah: FARMS, 1998); and Grant Hardy, ed., *The Book of Mormon: A Reader's Edition* (Urbana: University of Illinois Press, 2003), 122–25. Smith's New Translation of Isaiah largely follows the Book of Mormon redaction.

34. See also Robert A. Cloward, "Isaiah 29 and the Book of Mormon," in Parry and Welch, *Isaiah*, 191–247. I thank the 2009 Mormon Theology Seminar for refining my thinking on this topic.

35. 2 Nephi 27:5; compare Isaiah 29:10.

36. 2 Nephi 27, esp. vv. 5–6, 9, 13.

37. 2 Nephi 26:15–16; see also 2 Nephi 3:19–20, 27:9.

38. Mormon 8:23–26, 2 Nephi 1:14–23, 1 Nephi 22:14, Ether 8:24.

39. 2 Nephi 33:13.

40. Moroni 10:27–28. Robert Hullinger, *Joseph Smith's Response to Skepticism* (Salt Lake City: Signature Books, 1992), 73, misinterprets these passages.

41. "New Hymns," *EMS* 1:9 (February 1833): 72, and "An Angel Came Down," in Smith, *Sacred Hymns*, 22–23.

42. Brigham Young et al., *A Collection of Sacred Hymns, for the Church of Jesus Christ of Latter-day Saints, in Europe* (Liverpool: R. Hedlock and T. Ward, 1844), 218–19.

43. *EMS* 1:8 (January 1833): 57. On the persistence of this belief, see *JD* 17:284 and the chapter heading of the 1981 Mormon edition of the KJV.

44. William Phelps, "The Book of Mormon," *EMS* 1:7 (December 1832): 59; see also William Phelps, "The Answer," *T&S* 5:24 (January 1, 1845): 757.

45. Parley Pratt, "A Letter to the Queen of England," *T&S* 3:2 (November 15, 1841): 594.

46. Dean C. Jessee, "Joseph Knight's Recollection of Early Mormon History," *BYU Studies* 17:1 (autumn 1976), 35. Orson Pratt preached on the same topic on June 25, 1833, as recorded in his diary (MS 587, CHL).

47. The interplay of folk and academic scholarship on hieroglyphs was complex, but the scriptures told Smith and Harris to take their record to the learned. See Richard L. Bushman, *Joseph Smith: Rough Stone Rolling* (New York: Knopf, 2005), 63–66, on Harris's meeting with the scholars. Bushman is probably incorrect, *pace* Jan Shipps, "The Reality of the Restoration Ideal in the Mormon Tradition," in *The American Quest for the Primitive Church*, ed. Richard Hughes (Urbana: University of Illinois Press, 1988), 185, in

believing that Smith and Harris only saw the encounter as fulfilling prophecy in retrospect, though the documentation is sparse. Believing they were consciously acting out the prophecy does not require the reading of Hullinger (*Response to Skepticism*, 75–99) that Smith staged the encounter with the scholars to dupe Harris.

48. D. Michael Quinn, *Early Mormonism and the Magic World View* (Salt Lake City: Signature Books, 1987), 152.

49. Scholars generally see magic as a question of power and social status rather than a useful descriptor of belief systems. I generally agree. See, e.g., Jonathan Z. Smith, *Relating Religion: Essays in the Study of Religion* (Chicago: University of Chicago Press, 2004), 215–29.

50. 1 Nephi 3:19; 4:14–16.

51. See, e.g., Walter J. Ong, *Orality and Literacy: The Technologizing of the Word*, 2d ed. (New York: Routledge, 2002).

52. The reference to Abel's faith, such that "He, being dead, yet speaketh" (Hebrews 11:4) was popular as a description of the power of memorials. Pratt added it to the 1841 edition of his *A Voice of Warning and Instruction to All People* (New York: W. Sandford, 1837): Peter Crawley, *A Descriptive Bibliography of the Mormon Church*, 2 vols. (Provo, Utah: Religious Studies Center, Brigham Young University, 1997), 1:172–73.

53. William Phelps, "Writing Letters," *EMS* 1:4 (September 1832): 25.

54. John Mason Good, *The Book of Nature* (New York: J. & J. Harper, 1828), 319, Erich Robert Paul, "Joseph Smith and the Manchester (New York) Library," *BYU Studies* 22:3 (summer 1982): 333–56. On Mormon use of Good, see Orson Pratt, *Absurdities of Immaterialism, or, A Reply to T. W. P. Taylder's Pamphlet Entitled "The Materialism of the Mormons or the Latter-day Saints, Examined and Exposed"* (Liverpool: H. James, 1849), 1–2.

55. Moses 6:5–6, 45–46. Manuscript 1 for vv. 5–6 has Moses "write with the finger of inspiration," just as God would in vv. 45–46, and in an echo of the encounter between Jesus and Moriancumer in Ether 3. Manuscript 2 corrects it to the published "spirit of inspiration." *NewT*, 97, 100, 608. The Book of Moses, along with other distinctive Mormon scriptures, was canonized in *The Pearl of Great Price* in the latter nineteenth century. *The Pearl of Great Price* remains scripture for the modern Mormon Church.

56. John Brooke, *The Refiner's Fire: The Making of Mormon Cosmology, 1644–1844* (Cambridge: Cambridge University Press, 1994), 195–97, misapprehends the Book of Remembrance.

57. Jessee, *Personal Writings*, 286.

58. Revelation 20:12–15; see also Taves, *Experiencing Religion*, 30–32, 69–70, Juster, *Doomsayers*, 163, and Ann Kirschner, " 'Tending to Edify, Astonish, and Instruct': Published Narratives of Spiritual Dreams and Visions in the Early Republic," *Early American Studies* 1:1 (spring 2003): 198–229.

59. Irene Bates and E. Gary Smith, *Lost Legacy: The Mormon Office of the Presiding Patriarch* (Urbana: University of Illinois Press, 1996).

60. *EPB*, 76. See similar blessings in ibid., 12, 14–17, 39, 58, 71, 87, 96, 99, 124, 162–63, 186–87.

61. *EPB*, 12.

62. Alex Smith, "Joseph Smith's Nauvoo Journals: Understanding the Documents," paper presented at the meeting of the Mormon History

Association, Casper, Wyo., May 2006. The diary covers December 11, 1841–December 20, 1842.

63. Dean Jessee, comp. and ed., *The Papers of Joseph Smith: Journal, 1832–1842* (Salt Lake City: Deseret Book, 1992), 440–41.

64. *EMD* 1:470.

65. Jessee, *Journal, 1832–1842*, 416.

66. See Colleen McDannell, *The Christian Home in Victorian America, 1840–1900* (Bloomington: Indiana University Press, 1994), 83–84, and Paul Gutjahr, *An American Bible, A History of the Good Book in the United States, 1777–1880* (Stanford: Stanford University Press, 1999), 143–46.

67. "Speech Delivered by Heber C. Kimball," *T&S* 6:13 (July 15, 1845): 972.

68. On this history see Dean Jessee, "The Writing of Joseph Smith's History," *BYU Studies* 11:4 (summer 1971): 439–73, and Howard Searle, "Early Mormon Historiography" (Ph.D. diss., University of California, Los Angeles, 1977). Brigham Young specifically invoked "the Law of the Lord" in his copyright for the *History of the Church*: MS 4066, CHL.

69. *EPB*, 216.

70. Gregory Prince, *Power from On High: The Development of Mormon Priesthood* (Salt Lake City: Signature Books, 1995), 89.

71. Richard L. Bushman, *Believing History: Latter-day Saint Essays* (New York: Columbia University Press, 2004), 72, and *Rough Stone*, 31.

72. Alexander Baugh, "Parting the Veil: Joseph Smith's Seventy-six Documented Visionary Experiences," in *Opening the Heavens: Accounts of Divine Manifestations, 1820–1844*, ed. John W. Welch (Salt Lake City: Deseret Book, 2004), 301–302, Dean C. Jessee, "Joseph Smith's July 19, 1840 Discourse," *BYU Studies* 19:3 (spring 1979): 393.

73. Philippe Ariès, *The Hour of Our Death* (New York: Knopf, 1981), 161.

74. On Lutheran practice, see Beth Shumway Moore, *Patterned Lives: The Lutheran Funeral Biography in Early Modern Germany* (Wiesbaden: Harrassowitz, 2006). On colonial New England, see Jeannine Hensley, ed., *The Works of Anne Bradstreet* (Cambridge, Mass.: Harvard University Press, 1967), 241; David Hall, *Worlds of Wonder: Days of Judgment* (New York: Knopf, 1989), 28; and Cotton Mather, *Magnalia Christi America: Or, The Ecclesiastical History of New England, From its First Planting in the Year 1620, Unto the Year of Our Lord, 1698 in Seven Books* (Hartford: Silas Andrus, 1820).

75. Joseph A. Conforti, *Jonathan Edwards: Religious Tradition and American Culture* (Chapel Hill: University of North Carolina Press, 1995), 62–63, 73–75.

76. Towle, *Vicissitudes*, unpaginated front matter, 121, 209–12.

77. Brigham Young and Willard Richards, "Proclamation to the Saints in Nauvoo," *Wasp* 1:37 (January 14, 1843): 3, and Samuel M. Brown, "The Translator and the Ghostwriter: Joseph Smith and William Phelps," *Journal of Mormon History* 33:4 (winter 2007): 36.

78. Josiah Priest, *American Antiquities, and Discoveries in the West*, 2d ed., rev. (Albany: Hoffman and White, 1833), 22; compare "All Flesh," *EMS* 2:13 (June 1833): 102.

79. See context in Samuel M. Brown, "Joseph (Smith) in Egypt: Babel, Hieroglyphs, and the Pure Language of Eden," *Church History* 78:1 (March 2009): 26–65.

80. Ether 1:34–39, 3:6–9. [Oliver Cowdery], "Rise of the Church, Letter VI," *T&S* 2:11 (April 1, 1841), 362; compare Ether 2:13.

81. Smith distinguished the "Insp[ire]d. man" from "an old Jew" "witht. any auth[orit]y" who corrupted the text: *WJS*, 345, 350–51. See Charles Buck, *Theological Dictionary* (Philadelphia: Edwin T. Scott, 1823), 53–64, 216–17, 574–76, for Protestant context for such claims. The Book of Mormon maintained a similar view. See, e.g., 1 Nephi 13:29.

82. *FWR*, 23.

83. Later followers called the New Translation the Joseph Smith Translation (JST) or Inspired Version (IV). The manuscripts are published as *NewT*.

84. Philip Barlow, "Joseph Smith's Revision of the Bible: Fraudulent, Pathological, or Prophetic?" *Harvard Theological Review* 83:1 (January 1990): 45–64, and Kevin Barney, "The Joseph Smith Translation and the Ancient Texts of the Bible," *Dialogue* 19:3 (fall 1986): 85–102.

85. "History of Joseph Smith," *T&S* 5:14 (August 1, 1844): 592. See also Bushman, *Rough Stone*, 484.

86. Campbell's work—*The Sacred Writings of the Apostles and Evangelists of Jesus Christ, Commonly Styled the New Testament* (Buffaloe, Va.: Alexander Campbell, 1826), popularly known as the "Living Oracles"—was a slightly if pointedly revised compilation of various recent New Testament translations. See Cecil K. Thomas, *Alexander Campbell and His New Version* (St. Louis: Bethany Press, 1958).

87. Kathleen Flake, "Translating Time: The Nature and Function of Joseph Smith's Narrative Canon," *Journal of Religion* 87:4 (October 2007): 497–527.

88. *JSPR1*, 16–19 [*D&C* 7].

89. On "reformed Egyptian," see Mormon 9:32 and "Church History," *T&S* 3:8 (February 15, 1842): 707. Phelps used "short-hand" in an 1831 letter printed in E. D. Howe, *History of Mormonism: Or, A Faithful Account of that Singular Imposition and Delusion with Sketches of the Characters of its Propagators* (Painesville: E. D. Howe, 1840), 273. See also Parley Pratt, "Discovery of an Ancient Record in America," *MS* 1:2 (June 1840): 30.

90. Henry Caswall, *The City of the Mormons; or, Three Days at Nauvoo, in 1842* (London: J. G. & F. Rivington, 1842), 28; compare "Notices," *MS* 3:2 (June 1, 1842): 32.

91. Oliver Cowdery, "Egyptian Mummies—Ancient Records," *M&A* 2:3 (December 1835): 234, 237.

92. See *T&S* 3:9 (March 1, 1842): 704–6, 3:10 (March 15, 1842): 719–22, and *MS* 3:3 (July 1842): 34–36, 3:4 (August 1842): 49–53.

93. Brian Hauglid, *A Textual History of the Book of Abraham: Manuscripts and Editions* (Provo, Utah: Neal A. Maxwell Institute for Religious Scholarship, Brigham Young University, 2010), 7, summarizes the designations for these documents; originals at CHL.

94. *MS* 3:4 (August 1842): 70–71; see also *MS* 3:2 (June 1842): 32.

95. EN1, title page, CHL.

96. [Phelps for Smith], "For the Times and Seasons," *T&S* 4:24 (November 1, 1843): 374; see also "Notices," *MS* 3: 2 (June 1, 1842): 32, and *MS* 3:3 (July 1, 1842): 46–47.

97. Classicists understood the significance of Champollion's findings: "Egyptian Antiquities," *North American Review* 29 (October 1829): 361–88.

98. John Irwin, *American Hieroglyphics: The Symbol of the Egyptian Hieroglyphics in the American Renaissance* (New Haven: Yale University Press, 1980), 8–9. Kircher influenced thinking on hieroglyphics for centuries via his 1652 *Oedipus Aegyptiacus*: James Knowlson, *Universal Language Schemes in England and France 1600–1800* (Toronto: University of Toronto Press, 1975), 13.

99. Noah Webster, *American Dictionary of the English Language* (New York: S. Converse, 1828), s.v. "hieroglyphic."

100. W. W. Phelps, "Reflections for the Fourth of July, 1834," *EMS* 2:22 (July 1834): 173. See also Cowdery, "Egyptian Mummies," 235, amplified in "Egyptian Antiquities," *Wasp* 1:4 (May 7, 1842): 3, and *T&S* 3:13 (May 2, 1842): 774.

101. The quest for sacred language demonstrates the difficulty in tying Smith directly to hermetic texts when the tenets of the secret quest were easily accessible in cultural commonplaces about the meaning of hieroglyphs. The failure to explore the broader dissemination, separate from original traditions, of these sensibilities mars the standard treatment of Mormonism and hermeticism: Brooke, *Refiner's Fire*; see also Quinn, *Magic*, 151–52.

102. "The Jews," *T&S* 4:14 (June 1, 1843): 220–22, and 4:15 (June 15, 1843): 233–34.

103. *WWJ* 1:535, and "Letter from William Rowley," *T&S* 3:22 (September 15, 1842): 925.

104. Hebrew, Chinese, and Mesoamerican languages were grouped with Egyptian as hieroglyphic by most observers. "Progress of Ethnology, Continued," *Nauvoo Neighbor* 1:32 (December 6, 1843), and Jeffrey Russell, *View of Ancient and Modern Egypt* (Edinburgh: Oliver and Boyd, 1831), 178, 185 (a book circulating in New York: Paul, "Manchester Library"). Such beliefs about Chinese date at least to Francis Bacon: Knowlson, *Universal Language*, 16. Moses Stuart's Hebrew primer, one the Latter-day Saints used in their Kirtland Hebrew School, emphasized the pictographic nature of the Hebrew alphabet: *Grammar of the Hebrew Language* (Andover, Mass.: Flagg and Gould, 1831), 2.

105. EA, 1, and GAEL, 2.

106. GAEL, 5, 14.

107. GAEL, 31; compare Abraham 3:24.

108. GAEL, 4, 9.

109. GAEL, 6. Compare Swedenborg's attention to "the copious meanings hidden in 'the very flexures and curvatures' of the Hebrew letters": Schmidt, *Hearing Things*, 208.

110. Brown, "Translator and Ghostwriter," 59–61.

111. Abraham 1:14. The relationship between the KEP, the facsimile interpretations, and the Book of Abraham is fluid and disputed. Generally, critics argue that the KEP represent a stylized draft of the Book of Abraham, while apologists argue that the KEP are separate from the Book of Abraham. The issue cannot be resolved on the basis of current evidence. Regardless of the direct textual relationships, the documents reflect a single interpretive framework. The facsimiles are published in *T&S* 3:9 (March 1, 1842): 703; 3:10 (March 15, 1842): 722a; 3:14 (May 16, 1842): 783–84.

112. Abraham 1:14; there is some uncertainty as to whether the first letter should be "K" or "R" in the original manuscripts—I have used the published variant. The Latter-day Saints delighted in the circulation of these facsimiles, even as they battled with critics. See *T&S* 3:14 (May 16, 1842): 790, and the reprint from the New York *Herald* in "The Mormons—A Leaf From Joe Smith," *T&S* 3:13 (May 2, 1842): 773–74, as well as "A Scared Editor," *Wasp* 1:2 (April 23, 1842): 3.

113. Irwin, *Hieroglyphics*, 3–13, 28; E. Brooks Holifield, *Theology in America: Christian Thought from the Age of the Puritans to the Civil War* (New Haven: Yale University Press, 2003), 458–59; Paul K. Conkin, *The Uneasy Center: Reformed Christianity in Antebellum America* (Chapel Hill: University of North Carolina Press, 1995), 236; Ralph Waldo Emerson, *Nature, Addresses and Lectures* (Boston: James Munroe, 1849), 27.

114. Horace Bushnell, *God in Christ: Three Discourses Delivered at New Haven, Cambridge, and Andover, with a Preliminary Dissertation on Language* (Hartford: Brown and Parsons, 1849), esp. 46–50, Russell, *Ancient and Modern Egypt*, 175–76, Priest, *American Antiquities*, 121. Priest cited Rafinesque, whose idiosyncratic and heavily pictographic forgery *Wallam-Olum* was first published in *American Nations: or, Outlines of a National History; of the Ancient and Modern Nations of North and South America* (Philadelphia: C. S. Rafinesque, 1836), 121–61. See Charles Boewe, "A Note on Rafinesque, the Walam Olum, the Book of Mormon, and the Mayan Glyphs," *Numen* 32:1 (July 1985): 101–13.

115. Schmidt, *Hearing Things*, 132, 201, 230.

116. See Patton E. Burchett, "The 'Magical' Language of Mantra," *Journal of the American Academy of Religion* 76:4 (December 2008): esp. 807–12, and Smith, *Relating Religion*, 215–29.

117. Knowlson, *Universal Language*, 9–10.

118. Priest, *American Antiquities*, 14, 19; Clarke, *Holy Bible*, 1:43; and Bushnell, *God in Christ*, 34.

119. *Deseret* is perhaps the best known, though some twentieth-century Latter-day Saints have sought an Egyptian origin for the term. See Ronan J. Head, "A Brief Survey of Ancient and Near Eastern Beekeeping," *FARMS Review* 20:1 (2008): 57–66.

120. "History of Brigham Young," *MS* 25:28 (July 11, 1863): 439, "In Memoriam," *Contributor* 3:5 (February 1882). See also Edward Partridge, "Dear Friends and Neighbors," *M&A* 1:4 (January 1835): 60, E. D. Howe, *Mormonism Unvailed* (Painesville, Ohio: by the author, 1834), 133, Lee Copeland, "Speaking in Tongues in the Restoration Churches," *Dialogue* 24:1 (spring 1991): 20–23, and Janet Ellingson, "Becoming a People: The Beliefs and Practices of the Early Mormons, 1830–1845" (Ph.D. diss., University of Utah, 1997), 43–48.

121. Schmidt, *Hearing Things*, 201–2. Though some other enthusiasts saw glossolalia as speaking the language of angels, few were so explicitly Adamic in focus.

122. *JD* 3:100. There are indirect echoes of Swedenborg's Martian language, though the systems are reasonably distinct. See Emanuel Swedenborg, *Concerning Heaven and its Wonders, and Concerning Hell* [1758] (Boston: Otis Clapp, 1837), 135–37, and Emanuel Swedenborg, *Concerning*

the Earths in our Solar System [1758] (Boston: Otis Clapp, 1839), 58, 74–76, 86.

123. *JSPR1*, 264–65; compare *JD* 2:342.

124. On Adam-ondi-Ahman, see chapter 4 herein. On *Zomar*, see GAEL, 23, and Ezra Booth (who renders it "Zomas") in Howe, *Mormonism Unvailed*, 199. Parley Pratt suggests it meant "Zion" in "One Hundred Years Hence. 1945," *MS* 6:9 (October 15, 1845): 141.

125. Ether 3:21–28; see also Mosiah 28; Alma 37:21–25; and George D. Smith, ed., *An Intimate Chronicle: The Journals of William Clayton* (Salt Lake City: Signature Books, 1995), 133. While it is not entirely certain that the Jaredite stones were Smith's translating stones, the evidence suggests close association if not absolute identity.

126. Mosiah 28:10–20; Richard S. Van Wagoner and Steven Walker, "Joseph Smith: 'The Gift of Seeing,'" *Dialogue* 15:2 (summer 1982), and Ashurst-McGee, "Prophethood," 334–35. *Gazelem* seems to refer to both sacred stones and the seer who wields them: *D&C* 78:9; Alma 37:23. Ashurst-McGee, "Prophethood," 273–76, and Quinn, *Magic*, 147–48.

127. Moses 5.

128. GAEL, 3, 9, 30. This glyph appears to combine the root of king (*Phah*) with a particle suggesting primacy (*eh*). Compare *Zub Zool* and *Zub Zool eh* on GAEL, 6, and see the expanded definition of *Phah eh* on GAEL, 30.

129. GAEL, 23; compare "Israel Will Be Gathered," *EMS* 2:13 (June 1833): 101. The interpretation of a mirror image of the Hebrew letter as *Hi* ("same as Beth") in GAEL, 2, suggests they saw this line as a wall of the Hebrew pictogram *beth*, meaning "house."

130. Webster's 1828 *Dictionary* may have supported this interpretation in a secondary definition of "degree" as "a certain distance or remove in the line of descent, determining the proximity of blood."

131. GAEL, 1.

132. GAEL, 10.

133. Smith returned to grammar, this time a slight misreading of Hebrew plural forms, in 1843 to describe the sacred "lives" associated with Eve's name: Smith, *Intimate Chronicle*, 103. He appears to have been pointing toward the "breath of life" (*ruakh khayyim*) of Genesis 6:17 as a play on Eve (*khawwah*, "life") as the "mother of all living" (*'em kol-khay*) in Genesis 3:20, in an ostensible exegesis of Genesis 2:7, in which a soul is breathed into Adam. I thank Kevin Barney for this analysis.

134. GAEL, 3–4, 21.

135. GAEL, 18.

136. Alexander Campbell, "A Restoration of the Ancient Order of Things," *Christian Baptist*, 2d ed. rev. (Cincinnati, 1835), 2:11 (June 6, 1825): 159.

137. Samuel Hopkins, *Treatise on the Millennium* [1793] (Providence: Brown and Danforth, 1824), 110–14, Juster, *Doomsayers*, 159.

138. Clarke, *Holy Bible*, 4:758–59. See also [Oliver Cowdery], "The Prophecy of Zephaniah," *EMS* 2:18 (March 1834): 141–42.

139. Schmidt, *Hearing Things*, 206. For Swedenborg's complex views on angelic language, see his *Heaven and Hell*, 135–37, and *Solar System*, 58, 74–76, 86.

140. "All Flesh," *EMS* 2:13 (June 1833): 102.

141. GAEL, 31.
142. For a similar view among some German Reformed, see Mark S. Schantz, *Awaiting the Heavenly Country: The Civil War and America's Culture of Death* (Ithaca: Cornell University Press, 2008), 49.
143. *D&C* 107:53–57; and *EPB*, 4, 8.
144. Warren Cowdery, "Brother O. Cowdery," *M&A* 3:2 (November 1836): 411.
145. Van Wagoner and Walker, "Seeing," 60, and *WWJ* 2:155.
146. "Proclamation to the Saints in Nauvoo," *Wasp* 1:37 (January 14, 1843): 3; compare *APR*, 427.

Chapter 6

1. *WWJ* 2:364; see also *WJS*, 327–36, 389–92, and "Communicated," *Nauvoo Neighbor* 1:47 (March 20, 1844): 2. (The so-called King Follett Discourse was delivered at the church conference a month later.)
2. *HC* 6:253. The term "crafty" had primarily negative connotations but could be used in a positive sense then as now. I do not believe that "crafty" was a veiled reference to Masonry. Mormons used "crafty" in, e.g., *M&A* 2:2 (November 1835): 223–24; *M&A* 3:12 (September 1837): 570–71; and *T&S* 5:8 (April 15, 1844): 508.
3. *WWJ* 2:359.
4. Douglas Davies, *The Mormon Culture of Salvation* (Aldershot, England: Ashgate, 2000), 39, 92, correctly highlights the death emphasis of the Mormon temple.
5. On "words against death," see Douglas Davies, *Death, Ritual, and Belief: The Rhetoric of Funeral Rites*, 2d ed. (London: Continuum, 2002), 125–27.
6. Gregory Prince, *Power from On High: The Development of Mormon Priesthood* (Salt Lake City: Signature Books, 1995), 155–72.
7. Bonnie Magness-Gardiner, "Seals, Mesopotamian," in *Anchor Bible Dictionary*, ed. David Noel Freedman, 6 vols. (New Haven: Yale University Press, 1992), 5:1062–63. Seal also referred to the cylindrical object that left the imprint.
8. Ether 3:22; *JSPR1*, 258–65 [*D&C* 77]; and 2 Nephi 27:7–8.
9. See, e.g., Mosiah 5:15 and 2 Nephi 33:15.
10. E. Brooks Holifield, *Theology in America: Christian Thought from the Age of the Puritans to the Civil War* (New Haven: Yale University Press, 2003), 68.
11. See, e.g., Nathan Bangs, "The Christian Spectator *versus* John Wesley and the Witness of the Spirit," *The Methodist Magazine and Quarterly Review* 18:4 (October 1836): 266; Matthew Richey, "Sermon III on the Witness of the Spirit," *The Methodist Preacher; Or, Monthly Sermons from Living Ministers* (Boston: Kane & Co., 1833), 48; and William Smithson, *The Methodist Pulpit, South*, 3d ed. (Washington, D.C.: for the Author, 1859), 367.
12. Revelation 7:2–8.
13. *WJS*, 233.
14. Charles Buck, *Theological Dictionary* (Philadelphia: Edwin T. Scott, 1823), 558; "Try the Spirits," *T&S* 3:11 (April 1, 1842): 745–48; and Susan Juster, *Doomsayers: Anglo-American Prophecy in the Age of Revolution* (Philadelphia: University of Pennsylvania Press, 2003), 171.
15. On baptism as seal, see Buck, *Theological Dictionary*, 41.

16. *EPB*, 105.
17. Prince, *Power*, 119–21.
18. *FWR*, 20–23.
19. *JSR*, 166 [*D&C* 1:8–9].
20. The same image was present in the Book of Mormon: Alma 34:35.
21. *EPB*, 71; *JSPJ1*, 176; see also *EPB*, 39, and *JSPJ1*, 177.
22. Letters & Patriarchal Blessings, December 19, 1843 (MS 1330, *SelCol* 1:31).
23. Joseph Smith Jr. to William Phelps, July 31, 1832, CHL, 7.
24. Prince, *Power*, 162–63 (though a reference to Jared Carter may be a distinct practice). See also Rex Eugene Cooper, *Promises Made to the Fathers: Mormon Covenant Organization* (Salt Lake City: University of Utah Press, 1990), 64.
25. Pratt, Diary, July 8, August 26, and September 8, 1833, CHL; Prince, *Power*, 156–57; Dean C. Jessee, "Joseph Knight's Recollection of Early Mormon History," *BYU Studies* 17:1 (autumn 1976): 39, and Jan Shipps and John W. Welch, eds., *The Journals of William E. McLellin: 1831–1836* (Provo, Utah: Brigham Young University Press, 1994), 131. The practice recapitulated on a small scale the translation of Enoch's city Zion: *NewT*, 104–5 [Moses 7:18–23].
26. James Russell Rohrer, *Keepers of the Covenant: Frontier Missions and the Decline of Congregationalism, 1774–1818* (New York: Oxford University Press, 1995), 46–47. The vast literature on Puritan covenants is briefly but thoughtfully outlined in Holifield, *Theology*, 53–55.
27. Rohrer, *Keepers of the Covenant*, esp. 9–10.
28. See, e.g., Janet Moore Lindman, *Bodies of Belief: Baptist Community in Early America* (Philadelphia: University of Pennsylvania Press, 2008), 53, 62, 92–94, and John Peck and John Lawton, *An Historical Sketch of the Baptist Missionary Convention of the State of New York* (Utica: Bennett and Bright, 1837), 11, 13, 23, 41.
29. David H. Tripp, *The Renewal of the Covenant in the Methodist Tradition* (London: Epworth, 1969), and Karen B. Westerfield Tucker, *American Methodist Worship* (Oxford: Oxford University Press, 2001), 67–68, 73, 88, 110–13.
30. Nancy Towle, *Vicissitudes Illustrated in the Experience of Nancy Towle, in Europe and America*, 2d ed. (Portsmouth, N.H.: John Caldwell, 1833), 75.
31. *JSR*, 110, 112 [*D&C* 42:67]. The reference to church covenants was added in 1835.
32. *FWR*, 1; compare the October 5, 1831, ordination certificate for William Smith, Community of Christ Library-Archives, Independence, Missouri.
33. *KEQR*, 38; see also Amasa Lyman, Journal, January 6 and 31, 1843, CHL.
34. See *T&S* 3 (April 15, 1842): 761–62; *WJS*, 111; and "Elders Orson Hyde and John E. Page," *T&S* 2:6 (January 15, 1841): 287.
35. See, e.g., *D&C* 42:30. On communitarian experiments, see Leonard J. Arrington et al., *Building the City of God: Community and Cooperation Among the Mormons* (Urbana: University of Illinois Press, 1992).
36. Buck, *Theological Dictionary*, 119–21.
37. George Fox, *Works* [1706], 3 vols. (Philadelphia: Marcus T. C. Gould, 1831), 3:41.

38. On Mosaic law, see, e.g., Richard Watson, *Biblical and Theological Dictionary* (New York: Waugh and Mason, 1832), 438, 877. On millennial restoration, see, e.g., Elhanan Winchester, *Universal Restoration* (Bellows Falls, Vt.: Bill Blake, 1819), 168.

39. *JSPR1*, 34–35 [*D&C* 22].

40. Thomas Alexander, "The Reconstruction of Mormon Doctrine: From Joseph Smith to Progressive Theology," *Sunstone* 10:5 (May 1985): 8–19.

41. See, e.g., "To the Saints scattered abroad," "Dear brethren," and "Elder D. C. Smith," in *T&S* 1:2 (December 1839): 20, 27–28.

42. "Death of Col. Robert B. Thompson," *T&S* 2:21 (September 1, 1841): 519.

43. See, e.g., *JSPJ1*, 104.

44. *JSR*, 229 [*D&C* 88:130–33].

45. *JSPJ1*, 23.

46. Among Mormons, see Danny L. Jorgensen, "Dissent and Schism in the Early Church: Explaining Mormon Fissiparousness," *Dialogue* 28:3 (fall 1995): 15–39. On Protestants, see Ann Taves, *Fits, Trances & Visions: Experiencing Religion and Explaining Experience from Wesley to James* (Princeton: Princeton University Press, 1999), and Clarke Garrett, *Spirit Possession and Popular Religion: From the Camisards to the Shakers* (Baltimore: Johns Hopkins University Press, 1987).

47. Stephen Stein, *The Shaker Experience in America* (New Haven: Yale University Press, 1994), 166, and Stephen Taysom, *Shakers, Mormons, and Religious Worlds: Conflicting Visions, Contested Boundaries* (Bloomington: University of Indiana Press, 2010), 154–69.

48. *JSPR1*, 104–5, 108–13 [*D&C* 43].

49. *JSR*, 100 [*D&C* 38:32].

50. Prince, *Power*, 115–48, reprints several primary sources. Richard F. Burton, *The City of the Saints, and Across the Rocky Mountains to California* (New York: Harper & Brothers, 1862), 244, notes that Mormons in 1850s Utah still pronounced the term "On-dewment." Webster (in his 1828 *Dictionary*) maintained "enduement" as distinct from "endowment"; the Latter-day Saints did not.

51. Luke 24; Acts 2; and Joel 2:28–32.

52. Adam Clarke, *The New Testament of our Lord and Saviour Jesus Christ* (Philadelphia: Thomas Cowperthwait and Co., 1838), 336–38, and Buck, *Theological Dictionary*, 163–64.

53. This was at times opposed to traditional ordination: William Pitts, *The Gospel Witness* (Catskill, N.Y.: Junius Lewis and Co., 1818), 26–27, 37.

54. Holifield, *Theology*, 272; see also Charles Finney's sermon "The Enduement of Power," in *The Baptism of the Holy Ghost by Rev. Asa Mahan and The Enduement of Power by Rev. C. G. Finney* (London: Elliot Stock, 1876), 241–54.

55. John Fea, "Power from On High in an Age of Ecclesiastical Impotence: The 'Endument of the Holy Spirit' in American Fundamentalist Thought, 1880–1936," *Fides et Historia* 1 (summer 1994): 22–35.

56. On the Kirtland Temple, see Elwin C. Robison, *The First Mormon Temple: Design, Construction, and Historic Context of the Kirtland Temple* (Provo, Utah: Brigham Young University Press, 1997), and Laurel Andrew, *The Early Temples of the Mormons: The Architecture of the Millennial Kingdom*

in the American West (Albany: State University of New York Press, 1978).

57. *JSPJ1*, 55.

58. *JSPR1*, 306–7 [*D&C* 88:119].

59. Sidney Rigdon may have played a role in Smith's use of foot-washing: Mark L. Staker, *Hearken O Ye People: The Historical Setting of Joseph Smith's Ohio Revelations* (Salt Lake City: Kofford Books, 2009), 40.

60. *JSPR1*, 308–11 [*D&C* 88:138–41].

61. *NewT*, 465 [John 13:10].

62. One Baptist weekly considered the ancient tradition of foot-washing but refused to endorse the practice: "Pedilavium…Or Feet-Washing," *Columbian Star and Christian Index* 4:24 (June 11, 1831): 369–70. See also Morgan Edwards, *Customs of Primitive Churches* (Philadelphia: n.p., 1768), 93, and Catherine A. Brekus, *Strangers and Pilgrims: Female Preaching in America, 1740–1845* (Chapel Hill: University of North Carolina Press, 1998), 65, 156, 292. The Winebrennerian Baptists also practiced foot-washing—David Benedict, *General History* (New York: Lewis Colby, 1850), 914—as did the Moravians: Alexander Chalmers, *The General Biographical Dictionary*, 32 vols. (London: J. Nichols, 1817), 32:446. The Mennonites were the best known of the Anabaptist groups to openly practice it: I. Daniel Rupp, *He Pasa Ekklesia: An Original History of the Religious Denominations at Present Existing in the United States* (Philadelphia: J. Y. Humphreys, 1844), 507.

63. Some refused to celebrate foot-washing with other sectarian groups: "Annual Meeting of 1812," *Minutes of the Annual Meetings of the Church of the Brethren* (Elgin, Ill.: Brethren, 1909), 30. I thank Jonathan Stapley for this reference.

64. See, e.g., the case of Henry Moore in *KEQR*, 50–51.

65. Fred C. Collier and William Harwell, eds., *Kirtland Council Minute Book*, 2d ed. rev. (Salt Lake City: Collier's, 2002), 6.

66. Andrew, *Early Temples of the Mormons*, 30–35.

67. *JSPJ1*, 68.

68. Smith later extended foot-washing to private (unordained) members: William Phelps, letter of April 1836, HBLL.

69. *JSPJ1*, 98.

70. *JSPJ1*, 123.

71. Smith told his brother Samuel that he "shall be made a teacher in the house of the Lord, among the school of the prophets." *EPB*, 5; compare *JSPJ1*, 84–85, 129.

72. *JSPJ1*, 83.

73. *JSPJ1*, 98, an allusion to New Testament apostles (Mark 16:15–18) and their American counterparts (4 Nephi 1:5).

74. See, e.g., the case of Stephen Post in Steven C. Harper, "'A Pentecost and Endowment Indeed': Six Eyewitness Accounts of the Kirtland Temple Experience," in *Opening the Heavens: Accounts of Divine Manifestations, 1820–1844*, ed. John W. Welch (Salt Lake City: Deseret Book, 2004), 352.

75. *JSPJ1*, 97.

76. Leonard J. Arrington, ed., "Oliver Cowdery's Kirtland, Ohio, 'Sketchbook,'" *BYU Studies* 12:4 (summer 1972): 416.

77. 1 Corinthians 6:11.
78. Charles Rosenberg, *The Cholera Years: The United States in 1832, 1849, and 1866* (Chicago: University of Chicago Press, 1987), 18.
79. Robert Abzug, *Cosmos Crumbling: American Reform and the Religious Imagination* (New York: Oxford University Press, 1994), and Stephen Nissenbaum, *Sex, Diet, and Debility in Jacksonian America: Sylvester Graham and Health Reform* (Chicago: Dorsey Press, 1988).
80. Susan Cayleff, *Wash and Be Healed: The Water-Cure Movement and Women's Health* (Philadelphia: Temple University Press, 1991), 19–48.
81. Arrington, "Cowdery's Sketchbook," 419.
82. Exodus 30:34–38; This practice persisted in the cultus—the Nauvoo rites incorporated lavender in the anointing oil: Emmeline, "Mormon Endowments," *Warsaw Signal* (April 15, 1846). Psalm 23 may also have been an antecedent: James Montgomery's rendering (*Sacred Poems and Hymns* [New York: D. Appleton, 1854], 40) reads "with perfume and oil thou anointest my head." See also Emma Smith, *A Collection of Sacred Hymns, for the Church of Jesus Christ of Latter Day Saints* (Kirtland, Ohio: F. G. Williams, 1835), 113.
83. *JSPR1*, 310–13 [*D&C* 89], and *WWJ* 1:110–11.
84. Samuel M. Brown, "Escaping the Destroying Angel: Immortality and the Word of Wisdom in Early Mormonism," presentation at the meeting of the Mormon History Association, Springfield, Ill., May 2009. On Anglo-American immortalism, see John Brooke, *The Refiner's Fire: The Making of Mormon Cosmology, 1644–1844* (Cambridge: Cambridge University Press, 1994), 56–57.
85. Towle, *Vicissitudes*, 156–57; see also Pitts, *Gospel Witness*, 131.
86. James Ewell, *The Medical Companion, or Family Physician; Treating the Diseases of the United States, with their Symptoms, Causes, Cure, and Means of Prevention* (Washington: Printed for the Proprietors, 1827), 257; compare "Dr. John Thomson's Stimulating Liniment," *Southern Botanic Journal* 1:5 (April 1, 1837): 80; R. M. Huston, "Remarks on Phlegmasia Dolens," *North American Medical and Surgical Journal* 5:10 (April 1828): 281; and T. F. Cornell, "Scarlatina Connected with Cerebral Symptoms," *New-York Quarterly Journal of Medicine and Surgery* 4:8 (January 1841): 52.
87. *JSPJ1*, 166–71; see also Harper, "Pentecost," 344–45.
88. Peck and Lawton, *Historical Sketch*, 120.
89. Pitts, *Gospel Witness*.
90. Some, like the Dunkers, also used it for healing: Jonathan A. Stapley and Kristine Wright, "The Forms and the Power: The Development of Mormon Ritual Healing to 1847," *Journal of Mormon History* 35:3 (summer 2009): 50–51. See also Adam Clarke, *The Holy Bible Containing the Old and New Testaments*, 6 vols. (New York: T. Mason and G. Lane, 1837), 1:456–57, and Buck, *Theological Dictionary*, 180, 530–31.
91. Arrington, "Cowdery's Sketchbook," 419.
92. Exodus 40:15.
93. Exodus 29:21.
94. Ether 9:4–22.
95. Arrington, "Cowdery's Sketchbook," 419–21. For other anointings see *JSPJ1*, 171, 174, 181–82.

96. See Kris Wright, "Consecrating a Community: Uses and Perceptions of Holy Oil, 1834–1955," presentation at the meeting of Mormon History Association, Springfield, Ill., May 2009.
97. On oil-based healings see, e.g., *JSPJ1*, 190, and Stapley and Wright, "Forms and Power."
98. See, e.g., *JSPJ1*, 98, 168.
99. See, e.g., the healing of Elder Clark (*JSPJ1*, 112) or the attempted healing of Samuel Brannan (*JSPJ1*, 122).
100. *EPB*, 176.
101. *JSPJ1*, 172.
102. *JSPJ1*, 174.
103. Arrington, "Cowdery's Sketchbook," 420.
104. The anniversary was important to the festival: *JSPJ1*, 213.
105. On anointings, see *KEQR*, 2, 5–10, 13, 17–18, 27–29.
106. Harper, "Pentecost," 345–46; Arrington, "Cowdery's Sketchbook," 422; *JSPJ1*, 181–82; and *KEQR*, 6.
107. See, e.g., *KEQR*, 6, 9, 11–12, 27.
108. Smith, *Sacred Hymns*, 94, 121. Phelps may have been alluding to the Olive Leaf revelation. This hymn, now called "The Spirit of God," no longer contains the verse regarding washing and anointing.
109. Harper, "Pentecost," presents several important accounts. See also William Phelps, letter of April 1836, HBLL.
110. Arrington, "Cowdery's Sketchbook," 417, 420, and *JSPJ1*, 99; compare *D&C* 93:1.
111. Richard L. Bushman, *Joseph Smith: Rough Stone Rolling* (New York: Knopf, 2005), 451, and Taves, *Experiencing Religion*, 46.
112. *JSPJ1*, 138.
113. See Lauritz Petersen, "The Kirtland Temple," *BYU Studies* 12:4 (summer 1972): 400–409, on the configuration and titles of the pulpits.
114. *JSPJ1*, 200.
115. *JSPJ1*, 201n421.
116. *JSPJ1*, 205.
117. *JSPJ1*, 207 [*D&C* 109:35–38].
118. *JSPJ1*, 208, 210.
119. *JSPJ1*, 216 and n461; see also Harper, "Kirtland Temple," 346.
120. Leigh Eric Schmidt, *Holy Fairs: Scotland and the Making of American Revivalism*, 2d ed. (Grand Rapids, Mich.: Eerdmans, 2001), and Christopher Jones, "'We Latter-day Saints Are Methodists': The Influence of Methodism on Early Mormon Religiosity" (M.A. thesis, Brigham Young University, 2009), 93–111.
121. George Albert Smith recalled in 1855 that excluded women believed "that some mischief was going on" in the temple, and "some of them were right huffy about it." *JD* 2:215.
122. See, e.g., accounts in Janiece Johnson, "Give It All Up and Follow Your Lord: Mormon Female Religiosity, 1831–1843" (M.A. thesis, Brigham Young University, 2001), 30–32, and William Phelps, letter of April 1836, HBLL (my quotation merges two accounts).
123. See, e.g., Arrington, "Cowdery's Sketchbook," 426, and *JSPJ1*, 211n443.

124. See, e.g., Arrington, "Cowdery's Sketchbook," 417, 420, and *JSPJ1*, 26, 1:205.
125. William Harris, *Mormonism Portrayed* (Warsaw, Ill.: Sharp & Gamble, 1841), 31–32, reports that Smith told his followers they would not be intoxicated by drinking consecrated wine, with obvious effects. William McLellin concurred: Stan Larson and Samuel J. Passey, eds., *The William E. McLellin Papers, 1854–1880* (Salt Lake City: Signature Books, 2007), 436, 512, 516. Erastus Snow, "Autobiography," CHL, 22–30, confirms drinking wine "untill they were filled" but does not mention the promise of sobriety or the fact of intoxication. John Corrill, *A Brief History of the Church of Christ of Latter Day Saints* (St. Louis: Printed for the Author, 1839), 23, noted that "every man must answer for himself," while reminding readers that similar accusations were made at the New Testament Pentecost. The accusations may reflect stigmatization of even temperant drinking by some evangelicals; it seems unlikely that many Mormon worshippers were drunk, though minor intoxication seems possible. See also *JSPJ1*, 211–13 and 213n448.
126. Milton Backman, *The Heavens Resound: A History of the Latter-day Saints in Ohio, 1830–1838* (Salt Lake City: Deseret Book, 1983), 300, and *JSPJ1*, 215–16.
127. *KEQR*, 18; see also *JSPJ1*, 222.
128. *WWJ* 1:128–30.
129. Jonathan Stapley introduced me to one source suggesting a recapitulation of the Kirtland liturgy in 1839: Theodore Turley, Missionary Diary, vol. 1, 1839–1840, HBLL, 12–14.
130. *JSPJ1*, 222. See also William Phelps, Letter of April 1836, HBLL.
131. Smith recalled around this time that this scripture occupied a central place in Moroni's communications of the 1820s: *JSPJ1*, 89.
132. Warren Parrish, "Dear Parents," *M&A* 2:6 (March 1836): 282.
133. 1 Kings 17:17–24. See also Samuel M. Brown, "The Prophet Elias Puzzle," *Dialogue* 39:3 (fall 2006): 3–4.
134. Brown, "Elias." Brooke, *Refiner's Fire*, esp. 15, 19, 221, misapprehends the significance of Elias in early Mormonism. Many traditions invoked Elijah as the harbinger of an age of salvation or enlightenment, not just the hermetic "artist."
135. *EPB*, 65.
136. See, e.g., *EPB*, 38, 96, 177.
137. *JSPJ1*, 247.
138. Brown, "Elias."
139. *WJS*, 43.
140. *NewT*, 851.
141. *WJS*, 318.
142. *WJS*, 239.
143. *WJS*, 240.
144. David Fischer, *Albion's Seed: Four British Folkways in America* (Oxford: Oxford University Press, 1989), 112–13, and David Stannard, *The Puritan Way of Death: A Study of Religion, Culture, and Social Change* (New York: Oxford University Press, 1977), 83.

145. Ann Douglas, *The Feminization of American Culture* (New York: Knopf, 1977), 131.

146. David Stannard, "Death and the Puritan Child," in *Death in America*, ed. David Stannard (Philadelphia: University of Pennsylvania Press, 1977), 24.

147. Stannard, *Puritan Way of Death*, 52, 60.

148. Colleen McDannell and Bernhard Lang, *Heaven: A History*, 2d ed. (New Haven: Yale University Press, 2001), 92, 258.

149. Paul K. Conkin, *The Uneasy Center: Reformed Christianity in Antebellum America* (Chapel Hill: University of North Carolina Press, 1995), 109–12, and George M. Marsden, *Jonathan Edwards: A Life* (New Haven: Yale University Press, 2004), 335–36.

150. Baptists were split over the issue: Bill J. Leonard, *Baptist Ways: A History* (Valley Forge, Pa.: Judson Press, 2003).

151. A. Gregory Schneider, "The Ritual of Happy Dying Among Early American Methodists," *Church History* 56:3 (September 1987): 348–63; and Paul Johnson, *A Shopkeeper's Millennium: Society and Revivals in Rochester, New York, 1815–1837*, rev. ed. (New York: Hill and Wang, 2004), 98.

152. *WJS*, 368.

153. *APR*, 398–99. William Phelps elaborated a similar theme during a meeting on February 27, 1845: "if we die let us all die together, & there will be a jolly lot of spirits dancing into the next world—it wont be to hell, for there is no fiddle there." (CR 100 318, box 1, folder 30; *SelCol* 1:18).

154. *APR*, 366–67.

155. *WJS*, 240.

156. 2 Peter 1:10. The Greek (*klesis*, invitation or summons; *ekloge*, being chosen) probably refers to the early Christian theology of adoption into the family of God. See the Arminian reading of Adam Clarke: *New Testament*, 450–51.

157. *WJS*, 4; compare Ephesians 1:13–14 and Acts 2:33. See also Charles G. Finney, "Lecture XIV," *Oberlin Evangelist* 1:18 (August 14, 1839): 138–39.

158. See, e.g., the blessing of Lyman Sherman in *JSR*, 277–78 [*D&C* 108:2, 8].

159. *WWJ* 2:362, 365.

160. See, e.g., Pitts, *Gospel Witness*.

161. *WJS*, 335.

162. *WJS*, 240.

163. *WWJ* 2:362.

Chapter 7

1. Smith explained *Nauvoo* in "Proclamation," *T&S* 2:6 (January 15, 1841): 273–74, as "a beautiful situation, or place, carrying with it, also, the idea of *rest*." See Louis Zucker, "Joseph Smith as a Student of Hebrew," *Dialogue* 3:2 (summer 1968): 68, and Glen Leonard, *Nauvoo: A Place of Peace, a People of Promise* (Salt Lake City: Deseret Book, 2002), 58–59n48. Smith, following Joshua Seixas, appears to have imputed an unusual term for "beautiful" (used in Isaiah 52:7) to Psalm 48:2, which uses a more common term for "beautiful." Smith meant *Nauvoo* as a synonym for Zion. He may also have intended an echo of the "perfection of beauty" of Zion (Psalm 50:2), which

the Saints had applied to Missouri: Amasa Lyman, Journal, July 13, 27, 1834, CHL.

2. Janet Ellingson, "Becoming a People: The Beliefs and Practices of the Early Mormons, 1830–1845" (Ph.D. diss., University of Utah, 1997), 279, 282, independently suggests the metaphor of translation to describe the relationship between Mormonism and Masonry.

3. The actual age of Freemasonry (a synonym for Masonry) is uncertain and largely a question of perspective. Some traditions maintain origins in Solomon's Temple, Enoch's lost temple, or the creation of the earth, while many outsiders and modern insiders see Masonry as evolving from late medieval stonemasons' guilds that became recognizable in the seventeenth century with input from Rosicrucianism. See David Stevenson, *The Origins of Freemasonry: Scotland's Century, 1590–1710* (Cambridge: Cambridge University Press, 1988). Freemasonry arrived in America around 1730: Steven Bullock, *Revolutionary Brotherhood: Freemasonry and the Transformation of the American Social Order, 1730–1840* (Chapel Hill: University of North Carolina Press, 1996), 46.

4. Bullock, *Revolutionary Brotherhood*, 74–75, 137.

5. This demographic generalization is not entirely true. Occasional Blacks participated, and in some areas propertyless whites were included: Bullock, *Revolutionary Brotherhood*, 160.

6. Bullock, *Revolutionary Brotherhood*, 164–65, 167, 185, 191. On Masonic anti-sectarianism, see William Morgan, *Illustrations of Masonry by One of the Fraternity* ([Rochester, N.Y.]: For the Proprietor, 1827), 26, 32.

7. Some date the introduction of the focus on Adam to the early eighteenth century: Michael Homer, "'Similarities of Priesthood in Masonry': The Relationship Between Freemasonry and Mormonism," *Dialogue* 27:3 (fall 1994): 4; and Laurence Dermott, *Ahiman Rezon: or, A Help to all that are or would be Free and Accepted Masons*, 2d ed. (London: Robert Black, 1764), 1–2. On ancient Greeks, see Samuel Cole, *The Freemason's Library and General Ahiman Rezon* (Baltimore: Benjamin Edes, 1817), 9–10, 187–88. Christ's apostles were also popular candidates: Bullock, *Revolutionary Brotherhood*, 184.

8. Bullock, *Revolutionary Brotherhood*, 145–48. On education, see Daniel Walker Howe, *What Hath God Wrought: The Transformation of America, 1815–1848* (New York: Oxford University Press, 2007), 350.

9. Bullock, *Revolutionary Brotherhood*, 86–89, 163–83.

10. The Morgan affair demonstrated to Americans the ominous extralegal power of Masonry: David Brion Davis, "Some Themes in Counter-Subversion: An Analysis of Anti-Masonic, Anti-Catholic, and Anti-Mormon Literature," *Mississippi Valley Historical Review* 47:2 (September 1960): 212. I am not persuaded by polemics denying Morgan's Masonic membership.

11. Kathleen Smith Kutolowski, "Freemasonry and Community in the Early Republic: The Case for Anti-Masonic Anxieties," *American Quarterly* 34:5 (winter 1982): 543–61.

12. Bullock, *Revolutionary Brotherhood*, 312, 317.

13. Bullock, *Revolutionary Brotherhood*, 282–83. On American fraternalism see Mary Ann Clawson, *Constructing Brotherhood: Class, Gender, and Fraternalism* (Princeton, N.J.: Princeton University Press, 1989).

14. See, e.g., John Brooke, *The Refiner's Fire: The Making of Mormon Cosmology, 1644–1844* (Cambridge: Cambridge University Press, 1994).

15. For Mormon treatments of Masonry, see Homer, "Freemasonry and Mormonism," 1–3.

16. In 1974 Reed Durham delivered an informal and controversial speech, "Is There No Help for the Widow's Son?," that has been recirculated against Durham's wishes by various Mormon critics, most accessibly in *Joseph Smith and Masonry* (Nauvoo, Ill.: Martin, 1980).

17. Bullock, *Revolutionary Brotherhood*, 240.

18. See, e.g., Morgan, *Illustrations of Masonry*, and John G. Stearns, *An Inquiry into the Nature and Tendency of Speculative Free-Masonry* (Utica: Northway and Porter, 1829).

19. See, e.g., William Preston, *Illustrations of Masonry*, 2d ed. (London: J. Wilkie, 1775), Salem Town, *A System of Speculative Masonry, in its Origin, Patronage, Dissemination, Principles, Duties, and Ultimate Designs, Laid Open for the Examination of the Serious and Candid* (Salem, N.Y.: Dodd and Stevenson, 1818), and Thomas Webb, *The Freemason's Monitor: or, Illustrations of Masonry in Two Parts* (Boston: Cushing & Appleton, 1808). Jeremy L. Cross, *The True Masonic Chart: or, Hieroglyphic Monitor; Containing All the Emblems Explained* (New Haven: T. G. Woodward & Co., 1826), largely derives from Webb.

20. Rob Morris, *The Masonic Martyr: The Biography of Eli Bruce, Sheriff of Niagara County, New York* (Louisville, Ky.: Morris & Monsarrat, 1861), 266–67.

21. Helaman 2, 6–8, 11; 3 Nephi 2–3; Mormon 1–2.

22. "Delusions," *Millennial Harbinger* 2:2 (February 7, 1831): 85–96. These comparisons persisted: James H. Hunt, *Mormonism: Embracing the Origin, Rise and Progress of the Sect, With an Examination of the Book of Mormon* (St. Louis: Ustick and Davies, 1844), 44, 46. See also Homer, "Freemasonry and Mormonism," 20. On Book of Mormon anti-Masonry, see Dan Vogel, "Mormonism's Anti-Masonick Bible," *John Whitmer Historical Association Journal* 9 (1989): 17–29, versus Richard L. Bushman, *Joseph Smith and the Beginnings of Mormonism* (Urbana: University of Illinois Press, 1981), 129–31, and "The Book of Mormon and the American Revolution," *BYU Studies* 17:1 (autumn 1976): 3–20.

23. One exception appears to be a quotation from David Whitmer in 1831, which did not circulate widely: Vogel, "Anti-Masonick Bible."

24. Durham, "Widow's Son." Even the otherwise persuasive Bullock (*Revolutionary Brotherhood*, 268) falls into this easy but unconvincing comparison.

25. Chapters 3 and 4 herein demonstrate the complexity of the cultural context for buried records.

26. On Danites, see Leland Gentry, "The Danite Band of 1838," *BYU Studies* 14:4 (summer 1974): 421–50, and Stephen LeSueur, "The Danites Reconsidered: Were They Vigilantes or Just the Mormon Version of the Elks Club?," *John Whitmer Historical Association Journal* 14 (1994): 35–51.

27. Missouri Secretary of State, *Document Containing the Correspondence, Orders, &c., in Relation to the Disturbances with the Mormons: and the Evidence Given Before the Hon. Austin A. King, Judge of the Fifth Judicial Circuit of the State of Missouri at the Court-house in Richmond in a Criminal Court of Inquiry Begun November 12, 1828, on the Trial of Joseph Smith, Jr., and Others for High Treason and Other Crimes Against the State* (Fayette, Mo.: Boon's Lick Democrat, 1841). See also Gentry, "Danite Band," 431, 433. The distress signal was the right ear cupped between thumb and forefinger. John Bennett invoked the Danites as an antecedent once Mormons began to practice Masonry (*The History of the Saints; or, An Expose of Joe Smith and Mormonism* [Boston: Leland and Whiting, 1842], 265, 277).

28. See Dean Jessee, comp. and ed., *The Papers of Joseph Smith: Journal, 1832–1842* (Salt Lake City: Deseret Book, 1992), 2:256, 262, 268.

29. See, e.g., Durham, "Widow's Son," 16, and Elwin C. Robison, *The First Mormon Temple: Design, Construction, and Historic Context of the Kirtland Temple* (Provo, Utah: BYU Press, 1997). I thank Lachlan Mackay for his insight on this topic.

30. In December 1835, Joseph Smith preached a sermon after a sumptuous patriarchal blessing meeting to a crowded congregation. He later discovered that several Presbyterians had been present as he "exposed their [Protestants' theological and ecclesiastical] abominations in the language of the scriptures." Hoping to have converted his listeners, he prayed "that it may be like a nail in a sure place, driven by the master of assemblies." *JSPJ1*, 139. David John Buerger, *The Mysteries of Godliness: A History of Mormon Temple Worship* (Salt Lake City: Signature Books, 2002), 48, adduces this as evidence of Masonic influence, but in fact it was a common term for potent testimony, drawn from Isaiah 22:23–25 and Ecclesiastes 12:11. See, e.g., Robert Robinson, *Seventeen Discourses on Several Texts of Scripture: Addressed to Christian Assemblies, in Villages Near Cambridge* (Boston: Cummings, Hilliard, & Co., 1824), 406, and Richard Storrs, comp. and ed., *Memoir of the Rev. Samuel Green: Late Pastor of Union Church, Boston* (Boston: Perkins & Marvin, 1836), 43.

31. Catherine Albanese, *A Republic of Mind and Spirit: A Cultural History of American Metaphysical Religion* (New Haven: Yale University Press, 2007), 134.

32. Oliver Cowdery, "Egyptian Mummies—Ancient Records," *M&A* 2:3 (December 1835): 236. Cf. Flavius Josephus, *The Works of Flavius Josephus: The Learned and Authentic Jewish Historian and Celebrated Warrior*, trans. William Whiston (Baltimore: Armstrong and Plaskitt, 1830), 27 (1:2:3), the probable source of Masonic speculation.

33. Hyrum Smith's copy of the Whiston translation is at CHL. Bullock, *Revolutionary Brotherhood*, 20.

34. See Durham, "Widow's Son," and the published vignettes in *T&S* 3:9 (March 1, 1842): 703; 3:10 (March 15, 1842): 722a; 3:14 (May 16, 1842): 783–84.

35. On Lucinda, see Todd Compton, *In Sacred Loneliness: The Plural Wives of Joseph Smith* (Salt Lake City: Signature Books, 1997), 43–54; Lucinda was a dual wife.

36. Lucinda owned Stearns, *Speculative Free-Masonry*: "The Prophet's Death," *Chicago Times* 20 (November 20, 1875): 1.

37. Kenneth Godfrey, "Joseph Smith and the Masons," *Journal of the Illinois State Historical Society* 64:1 (spring 1971): 79.

38. Brooke, *Refiner's Fire*, 244–48, argues that Smith was merely following the wane of anti-Masonry, but Masonry was already recovering by the 1830s, and Mormons engaged in little if any anti-Masonry even in the latter 1820s.

39. Homer, "Freemasonry and Mormonism," 27, Godfrey, "Smith and the Masons," 85. On Bennett, see Andrew F. Smith, *The Saintly Scoundrel: The Life and Times of Dr. John Cook Bennett* (Urbana: University of Illinois Press, 1997). On the exposés available in Nauvoo, see Homer, "Freemasonry and Mormonism," 16.

40. James Allen, "Nauvoo's Masonic Hall," *John Whitmer Historical Association Journal* 10 (1990): 43, and Godfrey, "Smith and the Masons," 83.

41. Allen, "Masonic Hall," 43. There is a minor debate over precisely how Jonas raised Smith, i.e., whether it was "on sight."

42. Immediate rise to Master Mason was usually forbidden. Morgan, *Illustrations of Masonry*, 74. See Godfrey, "Smith and the Masons," 84, 87.

43. Horace Cummings, "Autobiography," 1–1, CHL.

44. Bullock, *Revolutionary Brotherhood*, 254.

45. Bullock, *Revolutionary Brotherhood*, 263.

46. R. Laurence Moore, "The Occult Connection? Mormonism, Christian Science, and Spiritualism," in *The Occult in America: New Historical Perspectives*, ed. Howard Kerr and Charles L. Crow (Urbana: University of Illinois Press, 1983), 142, and Bullock, *Revolutionary Brotherhood*, 19–20, 268. Some seceders complained that almost no Masons understood the esoteric rites of Masonry: Bullock, *Revolutionary Brotherhood*, 158, and Morgan, *Illustrations of Masonry*, 48, 61.

47. Stevenson, *Origins of Freemasonry*, 160–61.

48. Morgan, *Illustrations of Masonry*, 69. Abiff is mentioned in 2 Chronicles 2.

49. Albanese, *Mind and Spirit*, 128; compare Morgan, *Illustrations of Masonry*, 84–85.

50. Some traditions had Masons raising Noah from the grave in like manner: Stevenson, *Origins of Freemasonry*, 144.

51. Morgan, *Illustrations of Masonry*, 83, 9, and Bullock, *Revolutionary Brotherhood*, 25–26.

52. Morgan, *Illustrations of Masonry*, 56; see also *Hamlet*, act 3, scene 1.

53. Morgan, *Illustrations of Masonry*, 85, 101.

54. Bullock, *Revolutionary Brotherhood*, 261.

55. Bullock, *Revolutionary Brotherhood*, 16–17. On cremation, see Stephen Prothero, *Purified by Fire: A History of Cremation in America* (Berkeley: University of California Press, 2001).

56. Morgan, *Illustrations of Masonry*, 22, 52, 75.

57. Bullock, *Revolutionary Brotherhood*, 254.

58. Morgan, *Illustrations of Masonry*, 25–26.

59. Stevenson, *Origins of Freemasonry*, 150–51; Bullock, *Revolutionary Brotherhood*, 11, 18.

60. Avery Allyn, *A Ritual of Freemasonry: Illustrated by Numerous Engravings, to which is added a Key to the Phi Beta Kappa, the Orange, and Odd Fellows*

Societies (New York: William Gowans, 1853), 123–24. The best treatment of this word, which appears to be a complex, folk-kabbalistic misreading of the Hebrew word for "stone," is in Arturo de Hoyos, "The Mystery of the Royal Arch Word," in *Freemasonry in Context: History, Ritual, Controversy,* ed. Arturo de Hoyos and S. Brent Morris (Lanham, Md.: Lexington Books, 2004). See also Bullock, *Revolutionary Brotherhood,* 266.

61. See Craig James Hazen, *The Village Enlightenment in America: Popular Religion and Science in the Nineteenth Century* (Urbana: University of Illinois Press, 2000), and Erich Robert Paul, *Science, Religion, and Mormon Cosmology* (Urbana: University of Illinois Press, 1992).

62. See, e.g., "Extraordinary Phenomenon" and "Science," *Wasp* 1:35 (December 31, 1842): 2, 3, and the mocking reprint from the *Lancaster Examiner* in "Hymenial Statistics," *Wasp* 1:52 (April 26, 1843): 2.

63. Morgan, *Illustrations of Masonry,* 60.

64. Cole, *Freemason's Library,* 187.

65. Though the association is likely overplayed (Fawn M. Brodie, *No Man Knows My History: The Life of Joseph Smith, the Mormon Prophet,* 2d ed. rev. and enlarged [New York: Knopf, 1971], 171), Mormons quoted Thomas Dick, an important proponent of this view, on several occasions. See, e.g., Thomas Dick, "Philosophy of Religion," *M&A* 3: 5 (February 1837): 461–63, and discussion in Samuel M. Brown, "The Early Mormon Chain of Belonging," *Dialogue* 44:1 (spring 2011): 1–52.

66. On Masonic political power, see Kutolowski, "Freemasonry and Community."

67. On perfectionism, see Timothy L. Smith, *Revivalism and Social Reform: American Protestantism on the Eve of the Civil War* (Baltimore: Johns Hopkins University Press, 1980), and Spencer Klaw, *Without Sin: The Life and Death of the Oneida Community* (New York: Penguin, 1994).

68. Brooke, *Refiner's Fire,* 248.

69. I thank Philip Barlow for this analogy. For sample Mormon views of the genealogy of temple rites see the essays in Donald Parry, ed., *Temples of the Ancient World* (Salt Lake City: Deseret Book, 1994).

70. Larry Porter and Milton Backman, "Doctrine and the Temple in Nauvoo," *BYU Studies* 32:1–2 (winter-spring 1991): 45.

71. Out of respect for Mormon tradition—see Kathleen Flake, "'Not to Be Riten': The Nature and Effects of the Mormon Temple Rite as Oral Canon," *Journal of Ritual Studies* 9:2 (summer 1995): 1–21—I follow the practice of official sources by describing the Nauvoo Temple endowment only in very general terms. Official sources include Boyd K. Packer, *The Holy Temple* (Salt Lake City: Deseret Book, 1982); James E. Talmage, *The House of the Lord: A Study of Holy Sanctuaries Ancient and Modern* (Salt Lake City: Deseret News Press, 1912); and relevant entries in Daniel H. Ludlow, ed., *The Encyclopedia of Mormonism* (New York: Macmillan, 1992).

72. On the Quorum, see Andrew Ehat, "Joseph Smith's Introduction of Temple Ordinances and the 1844 Mormon Succession Question" (M.A. thesis, Brigham Young University, 1982), and Devery Anderson, "The Anointed Quorum in Nauvoo, 1842–45," *Journal of Mormon History* 29:2 (fall 2003): 137–57.

73. See, e.g., John Gillies, *The History of Ancient Greece: Its Colonies and Conquests* (Philadelphia: Thomas Wardle, 1831), esp. 250, and John

Fellows, *An Exposition of the Mysteries: or, Religious Dogmas and Customs of the Ancient Egyptians, Pythagoreans, and Druids; Also an Inquiry into the Origin, History, and Purport of Freemasonry* (New York: for the Author, 1835).

74. Alan Segal, *Life after Death: The Afterlife in Western Religions* (New York: Doubleday, 2004), 216–17.

75. "Ancient History.—No. 5. GREECE," *M&A* 3:9 (June 1837): 526.

76. Ehat, "Mormon Succession," 27.

77. George D. Smith, ed., *An Intimate Chronicle: The Journals of William Clayton* (Salt Lake City: Signature Books, 1995), 205.

78. Devery Anderson and Gary Bergera, eds., *The Nauvoo Endowment Companies, 1845–1846: A Documentary History* (Salt Lake City: Signature Books, 2005), 29, and Emma Smith, *A Collection of Sacred Hymns, for the Church of Jesus Christ of Latter Day Saints* (Kirtland, Ohio: F. G. Williams, 1835), 29–30.

79. Talmage, *House of the Lord*, 99–100.

80. On the cosmological drama, see *Encyclopedia of Mormonism*, s.v. "Temples."

81. Dan Vogel and Brent Metcalfe, "Joseph Smith's Scriptural Cosmology," in *The Word of God: Essays on Mormon Scripture*, ed. Dan Vogel (Salt Lake City: Signature Books, 1990), 187–220.

82. Mormon scripture contains several ascension visions: 1 Nephi 1: 8–15; 1 Nephi 11; Alma 36; Moses 7: 21–23; Abraham 3–5; esp. 3:1, 12, 22. Smith's Vision (*D&C* 76) is similar. On contemporary Protestant ascension visions, see Richard L. Bushman, "The Visionary World of Joseph Smith," *BYU Studies* 37:1 (1997): 183–204.

83. See Homer, "Freemasonry and Mormonism," esp. 68–70.

84. Godfrey, "Smith and the Masons," 86.

85. Willard Richards to Levi Richards, March 7–25, 1842, Richards Family Letters (MS 1558 2, CHL).

86. Andrew Ehat, "'They Might Have Known That He Was Not a Fallen Prophet'—The Nauvoo Journal of Joseph Fielding," *BYU Studies* 18:2 (winter 1979): 145, 147.

87. Heber Kimball to Parley Pratt, June 17, 1842, CHL.

88. Ehat, "Mormon Succession," 104. Bennett, *History of the Saints*, 3, 56, 191, 247.

89. Godfrey, "Smith and the Masons," 89.

90. Ehat, "Mormon Succession," 17.

91. See, e.g., "Masonic Notice," *Wasp* 1:29 (November 5, 1842): 3.

92. Allen, "Masonic Hall," 46.

93. Allen, "Masonic Hall," 44–45.

94. Bullock, *Revolutionary Brotherhood*, 16. "Full Particulars of the Wonderful Sights," *T&S* 4:10 (April 1, 1843), 149–50, reprinted in *Wasp* 1:51 (April 19, 1843): 2. The author of this piece was not Mormon, despite some confusion on the part of later readers. I thank Nick Litterski for help on this point.

95. Homer, "Freemasonry and Mormonism," 33.

96. Bullock, *Revolutionary Brotherhood*, 129.

97. Godfrey, "Smith and the Masons," 87.

98. Richard L. Bushman, *Joseph Smith: Rough Stone Rolling* (New York: Knopf, 2005), 449–51, represents a moderate view.
99. Many Masons imagined angels and ancient patriarchs as members of the fraternity. Smith's approach to this was dramatically more literal than that of most Masons.
100. It also, of course, had antecedents in kabbalah and formal esotericism. See, e.g., Frances Yates, *The Occult Philosophy in the Elizabethan Age* [1979] (New York: Routledge Classics, 2001), 23, 96, 178.
101. 1 Corinthians 12:10; compare *D&C* 46 and Ehat, "Mormon Succession," 31–35. On discernment among other radical movements see Susan Juster, *Doomsayers: Anglo-American Prophecy in the Age of Revolution* (Philadelphia: University of Pennsylvania Press, 2003), 35, 58, 166.
102. Ehat, "Mormon Succession," 33.
103. Oliver Cowdery, "Letter VIII," *M&A* 2:1 (October 1835): 197–99.
104. "Commandment, Given March 8, 1831," and "Commandment, Given May 9, 1831," *EMS* 1:3 (August 1832): 17 [*D&C* 46, 50]. For background see Parley Pratt, *The Autobiography of Parley Parker Pratt* (New York: Russell Brothers, 1874), 65–70; Bruce N. Westergren, ed., *From Historian to Dissident: The Book of John Whitmer* (Salt Lake City: Signature Books, 1995), 37–38, 57–58; Jared Carter, Journal, CHL, 20–29.
105. *T&S* 3:23 (October 10, 1842): 936 [*D&C* 128:20]; compare 2 Corinthians 11:14 and the concerns over "false Christs" in *FWR*, 23.
106. *WJS*, 6.
107. *WJS*, 44.
108. *WJS*, 6. See also *D&C* 129:4–5; compare Smith, *Intimate Chronicle*, 520, and James B. Allen, *Trials of Discipleship: The Story of William Clayton, a Mormon* (Urbana: University of Illinois Press, 1987), 121 and n30.
109. Frances Trollope, *Domestic Manners of the Americans*, New York reprint, 4th ed. (London: Whittaker, Treacher & Co., 1832), 94–95, 123, bemoans "the eternal shaking hands" of the vulgar Americans.
110. See, e.g., *JSPJ1*, 160.
111. They also recapitulated the experience of Jesus with his disciples after the resurrection: *WJS*, 255.
112. William Clayton, "Observations on the Sectarian God," *SelCol* 1:20. The power of humans over unembodied demons may reflect in part an expansive exegesis of Philippians 3:31.
113. Ann Taves, *Fits, Trances & Visions: Experiencing Religion and Explaining Experience from Wesley to James* (Princeton: Princeton University Press, 1999).
114. *WJS*, 116–17, and Ehat, "Mormon Succession," 32.
115. *WJS*, 119–20.
116. See, e.g., John Peck and John Lawton, *An Historical Sketch of the Baptist Missionary Convention of the State of New York* (Utica: Bennett and Bright, 1837), 16–17, 46.
117. Paul Johnson, *A Shopkeeper's Millennium: Society and Revivals in Rochester, New York, 1815–1837*, rev. ed. (New York: Hill and Wang, 2004), 25–27.
118. Heber Kimball to Parley Pratt, June 17, 1842, CHL.
119. On temple names, see Bruce R. McConkie, *A New Witness for the Articles of Faith* (Salt Lake City: Deseret Book, 1985), 315, and Truman Madsen,

"'Putting on the Names': A Jewish-Christian Legacy," and Bruce Porter and Stephen Ricks, "Names in Antiquity: Old, New, and Hidden," in *By Study and also by Faith*, vol. 1, ed. John Lundquist and Stephen Ricks (Salt Lake City: Deseret Book, 1990), 458–82, 501–22.

120. Smith did not revise this verse for his New Translation: *NewT*, 826–27.

121. Smith, *Sacred Hymns*, 21, *EMS* 1:5 (October 1832): 37, 40, and *M&A* 3:3 (December 1836): 419.

122. Mosiah 1:12.

123. *EPB*, 139.

124. Adam Clarke, *The New Testament of our Lord and Saviour Jesus Christ* (Philadelphia: Thomas Cowperthwait and Co., 1838), 499.

125. Among Presbyterians, communion tokens were small coinlike objects distributed the day before communion to assure that only approved members participated in the Lord's Supper: Leigh Eric Schmidt, *Holy Fairs: Scotland and the Making of American Revivalism*, 2d ed. (Grand Rapids, Mich.: Eerdmans, 2001), 108–11.

126. See, e.g., Eugene England, ed., "George Laub's Nauvoo Journal," *BYU Studies* 18:2 (winter 1978): 174–75, a transcription of a sermon from May 1844. Smith's translations were consistent with traditional Protestant interpretations of these names.

127. David J. Whittaker, "Substituted Names in the Published Revelations of Joseph Smith," *BYU Studies* 23:1 (winter 1983): 103–12.

128. Douglas Davies, *The Mormon Culture of Salvation* (Aldershot, England: Ashgate, 2000), 71; Ehat, "Mormon Succession," 28; George Laub, Journal, CHL, 101.

129. *WJS*, 38–39.

130. *WJS*, 64.

131. Anderson and Bergera, *Nauvoo Endowment Companies*, 204, reprinting the Clayton minutes. Compare Smith, *Intimate Chronicle*, 238.

132. Smith, *Intimate Chronicle*, 133.

133. Anderson and Bergera, *Nauvoo Endowment Companies*, 211.

134. Lorenzo Snow Journal, MS 1330 1, *SelCol* 1:31.

135. *WJS*, 358.

136. *WJS*, 351.

137. Smith applied similar logic in his own life. Hoping to evade legal proceedings, Smith claimed in June 1843, subsequent to his father's death, that he was "Joseph Smith Sr." rather than the "Joseph Smith Jr." named in the warrant. See "MISSOURI vs JOSEPH SMITH," *T&S* 4:16 (July 1, 1843): 244–46. Compare Municipal Court Record (MS 3434, CHL), 56–58, and Joseph Smith statement, June 30, 1843 (MS 155, box 4, folder 13, CHL). I thank Robin Jensen for assistance with these sources.

138. *WJS*, 64. Kabbalistic antecedents may also help to contextualize Smith's statements on this point.

139. Latter-day Saints publicly discussed the power of the new names for decades. See, e.g., Charles Rich, "Blessing the Result of Obedience," *JD* 19:250–51.

140. Andrew Ehat, "'Who Shall Ascend into the Hill of the Lord?' Sesquicentennial Reflections of a Sacred Day: 4 May 1842," in *Temples of the Ancient*

World, ed. Donald Parry (Salt Lake City: Deseret Book, 1994), 48–62; compare *HC* 5:1–2.

141. The precise relationship between Jehovah and Elohim in early, as opposed to later, Mormonism is not certain.

142. *JD* 2:31, 315; 5:133; 6:63, 154–55; 8:339; 9:25–26, 91; 10:172; 11:27; 18:132; 19:250; and Smith, *Intimate Chronicle*, 225.

143. On the second blessing, see, e.g., "European Missions," *Wesleyan-Methodist Magazine, for the Year 1833* (London: J. Mason, 1833): 821, Charles E. Hambrick-Stowe, *Charles G. Finney and the Spirit of American Evangelicalism* (Grand Rapids, Mich.: Eerdmans, 1996), 190–91, 251, and Catherine A. Brekus, *Strangers and Pilgrims: Female Preaching in America, 1740–1845* (Chapel Hill: University of North Carolina Press, 1998), 180.

144. Stanley B. Kimball, *On the Potter's Wheel: Diary of Heber C. Kimball* (Salt Lake City: Signature Books, 1987), 56–57. See also Bushman, *Rough Stone*, 497–98, and Davies, *Culture of Salvation*, 124.

145. See, e.g., Mark 16:1; John 12:3; Matthew 26:12.

146. *EPB*, 216. See also the blessing of Joseph Kingsbury, ibid.

147. See, e.g., John Pack, Journal (private possession, copy of holograph available at www.johnpackfamily.com/gallery/v/journal/), 10. I thank Jonathan Stapley for this reference.

148. Jonathan Stapley, "Last Rites and the Dynamics of Mormon Liturgy," *BYU Studies* 50:2 (2011): 96–128.

149. Antinomianism was central to the criticism of the Nauvoo *Expositor* group of seceders: *Nauvoo Expositor* 1:1 (June 7, 1844), and "Buckeye's Lamentation for Want of More Wives," *Warsaw Message* 1:47 (February 7, 1844): 1. See also Henry Caswall, *Prophet of the Nineteenth Century* (London: J. G. & F. Rivington, 1843), 9, and David Brion Davis, "The New England Origins of Mormonism," *New England Quarterly* 26:2 (June 1953): 156, 164. See also J. C. Davis, *Fear, Myth, and History: The Ranters and the Historians* (Cambridge: Cambridge University Press, 2002), 122.

150. On enthusiasm as antinomianism see Taves, *Experiencing Religion*, 49, and Clarke Garrett, *Spirit Possession and Popular Religion: From the Camisards to the Shakers* (Baltimore: Johns Hopkins University Press, 1987), 84.

151. On the Antinomian controversy, see Emery Battis, *Saints and Sectaries: Anne Hutchinson and the Antinomian Controversy in the Massachusetts Bay Colony* (Chapel Hill: University of North Carolina Press, 1962), and David Hall, *Worlds of Wonder, Days of Judgment* (New York: Knopf, 1989), 96.

152. Brooke, *Refiner's Fire*, 262.

153. Mosiah 26:20.

154. Helaman 10: esp. 5–7.

155. Ehat, "Mormon Succession."

156. *NewT*, 105–9 [Moses 7: esp. 13, 19–24].

157. *JSR*, 323–28 [D&C 132: esp. 19, 26].

158. Brodie, *No Man Knows*, 334–47.

159. *WJS*, 327–32. Smith had been preaching this for years: *WJS*, 62.

160. *WJS*, 80, with critical response in "Buckeye's Lamentation."

161. Ronald D. Dennis, ed., "The Martyrdom of Joseph Smith and His Brother Hyrum by Dan Jones," *BYU Studies* 24:1 (winter 1984), 88.

162. Anderson and Bergera, *Nauvoo Endowment Companies*, 277. See also the blessing of Zebedee Coltrin: *JSPJ1*, 42, 68, 111.

163. *WJS*, 124.

164. Ehat, "Mormon Succession," 52.

165. See, e.g., *WJS*, 36–37.

166. *T&S* 2 (October 15, 1841): 567–69.

167. Jonathan Stapley and Kristine Wright, "'They Shall Be Made Whole': A History of Baptism for Health," *Journal of Mormon History* 34:4 (fall 2008): esp. 75–78, 81–83.

168. On garments as angelic clothing, see Samuel M. Brown, "William Phelps's 'Paracletes': An Early Witness to Joseph Smith's Divine Anthropology," *International Journal of Mormon Studies* 2:1 (spring 2009): 82.

169. Bennett, *History of the Saints*, 277.

170. Smith and his brother had apparently removed the garment to avoid its exposure during their incarceration, although Phelps argued they had done so because of the heat: Smith, *Intimate Chronicle*, 224. On the protective quality of the temple garment, see Linda King Newell and Valeen Tippetts Avery, *Mormon Enigma: Emma Hale Smith*, 2d ed. (Urbana: University of Illinois Press, 1994), 189, and Abraham Smoot, Missionary Diary, vol. 1, 1836–1846, HBLL, 242.

171. This is the persuasive argument of Ehat, "Mormon Succession."

172. Heber Kimball prayed in late 1844 that God would "Preserve our President & his wife for we must receave our endewments through them." Laub, Journal, December 30, 1844.

173. Bushman, *Rough Stone*, 451, and Taves, *Experiencing Religion*, 46.

174. *NewT*, 86. Brackets indicate material added for the published version (Moses 1:39).

Chapter 8

1. On Bernhisel, see Gwynn Barrett, "John M. Bernhisel: Mormon Elder in Congress" (Ph.D. diss., Brigham Young University, 1968).

2. *APR*, 424, October 26, 1843, inserted retrospectively in hand of Robert Campbell, with John Bernhisel's signature appended. See also Lyndon Cook, *Nauvoo Marriages Proxy Sealings 1843–1846* (Provo: Grandin Book, 2004), 22–25.

3. Devery Anderson and Gary Bergera, eds., *The Nauvoo Endowment Companies, 1845–1846: A Documentary History* (Salt Lake City: Signature Books, 2005), 29, 566.

4. Cook, *Nauvoo Marriages*, 185, 214. On Mormon levirates, see Todd Compton, *In Sacred Loneliness: The Plural Wives of Joseph Smith* (Salt Lake City: Signature Books, 1997), 61, 154–56.

5. Van Wagoner and Steven Walker, *A Book of Mormons* (Salt Lake City: Signature Books, 1982), 16. See also Historian's Office Journal (CR 100, 1, vol. 30; *SelCol* 1:17), 53.

6. See, e.g., George M. Marsden, *Jonathan Edwards: A Life* (New Haven: Yale University Press, 2004), 55, 94, 429, 494. See also David Hall, *Worlds of Wonder: Days of Judgment* (New York: Knopf, 1989), 207–10, 218–19.

7. See Colleen McDannell and Bernhard Lang, *Heaven: A History*, 2d ed. (New Haven: Yale University Press, 2001), 58, 92, 155, 258. For contrary views, see reviews by Alan Bernstein in *Speculum* 66:1 (January 1991): 200–202, and Caroline Walker Bynum in *Church History* 62:2 (June 1993): 315–17.

8. On Swedenborg, see McDannell and Lang, *Heaven*, 183, 217–18.

9. Drew Gilpin Faust, *This Republic of Suffering: Death and the American Civil War* (New York: Knopf, 2008), and Mark S. Schantz, *Awaiting the Heavenly Country: The Civil War and America's Culture of Death* (Ithaca: Cornell University Press, 2008).

10. McDannell and Lang, *Heaven*, 126, 140, 183, 233, 236. Randy J. Sparks, "The Southern Way of Death: The Meaning of Death in Antebellum White Evangelical Culture," *Southern Quarterly* 44:1 (fall 2006): 40–41. Ann Douglas, *The Feminization of American Culture* (New York: Knopf, 1977), 202–3, argues that it also gave power to evangelical ministers and women.

11. See Daniel Walker Howe, *What Hath God Wrought: The Transformation of America, 1815–1848* (New York: Oxford University Press, 2007), on the dislocations and innovations of the period. See Nathan Hatch, *The Democratization of American Christianity* (New Haven: Yale University Press, 1989), on religious voluntarism and populism.

12. On the domestic heaven and rising individualism, see Rex Eugene Cooper, *Promises Made to the Fathers: Mormon Covenant Organization* (Salt Lake City: University of Utah Press, 1990), 92. On the prior model, see Paul Johnson, *A Shopkeeper's Millennium: Society and Revivals in Rochester, New York, 1815–1837*, rev. ed. (New York: Hill and Wang, 2004), 27, 43, and Steven Mintz and Susan Kellogg, *Domestic Revolutions: A Social History of American Family Life* (New York: Free Press, 1988), 6, 18–19, 22–23, 43, 45–46, 63–64.

13. Emma Disley, "Degrees of Glory: Protestant Doctrine and the Concepts of Rewards Hereafter," *Journal of Theological Studies* 42:1 (April 1991): 77–105.

14. See Elizabeth Stuart Phelps, *The Gates Ajar* (Boston: Fields, Osgood, & Co., 1869), 16, McDannell and Lang, *Heaven*, 265–70, and Barton Levi St. Armand, "Paradise Deferred: The Image of Heaven in the Work of Emily Dickinson and Elizabeth Stuart Phelps," *American Quarterly* 29:1 (spring 1977): 55–78.

15. See Nancy Towle, *Vicissitudes Illustrated in the Experience of Nancy Towle, in Europe and America*, 2d ed. (Portsmouth, N.H.: John Caldwell, 1833), esp. 117, 134–38, 144, 162–63, 191, 207, 209–13. Itinerants Jarena Lee and Francis Asbury were similarly separated from family during proselytizing tours.

16. *APR*, 339 [*D&C* 130:2].

17. *JSPJ1*, 134.

18. This section condenses the evidence and arguments of my "Early Mormon Adoption Theology and the Mechanics of Salvation," *Journal of Mormon History* 37:3 (summer 2011): 3–52.

19. Romans 8:14–15. The Greek term, *huiothesia*, means "making a son." See also Romans 8:23; 9:4; Galatians 4:5; Ephesians 1:5.

20. Cooper, *Covenant Organization*; Robert G. Pope, *The Halfway Covenant: Church Membership in New England* (Princeton, N.J.: Princeton University Press, 1969); E. Brooks Holifield, *Theology in America: Christian Thought from the Age of the Puritans to the Civil War* (New Haven: Yale University Press, 2003), 68.

21. James Russell Rohrer, *Keepers of the Covenant: Frontier Missions and the Decline of Congregationalism, 1774–1818* (New York: Oxford University Press, 1995).

22. Charles Buck, *Theological Dictionary* (Philadelphia: Edwin T. Scott, 1823), 11–13. Compare Adam Clarke, *The New Testament of our Lord and Saviour Jesus Christ* (Philadelphia: Thomas Cowperthwait and Co., 1838), 508.

23. Hatch, *Democratization*.

24. Holifield, *Theology*, 269.

25. See discussion in Ann Taves, *Fits, Trances and Visions: Experiencing Religion and Explaining Experience from Wesley to James* (Princeton: Princeton University Press, 1999), 50–51.

26. William Pitts, *The Gospel Witness* (Catskill, N.Y.: Junius Lewis and Co., 1818), 104.

27. Even the conservative Methodist Clarke saw adoption as "the redemption of our mystical body," Clarke, *New Testament*, 51, 53.

28. See, e.g., John Peck and John Lawton, *An Historical Sketch of the Baptist Missionary Convention of the State of New York* (Utica: Bennett and Bright, 1837), 127, 138, Towle, *Vicissitudes*, 43–44, 60, 65, 67, 70, 75, 93, 159, 186, 283, and Clarke, *New Testament*, 210.

29. Mosiah 27:25.

30. Mosiah 5:7–9; see also Moroni 7:26, 48, and 1 John 3:2.

31. Parley Pratt, *A Voice of Warning and Instruction to All People* (New York: W. Sandford, 1837), 96.

32. Pratt, *Voice of Warning*, 99.

33. Pratt, *Voice of Warning*, 103–5, 109–11.

34. "The Gathering," *MS* 3:12 (April 1843): 195, and "The Law of Adoption," *MS* 4:2 (June 1843): 17–19.

35. Wilford Woodruff, "President O. Cowdery, Dear Brother," *M&A* 3:3 (December 1836): 432, and Addison Pratt, "My Dear Wife," *T&S* 6:8 (May 1, 1845): 882.

36. Erastus Snow and Benjamin Winchester, "An Address to the Citizens of Salem," *T&S* 3:1 (November 1, 1841): 578.

37. See also V. H. Bruce, "Water Baptism," *T&S* 6:21 (January 15, 1846): 1095.

38. Abraham 2:10.

39. *WJS*, 73–74; see also *WWJ* 2:142.

40. *WJS*, 256.

41. *WJS*, 6; compare *HC* 3:381.

42. The deathbed image was strongly present in early blessings: Orson Hyde, *A Cry from the Wilderness, A Voice from the Dust: A Brief Sketch of the Origin and Doctrines of the "Church of Jesus Christ of Latter Day Saints" in America, known to some as: "The Mormons,"* trans. Justus Ernst (Frankfurt, Germany, 1842), 62.

43. Joseph Sr.'s deathbed is detailed in *LB*, 716–17. On Hyrum's patriarchal sealing power, see the 1841 revelation canonized as *D&C* 124:93, 124,

with discussion in Irene Bates and E. Gary Smith, *Lost Legacy: The Mormon Office of the Presiding Patriarch* (Urbana: University of Illinois Press, 1996), 49–50.

44. See, e.g., *JSPJ1*, 139, 146.
45. J. B. Turner, *Mormonism in All Ages: or the Rise, Progress, and Causes of Mormonism* (New York: Platt & Peters, 1842), 245–47.
46. See, e.g., John C. Bennett, *The History of the Saints; or, An Expose of Joe Smith and Mormonism* (Boston: Leland and Whiting, 1842), 42–43, and William Swartzell, *Mormonism Exposed, being a Journal of a Residence in Missouri from the 28th of May to the 20th of August, 1838* (Pekin, Ohio: by the author, 1840), iv.
47. See, e.g., *EPB*, 72, 95–96, 105, 187.
48. Abraham 1:18.
49. Abraham 1:2–4.
50. *EPB*, 40, 44, 65.
51. *EPB*, 187.
52. *T&S* 1:11 (September 1840): 172.
53. Kimball's comments are in Brigham Young, "From England: Preston, April 17th, 1840," *T&S* 1:8 (June 1840): 121.
54. *EPB*, 56, 67, 13. On Abraham's father, see Abraham 1:5–7, 27.
55. *EPB*, 16.
56. *EPB*, 175.
57. *EPB*, 70; compare 64.
58. *EPB*, 183.
59. *EPB*, 188.
60. Compare the experience of Zina D. Huntington, who received simultaneous blessings from her father and an unrelated patriarch on September 8, 1836 (copy of holograph in author's possession).
61. *EPB*, 187.
62. *EPB*, 71.
63. Armand Mauss, *All Abraham's Children: Changing Mormon Conceptions of Race and Lineage* (Urbana: University of Illinois Press, 2003), 17–40, discusses early Mormon beliefs about created lineage from a sociological perspective. See also Cooper, *Covenant Organization*, 74.
64. Bates and Smith, *Lost Legacy*, 67.
65. *EPB*, 76, 163.
66. *EPB*, 104–5; compare 120.
67. *EPB*, 72.
68. *LB*, 710–11.
69. *EPB*, 183.
70. *EPB*, 56.
71. *EPB*, 64.
72. *EPB*, 95.
73. *EPB*, 87.
74. *EPB*, 108.
75. *EPB*, 149.
76. *JSPJ1*, 146.
77. M. Guy Bishop, "'What Has Happened to Our Fathers?': Baptism for the Dead at Nauvoo," *Dialogue* 23:2 (summer 1990): 85–97, and *LB*, 332n13.

78. *WJS*, 37, 49n1.

79. *EMD* 1:513, and Gregory Prince, *Power from On High: The Development of Mormon Priesthood* (Salt Lake City: Signature Books, 1995), 87–88, 126, 143–44.

80. Bishop, "Baptism for the Dead."

81. Baugh, "Baptism for the Dead," and Prince, *Power*, 145. Mormons even baptized famous figures who were not related to them: Bishop, "Baptism for the Dead," 90, and Richard L. Bushman, *Joseph Smith: Rough Stone Rolling* (New York: Knopf, 2005), 422.

82. Smith preached, "We should build our house to his name that we might be Baptized for the Dead": *WJS*, 62.

83. On the uses of the font, see Jonathan Stapley and Kristine Wright, "'They Shall Be Made Whole': A History of Baptism for Health," *Journal of Mormon History* 34:4 (fall 2008): 69–112.

84. Brown, "Early Mormon Adoption Theology," 35–36.

85. Kim Östman, *The Introduction of Mormonism to Finnish Society, 1840–1900* (Åbo: Åbo Akademi University Press, 2010), 132.

86. *WJS*, 74, 77.

87. Thus, for example, Smith's followers called him "the Prophet and our Savior" at the Young and Richards Family Meeting; Minutes, January 8, 1845, *SelCol* 1:18, 2. See also John Hardy, comp., *A Collection of Sacred Hymns* (Boston: Dow and Jackson, 1843), 101. Brown, "Early Mormon Adoption Theology," 36, 44–49, and Douglas Davies, *Joseph Smith, Jesus, and Satanic Opposition* (Surrey, England: Ashgate, 2010), 134–35, also discuss secondary saviors.

88. *WJS*, 368.

89. Samuel M. Brown, "The Prophet Elias Puzzle," *Dialogue* 39:3 (fall 2006): 7–10.

90. "Special Meeting," *T&S* 5:16 (September 2, 1844): 638.

91. Eugene England, ed., "George Laub's Nauvoo Journal," *BYU Studies* 18:2 (winter 1978): 174; compare *WWJ* 2:388 and *WJS*, 365–69.

92. Douglas Davies, *The Mormon Culture of Salvation* (Aldershot, England: Ashgate, 2000), 146–47.

93. "Letter from Joseph Smith," *T&S* 3:23 (October 1, 1842): 935; compare *D&C* 128. See also *WWJ* 2:361–64, 2:386, 3:130–37.

94. Thomas F. O'Dea, *The Mormons* (Chicago: University of Chicago Press, 1957), 57.

95. *WJS*, 352–53.

96. See, e.g., *M&A* 1:1 (October 1834): 13.

97. *FWR*, 185; compare *WWJ* 1:118.

98. *JSR*, 320 [*D&C* 128:12].

99. *JSR*, 320 [*D&C* 128:13]. The original reads "simile of the grave."

100. Catherine Albanese, *A Republic of Mind and Spirit: A Cultural History of American Metaphysical Religion* (New Haven: Yale University Press, 2007), and Stephen Stein, *The Shaker Experience in America* (New Haven: Yale University Press, 1994).

101. "Speech," *T&S* 6:1 (July 1, 1845): 953–56.

102. Keith Thomas, *Religion and the Decline of Magic* (New York: Oxford University Press, 1997), and Eamon Duffy, *The Stripping of the Altars:*

Traditional Religion in England, 1400–1580 (New Haven: Yale University Press, 2002). On one of the rare sects practicing baptism for the dead, see William Knecht, "Mysteries of the Kingdom: More or Less," *BYU Studies* 5:3–4 (spring-summer 1964): 231–40.

103. Arthur O. Lovejoy, *The Great Chain of Being: A Study of the History of an Idea,* 1933 William James Lectures (Cambridge, Mass.: Harvard University Press, 1948). This section summarizes and abridges Samuel M. Brown, "The Early Mormon Chain of Belonging," *Dialogue* 44:1 (spring 2011): 1–52.

104. Alexander Pope, *An Essay on Man: in Four Epistles to Henry St. John, Lord Bolingbroke* (Troy, N.Y.: W. & H. Merriam, 1844), 11, 24 (discussion in Herbert Leventhal, *In the Shadow of the Enlightenment: Occultism and Renaissance Science in Eighteenth-century America* [New York: New York University Press, 1976], 219), and Agnes Marie Sibley, *Pope's Prestige in America, 1725–1835* (New York: King's Crown Press, 1949). See also "The Gathering," *T&S* 5:2 (January 15, 1844): 407.

105. On the associations between Smith's Egyptian project and the Chain of Being, see Brown, "Chain of Belonging," 12–19. Some evidence suggests that early Latter-day Saints associated the papyri directly with Jacob's Ladder, the biblical inflection of the Chain of Being: Brian Hauglid, *A Textual History of the Book of Abraham: Manuscripts and Editions* (Provo, Utah: Neal A. Maxwell Institute for Religious Scholarship, Brigham Young University, 2010), 4, 216 (and n27), with corroboration in Henry Caswall, *The City of the Mormons; or, Three Days at Nauvoo, in 1842* (London: J. G. & F. Rivington, 1842), 23.

106. See, e.g., Alma 11:42–45, 40:1–26; 1 Nephi 15:32–36.

107. "A Vision," *EMS* 1:2 (July 1832): 2–3 [*D&C* 76].

108. *JSR,* 186. Dick referred to the Chain as "the economy of the universe" in a passage reprinted by Mormons as "Philosophy of Religion," *M&A* 3:5 (February 1837): 462. Though later applied to dispensationalism, "economy," from the Greek *oikonomia,* "rules of the household," described God's order for the universe.

109. "History of Joseph Smith," *T&S* 5:14 (August 1, 1844): 592, and *EMS* 2:23 (August 1834): 179.

110. Michael Walzer, *The Revolution of the Saints: A Study in the Origins of Radical Politics* (Cambridge, Mass.: Harvard University Press, 1965), 156–57.

111. *JSPR1,* 297 [*D&C* 88:37].

112. *JSPR1,* 299 [*D&C* 88:51–61]; compare Matthew 20:1–16.

113. Grant Underwood, *The Millenarian World of Early Mormonism* (Urbana: University of Illinois Press, 1993), 53–54. There are occasional counterexamples, but Underwood's generalization of early Mormons as ignoring the formally tripartite heaven is largely correct. See Orson Hyde, "A Prophetic Warning," *M&A* 2:10 (July 1836), 346, as one example among many.

114. George D. Smith, ed., *An Intimate Chronicle: The Journals of William Clayton* (Salt Lake City: Signature Books, 1995), 101–2, May 16, 1843 [*D&C* 131:1–4].

115. Michael Hicks, "Joseph Smith, W. W. Phelps, and the Poetic Paraphrase of 'The Vision,'" *Journal of Mormon History* 20:2 (fall 1994): 63–84.

116. [William Phelps for Joseph Smith], "The Answer," *T&S* 4:6 (February 1, 1843): 85.

117. *WJS*, 381.
118. Brigham Young, Dream, February 17, 1847, CHL.
119. *WJS*, 9.
120. "Minutes of a Conference," *T&S* 2:23 (October 1, 1841): 577.
121. Joseph Smith, Revelation of July 27, 1842, *SelCol* 1:19.
122. Lovejoy, *Chain of Being*, 76, 232–35; Phelps, "Despise Not Prophesyings," *T&S* 2:7 (February 1, 1841): 299.
123. *WJS*, 40.
124. *WWJ* 3:131.
125. Cooper, *Covenant Organization*, 138.
126. Andrew Ehat, "'They Might Have Known That He Was Not a Fallen Prophet'—The Nauvoo Journal of Joseph Fielding," *BYU Studies* 18:2 (winter 1979): 154.
127. Cooper, *Covenant Organization*, 171.
128. Phelps wrote to his wife that "instead of saving myself only I must labor faithfully to save others that I may obtain a crown of many stars." Bruce Van Orden, "Writing to Zion: The William W. Phelps Kirtland Letters (1835–1836)," *BYU Studies* 33:3 (1993): 559, see also Sally Randall, letter of June 1, 1846, CHL.
129. Lovejoy, *Chain of Being*, chapter 9, and Lia Formigari, "Chain of Being," in *Dictionary of the History of Ideas*, ed. Philip Wiener, 4 vols. (New York: Scribner, 1973–74), 1:325–35.
130. *WWJ* 3:136.
131. *MS* 9 (January 15, 1847): 23–24.
132. Comparisons of this diagram to kabbalistic figures like Robert Fludd's Sephiroth (e.g., Lance Owens, "Joseph Smith and Kabbalah: The Occult Connection," *Dialogue* 27:3 [fall 1994]: 185–86) are unconvincing.
133. See Kathryn Daynes, *More Wives Than One: Transformation of the Mormon Marriage System, 1840–1910* (Urbana: University of Illinois Press, 2001); Compton, *Sacred Loneliness*; Louis J. Kern, *An Ordered Love: Sex Roles and Sexuality in Victorian Utopias—the Shakers, the Mormons, and the Oneida Community* (Chapel Hill: University of North Carolina Press, 1981); Lawrence Foster, *Women, Family, and Utopia: Communal Experiments of the Shakers, the Oneida Community, and the Mormons* (Syracuse: Syracuse University Press, 1992); B. Carmon Hardy, *Doing the Works of Abraham: Mormon Polygamy, Its Origin, Practice, and Demise* (Norman, Okla.: Arthur H. Clark, 2007), and Richard Van Wagoner, *Mormon Polygamy: A History*, 2d ed. (Salt Lake City: Signature Books, 1992).
134. For documentation of proto-polygamy among Smith's followers, see George Smith, *Nauvoo Polygamy: "...But We Called It Celestial Marriage"* (Salt Lake City: Signature Books, 2008), 241–354.
135. Sidney Ditzion, *Marriage, Morals, and Sex in America: A History of Ideas* (New York: Farrar, Straus and Giroux, 1975), 94, 99.
136. See, e.g., Laura Damon, "Notice," *Wasp* 1:20 (September 3, 1842): 3.
137. Karen Lystra, *Searching the Heart: Women, Men, and Romantic Love in the Nineteenth Century* (New York: Oxford University Press, 1992), esp. 229; compare Marsden, *Edwards*, 55, 326.
138. 1 Corinthians 7:9.

139. Erik R. Seeman, "'It Is Better to Marry Than to Burn': Anglo-American Attitudes Toward Celibacy, 1600–1800," *Journal of Family History* 24:4 (1999): 397–419.

140. *JSPR1*, 132–37 [*D&C* 49].

141. Matthew 22: 23–33; Mark 12:18–27; Luke 20:27–39.

142. *NewT*, 345–46.

143. There are rare exceptions, such as the Methodist James Rogers (1749–1807), who anticipated reunion with both of his dead wives in the after-life: Phyllis Mack, *Heart Religion in the British Enlightenment: Gender and Emotion in Early Methodism* (Cambridge: Cambridge University Press, 2008), 107–8. I thank Christopher Jones for this source.

144. Clarke, *New Testament*, 108.

145. William to Sally Phelps, September 16, 1835, CHL; *D&C* 132:16 (compare *HC* 6:442); "Remarks," *T&S* 6:20 (January 1, 1846): 1084; and "Celestial Marriage," *Seer* 1:3 (March 1853): 43.

146. *Nauvoo Neighbor* 2 (June 17, 19, 1844).

147. *NewT*, 503; 1 Corinthians 7: esp. 29.

148. *WWJ* 2:136.

149. On other sexual experiments, see Foster, *Communal Experiments*, esp. 126–28, 165, and Van Wagoner, *Mormon Polygamy*, esp. 42–43. Kern, *Ordered Love*, 140, is an extreme example of a tendency to see polygamy as primarily about sex. Davies correctly rejects this view in his *Culture of Salvation*, 100. Bushman has also argued that Smith "did not lust for women so much as he lusted for kin": *Rough Stone*, 440.

150. Schantz, *Culture of Death*, esp. 62–63.

151. Buck, *Theological Dictionary*, 341.

152. On Alger, see Compton, *Sacred Loneliness*, 25–42.

153. For discussion of the Articles, see Van Wagoner, *Mormon Polygamy*, 6.

154. "On Marriage," *T&S* 3:23 (October 1, 1842): 939. On Bennett's scandal, see Andrew F. Smith, *The Saintly Scoundrel: The Life and Times of Dr. John Cook Bennett* (Urbana: University of Illinois Press, 1997), 81–90.

155. *JSPJ1*, 146.

156. Martha Sonntag Bradley and Mary Brown Firmage Woodward, *4 Zinas: A Story of Mothers and Daughters on the Mormon Frontier* (Salt Lake City: Signature Books, 2000), 66; William to Sally Phelps, May 26, 1835, HBLL.

157. William to Sally Phelps, September 16, 1835, HBLL.

158. William Phelps, "Letter No. 8," *M&A* 1:9 (June 1835): 130.

159. See Kathleen Flake, "Making Sense of LDS Sealings: A Liturgical Analysis," presentation at the meeting of the Mormon History Association, Springfield, Ill., May 2009.

160. William G. Hartley, "Newel and Lydia Bailey Knight's Kirtland Love Story and Historic Wedding," *BYU Studies* 39:4 (2000): 6–22, and M. Scott Bradshaw, "Joseph Smith's Performance of Marriages in Ohio," *BYU Studies* 39:4 (2000): 23–69.

161. *JSPJ1*, 110, and Smith, *Sacred Hymns*, 81–82.

162. Buck, *Theological Dictionary*, 341, and McDannell and Lang, *Heaven*, 230–32.

163. Samuel M. Brown, "Joseph (Smith) in Egypt: Babel, Hieroglyphs, and the Pure Language of Eden," *Church History* 78:1 (March 2009): 57–58.

164. Hartley, "Historic Wedding," 18. The argument of Bradshaw, "Marriages," 31–32, that the union was not bigamous appears incorrect and is largely irrelevant since the participants believed it was bigamy.

165. *JSPJ1*, 166.

166. Joseph Smith, Revelation of July 27, 1842, *SelCol* 1:19.

167. Compton, *Sacred Loneliness*, 348–49.

168. Davies, *Culture of Salvation*, 155.

169. *WJS*, 205; compare Andrew Ehat, "Joseph Smith's Introduction of Temple Ordinances and the 1844 Mormon Succession Question" (M.A. thesis, Brigham Young University, 1982), 56.

170. *D&C* 132:4.

171. *WJS*, 239–40.

172. Smith, *Intimate Chronicle*, 102.

173. Cook, *Nauvoo Marriages*, xix.

174. Kingsbury, "Diary," Special Collections, Marriott Library, University of Utah, Salt Lake City, 14–15; compare *EPB*, 216.

175. Kingsbury, "Diary," 21–22.

176. Prince, *Power*, 155–72, Compare *WWJ* 2:340–41.

177. "Celestial Marriage," *Seer* 1 (February 1853): 31–32, reprinted in *MS* 15:14 (April 2, 1853): 214–15.

178. Foster, *Communal Experiments*, 151. John C. Bennett made a similar argument: Ehat, "Mormon Succession," 63.

179. Ehat, "Mormon Succession," 64–65; Hyrum Smith, Address, April 8, 1844, Thomas Bullock Report, CHL; and Brigham Young, Address, October 8, 1866, CHL.

180. See, e.g., Adam Clarke, *The Holy Bible Containing the Old and New Testaments*, 6 vols. (New York: T. Mason and G. Lane, 1837), 1:60, and Clarke, *New Testament*, 90–91.

181. See, e.g., Clarke, *Holy Bible*, 1:43–44.

182. Jacob 2: esp. 30.

183. *D&C* 132:37; compare Genesis 16. Kern, *Ordered Love*, 142, suggested that Smith had this story on his mind personally, as more than half of his first wife's children died in childhood, including the first three stillborn. Abraham had his Hagar to assure offspring, and so would the Latter-day Saints. Though such a claim seems somewhat far-fetched, it is an interesting parallel.

184. Buck, *Theological Dictionary*, 7–8, 19–20, 108, 288–89, 419, 457–58. See also Clarke, *Holy Bible*, 1:60, 791, 2:319, and Clarke, *New Testament*, 27.

185. Bennett, *History of the Saints*, 304–6, and Samuel M. Brown, "Joseph Smith and Charles Buck: Enthusiasm, Common Sense, and the Living Witness of History," presentation at the meeting of the Mormon History Association, Sacramento, Calif., May 2008.

186. Spencer Fluhman, "Anti-Mormonism and the Making of American Religion in Antebellum America" (Ph.D. diss., University of Wisconsin, 2006), 151.

187. Foster, *Communal Experiments*, 131, is incorrect on this point.

188. Brigham Young followed this pattern in his organization of the 1846–1847 Mormon migration to the Rocky Mountains, merging the metaphor of the Army of Israel with the heaven family.

189. Paul Johnson and Sean Wilentz, *The Kingdom of Matthias* (New York: Oxford University Press, 1994), 9–10; Ditzion, *Marriage*, 94, 99.

190. Dean C. Jessee, *Personal Writings of Joseph Smith*, rev. ed. (Salt Lake City: Deseret Book, 2002), 517.

191. McDannell and Lang, *Heaven*, 321.

192. Minutes of Church General Conference, October 8, 1845, Nauvoo, Illinois, *SelCol* 1:18, 8.

193. See, e.g., Matthew 10:34–39; Luke 14: 26–27. The Greek term used in Luke, *miseo*, is correctly translated as "hate." On early Christianity, see, e.g., Peter R. L. Brown, *The Body and Society: Men, Women, and Sexual Renunciation in Early Christianity* (New York: Columbia University Press, 1988), 89. On Smith, see his letter to William Phelps, July 31, 1832, *SelCol* 1:20.

194. Whitney Cross, *The Burned-over District: The Social and Intellectual History of Enthusiastic Religion in Western New York, 1800–1850* (Ithaca: Cornell University Press, 1950), 338.

195. Richard S. Van Wagoner and Steven Walker, "The Joseph/Hyrum Smith Funeral Sermon," *BYU Studies* 23:1 (winter 1983): 13. I deleted a duplicate "of" for readability.

196. Heber Kimball and Orson Hyde are best known. Others included Orson Pratt, William Law, and John Taylor. See Bushman, *Rough Stone*, 439.

197. Foster, *Communal Experiments*, 148–49, has proposed "proxy husband" as a replacement for "polyandry," but that term is also deficient. I prefer "dual wives" to describe the status of these women.

198. Van Wagoner, *Mormon Polygamy*, 41–42, describes the trope of proposals to dual wives as an Abrahamic test, probably the most common Mormon account of this practice.

199. First Great Awakening revivalists discussed the need to separate from legally married unconverted spouses: Douglas L. Winiarski, "Jonathan Edwards, Enthusiast? Radical Revivalism and the Great Awakening in the Connecticut Valley," *Church History* 74:4 (December 2005): 734.

200. Compton, *Sacred Loneliness*, 71–113. See also Bradford and Woodward, 4 *Zinas*, 107–14, 132–34, 197–202.

201. Van Wagoner, *Mormon Polygamy*, 45.

202. Van Wagoner and Walker, *A Book of Mormons*, 417, reprinting an interview in *New York World*, dated November 19, 1869.

203. See, e.g., Cooper, *Covenant Organization*, 138, and Smith, *Intimate Chronicle*, 226.

204. *WJS*, 239.

205. *WJS*, 244.

206. *JSPR1*, 274–89 [*D&C* 84].

207. *WJS*, 238–42.

208. Smith, *Intimate Chronicle*, 115–16. Higbee's sons were budding dissidents—their dissent may have directed Smith's reassuring comments.

209. See, e.g., the discussions Young led at the Young and Richards Family Meeting on January 8, 1845: General Church Minutes, *SelCol* 1:18.

210. See James B. Allen, *Trials of Discipleship: The Story of William Clayton, a Mormon* (Urbana: University of Illinois Press, 1987), 154, 199; *WWJ* 2:340; and Van Wagoner, *Mormon Polygamy*, 39.

211. Kern, *Ordered Love*, 144.
212. Compton, *Sacred Loneliness*, 11, 33, 81; and Bushman, *Rough Stone*, 445. Critics were aware of the doctrine before Smith's death: "Buckeye's Lamentation for Want of More Wives," *The Warsaw Message* 1:47 (February 7, 1844): 1.
213. Van Wagoner, *Mormon Polygamy*, 53, Compton, *Sacred Loneliness*, 348–51, 463, 497–501, and Foster, *Communal Experiments*, 137.
214. Van Wagoner and Walker, "Funeral Sermon," 11.
215. Parley Pratt, "Celestial Family Organization," *MS* 5:12 (May 1845): 193.

Chapter 9

1. "Come to Me," *T&S* 6:1 (January 15, 1845): 783.
2. See Samuel M. Brown, "William Phelps's 'Paracletes': An Early Witness to Joseph Smith's Divine Anthropology," *International Journal of Mormon Studies* 2:1 (spring 2009), 62–81. On *parakletos*, a controversial Johannine term understood to refer to either Jesus or the Holy Ghost, see Gerhard Kittel, *Theological Dictionary of the New Testament*, 10 vols. (Grand Rapids, Mich.: Eerdmans, 1964), 5:800–14. See also Charles Buck, *Theological Dictionary* (Philadelphia: Edwin T. Scott, 1823), 425.
3. Phelps used Joshua Seixas's Sephardic transliteration scheme for the Hebrew letters. The prefix *mil* probably refers to the seven angels of God (tied to the seven millennia of sacred history in popular tradition; see Revelation 5), on the basis of the Olive Leaf revelation (*D&C* 88). The Hebrew root for king, **MLK*, is less likely.
4. Brown, "Paracletes," 72.
5. Brown, "Paracletes," 63.
6. On *Ahman*, see *WJS*, 64, chapter 5 herein, and *D&C* 95:17 (June 1, 1833), and 78:20 (March 1832).
7. Terryl Givens, *When Souls Had Wings: Pre-mortal Existence in Western Thought* (New York: Oxford University Press, 2009), esp. 212–20.
8. *NewT*, 88–89 [Moses 2:30–33:17].
9. *JSPR1*, 134–35 [*D&C* 49:17].
10. *NewT*, 90 [Moses 4:1–4].
11. *NewT*, 83–84, 88 [Moses 1:6, 13, 16, and 2:27].
12. See Lecture 7 of the Lectures on Faith, in *Joseph Smith Papers, Revelations and Translations*, vol. 2, *Published Revelations*, ed. Robin Jensen et al. (Salt Lake City: Church Historian's Press, 2011), 378–80. On recasting Jesus, see Stephen Prothero, *American Jesus: How the Son of God Became a National Icon* (New York: Farrar, Straus and Giroux, 2003).
13. On others who saw human pre-existence as an *imitatio Christi*, see Givens, *Souls*, 52, 87, 267–68.
14. *JSR*, 238 [*D&C* 93:21–23, 29–30].
15. "Songs of Zion," *EMS* 1:12 (May 1833): 96; compare the glossalalic hymn dated February 27, 1833: *JSPR1*, 508–11. I concur with Michael Hicks, *Mormonism and Music: A History* (Urbana: University of Illinois Press, 2003), 36, that Phelps likely edited the hymn for publication, though Frederick G. Williams may have played a role. A probably Nauvoo-era broadside ("Mysteries of God," n.d., n.p., HBLL) suggests Rigdon as the

author, though collaborative authorship seems likely. I thank David Golding for this source.

16. Abraham 5:7–8.

17. William Phelps, "Letter No. 8," *M&A* 1:9 (June 1835): 130.

18. Abraham 3:21–28. Smith had been emphasizing the devil's minions in the pre-existent life since at least 1830: *D&C* 29:36. On the fallen angel see, e.g., John Reynolds, *Inquiries Concerning the State and Economy of the Angelical Worlds* (London: John Clark, 1723), 9–25.

19. *WJS*, 9, 33, 60, Henry Perkins, "The Mormons," *State Gazette* [Trenton], July 22, 1840, and J. B. Turner, *Mormonism in All Ages: or the Rise, Progress, and Causes of Mormonism* (New York: Platt & Peters, 1842), 241–42.

20. John Mason Good, *The Book of Nature* (New York: J. & J. Harper, 1828), 27.

21. Kevin Barney, "Joseph Smith's Emendation of Genesis 1:1," *Dialogue* 30:4 (winter 1997): 103–35. Mormons, following Seixas, transliterated the word *baurau*. For a contemporary example of another use of *BR'* in this sense, see Good, *Book of Nature*, 28.

22. While it is certainly possible that Smith had been exposed to some version of Lucretius's argument, perhaps through John Mason Good's translation of *The Nature of Things*, it seems more likely that he was responding to the same concepts as Lucretius rather than proposing an explicit rebuttal.

23. "Extract from a New Work Just Published," *T&S* 5:7 (April 1, 1844): 487.

24. Givens, *Souls*. See also Buck, *Theological Dictionary*, 7–8, 122, 173, 421–22, 445, 481.

25. Adam Clarke, *The Holy Bible Containing the Old and New Testaments*, 6 vols. (New York: T. Mason and G. Lane, 1837), 3:168, described these morning stars as "intelligent beings" or the "angelic host."

26. See, e.g., Jeremiah 1:5; Ephesians 1:4; and 1 Peter 1:20: Brown, "Paracletes," 75; compare Emma Smith, *A Collection of Sacred Hymns, for the Church of Jesus Christ of Latter Day Saints* (Kirtland, Ohio: F. G. Williams, 1835), 95–96.

27. On Hebrew angels, see Susan Garrett, *No Ordinary Angel: Celestial Spirits and Christian Claims about Jesus* (New Haven: Yale University Press, 2008).

28. On the names of angelic orders in the New Testament, see Ephesians 3:10, 6:12, and Colossians 1:16; see also Dick, *Future State*, 210, 231, 258, and Peter Marshall and Alexandra Walsham, "Migrations of Angels in the Early Modern World," in *Angels in the Early Modern World*, ed. Peter Marshall and Alexandra Walsham (Cambridge: Cambridge University Press, 2006), 12.

29. In Genesis 28:11–19 Jacob sees a ladder on which angels move between heaven and earth, an image central to the temporal Chain of Being: Lovejoy, *Chain of Being*, 205, 248.

30. On Christ's transfiguration, see Matthew 17:1–9, Mark 9:2–8, Luke 9:28–36. On the 1836 recapitulation, see *JSR*, 279–80 [*D&C* 110].

31. Givens, *Souls*, 14–16 and Segal, *Life after Death*, 374.

32. On medieval angelology, see David Keck, *Angels and Angelology in the Middle Ages* (New York: Oxford University Press, 1998).

33. Philip M. Soergel, "Luther on the Angels," in Marshall and Walsham, *Angels in the Early Modern World*, 64–82.

34. Joad Raymond, "'With the Tongues of Angels': Angelic Conversations in Paradise Lost and Seventeenth Century England," in Marshall and Walsham, *Angels in the Early Modern World*, 256–81. See use of Milton in Buck, *Theological Dictionary*, 23.

35. Reynolds, *Angelical Worlds*, esp. 171–76.

36. Increase Mather, *Angelographia: or, A Discourse Concerning the Nature and Power of the Holy Angels* (Boston: Green and Allen, 1696). On Edwards, see George M. Marsden, *Jonathan Edwards: A Life* (New Haven: Yale University Press, 2004).

37. See the essays in Marshall and Walsham, *Angels in the Early Modern World*.

38. See, e.g., Reynolds, *Angelical Worlds*, 131.

39. David Tappan strongly endorsed the angelic chain in exegesis of Ephesians 3:8–10: *Sermons on Important Subjects by the Late Rev. David Tappan* (Boston: W. Hilliard and Lincoln & Edmands, 1807), 246–68, esp. 259–62. See also Reynolds, *Angelical Worlds*, 100. On democratic power, see Elizabeth Reis, "Otherworldly Visions: Angels, Devils and Gender in Puritan New England," in Marshall and Walsham, *Angels in the Early Modern World*, 294–95.

40. See, e.g., Reis, "Otherworldly Visions," 295–96.

41. Buck, *Theological Dictionary*, 21–23.

42. Ann Kirschner, "'Tending to Edify, Astonish, and Instruct': Published Narratives of Spiritual Dreams and Visions in the Early Republic," *Early American Studies* 1:1 (spring 2003): 198–229. See also R. C. Finucane, *Ghosts: Appearances of the Dead and Cultural Transformation* (Amherst, N.Y.: Prometheus Books, 1996).

43. Swedenborg, *Concerning Heaven and its Wonders, and Concerning Hell* [1758] (Boston: Otis Clapp, 1837), 135–37, 9–10, 20–21, and Swedenborg, *Concerning the Earths in our Solar System* [1758] (Boston: Otis Clapp, 1839), 46, with discussion in Colleen McDannell and Bernhard Lang, *Heaven: A History*, 2d ed. (New Haven: Yale University Press, 2001), 232.

44. Turner, *Mormonism*, 90.

45. Reis, "Otherworldly Visions."

46. See, e.g., Nancy Towle, *Vicissitudes Illustrated in the Experience of Nancy Towle, in Europe and America*, 2d ed. (Portsmouth, N.H.: John Caldwell, 1833), 137.

47. On Luther and Calvin, see Soergel, "Luther on the Angels." See also Towle, *Vicissitudes*, 54.

48. See the emblematic poetry of Smith, *Sacred Hymns*, 58, 60, 63.

49. Buck, *Theological Dictionary*, 21–23.

50. See, e.g., Scott Stephan, *Redeeming the Southern Family: Evangelical Women and Domestic Devotion in the Antebellum South* (Athens: University of Georgia Press, 2008), 213.

51. Alexander Baugh, "Parting the Veil: Joseph Smith's Seventy-six Documented Visionary Experiences," in *Opening the Heavens: Accounts of Divine Manifestations, 1820–1844*, ed. John W. Welch (Salt Lake City: Deseret Book, 2004), 301–302.

52. JSPR1, 264–65; compare JD 2:342.

53. NewT, 429 [Luke 20:36]; Smith substituted "children" for the "sons" of the KJV.

54. Mark S. Schantz, *Awaiting the Heavenly Country: The Civil War and America's Culture of Death* (Ithaca: Cornell University Press, 2008), 62, and Mark L. Staker, *Hearken O Ye People: The Historical Setting of Joseph Smith's Ohio Revelations* (Salt Lake City: Kofford Books, 2009), 440.

55. Though Smith reported an encounter with Raphael (*JSR*, 321–22 [*D&C* 128]), he never offered alternative identities for either Raphael or the fourth of the standard archangels, Uriel. See also *JSR*, 74.

56. *WJS*, 39; GAEL, 1, 6; Orson Pratt, "Zion of Enoch," *Seer* 2:5 (May 1854): 262; *D&C* 88:112; *D&C* 27:11; George D. Smith, ed., *An Intimate Chronicle: The Journals of William Clayton* (Salt Lake City: Signature Books, 1995), 517–18, and *WJS*, 8–12.

57. *WJS*, 10.

58. *WJS*, 9; compare *NewT*, 202, 278.

59. *WJS*, 40; compare Hebrews 11:4. Paul was generally believed to be the author of Hebrews at the time.

60. *WJS*, 40.

61. *WJS*, 41.

62. See discussion in Samuel M. Brown, "Joseph Smith and Charles Buck: Enthusiasm, Common Sense, and the Living Witness of History," presentation at the meeting of the Mormon History Association, Sacramento, Calif., May 2008.

63. *WJS*, 6.

64. *WJS*, 44.

65. *WJS*, 61.

66. *WJS*, 117.

67. *WJS*, 9.

68. *WJS*, 240, 253.

69. Phelps, "Letter No. 8," and Smith, *Sacred Hymns*, 77.

70. Sidney Rigdon, "Faith of the Church," *M&A* 1:11 (August 1835): 165.

71. Donald G. Godfrey and Kenneth W. Godfrey, *The Diaries of Charles Ora Card: The Utah Years, 1871–1886* (Provo, Utah: Religious Studies Center, Brigham Young University, 2006), 386.

72. *WJS*, 36–37; see also *LB*, 792. Smith may have been following the terminology of the Irvingites, a sect Mormons knew well as a competitor in Britain and Canada, for whom "angel" referred to a hierarch: Buck, *Theological Dictionary*, 21.

73. Reynolds, *Angelical Worlds*, 47.

74. *NewT*, 535.

75. *WJS*, 14.

76. *WJS*, 77.

77. "Minutes of a Special Conference," *T&S* 4:21 (September 15, 1843): 331. Smith's location of this theme in New Testament texts, particularly Hebrews 12, is recorded in another account of the sermon: *WJS*, 255. In the phrase of another recorder of the sermon, "Angels have advanced higher in knowledge & power than spirits": *WJS*, 254.

78. Swedenborg, *Heaven and Hell*, 142, 175–78, 277–81.

79. "The Angels," *T&S* 6:4 (March 1, 1845): 823–24.

80. *WJS*, 77.

81. McDannell and Lang, *Heaven*, 58.

82. *JSR*, 324 [*D&C* 132:16]; compare *WJS*, 232.

83. Samuel Bent et al., "The High Council of the Church of Jesus Christ to the Saints of Nauvoo," *T&S* 3: 8 (February 15, 1842): 700.

84. 1 Corinthians 6:2–3; compare *WJS*, 13 and *JD* 1:128.

85. *JD* 2:342–43, with discussion in Samuel M. Brown, "Joseph (Smith) in Egypt: Babel, Hieroglyphs, and the Pure Language of Eden," *Church History* 78:1 (March 2009): 53.

86. *WJS*, 344, 349.

87. John 5:19–20.

88. *WJS*, 382–83.

89. Parley P. Pratt, *An Answer to Mr. William Hewitt's Tract Against the Latter-day Saints* (Manchester, England: W. R. Thomas, 1840), 9. See Benjamin Park, "Salvation Through a Tabernacle: Joseph Smith, Parley P. Pratt, and Early Mormon Theologies of Embodiment," *Dialogue* 43:2 (summer 2010): 18–19, on Pratt's views.

90. Backman, "Truman Coe," 354. Coe may have been responding to Warren Cowdery, "I am the way, the truth, and the life," *M&A* 2:5 (February 5, 1836): 265. Grant Underwood, "A 'Communities of Discourse' Approach to Early LDS Thought," in *Discourses of Mormon Theology: Philosophical and Theological Possibilities*, ed. James M. McLaughlan and Loyd Ericson (Salt Lake City: Kofford Books, 2007), 27–38, misapprehends early Mormon embodiment beliefs.

91. Smith, ed., *Intimate Chronicle*, 516.

92. Not the Prophet, S.T.P., "To the Editor," *T&S* 5:8 (April 15, 1844): 503.

93. Henry Caswall, *The City of the Mormons; or, Three Days at Nauvoo, in 1842* (London: J. G. & F. Rivington, 1842), 11, 38–39. The Pratt brothers particularly derided the Protestant God as worthy of scorn.

94. "Poetry," *T&S* 6:2 (February 1, 1845): 799, with simultaneous publication in the Nauvoo *Neighbor*. The author of the parody remains unknown: Michael Hicks, "Poetic Borrowing in Early Mormonism," *Dialogue* 18:1 (spring 1985): 136–37.

95. *WJS*, 382.

96. See, e.g., Buck, *Theological Dictionary*, 218–19. The gendering of the Holy Ghost also derives from Mormon beliefs about the Holy Ghost's integration into the Chain of Belonging as an individual.

97. Swedenborg, *Solar System*, 93.

98. Thomas E. Jenkins, *The Character of God: Recovering the Lost Literary Power of American Protestantism* (New York: Oxford University Press, 1997), 118–19, 125–27. 129–30.

99. *JSPR1*, 249 [*D&C* 76:58].

100. *JSPR1*, 292–99, 306–7 [*D&C* 88: esp. 7–20, 28–29, 37, 42–61, 107]; compare Matthew 20:1–16.

101. Parley Pratt, *A Voice of Warning and Instruction to All People* (New York: W. Sandford, 1837), 145.

102. A probably ghostwritten early attack on Campbellites decried Campbellite leaders for "exalting themselves to the stations of gods": Joseph Smith [Sidney Rigdon?], "Dear Brother," *EMS* 2:24 (September 1834): 192.

103. Parley P. Pratt, *Mormonism Unveiled: Zion's Watchman Unmasked, and Its Editor, Mr. L. R. Sunderland, Exposed; Truth Vindicated; The Devil Mad, and*

Priestcraft in Danger! (New York City: for the author, 1838), 26–27; compare La Roy Sunderland, *Mormonism Exposed and Refuted* (New York: Piercy & Reed, 1838), 35.

104. Eliza R. Snow (Smith), *Biography and Family Record of Lorenzo Snow: One of the Twelve Apostles of the Church of Jesus Christ of Latter-day Saints* (Salt Lake City: Deseret News, 1884), 10, 46. The original text of this blessing is not extant (contrast *EPB*, 95). Snow may have been following Orson Pratt, whose 1844 "Mormon Creed" asked "What is his [humanity's] final destiny? To be like God. What has God been? Like man": Orson Pratt, *Prophetical Almanac for 1845* (New York: by the author, 1845), 5.

105. *WJS*, 247.

106. Matthew 5:48.

107. *WJS*, 382. As one example among many, an eighteenth-century evangelical layperson explained the paradox of Christ's Incarnation as "Shewing a God man to be necessary to be a fact—and yet to be Equal with God." Douglas L. Winiarski, "Jonathan Edwards, Enthusiast? Radical Revivalism and the Great Awakening in the Connecticut Valley," *Church History* 74:4 (December 2005): 738.

108. "The Living God," *T&S* 6:3 (February 15, 1845): 809.

109. William Phelps, "The Last Days," *EMS* 1:9 (February 1833): 67.

110. William Phelps, "Letter No. III," *M&A* 1: 4 (January 1835): 51.

111. Phelps, "Letter No. 8."

112. See Arthur O. Lovejoy, *The Great Chain of Being: A Study of the History of an Idea*, 1933 William James Lectures (Cambridge, Mass.: Harvard University Press, 1948), 242–87, esp. 246–48, 262–63.

113. *WJS*, 341, 345, 350, 358.

114. Eugene England, ed., "George Laub's Nauvoo Journal," *BYU Studies* 18:2 (winter 1978): 173; compare *WJS*, 362, and [Parley P. Pratt], "Materiality," *Prophet* 1:52 (May 24, 1845): 2.

115. "Conference Minutes," *T&S* 5:15 (August 15, 1844): 614; compare *WJS*, 350.

116. Brown, "Paracletes."

117. *WJS*, 212.

118. *WJS*, 369.

119. See Reynolds, *Angelical Worlds*, 126, 138.

120. *WJS*, 381.

121. Buck, *Theological Dictionary*, 78, 68, 460, 590.

122. Buck, *Theological Dictionary*, 48–49.

123. "Living God," 808. Compare Genesis 3:5, 22.

124. On divine councils, see Givens, *Souls*, 12–17, and Mark Smith, *The Early History of God: Yahweh and the Other Deities in Ancient Israel* (Grand Rapids, Mich.: Eerdmans, 2002).

125. Abraham 3:21–23, 4:1–22.

126. Psalm 82:1–7, and John 10:34–35.

127. Adam Clarke, *The New Testament of our Lord and Saviour Jesus Christ* (Philadelphia: Thomas Cowperthwait and Co., 1838), 293.

128. Clarke, *Holy Bible*, 3:479–80.

129. "Living God," 809.

130. Parley P. Pratt, *An Appeal to the Inhabitants of the State of New York: Letter to Queen Victoria (Reprinted from the tenth European Edition); the Fountain of Knowledge, Immortality of the Body, and Intelligence and Affection* (Nauvoo: John Taylor, 1844), 16.

131. "Extract," *T&S* 5:7 (April 1, 1844): 487.

132. William Harris, *Mormonism Portrayed* (Warsaw, Ill.: Sharp & Gamble, 1841), 20–23; see also John C. Bennett, *The History of the Saints; or, An Expose of Joe Smith and Mormonism* (Boston: Leland and Whiting, 1842), 130.

133. Turner, *Mormonism*, 241–42.

134. Caswall, *City of the Mormons*, 34.

135. Catherine Albanese, *A Republic of Mind and Spirit: A Cultural History of American Metaphysical Religion* (New Haven: Yale University Press, 2007), 312.

136. Albanese, *Mind and Spirit*, 229.

137. *WJS*, 239.

138. Smith revised "gods" to "God" in *NewT* 696–97 [Exodus 22:28]. See also *JSPR1*, 249 [D&C 76:54–59] and *JSPR1*, 307 [D&C 88:107].

139. Dean Jessee and Jack Welch, "Revelations in Context," *BYU Studies* 39:3 (2000): 138 [D&C 121:28–30].

140. Smith recalled in 1844 that he had discussed the issue with Joshua Seixas, presumably in 1836: *WJS*, 379. Later repetitions of this claim are in Parley Pratt's editorial in *MS* 3:4 (August 1, 1842): 71, and "Living God," 809.

141. Abraham 4:1–22; compare *NewT*, 86–89 [Moses 2], and GAEL, 4–5. Chapter 4 of the Book of Abraham was probably written in late 1841 or early 1842. Smith's March 1839 letter suggests that he had those themes in mind before 1842, but there is not certain evidence for an earlier date. I thank Bill Smith for insight on this topic.

142. Nonconfessional scholars generally see fragments of earlier polytheistic Canaanite or other Mesopotamian religions scattered throughout the received text of the Hebrew Bible. See, e.g., Smith, *History of God*.

143. See, e.g., Deuteronomy 10:17 and Joshua 22:22; compare *M&A* 1:8 (May 1835): 127.

144. "Living God," *T&S* 6:3 (February 15, 1845): 809.

145. *WJS*, 378; compare *HC* 6:476. In the New Translation Smith corrected the verse to a monotheistic reading: *NewT*, 567. On 2 Peter, see Brown, "Paracletes," 66n12.

146. "Living God," 808.

147. "Living God," 808.

148. *WJS*, 380–81, and Abraham 3:18.

149. Donald Q. Cannon, "The King Follett Discourse: Joseph Smith's Greatest Sermon in Historical Perspective," *BYU Studies* 18:2 (winter 1978), 188.

150. "Living God," 809.

151. Buck, *Theological Dictionary*, 408–9. The few who supported it did so as a description of Trinity: Clarke, *Holy Bible*, 1:25–26.

152. Franklin's "Articles of Belief and Acts of Religion" are discussed in I. Woodbridge Riley, *American Philosophy: The Early Schools* (New York: Dodd, Mead, 1907), 249–54.

153. Abraham 1:11.

154. Abraham 1:23–25, and GAEL, 3–4, 5, 10, 13. See also Brown, "Joseph (Smith) in Egypt," 60–61.

155. Abraham 4:27.

156. Phelps, "Letter No. 8"; compare 1 Corinthians 11:11.

157. *JSPR1*, 248–49 [*D&C* 76:56].

158. "Come to Me," *T&S* 6:1 (January 15, 1845): 783, with commentary by Brigham Young in Joseph G. Hovey, Reminiscences and Journal 1846–1856 (MS 1576 1, CHL), 38–39.

159. William Phelps, "The Answer," *T&S* 5:24 (January 1, 1845): 758, an exegesis of the proscription of matriolatry in Jeremiah 7:18.

160. Brown, "Paracletes," 76.

161. See Jill Mulvay Derr, "The Significance of 'O My Father' in the Personal Journey of Eliza R. Snow," *BYU Studies* 36:1 (1996–97): 84–138, and Jill Mulvay Derr and Karen Lynn Davidson, eds., *Eliza R. Snow: The Complete Poetry* (Provo, Utah: Brigham Young University Press; Salt Lake City: University of Utah Press, 2009), 312–14. By 1856, Snow called this poem "Invocation, or the Eternal Father and Mother." Eliza R. Snow, *Poems, Religious, Historical, and Political* (Liverpool: F. D. Richards, 1856), 1–2.

162. Schantz, *Culture of Death*, 110, quotes a representative memorial poem.

163. *T&S* 6:17 (November 15, 1845): 1039, Hicks, *Mormonism and Music*, 33–35.

164. Susa Young Gates, *History of the Young Ladies Mutual Improvement Association of the Church of Jesus Christ of Latter-day Saints from November 1869 to June 1910* (Salt Lake City: *Deseret News*, 1911), 15–16.

165. Orson Pratt, "Celestial Marriage," *Seer* 1 (October 1853): 159.

166. Ann Douglas, *The Feminization of American Culture* (New York: Knopf, 1977); see also Catherine A. Brekus, *Strangers and Pilgrims: Female Preaching in America, 1740–1845* (Chapel Hill: University of North Carolina Press, 1998).

167. Catherine Albanese, "Mormonism and the Male-female God: An Exploration in Active Mysticism," *Sunstone* 6:2 (March-April 1981): 55.

168. Albanese, *Mind and Spirit*, 185.

169. Linda P. Wilcox, "The Mormon Concept of a Mother in Heaven," in *Sisters in Spirit: Mormon Women in Historical and Cultural Perspectives*, ed. Maureen Ursenbach Beecher and Lavina Fielding Anderson (Urbana: University of Illinois Press, 1985), 65.

170. Josiah Priest, *The Anti-Universalist: Or History of the Fallen Angels of the Scriptures* (Albany, N.Y.: J. Munsell, 1839), 30.

171. One writer argued that Mormonism provided the idea to Transcendentalist Theodore Parker: Edward Tullidge, *The Women of Mormondom* (New York: Tullidge and Crandall, 1877), 188–89. See also Albanese, "Male-female God," 52–53.

172. Albanese, *Mind and Spirit*, 143.

173. As John Heeren et al., "The Mormon Concept of Mother in Heaven: A Sociological Account of Its Origins and Development," *Journal for the Scientific Study of Religion* 23:4 (December 1984): 396–411, have observed, the dyadic model of Albanese, "Male-female God" (as well as John Brooke, *The Refiner's Fire: The Making of Mormon Cosmology, 1644–1844* [Cambridge:

Cambridge University Press, 1994], 258), does not represent earliest Mormon belief on this point.

174. "Living God," 808, argues that "Jesus Christ had a father and mother of his spirit."

175. William Phipps, "The Case for a Married Jesus," *Dialogue* 7:4 (winter 1972): 44–49.

176. *WJS*, 200, 207.

177. William Phelps, "There Is No End," *Deseret News* 6:37 (November 19, 1859): 290.

Chapter 10

1. *HC* 6:555; compare "The Murder," *T&S* 5:13 (July 15, 1844): 585, and a similar phrase from 1838 in *HC* 3:227–28.

2. *HC* 6:555–56.

3. *HC* 6:549, 552; Ronald D. Dennis, ed., "The Martyrdom of Joseph Smith and His Brother Hyrum by Dan Jones," *BYU Studies* 24:1 (winter 1984): 84; Andrew Ehat, "Joseph Smith's Introduction of Temple Ordinances and the 1844 Mormon Succession Question" (M.A. thesis, Brigham Young University, 1982), 183.

4. Dennis, "Martyrdom," 85, 96.

5. D. Michael Quinn, "Joseph Smith III's 1844 Blessing and the Mormons of Utah," *Dialogue* 15:2 (summer 1982): 77; "Speech of Heber C. Kimball, Delivered June 1st, 1845," *T&S* 6:14 (August 1, 1845): 987; *HC* 7:120–21.

6. Murder and the sin against the Holy Ghost, a circumlocution for betrayal or apostasy, were the two sins that could negate salvational surety, as per *D&C* 132.

7. *WJS*, 258.

8. *HC* 6:549.

9. On the Masonic distress call, see "Murder," 585. Smith's use of the distress call is often seen as gamesmanship, but he might also have identified with the ancient widow's son as he died to protect the sacred name of God. I thank Kate Holbrook for this insight.

10. R. Laurence Moore, *Religious Outsiders and the Making of Americans* (New York: Oxford University Press, 1986), 25–47, and Nicole Kelley, "Philosophy as Training for Death: Reading the Ancient Christian Martyr Acts as Spiritual Exercises," *Church History* 75:4 (December 2006): 723–47.

11. Parley Pratt, "A History," *T&S* 1:8 (June 1840): 114.

12. Parley Pratt, *The Autobiography of Parley Parker Pratt* (New York: Russell Brothers, 1874), 197–98.

13. Beth Shumway Moore, *Bones in the Well: The Haun's Mill Massacre, 1838: A Documentary History* (Norman, Okla.: Arthur H. Clarke, 2007).

14. E. Robinson and D. C. Smith, "Address," *T&S* 1:1 (November 1839): 2.

15. Benjamin Andrews, "Appeal to the People of Maine," *T&S* 5:2 (January 15, 1844): 404. See also "Murder," *T&S* 5:13 (July 15, 1844): 585.

16. Caroline Walker Bynum, *Resurrection of the Body in Western Christianity, 200–1336* (New York: Columbia University Press, 1995), 44.

17. "Magna Est Veritas, et Praevalebit," *T&S* 5:15 (August 15, 1844): 621.

18. "Ex-Gov. L. W. Boggs" and "Missouri Mob Law," *Wasp* 1:22 (September 17, 1842): 2.

19. In Young's phrase, "we would say to all the saints who have made a covenant with the Lord by sacrifice, that inasmuch as you are faithful, you shall not lose your reward, although not numbered among those who were in the late difficulties in the west." "To the elders," *T&S* 1:1 (November 1839): 12.

20. "Speech of Mr. Smith," *Wasp* 1:37 (January 14, 1843): 2.

21. *Wasp* 1:11 (June 25, 1842): 4.

22. Robert Thompson, "A History of the Persecution," *T&S* 1:10 (August 1840): 148–49.

23. Moore, *Bones in the Well*, 117, and David W. Grua, "Memoirs of the Persecuted: Persecution, Memory, and the West as a Mormon Refuge" (M.A. thesis, Brigham Young University, 2008), 70–71.

24. "Persecution," *T&S* 2:21 (September 1, 1841): 527.

25. Edward Partridge, "Quincy, Adams co. Ill.," *T&S* 1:3 (January 1840): 37.

26. "Extract," *T&S* 1:1 (November 1839): 8.

27. Smith quoted the hymn with minor variation: Hannah More, *The Works of Hannah More*, 2 vols. (New York: Harper & Brothers, 1835), 1:54.

28. E. R. Snow, "Missouri," *T&S* 5:3 (February 1, 1844): 431.

29. David Hall, *Worlds of Wonder: Days of Judgment* (New York: Knopf, 1989), 60, 187–89, and "The Revival of the Inquisition and of Persecution," *T&S* 5:4 (February 15, 1844): 435.

30. The Book of Mormon provided one example of explaining martyrdom: Alma 14: esp. 11.

31. See, e.g., Grua, "Memoirs"; Lorenzo Snow, "Fighting the Good Fight," in *Collected Discourses Delivered by President Wilford Woodruff, His Two Counselors, the Twelve Apostles, and Others*, ed. Brian H. Stuy, 5 vols. (Burbank, Calif.: B.H.S., 1987), 1:42–44; Thomas Alexander, "Wilford Woodruff and the Mormon Reformation of 1855–57," *Dialogue* 25:2 (summer 1992): 30; and *JD* 7:289, 10:45–46. See also the exemplary eulogy for Brigham Young's father, Historian's Office, Brigham Young History Drafts (CR 100 475, CHL).

32. See *LB*, 752n125, versus Richard L. Bushman, *Joseph Smith: Rough Stone Rolling* (New York: Knopf, 2005), 9. Bushman is correct: *WWJ* 2:450.

33. Dean Jessee, comp. and ed., *The Papers of Joseph Smith: Journal, 1832–1842* (Salt Lake City: Deseret Book, 1992), 2:439; *LB*, 493.

34. *T&S* 1:11 (September 1840): 172.

35. *LB*, 752–53, 763–65, 767, *EMD* 1:488, and *T&S* 2 (August 16, 1841): 503–4.

36. On Samuel Smith, see *LB*, 207, 265, 750–51.

37. *LB*, 493.

38. William Phelps, "The Answer," *T&S* 5:24 (January 1, 1845): 760.

39. "History of Brigham Young," *MS* 27:7 (February 18, 1865): 103–4.

40. Phineas Richards to Wealthy Richards, January 7, 1839, photocopy in Richards Correspondence, HBLL. I thank David Grua for this source.

41. "Obituary," *T&S* 1:8 (June 1840): 127–28.

42. *Wasp* 1:27 (October 22, 1842): 3.

43. H. G. Sherwood [for the Nauvoo High Council], "Messrs. Editors," *T&S* 1:4 (February 1840): 56.

44. "Immigration," *T&S* 1:8 (June 1840): 123.

45. Daniel Kidder, *Mormonism and the Mormons: A Historical View of the Rise and Progress of the Sect of Self-styled Latter-day Saints* (New York: Land & Standford for the Methodist Episcopal Church, 1842), 155.

46. *JD* 5:71, and Robert Thompson, "A History of the Persecution," *T&S* 1:10 (August 1840): 153.

47. Richard S. Van Wagoner and Steven Walker, "The Joseph/Hyrum Smith Funeral Sermon," *BYU Studies* 23:1 (winter 1983): 9.

48. *WJS*, 347.

49. Richard L. Anderson, "Joseph Smith's Prophecies of Martyrdom," in *The Eighth Annual Sidney B. Sperry Symposium* (Provo, Utah: Brigham Young University, 1980), 1–14.

50. *T&S* 5:23 (December 15, 1844): 744.

51. Dennis, "Martyrdom," 93.

52. Joseph Fielding (Andrew Ehat), "'They Might Have Known That He Was Not a Fallen Prophet'—The Nauvoo Journal of Joseph Fielding," *BYU Studies* 18:2 [winter 1979]: 152) wrote: "I feel as though I want to ask their forgiveness that I have not mourned for them more deeply."

53. Dennis, "Martyrdom," 94.

54. Davis Bitton, *The Martyrdom Remembered* (Salt Lake City: Aspen, 1994), 8–9; compare "Zion in Captivity," *T&S* 1:4 (February 1840): 64, and "The Prophet's Death," *Chicago Times* 20 (November 20, 1875): 1.

55. Glen Leonard, *Nauvoo: A Place of Peace, a People of Promise* (Salt Lake City: Deseret Book, 2002), 411.

56. Wm. Burton, "Conference Minutes," *T&S* 5:16 (September 2, 1844): 629.

57. *T&S* 5:13 (July 15, 1844): 591; compare *HC* 7:15. The epigraph is from Psalm 79:10—"the blood of your servant is poured out." I thank Kevin Barney for the translation.

58. On earlier uses, see, e.g., Brigham Young et al., "To the Elders," *T&S* 1:1 (November 1839): 12.

59. "Murder," 585–86.

60. "The Prophet's Death," *Chicago Times* 20 (November 20, 1875): 1.

61. *T&S* 1:1 (November 1839): 9, Brigham Young, et al., "To the Elders," *T&S* 1:1 (November 1839): 12.

62. William E. Hunter, *Edward Hunter: Faithful Steward*, ed. Janath Russell Cannon (Salt Lake City: Mrs. William E. Hunter, 1970), 76–77.

63. Leonard, *Nauvoo*, 398–99.

64. Hunter, *Edward Hunter*, 70–71, 77.

65. Bitton, *Martyrdom*, 9.

66. Bitton, *Martyrdom*, 5.

67. Dennis, "Martyrdom," 94.

68. Dallin H. Oaks and Marvin S. Hill, *The Carthage Conspiracy: The Trial of the Accused Assassins of Joseph Smith* (Urbana: University of Illinois Press, 1975).

69. Allen Joseph Stout, Journal, CHL, 19.

70. George D. Smith, ed., *An Intimate Chronicle: The Journals of William Clayton* (Salt Lake City: Signature Books, 1995), 244; see also Hope Hilton, "Wild

Bill" Hickman and the Mormon Frontier (Salt Lake City: Signature Books, 1989), 14–15.

71. "Address to the Saints," *Supplement to the Millennial Star* (August 1844): 15.
72. Van Wagoner and Walker, "Smith Funeral Sermon," 15–16.
73. Smith, *Intimate Chronicle*, 243.
74. Devery Anderson and Gary Bergera, eds., *The Nauvoo Endowment Companies, 1845–1846: A Documentary History* (Salt Lake City: Signature Books, 2005), 29, 206.
75. See, e.g., Thomas Goodrich, *The Darkest Dawn: Lincoln, Booth, and the Great American Tragedy* (Bloomington: Indiana University Press, 2005), 225–30, 247–71, and W. J. Ferguson, *I Saw Booth Shoot Lincoln* (New York: Houghton Mifflin, 1930), 58–59.
76. Joab, a General in Israel [John C. Bennett], "Burglary! Treason!! Arson!!! Murder!!!!," *T&S* 1:11 (September 1840): 167.
77. Maureen Ursenbach Beecher, "'All Things Move in Order in the City': The Nauvoo Diary of Zina Diantha Huntington Jacobs," *BYU Studies* 19:3 (spring 1979): 292.
78. Charles Buck, *Theological Dictionary* (Philadelphia: Edwin T. Scott, 1823), 342, notes that prior martyrs were believed to be "shortening the times of persecution" through a similar mechanism. See also the *Nauvoo Neighbor* editorial of July 24, 1844, quoted in Bitton, *Martyrdom*, 17–18.
79. Bitton, *Martyrdom*, 14.
80. Beecher, "Nauvoo Diary," 303.
81. Beecher, "Nauvoo Diary," 303, 312.
82. Bitton, *Martyrdom*, 34.
83. *T&S* 5:12 (July 1, 1844): 560.
84. Eliza Snow, "The Assassination of Gen'ls Joseph and Hyrum Smith," *T&S* 5:12 (July 1, 1844): 575.
85. Walter D. Bowen, "The Versatile W. W. Phelps—Mormon Writer, Educator, and Pioneer" (M.A. thesis, Brigham Young University, 1958), 205; see also *T&S* 5:13 (July 15, 1844): 591.
86. William Daniels, *A Correct Account of the Murders of Generals Joseph and Hyrum Smith at Carthage on the 27th day of June, 1844* (Nauvoo, Ill.: John Taylor, 1845), 12.
87. See, e.g., *D&C* 135:7.
88. Alma 24:12–13.
89. 3 Nephi 9:5–11.
90. Mormon 8:27, 40–41; Ether 8:22–24; Alma 1:13; Alma 20:18–19; 2 Nephi 26:3, 2 Nephi 28:10; Mosiah 17:10.
91. Genesis 4:10–11.
92. Numbers 35:33; Deuteronomy 19:13, 32:43; Psalm 106:38.
93. 2 Kings 9:7; Matthew 23:30–35; and Luke 11:50–51.
94. Mary Ann Meyers, "Gates Ajar," in *Death in America*, ed. David Stannard (Philadelphia: University of Pennsylvania Press, 1977), 119–20.
95. Beecher, "Nauvoo Diary," 314.
96. Stuy, *Collected Discourses*, 1:77, 1:205, 2:48, 2:136.
97. *WWJ* 3:134.
98. Van Wagoner and Walker, "Smith Funeral Sermon," 10.

99. Samuel Richards to Franklin Richards, August 23, 1844, CHL.
100. Dennis, "Martyrdom," 109.
101. "Speech of Elder H. C. Kimball," *T&S* 6:1 (August 1, 1845): 988.
102. William Phelps, "A Voice from the Prophet. 'Come to Me,'" *T&S* 6:1 (January 15, 1845): 783, 794.
103. *HC* 7:237–38.
104. *T&S* 6:16 (November 1, 1845): 1014.
105. *T&S* 5:24 (December 25, 1844): 757–61.
106. William Huntington, Reminiscences and Journal [July 14, 1844], CHL, 16–17.
107. Smith, *Intimate Chronicle*, 238.
108. Gregory Prince, *Power from On High: The Development of Mormon Priesthood* (Salt Lake City: Signature Books, 1995), 153.
109. There is a polemical debate about collective memory surrounding this event. See Reid L. Harper, "The Mantle of Joseph: Creation of a Mormon Miracle," *Journal of Mormon History* 22:2 (fall 1996): 35–71, versus Lynne Watkins Jorgensen, "The Mantle of the Prophet Joseph Passes to Brother Brigham: A Collective Spiritual Witness," *BYU Studies* 36:4 (1996–97): 125–204.
110. Douglas Davies, *The Mormon Culture of Salvation* (Aldershot, England: Ashgate, 2000), 103.
111. Beecher, "Nauvoo Diary," 302.
112. Van Wagoner and Walker, "Smith Funeral Sermon," 16, and Bitton, *Martyrdom*, 33.
113. See, e.g., Dennis, "Martyrdom," 101.
114. *D&C* 135:3.
115. Leonard, *Nauvoo*, 407. Among these memorials, John Taylor's poems "The Seer" and "O Give Me Back My Prophet Dear"; Eliza Snow's poems; and William Phelps's now famous "Praise to the Man" are best known.
116. Joseph Smith, "Liberty Jail, Missouri, December 16, 1838," *T&S* 1:6 (April 1840): 83.
117. Ehat, "Nauvoo Journal," 151–52.
118. Daniels, *Correct Account*, 14.
119. Dennis, "Martyrdom," 105.
120. See, e.g., Sally Randall (quoted in Bitton, *Martyrdom*, 26), and Eliza R. Snow ("The Assassination," *T&S* 5:12 [July 1, 1844]: 575).
121. Beecher, "Nauvoo Diary," 304–5. "Sons" appears to be genitive, with reference to Joseph Smith.
122. John Taylor, "The Seer," *T&S* 5:24 (January 1, 1845): 767.
123. *HC* 7:257; compare *JD* 1:364, 8:320.
124. Daniels, *Correct Account*, 15.
125. Oaks and Hill, *Carthage Conspiracy*, 87–90.
126. Hunter, *Edward Hunter*, 76–77.
127. Dennis, "Martyrdom," 93. The use of the term "blood" to describe the fluids that likely drained from the brothers' bodies in the hot June weather is culturally significant if medically imprecise.
128. "The Prophet's Death," *Chicago Times* 20 (November 20, 1875): 1. See also Smith, *Intimate Chronicle*, 136.
129. Dennis, "Martyrdom," 93.

130. Leonard, *Nauvoo*, 402–3.

131. Joseph Johnstun, "'To Lay in Yonder Tomb': The Tomb and Burial of Joseph Smith," *Mormon Historical Studies* 5:2 (fall 2005): 163–80.

132. Beecher, "Nauvoo Diary," 293.

133. See Johnstun, "Tomb and Burial," and T. B. H. Stenhouse, *Rocky Mountain Saints* (New York: Appleton and Company, 1873), 174.

134. Chief Blackhawk's corpse was violated in 1840–41: Kerry Trask, *Black Hawk: The Battle for the Hearts of America* (New York: Macmillan, 2006), 303–4. The poem is Lyman O. Littlefield, "Black Hawk's Grave," *Wasp* 1:28 (October 29, 1842): 1.

135. Roger D. Launius, *Joseph Smith III: Pragmatic Prophet* (Urbana: University of Illinois Press, 1988), 39.

136. Johnstun, "Tomb and Burial."

137. Leonard, *Nauvoo*, 404.

138. Bennett to Strang, April 2, 1846, James Jesse Strang Collection, Yale Collection of Western Americana, Beinecke Rare Book and Manuscript Library, Yale University. I thank Robin Jensen for this source.

139. Barbara Bernauer, "Still Side by Side—The Final Burial of Joseph and Hyrum Smith," *John Whitmer Historical Association Journal* 11 (1991): 18–22.

140. Bernauer, "Side by Side," 17. On David Hyrum, see Valeen Tippetts Avery, *From Mission to Madness: Last Son of the Mormon Prophet* (Urbana: University of Illinois Press, 1998).

141. Bernauer, "Side by Side," 28.

142. Bernauer, "Side by Side," 31.

143. Bernauer, "Side by Side," 32.

144. There were, of course, theological differences between the two groups, but they were largely differences over elements like polygamy, theocracy, and temple that strongly supported the ecclesial over the biological model of kinship.

145. D. Michael Quinn, "The Mormon Succession Crisis of 1844," *BYU Studies* 16:2 (winter 1976): 187–233.

146. Phelps, "Answer," 761.

147. Brigham Young to Lucy Smith, April 4, 1847, CHL.

INDEX